Media and Protest Logics
in the Digital Era

Oxford Studies in Digital Politics

Series Editor: Andrew Chadwick, Professor of Political Communication in the Centre for Research in Communication and Culture and the Department of Social Sciences, Loughborough University

Media and Protest Logics in the Digital Era

THE UMBRELLA MOVEMENT IN HONG KONG

FRANCIS L. F. LEE

and

JOSEPH M. CHAN

OXFORD
UNIVERSITY PRESS

OXFORD
UNIVERSITY PRESS

Oxford University Press is a department of the University of Oxford. It furthers
the University's objective of excellence in research, scholarship, and education
by publishing worldwide. Oxford is a registered trade mark of Oxford University
Press in the UK and certain other countries.

Published in the United States of America by Oxford University Press
198 Madison Avenue, New York, NY 10016, United States of America.

© Oxford University Press 2018

CIP data is on file at the Library of Congress
ISBN 978–0–19–085678–6 (pbk.); 978–0–19–085677–9 (hbk.)

9 8 7 6 5 4 3 2 1

Paperback printed by WebCom, Inc., Canada
Hardback printed by Bridgeport National Bindery, Inc., United States of America

Contents

Acknowledgments

The authors need to thank many people who have helped in the research for the present volume. Gary Tang, Dennis Leung, and Chan Chi-kit helped coordinate and conduct the protest onsite surveys in early October and early November 2014. Also crucial to the successful completion of the onsite surveys were the numerous student helpers from the Chinese University of Hong Kong and Hang Seng Management College. Vincent Huang helped manage the data related to parts of the analysis of Chapter 2. Li Yungeng and Huang Peiying helped conduct the framing analysis of mainstream media discourse reported in Chapter 6. Nick Zhang contributed his expertise to the analysis of social media materials in Chapter 5. The first author was also lucky to have the responsible and competent assistantship of Amon Yiu and Vivien Zhang, without whom some of the analyses in the book could not be completed easily.

Many friends and colleagues have provided the authors with opportunities to present their observations and findings about the Umbrella Movement. These opportunities allowed the authors to test and revise their ideas as well as to learn from others. Colleague and old friend Jack Qiu invited us to present some of our findings at a conference about digital activism in April 2015. The presentation was then turned into an article for *Information, Communication, and Society*, from which parts of Chapter 5 were derived. Weng Shieu-chi invited the first author to contribute a piece to a special issue about the Umbrella Movement and Sunflower Movement in the *Journal of Communication Research and Practice*. John Flowerdew and Rodney Jones, former colleagues of the first author at the City University of Hong Kong, organized a special issue for the *Journal of Language and Politics* focusing on language and discourses in the Umbrella Movement. Their invitation provided an opportunity to work on media representation of public opinion during the Umbrella Movement, which became part of Chapter 6 of this book. Wang Wei-ching of National Taiwan Normal University invited the authors to participate in a workshop on digital media and social activism. Huang Yu of Hong Kong Baptist

University then invited the first author to turn his presentation there into a journal article for *Communication & Society*. The article was the source for part of Chapter 4.

It was a pleasure for the first author to participate in a couple of edited volumes and their associated workshops on the Umbrella Movement organized by prominent scholars in the study of Hong Kong politics and society. One was organized by Ma Ngok, and the other was organized by Lee Ching-kwan and Sing Ming. The author learned a lot about other aspects of the Umbrella Movement from the organizers and the work of the other participants.

Certainly, the authors need to thank the anonymous reviewers solicited by Oxford University Press and Andrew Chadwick, editor of the series, for their insightful and constructive critiques and comments on the book.

In early 2015, the first author undertook a sabbatical at the National Sun Yat-Sen University at Kaohsiung, Taiwan. The author had the opportunity to exchange ideas and observations with colleagues and students at the university's Institute of Political Science. The author also needs to thank Chen Wan-chi of the Department of Sociology at National Taipei University for providing another opportunity of exchange of ideas and observations related to student movements in Hong Kong and Taiwan. Beyond campuses, the hospitality of several colleagues at NSYSU, including Liao Da-chi, Alex Tan, and especially Frank Liu and his adorable family, made the stay at Kaohsiung highly enjoyable and memorable. It was very good fortune that the first author could concentrate on producing the first drafts of most of the chapters of this book during his stay in this most congenial city in Southern Taiwan.

Lastly, the authors would like to thank various publishers and publications for permitting us to incorporate parts of some previous publications into various chapters of this book. Chapter 2 is derived in part from the article titled "Triggering the protest paradigm: Examining factors affecting news coverage of protests," published in the *International Journal of Communication* (http://ijoc.org/index.php/ijoc/article/view/2873/1215). Chapter 3 is derived in part from "Social movement as civic education: Communication activities and understanding of civil disobedience in the Umbrella Movement," in the *Chinese Journal of Communication* (http://www.tandfonline.com/doi/full/10.1080/17544750.2015.1057192). Chapter 4 is derived in part from a Chinese article entitled "News media as the public monitor in a large-scale protest campaign: The case of Hong Kong's Umbrella Movement," published in *Communication & Society*.

Parts of Chapter 5 are derived from two articles. The first article is entitled "Digital media activities and mode of participation in a protest campaign: A study of the Umbrella Movement." It was published in the first issue in 2016 in *Information, Communication & Society* (http://www.tandfonline.com/doi/full/10.1080/1369118X.2015.1093530). The second article is entitled "Online media and the power and limitations of connective action: The case of the 2014 Umbrella Movement in Hong Kong." It was published in Chinese in the *Journal of Communication Research and Practice.* Lastly, Chapter 6 is derived in part from "Opinion polling and construction of public opinion in newspaper discourses during the Umbrella Movement," published in the *Journal of Language and Politics* (with kind permission by John Benjamins Publishing Company, Amsterdam/ Philadelphia. www.benjamins.com).

Media and Protest Logics
in the Digital Era

1

Introduction

This book is about the Umbrella Movement—the occupation protest calling for "genuine democracy" conducted by Hong Kong people from late September to mid-December 2014. According to university-conducted polls, about 20% of Hong Kong citizens went to the occupied areas to support the movement.[1] Even taking into account the probable oversampling of politically active citizens by polls, it is safe to state that at least hundreds of thousands of local people participated in the protest. The Umbrella Movement is the largest civil disobedience campaign in the history of Hong Kong. It is also the largest protest campaign on Chinese soil involving the occupation of public space since the 1989 student movement in Beijing.

The protest captured a large amount of international media attention. Besides the basic news values of the events (e.g., the scale of the protest, involvement of conflicts, the prominence of China, compelling visual images, etc.) and the presence of a large group of foreign correspondents in the city, the newsworthiness of the protest was arguably enhanced by how it fit into an existing image of a new type of protests occurring around the world. In fact, the Umbrella Revolution, the label coined and preferred by the international media when reporting about the protest campaign, signified how the international media characterized the Hong Kong protest and, by connotation, linked it to events in the Middle East and other countries in previous years.

For academics and observers familiar with the recent wave of occupation protests around the world since the late 2000s and early 2010s, the Umbrella Movement undeniably shared some of the characteristics of the other occupation protests. Besides the choice of occupation of public space as the main item of its action repertoire, the Umbrella Movement also exhibited a significant degree of spontaneous participation among huge number of participants and a quick scaling-up process. The rise of the protest campaign immediately brought about discussions in the international media regarding the role of digital and social media in mobilization and coordination.[2] We will return to the question of how the Umbrella Movement is similar to and different from other occupation protests below. But generally speaking, there is certainly a prima facie case for treating the Umbrella Movement as a member of an emerging family of occupation protests. Understanding what happened in the Umbrella Movement should thus contribute to our understanding of this family of occupation movements in general.

The aim of this book is therefore twofold. We provide an analysis of the role and impact of the media—both conventional mass media institutions and digital media platforms—in the formation and dynamics of the Umbrella Movement. This analysis is embedded in a holistic account of the movement, including the historical contexts and contingent events behind its emergence and the evolution of the movement from September to December 2014. Here, "holistic" does not entail "comprehensive." It is impossible for a single book with a relative emphasis on media and communication to cover all aspects of the movement. But one underlying emphasis of this book is the premise that a protest movement should be understood in relation to local dynamics and contextual conditions. Hence it is important to ground the analysis of the role of media and communication on a broader account of the Umbrella Movement at large.

More important, the contextualized account of the Umbrella Movement and the role of the media in its formation and dynamics should allow us to engage in theoretical dialogues with the extant literature on the relationship between media and new forms of social movements and protest logics. Our theoretical aim is not to develop another new theory about social movements and contentious politics in the digital era; rather, our premise is that, while the Umbrella Movement is not conceptually ideal-typical of a new form of protests, it may be considered typical of the majority of actual protest campaigns in its "mixed character." That is, we see the Umbrella Movement as a case in which old and new protest logics and movement formations engage and interact with each other. The Umbrella Movement should be capable of shedding light on a number of important issues, including, among others, how one may explain the rise of such seemingly digital media–enabled social movements, how one can conceptualize the relationship between digital media platforms and conventional media institutions, how the two can combine to facilitate social mobilization, the power and limitations of such occupation protests and new "action logics," and the continual significance of "old" protest logics of resource mobilization and collective action framing.

The latter parts of this introductory chapter will further explicate the theoretical orientation and presumptions underlying our analysis. But before the conceptual discussions, we will first offer a more "journalistic" account of what happened in the Umbrella Movement in order to help orient the readers.

The Umbrella Movement: Background and Happenings

The background of the Umbrella Movement is multifaceted and highly complicated. It is tied to issues such as the development of social mobilization in Hong Kong in the past decade, the rising sense of social injustice among local residents, and changes in young people's value orientations. Some of these issues will be addressed in Chapter 2. But putting aside the underlying issues and contextual factors, the explicit and imminent concern of the Umbrella Movement was democratization of the local political system. The Basic Law—the constitutional document for the Hong Kong Special Administrative Region (SAR)—stipulates[3] that the city shall undergo democratization with the goal of institutionalizing election with universal suffrage for the Chief Executive (CE) of the SAR government. However, democratization progressed at a snail's pace after the handover in 1997. The proportion of directly elected seats in the legislature did not increase between 1998 and 2012. For the CE election, the National People's Congress (NPC) of China ruled out, in 2004, direct elections of the CE in 2007. In late 2007, the NPC once again ruled out direct elections of the CE in 2012. But it promised that the city could directly elect its CE in 2017.

NPC's decision in late 2007 set up the time frame for direct elections of the CE. Public debate thus moved from "when" to "how." After all, what kind of "democratic elections" would an authoritarian country allow one of its cities to have? Some commentators predicted that China would set up the electoral procedures in such a way that only candidates it approves could stand. "Entrance barrier" of the election became a core issue. Debates about democratic reform became a matter of whether "genuine popular election" would be institutionalized.

For the democrats, an important question was how they could pressure the Chinese and Hong Kong government on the matter. In January 2013, law professor Benny Tai[4] suggested in a newspaper op-ed article the mounting of a civil disobedience campaign[5]—occupying roads in the financial district Central in order to paralyze business and financial activities. The idea caught fire. In March 2013, Tai initiated the "Occupy Central with Love and Peace" campaign together with sociology professor Chan Kin-man and the Reverend Chu Yiu-ming. The media dubbed them the Occupy Central Trio (the "Trio" hereafter).

Between March 2013 and August 2014, the Occupy Central campaign would recruit volunteers, organize deliberation days, conduct rehearsals, and engage in intensive discursive work explaining the concept and practices of civil disobedience. Meanwhile, the Hong Kong government began the first round of public consultation on the 2017 electoral arrangement in early 2014. Pro-democracy (as well as conservative) political parties and civic groups articulated various proposals. Proposals from the pro-democracy camp ranged from the most "principled and idealistic," such as the call for the institutionalization of civil nomination of candidates, which was rebuked by China as unconstitutional, to more moderate proposals aiming at securing the possibility for members of the pro-democracy political parties to become candidates in the popular election.

Despite the democrats' efforts, on August 31, 2014, the NPC announced a highly conservative framework for the 2017 election: only *two to three* persons who obtain *endorsement from more than half of the members of the nomination committee* can stand as candidates in the popular vote, and *the formation of the nomination committee shall remain unchanged*. Since the nomination committee is dominated by pro-China elites, the framework effectively allows the Chinese government to screen the candidates if it wants to.

In response to the decision, the Trio announced the initiation of the resistance movement. On September 23, 2014, Benny Tai publicized through the news media that Occupy Central would begin on October 1. The Hong Kong Federation of Students (HKFS), the organization composed of the student unions of all major universities in the city, initiated a week of class strike between September 22 and 26. Scholarism, a prominent civic association comprising mostly high school activists,[6] also called for a class strike by high school students. During the week, rallies were held in front of the Government Headquarters. The rally on the evening of Friday, September 26, extended into the weekend, with thousands of citizens, primarily youth, participating. There were calls among some protesters for the Trio to kick-start the occupation earlier than planned. Finally, in the early morning hours of Sunday, September 28, Benny Tai announced the beginning of Occupy Central.

Occupy Central was originally scripted as an action with strict discipline. The occupiers were expected to sit down to block traffic. But they were not expected to confront the police physically. They were requested not to resist and fight when the police evicted the area. In fact, the Trio originally expected the action to last for only several days.[7]

What the Trio could not predict were the events of the afternoon of September 28. Tens of thousands of citizens flocked to Admiralty, the district where the Government Headquarters are located. Many of these citizens probably did not aim at joining the occupation; many of them went there just to offer moral support.[8] Yet the police insisted on blocking the entrance to the area in front of the East Wing of the Government Headquarters, where the occupiers were located. Protesters inadvertently started the occupation of highways when the police failed to keep the increasing number of protesters staying on the pedestrian pathways. On the road, some protesters repeatedly attempted to charge the police's defense line. At around 6 p.m., the police fired tear gas into the crowd. The images that shocked the city and captivated the world were produced: tear gas flew over the urban landscape of metropolitan Hong Kong, and protesters protected themselves with the humble "weapon" of umbrellas. The international media quickly created the label "Umbrella Revolution" for the protest. The central leaders of the movement and pro-movement academics adjusted the label to Umbrella Movement.[9]

The police action backfired. The tear gas failed to drive the protesters home and arguably drove more people to the streets. In addition, as the police took action in Admiralty, some protesters quickly coordinated among themselves and initiated occupation actions in other districts. Within 24 hours, occupation "blossomed all over the place," as the activists would say. Immediate eviction of all areas became virtually impossible. The occupation action later consolidated into three main areas: the financial district of Admiralty, the shopping-cum-business district of Causeway Bay, and the grassroots[10] residential district of Mong Kok.

What happened inside the occupied areas is similar to occupation actions in other parts of the world in recent years. Protesters camped on the site, shared food, held occasional rallies, and engaged in personalized practices ranging from cultivating flowers and vegetables to various forms of artistic expressions. Pro-movement academics lectured in "mobile classrooms." In Admiralty, a study area was created for students. Part of the wall at one entrance to the Government Headquarters was treated as a Lennon Wall (inspired by the one in Prague), with an estimated 15,000 messages posted by the end of the occupation. In Mong Kok, a statue of the God of Kwan[11] was erected. Temporary churches were also set up in both Admiralty and Mong Kok. The occupied areas were creatively turned into places where protesters realized their visions of community and experimented with ways of life.

Actions extended beyond the occupied areas too. At universities, graduates brought yellow umbrellas with them onto the stage during graduation ceremonies. As one of the movement's highlights, a group of citizens hung a huge yellow banner with the slogan "I Demand Genuine Popular Election" on the hillside under the Lion Rock, making the banner visible from a large part of the urban areas in the Kowloon peninsula. The action triggered the hanging of banners on buildings around the city.

Moreover, movement supporters (and opponents) took symbolic actions in cyberspace. Many people changed their profile pictures on social media accounts into a yellow umbrella, a yellow ribbon, or other symbols of the movement, while many opponents of the movement also changed their profile pictures to a blue ribbon, which signified support for the police to take what they regarded as necessary actions against the occupation. Movement supporters also shared personal stories, observations, frontline experiences, rumor-dispelling information, photos, satirical pictures, and other creative artworks via social media platforms.

The protest, in other words, evolved into a range of improvisational, decentralized, and even individualized actions both within and outside the occupied areas, and both online and offline. While such a shift allowed more people to participate in their own ways, it also brought about a tension between centralized leadership and decentralized actions. The Trio, the HKFS, and Scholarism were seen as the leaders of the movement by the government and the news media, but not necessarily by all movement participants. For instance, before the leaders of the HKFS joined a televised dialogue with top Hong Kong government officials on October 21, many movement participants stated in social media that HKFS could *not* represent them. After the televised dialogue, the movement leaders announced the plan to conduct a referendum within the occupied areas to gauge participants' opinions about the "promises" made by the government during the dialogue. But some participants and groups suspected that the referendum was a preparation for retreating from the area. The leaders had to cancel the referendum later because of internal dissension.

As the Chinese and Hong Kong governments were unwilling to make any substantive concessions, internal debates regarding movement directions and strategies became more intense over time. Some movement supporters argued for a retreat from the occupied areas in order to preserve the movement's energy and avoid alienating the general public, whereas others called for escalating the actions. The Trio left the occupied areas in early November and returned to work (i.e., to university teaching for Tai and Chan). On November 30, the HKFS and Scholarism escalated the action by calling people to surround the whole Government Headquarters in order to paralyze the government. But the police succeeded in dispersing the crowd by force. On December 2, the Trio surrendered to the police to fulfill their promise of breaking the law without breaking the rule of law.

The movement seemingly lost steam. In fact, by mid-November, university-conducted opinion polls already showed that about 70% of the public, including many movement supporters, believed that it was time to retreat.[12] Earlier, anti-movement groups successfully applied for court injunctions ordering the protesters to leave the occupied areas. The Hong Kong Bar Association, which had been critical toward the NPC decision and therefore arguably an ally of the movement at least in its early stages, issued a statement arguing that not following court orders would damage the rule of law in Hong Kong. The Hong Kong police evicted the Mong Kok occupation site on November 25 and 26, then the occupied area in Admiralty on December 11, and finally the last occupied site in Causeway Bay on December 15.

The above summary is inevitably selective, but it should give readers a sense of the factual background and major happenings during the movement. It also points toward three interrelated aspects of the movement that are central to this book's analysis. First, through the transformation from the originally planned Occupy Central to more decentralized actions, the Umbrella Movement took up characteristics of what scholars have called "networked social movements" (Castells, 2012) and "connective actions" (Bennett & Segerberg, 2013). But the Umbrella Movement also significantly differs from such conceptual ideal types. Hence it would be better considered as a case in which old and new movement formations and logics coexist and interact.

Second, the movement occurred against the background of years of social and political development. Yet the contextual background by itself does not determine the occurrence of the movement at a specific temporal juncture. Rather, there were dynamics and contingencies that led to the evolution of the movement from a planned civil disobedience campaign to more dispersed and decentralized actions.

Third, both digital media and mass media played significant roles in shaping the dynamics of the movement. Digital media allowed supporters to follow the development of the protest, voice their opinions, and communicate and coordinate with each other. They also provided the platforms for online actions. Yet conventional mass media remained crucial in portraying the movement in the broader public arena and shaping public opinion toward the movement. How the Umbrella Movement evolved within a mediascape composed of digital media platforms and mass media institutions constitutes our analytical focus.

The next few sections will further elaborate on these three aspects of this book's analysis by linking them to the current literature. The discussion will help clarify the conceptual focuses of and the theoretical premises underlying the study.

Mixing Old and New Movement Formations and Action Logics

Since 2009, the world has witnessed a number of prominent protest movements occurring in different parts of the globe. The Iranian Revolution in 2009, the Arab Spring in 2010 and 2011, the Spanish Indignados in 2011, and Occupy Wall Street in 2012, Taiwan's Sunflower Movement in 2014, and campus occupations in various countries, among others, have captured the attention and imagination of the media, activists, and academics around the world. These events illustrate the capability and willingness of people to take on powerful and seemingly immovable targets. The protest movements generated a huge and still growing body of academic literature (e.g., Achcar, 2013; Carty, 2015; Della Porta, 2015; el-Nawawy & Khamis, 2013; Fuchs, 2014; Howard & Hussain, 2013; Hussain & Howard, 2013; Tripp, 2013). For scholars interested in social movements, these events are particularly worth examining not only because of their scale, prominence, and real-world significance, but also because the events seemingly involved new forms of social movements and new ways of organizing contentious actions.

Two of the most influential accounts of new movement formation and "logics" of contentious actions were offered by Castells (2012) and Bennett and Segerberg (2013). Castells (2012) saw the wave of popular protests from the Iranian Revolution and Iceland's Kitchenware Revolution in 2009 to Occupy Wall Street in 2012 as exemplars of "networked social movements," a term he coined more than a decade ago (Castells, 2001). Networked social movements are networked in multiple forms; they are "networks of networks," instead of networks of formal organizations. "This decentered structure maximizes chances of participation in the movement. . . . It also reduces the vulnerability of the movement to the threat of repression, since there are few specific targets to repress" (p. 221). The movements occupy urban space while simultaneously network through cyberspace, in the process constructing a hybrid "space of autonomy" that allows the movements to become both local and global. These movements construct their own "timeless time" through extending their actions "day by day" and through referring to an unlimited horizon of future possibilities.

Networked social movements are largely spontaneous in origin and viral in the way they are spread, "usually triggered by a spark of indignation either related to a specific event or to a peak of disgust with the actions of the rulers" (p. 223). The movements are leaderless. Although there can be influential individuals in the movement, these influential activists are accepted by the participants only so long as they do not make major decisions by themselves. The implicit rule "is the self-government of the movement by the people in the movement" (p. 223). Direct, participatory democracies are practiced through assemblies and other methods.

Moreover, the networked social movements are highly reflexive. "They constantly interrogate themselves as movements, and as individuals, about who they are, what they want, what they want to achieve, which kind of democracy and society they wish for, and how to avoid the traps and pitfalls of so many movements that have failed by reproducing in themselves the mechanisms of the system they want to change" (p. 225). Last but not least, these movements are mostly non-programmatic. They do not aim at promoting and implementing a concrete program of policy changes. They are social movements aiming at "changing the values of society. . . . They aim to transform the state but not to seize the state. They express feelings and stir debate but do not create parties or support governments, although they may become a target of choice for political marketing" (p. 227).

While Castells's (2012) conceptualization characterizes the broad parameters and features of networked social movements, Bennett and Segerberg (2013) are more concerned with forms of participation, mobilization, and coordination of protest actions. In some of his earlier writings, Bennett and his colleagues already noted the trend toward personalization of collective actions and the emergence of the "self-actualizing citizen" who often practice their citizenship outside conventional channels of political participation (Bennett, 2008; Bennett & Segerberg, 2011). In the later, book-length account, Bennett and Segerberg (2013) formalized what they called "the logic of connective action" in order to explain the formation of contemporary protest actions that scale up quickly, produce large mobilizations, display unusual flexibility, build up adaptive protest repertoires, and embrace an ethos of inclusiveness" (p. 25). Central to the possibility of such crowd-enabled connective action are the fundamental interests in expression on the part of the citizens, creation of personal action frames with which individuals can easily identify, the availability of personal digital communication technologies that facilitate the sharing of the personal action frames, and the capability of digital media communication to organize and coordinate actions.

Bennett and Segerberg (2013) contrasted the logic of connective action to the conventional logic of "organizationally brokered collective action," which involves movement organizations or coalitions of organizations pooling together resources, offering selective incentives, framing the issues, constructing shared identity, and mobilizing their supporters. They also discussed a hybrid form of "organizationally enabled connective action," which involves "loosely tied networks of organizations sponsoring multiple actions and causes around a general set of issues in which followers are invited to personalize their engagement" (p. 13). The tripartite typology of crowd-enabled connective action, organizationally enabled connective action, and organizationally brokered collective action thus present three ideal types to which empirical cases may approach to different extents.

Based on the descriptive account provided in the previous section, it is not difficult to see how the Umbrella Movement took up some of the characteristics of networked social movements involving crowd-enabled connective actions. Occupation of urban space was the most important form of action undertaken by the movement, and with vibrant online communication activities, a hybrid space of autonomy was created. Actions within and outside the occupied areas were also dispersed, decentralized, and sometimes individualized. Some of the most important frontline actions in the occupied areas, ranging from building road blockades to confronting the police, were often not coordinated and organized by the movement leaders. Rather, the occupiers coordinated among themselves on the spot, sometimes improvising the actions to be taken.[13]

The movement also exhibited a significant degree of reflexivity. Participants continually debated among themselves, in cyberspace and in the occupied areas, about issues ranging from the goal and strategies of the movement to the proper "atmosphere" in the occupied areas.[14] "Don't forget the original intention" was a common saying among the protesters. Meanwhile, the main "slogan" of the movement—"I demand genuine popular election"—can be regarded as the simple personal action frame that allowed many people to easily identify with and participate in the movement in their own ways.

But the Umbrella Movement also differed from the ideal-typical networked social movement and connective actions in important ways. The Umbrella Movement was not entirely spontaneous in its origin. While many citizens might have "spontaneously" joined the movement at the time they witnessed on television the firing of tear gas by the police, and the evolution of the movement was unpredicted, the occurrence of a large-scale civil disobedience campaign was pre-announced and carefully planned. More important, the movement did have its central leadership, even though there were tensions both among the three leading groups (the Trio, HKFS, and Scholarism) and between the leading groups and the large range of groups and individuals constituting the movement at large.

Nor did the Umbrella Movement constitute what Bennett and Segerberg (2013) labeled "organizationally enabled connective action." In the latter ideal type, the connective action was intentionally promoted and facilitated by the movement organizations at the center. In the Umbrella Movement, the connective action was generated from the bottom up and was unexpected by the central organizers.

Moreover, the Umbrella Movement was far from non-programmatic. In Castells's broader theoretical framework of communication power, social movements are peculiarly defined as "social actors aiming for cultural change (a change in values)" (Castells, 2009, p. 300). Although the organizers of the Umbrella Movement would also talk about how the action could lead to cultural changes, the protest did have the NPC's decision on the 2017 electoral framework in Hong Kong as its specific target. It had the concrete policy goals of urging the NPC to retract its decision, to restart the institutional procedure of determining the 2017 electoral framework, and to allow the institutionalization of civil nomination in the 2017 CE election. The fact that the movement had concrete and immediate policy goals meant that the movement could not live on "timeless time." Instead, the issue had to be resolved in time for the 2017 election. This also entailed the need for the movement to engage in direct interactions with the target authorities[15] and arguably necessitated the presence of some forms of leadership and representation.

The Umbrella Movement, therefore, involves a mixture of the characteristics of "old" and "new" types of movements and contentious actions. This is not surprising. While Castells and Bennett and Segerberg attempted to theorize about emerging forms of social movements and logics of contentious actions, a wide range of movements and protests co-exist in the contemporary world (e.g., Anduiza, Cristancho, & Sabucedo, 2014), and many protest campaigns can be seen as involving combinations of various ideal types. As Bennett and Segerberg (2013) themselves put it, "in reality, the three forms of network organization interact and overlap, and various tensions may arise when they come into conflict" (pp. 48–49). What may happen "when logics collide"? Bennett and Segerberg (2013) provided some preliminary discussions based on the case of Occupy Wall Street in 2011 to 2012. But the question deserves more attention and empirical analyses with different cases.

We believe that the Umbrella Movement constitutes a case illustrative of what may happen when the logic of connective action intervenes into a centrally planned and organized collective action, as well as what may happen when a programmatic movement with concrete policy goals faces the forces of decentralization. Notably, the logic of connective action intervened into the plan of Occupy Central, turning it into the Umbrella Movement, but without totally displacing the central organizers from their "leading position" and rendering all preparation work for the Occupy Central campaign completely irrelevant. The connective actions both empowered the movement and exacerbated existing tensions and internal dissensions. The leaders faced the challenge of assimilating the benefits of having the dispersed actions while maintaining their capability of steering the movement as a whole. An important question for observers of the movement is to what extent the tensions and internal dissensions originating from the collision of action logics contributed to the "failure" of the movement to achieve tangible results, as well as to what extent such problems and difficulties related to not only how the movement ended but also some of its aftermath.

Explaining a Movement: Historical Trajectories and Contingencies

Since the early 2000s, an increasing number of social movement scholars have recognized the changes brought about by digital media technologies in how people organize collective actions and mobilize each other. One observation shared by many scholars is the declining significance of formal movement organizations in collective action organization and mobilization. Buechler (2011, p. 221) discussed the Internet as an "organizational substitute" facilitating collective actions. Earl, Kimport, Prieto, Rush, and Reynoso (2010, p. 441) argued that studies assuming "that (only) SMOs produce protest risk missing whole swaths of protest organized outside of formal organization." Against this background, Bennett and Segerberg's (2013) account of the logic of crowd-enabled connective action is exactly a theory about how protest actions could emerge without resource mobilization centering on movement organizations. In one sense, the logic of connective action can be seen as a substitute of resource mobilization theory when explaining the emergence of specific types or cases of protest campaigns.

However, similar to conventional resource mobilization theory, Bennett and Segerberg's (2013) account is primarily a meso-level theory explicating *how* connective actions could arise without formal organizational processes. The logic of connective action itself does not offer explanations of *why* specific protests would arise at specific historical junctures and social contexts. For tackling the latter question, one may need to return to extant social movement theories for possible theoretical insights and conceptual tools.

Specifically, as resource mobilization theory in the 1970s evolved into the more comprehensive political process model (McAdam, 1982; Tilly, 1978) in the 1980s, "political opportunity structure" became one of the most prominent concepts that scholars use to make arguments about how macro-level contextual conditions can explain the emergence and/or success of a movement (e.g., Kitschelt, 1986; Kriesi, 2004). The dominance of the concept is signified not only by the number of scholars using it but also by its ability to produce conceptual "spin-offs," such as discursive opportunity structure (Ferree, Gamson, Gerhards, & Rucht, 2002) and mediation opportunity structure (Cammaerts, 2012). However, the concept has also received much criticism (Giugni, 2009, 2011). For analyzing the Umbrella Movement, three limitations of the concept are particularly relevant: its structural bias, its assumption of instrumental rationality, and its inadequacy when dealing with the dynamics in specific cases.

We can illustrate the problem by attempting a brief analysis of the political opportunity structure behind the Umbrella Movement. Summarizing the literature utilizing the concept from the 1970s to the mid-1990s, McAdam (1996) identified four major dimensions of political opportunity structure: (1) the degree to which the institutionalized political system is open to input from outside; (2) the degree of stability of elite alignment in the polity; (3) the presence of elite allies for social movements; and (4) the state's capability and propensity for repression. The basic expectation is that social movements are more likely to arise when the political opportunity structure is favorable to social mobilization, that is, when the political system is open, elite alignment is unstable, elite allies for social movements are present, and the risk of state repression is low.

For the Umbrella Movement, which had the stated goal of "genuine popular elections" in Hong Kong, the "polity" concerned is not just the Hong Kong government but also the Chinese state, since the latter holds the power to make authoritative decisions on the matter. In this case, it is not difficult to see how few political opportunities actually existed: the Chinese political system is "closed" and does not easily subject itself to the influence of non-institutionalized forces. There is no high degree of instability in how local and national political elites are aligned. While the local democrats can be considered the "elite allies" for the Umbrella Movement, they have virtually no influence on China, and the movement does not have major elite allies in the broader Chinese political system. Meanwhile, the Chinese state has a strong capacity of repression, if not necessarily a strong propensity for exercising repression in Hong Kong. In fact, the headquarters of the People's Liberation Army in Hong Kong are literally just around the corner of the Admiralty occupation. Therefore, adopting McAdam's (1996) conceptualization, the political opportunity structure was highly unfavorable to the Umbrella Movement.

Can there be other aspects of the political opportunity structure that favor the pro-democracy movement in Hong Kong? Perhaps one can identify some if one has to, such as the increasing propensity of citizens to join protests, or the high penetration rates of digital and social media. But if the latter are taken as dimensions of political opportunity structure, the concept of political opportunity structure itself will run into the problem noted by Gamson and Mayer (1996): "in danger of becoming a sponge that soaks up virtually every aspect of the social movement environment" (p. 275). The analysis will become arbitrary and tautological, as researchers can always identify some aspects of the social and political environment that are conducive to mobilization. To avoid tautological thinking, one also cannot make inferences about whether political opportunities existed based on the emergence or outcome of a movement.

Therefore, if we adopt the conceptual lens of political opportunity structure in the present case, either we use the concept very loosely to refer to whatever we can identify as conducive to the emergence of the Umbrella Movement and risk committing the mistake of tautology, or we follow McAdam's (1996) definition of the concept, which properly focuses on the characteristics of the political system as its main dimensions, and yet come to the conclusion that political opportunity structure does not bring us a good explanation of the emergence of the Umbrella Movement. In fact, thinking in terms of political opportunities would bring us an intriguing question: Why did the Umbrella Movement occur despite the seemingly highly unfavorable political opportunity structure?

Most fundamentally, the possibility of a large-scale movement despite the lack of opportunities resides in the fact that structural conditions do not determine behavior. Instrumental rationality does not always prevail, and the dynamics of a movement is inherently unpredictable. This is not to say that structural factors do not matter. But structural factors are not mechanical causes; they are the conditions that social agents react to and operate within. And agents do not always act based merely on instrumental calculations. For example, studies have shown that state repression can generate higher levels of more radical forms of mobilization despite the increase in the costs of protests; this is because repression can trigger moral indignation that drives people to act (Opp, 1994). The relationship between structural conditions and social actions and interactions is more similar to the relationship between the structure and conditions of a playing field and the "game" unfolding on it (Ferree et al., 2002). The structure of the playing field does affect the game, but the outcome of the game is ultimately the result of the dynamic interactions among the players.

Given the above considerations, instead of talking in terms of structural opportunities, our analysis of the Umbrella Movement will be built on an underlying emphasis on historical trajectories and conditioned contingencies. This emphasis is grounded in two interrelated recognitions. First, the Umbrella Movement was a "movement" only in a relatively loose sense. Broadly defined and enduring social movements, such as the environmental movement, the feminist movement, the antinuclear movement, etc., can consist of waves of prominent protest activities punctuated by periods of low-profile actions on the part of the hardcore activists (Melucci, 1989; Taylor, 1989). Considered in relation to enduring social movements, the Umbrella Movement can actually be better seen as a large-scale, intensive protest campaign belonging to the broader pro-democracy movement in Hong Kong. To explain the occurrence of the Umbrella Movement, therefore, is to explain why the newest and most powerful demonstration of the pro-democracy movement in Hong Kong would take the form of a large-scale civil disobedience campaign in year 2013 to 2014.

Second, when the "why" question is framed as above, there is a strong case for treating the context for the Umbrella Movement not as a static structure but as an evolving historical process. On July 1, 2003, half a million Hong Kong citizens protested on the street against the Hong Kong government, forcing the latter to postpone the then imminent national security legislation. This "July 1 protest" constituted a critical event for the Hong Kong society, altering elites and popular perceptions of reality and thus the political strategies of various actors (Lee & Chan, 2011). It reinvigorated the pro-democracy movement in the city and contributed to the broader growth and diversification of protest politics in Hong Kong (Cheng & Yuen, 2017). These happenings and processes, we contend, are the indispensable background without which the Umbrella Movement cannot be properly understood.

Nevertheless, an emphasis on historical trajectories also brings along an emphasis on contingencies. In any processes that unfold over time, what happens before conditions, but not necessarily determines, what happens afterwards. The past does not determine the present and the future partly because of the agencies of actors, and partly because social reality can often be substantially affected by accidents, mistakes, and unintended consequences.

In order to discuss the historical context for the Umbrella Movement more sys-tematically, we draw upon discussions of the "temporalities of social movements" (McAdam & Sewell, 2001), especially the brief but succinct conceptualization by Della Porta and Mattoni (2015). They argued that a movement is simultane-ously tied to a long-, a medium-, and a short-term temporality. In the long-term perspective, "social movements intertwine with 'cultural epochs of contention' in which specific templates of contention are available to protesters" (p. 46). The long-term temporality highlights the continuities and similarities across a range of protests and movements happening within the same socio-historical era. In the medium-term perspective, a movement can be considered as locating at a certain point in a protest cycle (Tarrow, 1989, 1998) or belonging to a wave of protests (Koopmans, 2004). Such a temporality emphasizes the ups and downs of social mobilization over time. In the short term, during the mobilization stage, the unfolding of protest actions is shaped by the occurrence of events and the interactions among agents.

We follow Della Porta and Mattoni (2015) in trying to identify three temporali-ties of the Umbrella Movement, but we do not adopt their exact definitions of the long, medium, and short term. We treat the three temporalities in relative terms, and we do not attempt to place the Umbrella Movement within an "epoch of conten-tion." This is based on the presumption that social movements in Hong Kong were experiencing rapid changes in the two decades before the Umbrella Movement. It may not be useful to treat contemporary Hong Kong as in the midst of a relatively stable "epoch of contention." Instead, Della Porta and Mattoni's (2015) "medium-term perspective" becomes our "long-term perspective"; that is, we first of all posit the Umbrella Movement within the rise and transformation of social mobilization in Hong Kong since the early 2000s.

Our medium-term perspective, then, refers to the two-year Occupy Central Campaign before the beginning of the collective actions in late September 2014. One important characteristic of the Umbrella Movement is that it occurred after a long period of planning and intensive discursive contestation surround-ing the nature, character, purpose, and justifiability of civil disobedience. For nearly two years, a large-scale collective action was pre-announced, anticipated, and prepared. The lengthy period of preparation was crucial because large-scale occupation of urban streets represents a "tactical innovation" in social protests in Hong Kong. The articulation of civil disobedience by the proponents of Occupy Central and the discursive contestation that ensued should have substantially shaped the general public's understanding and expectations. Such understand-ing and expectations could influence the onset and evolution of the protest actions even after Occupy Central was unexpectedly turned into the Umbrella Movement.

The short-term temporality, then, simply refers to the 79 days of occupation between September 28 and December 15, 2014. The occupation evolved as a result of the dynamic interactions among the movement leaders, the participants, the pro-democracy parties and civic organizations, the news media, the Hong Kong and Chinese governments, the police force, the pro-establishment politicians and social elites, and the anti-occupation protesters.

As Della Porta and Mattoni (2015) pointed out, paying attention to temporality allows researchers to "appreciate the dynamism of explanatory variables in the development of mobilizations" (p. 45). Different factors may play different roles and have different degrees of influences at different stages of the contentious action. Even the basic profile of the movement's participants may shift over time. The relationships among the three temporalities is a matter of conditioned contingency; that is, the evolution of a social movement within each temporality is to a large extent contingent upon the happening of events and the interactions among actors, but these contingencies do not arise out of a historical vacuum. The relatively more short-term temporality is grounded in the relatively more long-term temporality in the sense that the latter constitutes the conditions that shape the happenings in the former.

The identification of the three temporalities and the idea of conditioned contingency help organize our analysis and interpretation of the Umbrella Movement. As we will see throughout the later chapters, aspects of the Occupy Central campaign can be properly understood only when it is tied to the political culture and the transformation of protest actions in the city in the previous 15 years, and the Occupy Central campaign in turn exerted certain influences on the evolution of the Umbrella Movement.

The Roles of Digital and Mass Media

The wave of popular protests that was treated as exemplary of new movement phenomena by Castells (2012) and Bennett and Segerberg (2013) has also generated hyperbolic media discourses about the impact of the Internet on social movements, with phrases such as "Facebook Revolution" and "Twitter Revolution" being coined and celebrated. Meanwhile, a proliferating body of research has aimed at uncovering the roles and functions of digital media, and especially social media, in the protest wave (e.g., Gonzalez-Bailon & Wang, 2016; Mico & Casero-Ripolles, 2014; Papacharissi, 2016; Penney & Dadas, 2014; Poell, Abdulla, Rieder, Woltering, & Zach, 2016; Salem, 2015; Thorson et al., 2013; Tremayne, 2014).

Academics, expectably, are much more cautious not to exaggerate the power of technologies (Olorunnisola & Martin, 2014). Many researchers emphasize that digital media technologies did not "cause" the movements, or at least did not cause them single-handedly, while at the same time arguing that digital media did play significant roles in empowering and shaping the protests (e.g., Eltantawy & Wiest, 2011; Howard & Hussain, 2013; Kamel, 2014). As Castells (2012) put it:

> Neither the Internet, nor any other technology for that matter, can be a source of social causation. Social movements arise from the contradictions and conflicts of specific societies. . . . Yet, at the same time, it is essential to emphasize the critical role of communication in the formation and practice of social movements, now and in history. Because people can only challenge domination by connecting with each other, by sharing outrage, by feeling togetherness, and by constructing alternative projects for themselves and for society at large. Their connectivity depends on interactive networks of communication. (p. 229)

Digital media technologies are neither the necessary nor sufficient conditions for large-scale social movements. But in many contemporary "mediatized" societies (Hepp, 2012; Hjarvard, 2013), digital media have become ubiquitous and fully embedded in people's everyday lives. And Hong Kong is one of such societies.[16] Digital media are fast becoming not so much institutions producing contents for mass consumption as logistical tools essential for people to navigate their everyday living environment (e.g., Frith, 2015; Peters, 2015). It is difficult to imagine that digital media would play no role at all in any significant social phenomena. Nevertheless, several qualifications and conceptual considerations have to be kept in mind when analyzing the impact of digital media technologies in specific cases.

First, recognizing the general significance of the Internet does not mean that all kinds of digital media platforms are playing all sorts of roles in all specific movements. In fact, some studies have downplayed the role of specific social media platforms in the Middle East uprisings. Ems (2014) argued that Twitter mainly served to convey information from within Iran to the Western media during the Iranian Revolution in 2009. Aday et al. (2013) found that the consumers of the social media messages during the Arab Spring came mostly from outside the region. Social media was therefore mainly a "megaphone" that generated external attention (p. 912). Meanwhile, Theocharis, Lowe, van Deth, and García-Albacete (2015) analyzed tweets during Occupy Wall Street, Spain's Indignados, and the Greek Aganaktismenoi movement and found that only a very small proportion involved mobilization and coordination of actions. They concluded that Twitter "does not seem to have altered the underlying processes that drive collective action and organization" (p. 217). These studies illustrate the importance to pay attention to the questions of which digital media platforms really matter and what kinds of impact digital media platforms have *and do not have* in specific cases.

Second, the impact of the Internet is dependent on how people use it. There is no guarantee that activists, movement organizations, and citizens would use digital media in ways that would maximize the benefits and power of such technologies.

In fact, even before the advancement of social media, the Internet has long been regarded as capable of lowering the costs of information, coordination, mobilization, and participation for activists and participants (Coopman, 2011; Lupia & Sin, 2003). The Internet constitutes an important resource facilitating more efficient and effective mobilization processes (Hara & Huang, 2011). It also provides the platforms for movement groups to communicate with supporters more directly (Hajek & Kabele, 2010; Stein, 2009). However, as Earl and Kimport (2011) pointed out, the Internet's affordances are not always leveraged by movement organizations. Where individual citizens are concerned, there is also a well-established argument that the Internet creates a high-choice media environment in which selective exposure can be more easily exercised (Bennett & Iyengar, 2008; Iyengar & Hahn, 2009). The online public is fragmented into echo chambers within which people are exposed mainly to what they are interested in and/or agree with. The result is the enlargement of the existing participation gap between the politically interested and non-interested (Prior, 2007) and the polarization of public opinion (Sunstein, 2009, 2017). Internet use can bring people toward as well as away from social movements, depending on what people use the Internet for.

Third and most important, it is necessary to consider digital media as functioning within a broader media environment comprising both digital media platforms and conventional media institutions. A large part of the impact of digital media platforms on protests needs to be understood in relation to what the mass media institutions would and would not do. In the Arab Spring, for example, social media played an important role in communicating the events to the wider public and the international audience partly because the national news media in the Arab countries were tightly controlled by the state and hence did not report on the protest events at all. It thus left the room open for social media to take up the basic information dissemination function. But at the same time, even in the Arab Spring, certain mass media institutions—Al Jazeera in particular—remained crucial in communicating the events to the world and kept the actions of the Arab states under the monitoring by the international society. Al Jazeera and foreign media reported on the events partly by curating content from citizens via digital media platforms (Ahy, 2016; Howard & Hussain, 2013; Wolover, 2016). In other words, social media communication by the citizens during the Arab Spring could achieve their impact partly due to the amplification effect of mass media institutions.

It should be noted that digital media are often considered as having the potential of changing the unequal relationship between social movements and conventional media. The movement-media relationship is unequal because social movements are reliant on the mass media for communicating their messages to the general public, validating themselves as legitimate spokespersons on public matters, and enlisting the participation and support of third parties (Gamson & Wolfsfeld, 1993). But the news media are much less reliant on social movements because there are numerous news stories and events competing for journalists' attention on any given day.

Against this background, digital media may help address the inequality by allowing social movements to bypass the mainstream media and communicate with the public directly. However, as just pointed out, the Internet can also lead to heightened levels of selective exposure. Consequentially, the information and materials social movements offered online are likely to be accessed mainly by those who are already supportive toward the movement (Marmura, 2008, p. 261). Conventional mass media can remain significant if a social movement needs to preach beyond the choir.

Therefore, an analysis of the evolution of a social movement also needs to pay attention to mass media institutions, not only because it shapes the influence of digital media, but also because they have retained a substantial degree of power to set the agenda, represent reality, confer status, and amplify messages even in the era of digital media technologies (e.g., Molaei, 2015; Tufekci, 2013).

When considering the mass media–social movement nexus, one prominent, critical perspective adopted by many social movement scholars emphasizes the way the mainstream media are embedded in the dominant political economic structure of the society due to ownership patterns and reliance on advertising. The mainstream media thus constitute agents of social control and have the tendency either to ignore social movements altogether or to portray them as deviant and even threatening (Chan & Lee, 1984; Gitlin, 1980; Small, 1995; Boykoff, 2006). In the case of the Umbrella Movement, while the mainstream media could hardly ignore such a large-scale event, it would not be surprising if many news outlets exhibited biases against the movements given the political economy of the press in the city (Fung, 2007; Lee, 2015a).

Nevertheless, the mainstream news media are not a singular, undifferentiated entity. News organizations can have different political predilections. In Hong Kong, the presence of the strongly pro-democracy *Apple Daily* and a few other relatively liberal-oriented news outlets had pushed the boundaries of acceptable news discourses (Lee, 2015a). There can also be discrepancies between the news organizations' political predilections and the political and social attitudes of the individual journalists, especially the younger journalists working in the frontline. Around the world, frontline journalists are often found to hold more liberal progressive social and political views when compared to newsroom managers, and Hong Kong is not an exception to the pattern (Lee & Chan, 2009a). Moreover, despite political pressure, the news media and professional journalists cannot totally ignore some of their basic professional values and normative social roles. Therefore, the "mainstream media" should be seen as a complex configuration of media institutions subjected to a range of external and internal influences that are sometimes contradictory to each other.

The implication is that the mainstream news media can also have complex and contradictory influences on social movements, as well as multifarious relationships with digital media communications. On the one hand, the significance of much digital media communications—ranging from interpersonal communications among movement supporters via social media to content produced by online alternative news sites—resides in how they challenge the symbolic power of the mainstream media and the reality constructed in the dominant public sphere. In this regard, digital media may sustain the emergence of online counter-publics (Cayli, 2013; Downey & Fenton, 2003). But on the other hand, the "counter-public communications" via digital media can also be intertwined with and even reliant on mainstream media contents. In a large-scale protest campaign, as long as the mainstream media do not completely refrain from covering the facts about the protest and the actions and responses of the government and other stakeholders, the basic information disseminated by the mainstream media remains crucial raw materials based on which counter-public discourses can be developed. Besides, to the extent that the mainstream media system is internally diverse, digital media communications may work with the progressive elements of the mainstream media system to generate and propagate pro-movement discourses.

In sum, digital media play an important role in the formation of contemporary large-scale protests because of their pervasiveness in people's lives. But they do not constitute a "cause" in isolation from other institutions. Most important, while digital media platforms and mass media institutions are analytically distinctive from each other, they are closely intertwined in reality, forming an integrated media environment (Chadwick, 2011, 2013) within which information, discourses, and images are communicated to different sectors of the public. Given the presence of internal complexities within both the digital media arena and mass media institutions, digital media communications can work with and against different elements of the mainstream mass media system. Both digital and conventional media had multiple and potentially contradictory influences on the Umbrella Movement.

Analytical Approach and Chapter Outline

To recapitulate, this book attempts to provide an analysis of the role and impact of the media in the Umbrella Movement by grounding it into an overall account of the occurrence and evolution of the movement itself. We aim at using such an overall account of the Umbrella Movement to engage in theoretical dialogues with existing work on the media-movement nexus, especially certain influential works about the role of digital media in the rise of new forms of protests.

Specifically, we see the Umbrella Movement as taking up some, but not all, of the characteristics of new movement formations and action logics identified by scholars through examining recent protest movements. The Umbrella Movement can be considered a case in which connective actions generated through bottom-up processes intervened into a collective action with central leadership. In the process, connective actions both empower the movement and generate tensions. Our analysis will pay particular attention to the role of digital media platforms and mass media institutions, treated as forming an integrated media environment, in shaping citizens' participation and the dynamics of the movement as a whole.

Given the above-explained emphases on conditioned contingency and the dynamic development of a movement, the analysis and chapters are organized largely according to the temporal unfolding of the Umbrella Movement. We will put the Umbrella Movement into its historical context by emphasizing the rise and transformation of social mobilization in Hong Kong since the early 2000s as well as the Occupy Central Campaign immediately preceding it. We see the Umbrella Movement as a contingent product of the happening of events and the interactions among the key actors, including the large group of participants and the government, but the evolution of the movement cannot be totally dissociated from the conditions that can be identified through the long- and medium-term perspectives.

Within each chapter, our general goal is to provide a contextually and conceptually informed analysis of the specific stage or aspect of the movement concerned. The analyses in various chapters should be able to highlight the social, cultural, and theoretical import of the case under study.

The exact range of data and methods used in each chapter is partly constrained by data availability, partly driven by this book's relative emphasis on media and communications, and partly based on what we regard as most significant in the specific stage or aspect of the movement addressed in the chapter. For instance, our analysis of the Occupy Central campaign preceding the Umbrella Movement in Chapter 3 will emphasize the discursive work by the Trio and the ensuing discursive contestation in the public arena. Our analysis of the government's response to the Umbrella Movement in Chapter 6 will examine the counter-frames put forward by the government and the pro-establishment forces. But this is not because we have an underlying theoretical emphasis on "discourse" or "frames" throughout the book; it is because we believe that the discursive contestations surrounding the concept of civil disobedience constituted the most appropriate and accessible entry point if we need to understand how the Occupy Central campaign shaped the Umbrella Movement, and analyzing the counter-frames utilized by the government was also an appropriate entry point to discuss the government's more general "counter-movement strategies."

Therefore, while this introductory chapter has outlined the aims and certain theoretical principles of our analysis, more specific research questions and analytical issues will be articulated in various chapters to come. In the process, additional theoretical and conceptual tools will be introduced or developed.

Chapter 2 offers a discussion of the background of the Umbrella Movement from the "long-term perspective." We discuss the proliferation, and to a certain extent the normalization and routinization, of social protests in Hong Kong. In association, we discuss the development and mutation of "citizen self-mobilization" for social protests in the city. Moreover, since young people constituted the main participants of the Umbrella Movement, Chapter 2 also discusses the "post-material turn" among young people in Hong Kong as part of the background of the Umbrella Movement.

Chapter 3, then, discusses the Occupy Central campaign. We contend that the proposal of civil disobedience in the form of occupying urban streets was a response from the "pro-democracy moderates" to the movement sector's urge to radicalize. But putting forward a new and more radical type of collective actions requires intensive discursive work of justification. Chapter 3 examines the characteristics of such discursive work. Drawing upon population surveys, it also illustrates the "educational role" of the Occupy Central campaign and the impact of media and communication on citizens' understanding of civil disobedience.

Chapters 4 to 6 will then focus on the Umbrella Movement itself. Chapter 4 offers an analysis of the impact of the media on the quick scaling up of the movement on September 28 and on public opinion in the first few weeks of the movement. Specifically, the chapter develops the concept of the partially censored public monitor to understand the mixed and even contradictory impact of the media, especially television, on public opinion. Consistent with the notion of an integrated media environment, the analysis also emphasizes the role of digital media in enhancing the mainstream media's public monitor function.

Chapter 5 focuses on digital media use and connective actions. The chapter contends that digital media facilitated the spread of variegated and personalized participation. It strengthened people's involvement and thus empowered the movement, but also introduced decentralizing forces into it. Empirically, the chapter draws upon the protest onsite surveys to provide information about the protesters' online communication activities and evidences for the major contentions. The chapter then presents an exploratory analysis of Facebook public pages created in support for the movement. The analysis further illustrates the relationships between central leadership and bottom-up connective actions in the occupation campaign.

Chapter 6 discusses the dynamics toward the end of the protest campaign, focusing particularly on the discursive frames and counter-mobilization strategies adopted by the government. The chapter analyzes the editorials of the pro-government newspapers and illustrates three main counter-movement frames. It discusses how political strategies, coupled with discursive frames, were employed by the pro-government forces to undermine the movement. It also discusses how such discourses circulated in the online pro-government enclaves constructed by the conservatives.

Chapter 7 summarizes our account of the Umbrella Movement. The chapter discusses the implications of the analysis on theoretical understandings of the emergence of social movements in the era of networked digital media, the power and limitations of connective actions, and the role of mass and digital media in protest formation and participation. Such discussions would compare the Umbrella Movement to similar protest movements in other parts of the world in the past few years, ranging from the Arab Spring to Taiwan's Sunflower Movement in 2014. The chapter ends with a discussion of the possible impact of the Umbrella Movement on Hong Kong politics and society, as well as the future development of social mobilization in the city.

Notes on Data and Methods

The analysis in this book is based on a range of empirical data obtained before, during, and after the Umbrella Movement. Chapter 2, for example, draws upon the data from a number of studies conducted by the authors in the past. Chapter 3 draws upon a representative population survey conducted in 2013. Chapter 3 and Chapter 4 involve the analysis of media texts. Chapter 5 draws upon an analysis of Facebook public pages, focusing particularly on their interconnections and some basic content characteristics. Chapters 3 to 5 also draw upon a population survey and two onsite protester surveys conducted during the Umbrella Movement. While the population survey follows the standard approach of representative survey research, it would be worthwhile to briefly discuss the onsite protester surveys here.

Methodologically, the protester surveys follow what is by now a well-established approach in social movement studies for deriving samples of protesters from protest sites (Lee & Chan, 2011; Milkman, Luce, & Lewis, 2013; Walgrave & Verhulst, 2011). Specifically, teams of interviewers were ordered to walk along designated paths that would allow them to cover the occupied areas. They were asked to select every tenth person that they walked past as an interviewee. The interviewers were asked not to choose interviewees by their own predilections, but had to follow the procedure strictly and select the person who stood closest to them when several protesters stood together. The selected interviewees were asked to fill out the questionnaires by themselves. The procedure treats the temporal-spatial distribution of the protesters in the occupied areas as the sampling frame, and the orders given to the interviewers were aimed at minimizing biases introduced by interviewers.

In contrast to protests with a very tense and uncertain atmosphere on the site (e.g., Tufekci & Wilson, 2012), we could adopt this procedure largely because the occupied areas were largely peaceful and orderly most of the time throughout the movement. The participants were very cooperative. Due to resource constraints and various practical considerations, the October survey, conducted on October 4 and 5, was done only in Admiralty, while the November survey, conducted on November 2, covered Admiralty and Mong Kok. The sample sizes of the two surveys are 969 and 567, respectively, and the response rates are both higher than 95% (the Appendix provides the descriptive profiles of the participants derived from the onsite surveys).

The relative reliance on survey data in this book means that we differ methodologically from many studies that focus mainly on analyzing social media contents and networks. We did not conduct more comprehensive and elaborate analyses of social media contents and networks other than the Facebook page analysis to be reported in Chapter 5 partly because our analytical interests and concerns go beyond communications in the social media arena, and partly because the majority of the most important and relevant social media communication contents during the Umbrella Movement were inaccessible. Hong Kong citizens seldom used Twitter and similarly public-oriented social media sites. Rather, protesters used mostly Facebook and WhatsApp for communicating about the movement. The impossibility of accessing such privatized communications limits researchers' capability of tackling certain research questions, such as the exact ways social media helped ordinary participants to coordinate the occupation by themselves.

In the ideal world, conventional survey methods and content analyses should be combined with social media content data to offer a comprehensive examination of media communications in a protest campaign. But we have collected what we can feasibly collect given resource and reality constraints. We believe that the range of methods and data should be adequate for the range of questions and issues to be addressed in this book.

2

Social Transformation and the Rise of Protests, 2003–2014

Large-scale social protests are by no means rare in contemporary Hong Kong. On July 1, 2003, half a million citizens marched on the street to protest against the then upcoming national security legislation and government incompetence in general. The protest succeeded in forcing the government to postpone the national security legislation. Since then, the "July 1 protest" has become a series of annual protest activities, in which tens of thousands of citizens call for democratization and make a range of policy demands.

The July 1 protest in 2003 was a "critical event" (Staggenborg, 1991, 2001) that altered the perceptions of reality by both the political elites and ordinary citizens (Lee & Chan, 2011). The Chinese government was widely regarded as having shifted its strategies of governing Hong Kong after 2003, intervening more openly and directly into local political and social affairs (Poon, 2008; Tai, 2008). This intervention paved the way for increasing conflicts between the local society and the Chinese state in later years.

For the local society, the July 1, 2003, protest spurred the growth of new civic groups and political organizations. Pro-democracy political parties such as the Civic Party and the League of Social Democrats, established in 2005 and 2006, respectively, can be considered as organizational spin-offs of the 2003 protest. The emergence of the heritage protection movement and related civic associations since 2005 also can be regarded as having been propelled by the 2003 protest (Lee & Chan, 2011, p. 131). These new organizations and groups in turn contributed to the continual growth of social mobilization.

Therefore, while the Umbrella Movement surprised many local observers by its form and duration, the occurrence of a large-scale protest campaign on the issue of democratization in Hong Kong was itself unsurprising. The rise and transformation of social mobilization constitutes the crucial historical context for understanding the emergence of the Occupy Central campaign and the Umbrella Movement.

Drawing upon the literature in social movement studies, one way to describe and analyze the rise of protests in Hong Kong is to treat it as a protest cycle. The concept of a protest cycle, or cycle of contention, sees protests in a society as going through periods of ups and downs, largely as a result of resource mobilization and competition (Kitschelt, 1993; Mueller, 1999; Tarrow, 1989). A protest cycle begins with the initial success of social movements, which brings about the proliferation of movement groups, protest activities, and higher levels of public support for social movements. New movement organizations put forward new claims and develop new tactics. But as the movement sector continues to grow, competition for resources, supporters, and influences intensifies. This leads to the co-optation of some movement organizations into formal political institutions at one end, and the radicalization of some movement organizations on the other. Public support for movements thus goes downward.

On the surface, the success of the July 1 protest in 2003 and the subsequent growth of civic associations and public support correspond to the initial stages of the protest cycle model. There has also been a trend of movement radicalization in Hong Kong in recent years (Cheng, 2014), to be discussed further later. In one sense, the Umbrella Movement can be considered as located along the rising curve of a protest cycle.

However, by focusing mainly on the "ups and downs" of social movements, the protest cycle model does not give enough credence to the possibilities of long-term and enduring changes brought about by waves of mobilization. That is, although levels of social mobilization inevitably rise and fall over time, a society may not return simply to where it began after the end of a protest cycle. Given this consideration, another concept pertinent to understanding the rise of protests in Hong Kong is Meyer and Tarrow's (1998) notion of the social movement society. The notion was motivated by the observation that social movements and contentious politics have become normalized into a routine part of the political process in advanced Western liberal democracies (Dalton, 2002).

The social movement society has three major, interrelated characteristics. First, social movements and collective actions become diversified, not just by having more people participating in protests, but also by having a more diverse range of groups organizing protest activities addressing a more diverse range of issues and aiming at a more diverse set of targets (Rucht, 1998; Soule & Earl, 2005). Movement practices may even spread into various social arenas and be adopted by people to address issues other than public affairs as conventionally understood (Earl & Kimport, 2009).

Second, in a social movement society, the general public comes to accept the legitimacy and appropriateness of collective actions as a means for people to stake claims about their interests and goals. It does not mean that the public necessarily supports every single protest adopting any kind of tactics. In fact, as Della Porta (1999) pointed out, the normalization of certain forms of protests is often accompanied by the stigmatization of other protests as deviant and radical. What the movement society is expected to exhibit is a high level of "diffuse support" among the public for the generalized idea of social movement itself.

Third, uncertainties surrounding protest activities are reduced in a movement society. The state, the media, and the public can more easily predict what kinds of protests will happen where, when, and in what forms. The protest actions also become less disruptive and cause lower levels of damages (McAdam & Simpson, 2005). Closely associated with this trend is the increasingly cooperative relationship between protest groups and the police (McCarthy & McPhail, 1998).

As we will elaborate in the next section, there are aspects of the development of social mobilization in Hong Kong that are consistent with the concept of the social movement society, especially in terms of the rise of public support toward social movements. Where Hong Kong deviates from the social movement society model is the inability of its formal political institutions to absorb public opinion into the policy and political decision-making processes (Cheng, 2016). Social movements became valorized as one of the most important forms of public opinion expressions in the city. In such a situation, protests are normalized in the sense of being regarded as "normal" by many citizens, but they often fall short of having the effectiveness that citizens demand. As a result, significant frustrations toward routinized protests arose, which created the pressures and incentives for the social movement sector as a whole to radicalize. Radicalization also created a more strained and conflict-ridden relationship between the social movement sector and the police.

This chapter and part of the following one will elaborate on the above account of the development of protest politics in Hong Kong. The next section below will further describe the rise of social mobilization in the city and substantiate the claim that Hong Kong has taken up some features of the social movement society. We will then discuss a peculiar aspect of the evolution of protest actions in Hong Kong since 2003, namely, the rise and transformation of "citizen self-mobilization." This will illustrate the precedents of the use of digital media for protest organization and mobilization among ordinary citizens.

Finally, this chapter will take a detour away from protest politics itself and discuss the transformation in value orientations of the Hong Kong public, focusing especially on the "post-material turn" among the young people. Both the Umbrella Movement and protest politics in general are embedded in broader processes of social and cultural changes. While it is beyond the scope of this book to fully discuss various social and cultural changes of Hong Kong, the rise of a post-material generation and how they perceive the socioeconomic conditions of the city are highly relevant to the Umbrella Movement.

The Rise and Normalization of Protests

The first and most basic indicator of the rise of social mobilization in Hong Kong is the sheer increase in the number of collective actions undertaken over the years.

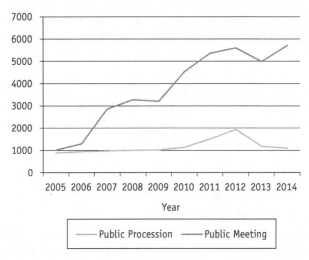

Figure 2.1 Number of public processions and meetings in Hong Kong, 2005–2014

Figure 2.1 shows the number of public processions and public meetings organized in Hong Kong, according to police statistics.[1]

Not all public processions or public meetings are protest actions. But it should be reasonable to assume that a significant proportion of rallies and marches are protests. Assuming that the proportion of non-contentious processions and meetings did not substantially increase over the years, the trends shown in Figure 2.1 should be representative of the trend of numbers of protests in the city.

The number of public processions increased from 887 in 2005 to over 1,000 in 2008, and then to 1,930 in 2012. The number dropped to 1,103 in 2014, but it was still higher than those in the period between 2005 and 2009. The increase in number of public meetings was even sharper and clearer: it grew from 1,013 in 2005 to 3,280 in 2008, and then further to 5,599 in 2012 and 5,715 in 2014, despite a drop in year 2013.

The sheer number of protests is only a small part of the story of the rise of social mobilization. What is also notable is the diversity of collective actions, the changing media image of protests, and increasingly positive public opinions toward the idea of social protests. The following sections discuss these developments by drawing upon data from a content analysis of newspaper coverage of social protests and findings from a range of surveys.

The content analysis, in particular, allows us to describe the characteristics of protests in the city and features of the media's protest coverage. In other words, we use the content analysis data both as a record of events and as news coverage constructed by journalists based on news judgments, production routines, and possibly political biases. Admittedly, these two treatments are based on different theoretical assumptions of the nature of news. We ultimately see news from a constructivist perspective. However, although scholars are well aware of the selection and description biases in protest coverage (e.g., Oliver & Maney, 2000; Oliver & Myers, 1999; McCarthy, McPhail, & Smith, 1996; Wilkes & Ricard, 2007), researchers have also found that other information sources, such as police records, can be even more selective and often lack the information of interest to researchers (Barranco & Wisler, 1999). Hence, in social movement studies, news reports remain the most frequently used basis for establishing protest event databases (e.g., Earl, Martin, McCarthy, & Soule, 2004; Jenkins & Perrow, 1977).

Methodologically, the content analysis examined news reports of protests published by four Chinese general-interest newspapers: *Apple Daily* (*Apple*), *Oriental Daily* (*Oriental*), *Ming Pao* (*MP*), and *Sing Tao Daily* (*STD*). *Apple* and *Oriental* are among the most widely circulated mass-oriented newspapers in the city, whereas *MP* and *STD* are two prominent middle-class oriented newspapers. Politically, *Apple* is strongly pro-democracy. *MP* emphasizes its professionalism and neutrality in news reporting, but also exhibits a somewhat liberal orientation when covering major political events. Both *Oriental* and *STD* are, broadly speaking, pro-government in political orientations.

News articles were derived from the electronic news archive Wise News via a keyword search.[2] Assistants vetted the articles to identify the relevant ones. A relevant article is a news report of a protest action in Hong Kong on the previous day. A protest action is defined as a public, performative action conducted by more than a single person making a claim that is against the interests and/or intention of another party. The procedures resulted in a sample of 1,767 articles: 512 from *Apple*, 485 from *Oriental*, 407 from *MP*, and 363 from *STD*.[3]

For analyzing the characteristics of social protests, the data set with news articles as the unit of analysis was further reconstructed into a data set with a protest action as the unit of analysis. The 1,767 articles reported a total of 795 unique protest actions. The basic characteristics of a protest were then derived by summarizing the information from the news reports.

DIVERSITY OF SOCIAL PROTESTS

Consistent with police statistics, the frequency of protests as registered in the news media increased over time. The sample of protest events included 53 distinctive protests in 2001 and 45 each in 2002 and 2003. The figure rose to 69 in 2006, and then to 103 and 94 for 2011 and 2012, respectively. There is a statistically significant correlation between year and number of protests in the sample ($r = 0.85$, $p < .001$, $n = 12$).

For this section, more important than sheer number of protests is the extent of diversity of the protests in terms of the issues addressed and the identities of the organizers and the targets. Information was collected through the content analysis. For presentational clarity, we broke down the sample into two time periods: 2001–2004 and 2005–2012. The end of 2004 is used as the cut-off point because the critical event of the July 1, 2003, protest is likely to have had an influence on the characteristics of collective actions, and yet such influence (e.g., the proliferation of new civic associations) may take some time to emerge.

As the top half of Table 2.1 shows, except for labor issues and the broad category of "economy, finance and business," none of the other specified issue categories was addressed by more than 10% of the recorded protests. There is also a significant proportion of protests addressing issue categories not specified in the coding scheme. Percentage-wise, there was a lower proportion—from 10.9% to 5.9%—of protests addressing political issues in the second period. Meanwhile, although the Hong Kong economy has improved since 2004 and 2005, the percentages of protests addressing labor issues and the economy have increased.

It is difficult to judge based on the percentages whether protests have become more diversified in topics. The five most prominent topics (excluding non–Hong Kong issues and "other Hong Kong issues") account for 47.5% of the reported protests in the first period and 50.9% of the protests in the second period. This does not indicate a trend of diversification.

However, diversification is arguably signified not by degree of concentration of protest topics, but simply by the emergence of protests about several issue categories, such as gender and sexual orientation, media and press freedom, and public finance. The rises in percentages of protests about these topics are not huge. But protests about such topics were almost nonexistent from 2001 to 2004 and started to appear only in the second period. In fact, looking at numbers of protests, we can see that the figures are invariably larger in the second period. Of course, the second period covers eight years as opposed to four. But even after adjusting the figures into number of protests per year, we can still see that, except for "Hong Kong politics" and "issues in other countries," numbers of protests per year addressing various issues have all increased. In other words, the rise of protests was not centered on specific issues. Protests on a wide range of issues have become more frequent.

The bottom half of Table 2.1 shows the identity of the protest organizers. Information about protest organizers was available for about 70% of the reported protests. "Civic groups" is a large category encompassing a full range of civil society organizations, with only labor unions treated as a separate category.[4] It is not surprising therefore that more than one-third of the protests captured in the sample (and more than half of the protests with information about organizers) were organized by civic groups. Yet there was a significant drop in the proportion of protests organized by civic groups.[5] Interestingly, the percentage of protests organized by labor unions also declined, even though the top half of Table 2.1 has shown an increase in percentages of protests addressing labor issues.

Directly related to the notion of diversification, there were more protests organized by entities that are conventionally less associated with non-institutionalized political actions, thus indicating that more types of groups and organizations have

Table 2.1 **Topics and Organizers of Protests in the News, 2001–2012**

	2001–2004	*2005–2012*	*Total*
Topics			
Hong Kong politics	10.9% (22)	5.9% (35)	7.2% (57)
Economy / finance / business	8.9% (18)	11.0% (65)	10.5% (83)
Public finance	1.0% (2)	3.2% (19)	2.7% (21)
Labor	16.8% (34)	23.1% (136)	21.5% (170)
Education	6.4% (13)	5.8% (34)	5.9% (47)
Social welfare	3.5% (7)	3.7% (22)	3.7% (29)
Environment	4.0% (8)	4.1% (24)	4.0% (32)
Gender / sexual orientation	0.5% (1)	1.9% (11)	1.5% (12)
(Re)development / heritage	3.0% (6)	3.2% (19)	1.5% (25)
Transportation	4.5% (9)	5.1% (30)	4.9% (39)
Public health / medical	1.5% (3)	2.2% (13)	2.0% (16)
Consumer	3.0% (6)	2.9% (17)	2.9% (23)
Media / press freedom	1.5% (3)	3.1% (18)	2.7% (21)
Other Hong Kong issues	25.2% (51)	18.1% (107)	19.9% (158)
Issues in China	5.0% (10)	5.1% (30)	5.1% (40)
Issues in other countries	4.5% (9)	1.7% (10)	2.4% (19)
Organizers			
Civic groups	41.6% (84)	34.9% (206)	36.6% (290)
Labor unions	19.9% (20)	12.4% (73)	11.7% (93)
Commercial / professional / occupational groups	1.5% (3)	3.0% (18)	2.7% (21)
Political parties	13.9% (28)	15.8% (93)	15.3% (121)
Self-organized citizens	0.0% (0)	2.0% (12)	1.5% (12)
Others	1.5% (3)	1.9% (11)	1.8% (14)
No information	31.7% (64)	30.0% (177)	30.4% (241)

Note: Each article belongs to only one category, as only the main protest topic / main protest organizer (in the case of a protest having multiple organizers) was coded. Entries are column percentages, and bracketed numbers are numbers of articles per year.

started to voice their claims through collective actions. The percentage and number of protests organized by "commercial, professional, or occupational groups" have increased slightly, but the sheer number rose from merely 3 in the first period to 18 in the second period. Political parties have also accounted for a larger percentage and number of protests reported. Most interesting, there was the emergence of protests reported as organized by ordinary citizens themselves.[6]

Besides organizers, the content analysis also coded the main protest targets. When coding targets, multiple answers were allowed. Hence there is a set of dichotomous variables about whether a specific entity is the target of the reported protest. The results show that the percentages of protests targeting the Hong Kong and Chinese government have remained stable: 61.4% and 61.9% for Hong Kong government and 5.4% and 6.4% for Chinese government in the two periods, respectively. By contrast, the percentage of protests targeting business organizations increased from 26.7% to 32.9%. On the whole, the percentage of protests targeting at least one non-government entity increased slightly from 48.5% to 51.9%, although this increase is not statistically significant.

CHARACTERISTICS OF MEDIA COVERAGE OF PROTESTS

Communication scholars have long criticized the mainstream news media for adopting the "protest paradigm" when covering social protests (Chan & Lee, 1984; McLeod & Hertog, 1998). Conceptually, the protest paradigm refers to a pattern of news coverage focusing on or even exaggerating violence and disruption, following the script of crime news, highlighting the protesters' (strange) appearance and/or ignorance, portraying protests as ineffective, centering on the theatrical aspects of the protests and neglecting the substantive issues raised, invoking public opinion against the protesters, and privileging sources supporting the targets of the protests. In sum, the protest paradigm is a pattern of coverage undermining and delegitimizing social protests.

Studies in the past decade in various countries have continued to illustrate the presence of the protest paradigm in the news (Di Cicco, 2010; McFarlane & Hay, 2003; Xu, 2013). But other studies have shown that the protest paradigm may be present to different degrees depending on the types of protests and media concerned (e.g., Boyle, McLeod, & Armstrong, 2012; McCluskey, Stein, Boyle, & McLeod, 2009; Weaver & Scacco, 2013). In societies where protests have become normalized, media coverage of protests should become relatively less negative (Cottle, 2008).

There have been studies showing the Hong Kong media's tendency to sensationalize, problematize, and delegitimize "violent" protests (Lee, 2008; Leung, 2009), and various movement groups have criticized the biases of the mainstream media. But these do not rule out the possibility that the news media may have become *relatively* less negative toward social protests in general. The content analysis allows us to examine this possibility. Several indicators of the "protest paradigm" are available. First, two indicators of emphasis on violence and disruption were constructed. The coders identified whether the headline or lead paragraph of an article mentions "arrests," "injuries or damages," "violence/conflict," and "disruption" (e.g., a traffic jam). A single dichotomous variable was created with 1 = at least one item was mentioned in headline or lead and 0 = none was mentioned. In addition, the coders identified whether other parts of the article mention "protesters' use of force," "scuffles," "damage to properties," "disruption of traffic," "disruption of business activities," "disruption of other aspects of everyday life," "arrests," and "injuries." They were originally coded separately and were then turned into a single dichotomous variable with 1 = at least one of the items was mentioned in the article and 0 = none was mentioned.[7]

In the whole sample, 10.4% of the articles mention violence or disruption in the headline or lead, and 14.1% mention violence or disruption in other parts of the article. When broken down into two time periods with end of 2004 as the break-off point, the percentage of news articles mentioning violence or disruption in the headline or lead declined, from 13.6% to 9.2%. The percentage of news articles mentioning violence of disruption in other parts of the article also declined, from 16.6% to 13.3%.[8] The figures are suggestive of relatively less negative media coverage over time.

The media's attitude toward social protests can also be gauged through their use of sources. Whether the protesters are quoted is an important (if far from perfect) indicator of whether the protesters' concerns are communicated in the news. The coders counted the total number of sources used in an article and the characteristics of up to the first 10 sources. Each source was categorized according to the source's relation to the protest.[9] Two variables about inclusion of the protesters' voices were created. The first is *number of protester-sources quoted*, i.e., number of sources who were the protest's "organizers/leaders" or "participants." But the sheer number does not necessarily reflect the extent to which the protester-sources dominate an article. An article can have one protester-source and no other sources; it can also quote multiple protester-sources and an even larger number of other sources. Therefore, the second variable is *protester-sources' share of voice*, which refers to the proportion of sources within a given article being protester-sources.

In addition, the content analysis allows us to construct an indicator of whether the coverage invoked positive or negative public opinion toward the protests. The coders registered whether the sources belonging to the "bystander/observer" or "others" category explicitly praised and criticized the protests or protesters. *Explicit praises and criticisms* is the total number of explicit praises minus the total number of explicit criticisms in an article. Higher scores thus represent the invocation of a more positive public opinion.

When only the first 10 sources are counted, the news articles quoted 0.96 protester-sources on average. The average share of voice of protester-sources is

51.5%, indicating that the voices of the protesters are not seriously marginalized. The "tone of public opinion invoked" variable ranges from −4 to 3 and has a mean score of −.01. But it should be noted that 96% of the news articles score zero on the indicator: most articles did not invoke bystander opinion or the opinions invoked did not constitute explicit praises or criticisms.

We are interested in whether the prominence of protesters' voices and the tone of public opinion invoked have changed over time. As Table 2.2 shows, the "year" variable correlates significantly positively with number of protester-sources and protesters' share of voice. Despite the small coefficients, the findings do support the claim that news coverage has put relatively more emphasis on the voices of the protesters over time. Public opinion invoked does not correlate significantly with "year," but the coefficient is also positive in sign.

On the whole, although the over-time change is not statistically significant for every indicator, all the findings are consistent in direction. They all point toward relatively less negative media coverage of protests from 2001 to 2012. Of course, there could be different interpretations regarding what actually caused the trend. Specifically, the extent to which media coverage would feature violence and disruption is partly dependent on the events themselves. The media could not report on arrests and police-protester conflicts unless the latter did occur. Therefore, it is logically possible that the generally low and declining percentages of articles mentioning disruption and violence may signify an actual decline in disruption and violence in social protests, and the changes in the characteristics of social protests in turn led to a shift in the media's attitude. However, for the present discussion, the important point is that there was a change in media coverage of protests over time. The trend itself indicates the normalization of protests in the city in the period analyzed.

Table 2.2 **Correlations between "year" and the use of news sources**

	Number of protester-sources	Protesters' share of voice	Explicit praises or criticisms
Year	.051*	.066*	.045
Number of protester-sources		.578***	.092***
Protesters' share of voice			.126***

Notes: Entries are Pearson correlation coefficients. $N = 1{,}437$ for correlations involving protesters' share of voice because 330 news articles did not quote any news source and therefore share of voice cannot be calculated. $N = 1{,}767$ for the others. *** $p < .001$; * $p < .05$.

PUBLIC OPINION TOWARD COLLECTIVE ACTIONS AND SOCIAL MOVEMENTS

Another characteristic of a social movement society is that the public holds generally positive views toward social movements and collective actions. Of concern here is not people's support for specific movements. Whether a citizen is supportive toward the gay rights movement or the anti-nuclear movement is likely to depend most heavily on one's attitude toward the issue itself. But people may have positive or negative attitudes toward social movements and collective actions considered generally. Available survey data allow an examination of such general attitudes in three ways: collective efficacy, generalized action potential, and perceived representativeness of social movements.

Political efficacy is people's beliefs about their ability to make a difference in politics. Political scientists have conventionally differentiated between internal and external efficacy, that is, people's perceptions of their own ability to understand and participate in politics, and their beliefs about whether the political system is responsive to their views (see Abramson, 1983). But past research has shown that Hong Kong people exhibit relatively high levels of collective efficacy, which refers to people's beliefs about the capability of the public to effect social change as a collective actor (Lee, 2006a). Collective efficacy has also been shown to have effects on political behavior independent of internal and external efficacy (Lee, 2010).

Table 2.3 summarizes Hong Kong people's levels of internal, collective, and external efficacy over the years.[10] In March 2004, Hong Kong people's level of collective efficacy stood at a very high level, probably encouraged by the success of the July 1 protest in year 2003. The mean scores of the two items are clearly above the midpoint of the scale. Notably, people's level of internal efficacy was not high. That is, Hong Kong people in 2004 were not particularly confident about their individual abilities to understand and participate in politics, but they were quite confident about the capability of the public as a collective actor.

Over the years, people's level of collective efficacy seems to have declined somewhat. The mean score of the first collective efficacy statement dropped from 3.61 in 2004 to 3.49 in 2014, while the mean score of the second statement declined from 3.46 to 3.14 in the same period. But the decline is not substantial. In fact, the most important point one could note from Table 2.3 is the persistence of the basic pattern. Despite the many political events that have transpired in the decade, Hong Kong people's level of collective efficacy remains higher than their level of internal efficacy, and internal efficacy is similarly consistently higher than external efficacy.

Gamson (1968) has articulated the classic argument that people participate in protests when they are confident about their ability to effect change *and* are dissatisfied with the system. The combination of high levels of collective efficacy and low levels of external efficacy thus arguably provide the condition for mobilization. In fact, Hong Kong people have exhibited a substantial level of generalized action potential, that is, a generalized willingness to take part in collective actions (Jenkins

Table 2.3 **Hong Kong citizens' levels of political efficacy**

	2004/03	2005/09	2008/07	2010/01	2012/02	2014/03
Internal efficacy						
I have enough ability to understand politics	3.01	2.83	2.96	3.13	3.24	3.15
I have enough ability to participate in public affairs	3.00	2.68	2.86	—	—	2.82
Collective efficacy						
Collective actions of HK people have huge influence on public affairs	3.61	3.73	3.52	3.26	3.48	3.49
Collective actions of HK people can improve the society	3.46	3.41	3.42	—	—	3.14
External efficacy						
The current HK political system can effectively respond to citizens' demand	2.49	2.82	2.76	–	–	2.50
The current SAR government can effectively respond to public opinion	2.24	2.80	2.62	—	—	2.36

Notes: The entries are mean scores based on a five-point Likert scale ranging from 1 = strongly disagree to 5 = strongly agree. Ns range from 706 (March 2014) to 1016 (February 2012) for the six surveys.

& Wallace, 1996; Oegema & Klandermans, 1994). In a series of surveys conducted by the Centre for Communication and Public Opinion Survey at the Chinese University of Hong Kong, respondents were asked whether they would agree with the statement "I am likely to participate in collective actions such as protest marches in the future to strive for my rights and interests." In January 2010, 38.5% of the respondents disagreed with the statement, whereas 36.5% agreed. The figure means that more than 2 million Hong Kong citizens were then receptive toward the general idea of protest participation.

Remarkably, when the same question was asked in February 2012, the percentage of respondents disagreeing with the statement declined to 27.3%, while the percentage agreeing with the statement rose to 42.4%. The March 2014 survey found that the percentages disagreeing and agreeing with the statement changed further to 19.1% and 46.8%, respectively. In other words, the proportion of citizens who were receptive toward the idea of protest participation kept increasing in the years before the Umbrella Movement.

The same series of surveys also asked the respondents to evaluate whether a number of media platforms, political organizations, and forms of opinion expression were representative of public opinion. Respondents were asked to rate the items using a 0–10 scale. As Table 2.4 shows, Hong Kong citizens rated the Hong Kong government, political parties, and legislators very low. The mean scores of the three items were below the midpoint of the scale in 2010, and they declined further in 2012 and 2014. Media channels fared relatively better. In 2010, the most positively rated items were television news, public affairs commentators, radio phone-in shows, and polling agencies. Public evaluations of media platforms remained stable between 2010 and 2012. However, by 2014 there was a sharp decline of perceived representativeness of all media platforms. Television news, in particular, changed from being the most positively evaluated item on the list to being the least positively evaluated among the media-related items. We will return to this point below.

Against the background of the declining scores of almost all other items, it is highly significant that perceived representativeness of social movements remained

Table 2.4 **Perceived representativeness of channels and forms of opinion expression**

	2010	2012	2014
Channels/forms of expression			
Political parties	4.42	4.46	4.08
Legislators	4.62	4.69	4.10
Hong Kong government	4.84	4.55	3.79
Public affairs commentators	5.65	5.58	4.51
Newspapers	5.48	5.44	4.56
Television news	6.00	6.01	4.43
Radio phone-in talk shows	5.60	5.65	4.82
Polling agencies	5.60	5.65	5.54
Social movements	5.19	5.22	5.23

Notes: Entries are mean scores on a 0–10 scale: 0 = absolutely cannot represent public opinion and 10 = absolutely can. N = 1,007, 1,016, and 1,037 for the 2010, 2012, and 2014 surveys, respectively.

stable. In January 2010, social movements already obtained a mean score higher than the midpoint of the scale. In 2014, the mean score remained above the midpoint of the scale: it even increased nominally to 5.23. And because of the decline in perceived representativeness of the full range of media platforms, social movements became the second most representative entity in the 2014 survey, falling only behind polling agencies.

SOCIAL MOVEMENT AS PUBLIC OPINION

The previous sections have presented evidence showing that Hong Kong society has taken up some of the features of a social movement society since the 2000s: protest actions have become more frequent; they are diverse in terms of topics, organizers, and targets; most protests are relatively non-disruptive; media coverage has become relatively less negative toward protest actions over time; and the public has exhibited an overall positive orientation toward the generalized ideas of social movements and collective actions.

Many of the changes over time illustrated in the previous sections are not substantial; for example, there was no clear linear trend toward diversification of protest topics and organizers, and the trend toward relatively less negative media coverage was weak. This is partly because the rise of protest politics in Hong Kong did not begin only in the early 2000s. Instead, local sociologists have long argued that social movements have constituted an important undercurrent in Hong Kong politics since the late 1960s (Lui & Chiu, 2000). In the mid- to late 1990s, local political scientists (e.g., DeGolyer, 1996; W. M. Lam, 2004) also pointed toward people's experiences in protest participation as evidence against the "myth" of an apathetic citizenry constructed in earlier works on the city's political culture (e.g., Lau, 1982; Lau & Kuan, 1988). Nevertheless, social mobilization has undoubtedly grown further since the early 2000s, especially after the critical event of the July 1, 2003, protest.

Some scholars link the rise of protests in Hong Kong to broader social and cultural changes (Ma, 2011; A. So, 2011). We will discuss the notion of the "post-material turn" later in this chapter. But in relation to the data presented above, it is worth focusing on Table 2.4 again: by 2014, social movements stood out as one of only two means of public opinion expression regarded by the public as representative of public opinion. The rise of protests can therefore be understood in relation to the failure of other social and political institutions in mediating between the polity and the society.

In the colonial era, the Hong Kong society was governed by the technique famously described by sociologist Ambrose King (1975) as the "administrative absorption of politics." Local elites were brought into the political institutions through mechanisms such as inclusion into the Executive and/or Legislative Councils, the appointment of Justices of Peace, and the establishment of consultation committees. However, one condition for the technique to work was the general lack of societal demand for governmental intervention (Lau, 1982). Hong Kong people at the time tended to rely on their familial networks to resolve livelihood problems. But as the society modernized and pluralized, public expectation toward the government increased. Conflicts between societal interests could no longer be easily "absorbed" into the administrative system. Although the SAR government has set up an increasing number of consultative bodies and committees (Ma, 2007), scholars have provided largely negative evaluations of the performance of the consultation system (Cheung, 2011).

Meanwhile, local political parties emerged in the early 1990s as partial democratization was introduced into the political system. But citizens had long exhibited a substantial level of distrust toward politicians and political parties, partly because of the deep-rooted cultural idea that "politics is dirty" (W. M. Lam, 2004), and partly because the absence of democracy and the configuration of the political system have undermined the development of political parties. The Chief Executive of the SAR government, by law, cannot be a political party member. As parties have no chance of actually governing, their role becomes highly restricted to either the government's helper or the perpetual opposition (J. Lam, 2002). The system does not encourage political parties to take their interests aggregation and articulation roles seriously.

The lack of democracy and the weaknesses of the formal political institutions have left open the space for the mass media to articulate and communicate public opinion. In the immediate years after the handover, Chan and So (2004) argued that the Hong Kong media had a surrogate democracy function. With a journalistic corps largely subscribing to the liberal model of journalistic professionalism (So & Chan, 2007), the media provided timely coverage of social issues, communicated diverse viewpoints, provided the platforms for public debates, and monitored the exercise of power. However, the media were also under rising levels of political pressure. Media owners in the city were mostly business people with huge business interests in China. Some of them held formal political appointments in the Chinese political system (Fung, 2007).[11] Although China could not exercise direct control of the Hong Kong press, indirect control through the owners and the utilization of other means of influence, ranging from severe public criticisms to occasional frontline harassment of Hong Kong journalists working in the mainland (Lee, 2007, 2015a), led to widespread self-censorship on politically sensitive matters (Au, 2016; Lee & Chan, 2009a).

The decline of trust in the news media was gradual. As Table 2.4 shows, in January 2010, the Hong Kong public still evaluated various media platforms relatively positively. The situation worsened quickly between 2012 and 2014, probably due to a series of high-profile incidents related to press freedom.[12] Besides, as discussed in Chapter 1, the media system was not completely homogeneous. In addition to a few relatively more liberal-oriented news outlets, radio phone-in talk shows played an important role in communicating public opinion in the city (Lee, 2014). But talk radio could not totally dissociate itself from the mainstream media at large. By 2014, public evaluation of talk radio also substantially declined and fell below the midpoint of the scale.

When even the mass media failed to mediate between the society and the polity, many citizens turned to social movements. In our study of the July 1 protests, we found that many citizens who repeatedly joined the July 1 protests treated protests as a means to voice their opinions without the mediation by other agents (Lee & Chan, 2011, pp. 177–179). The rise of social movements in Hong Kong can be taken as signifying a desire of the citizenry to take their destiny in their own hands when various "representative institutions" have failed.

However, despite people's beliefs in the value of protests for expressing opinions, can the public opinion expressed through protests affect political decision making? If the political system fails to effectively absorb the public opinion expressed through social movements, would people still believe in the power of movements in the long run? As noted earlier, protests have been normalized and routinized in Hong Kong to a certain extent, but the normalization and routinization were by no means celebrated by all in the movement sector. Instead, normalization weakened social movements' symbolic power and ability to disrupt. Normalization of movements thus led to a vocal critique of "ritualistic protests" (Lee & Chan, 2011) and a call for more-radical tactics. Occupy Central, against this background, was the response to the urge to radicalize from parts of the pro-democracy movement.

We will further elaborate on the relationship between movement radicalization and Occupy Central in the next chapter. Before that, the remaining sections of this chapter will discuss two other aspects of the context for the Umbrella Movement, namely the rise of citizen self-mobilization and changes in cultural values of the young citizens.

Mutation of Citizen Self-mobilization

In the face of large-scale social mobilization, conservative politicians and the government regularly attempted to downplay the significance of protests by resorting to various delegitimizing discourses. One theme sometimes evoked by the conservatives describes the protesters as being manipulated or misled by politicians (Lee & Chan, 2011, pp. 74–75). Partly as a response to this negative description of the protesters, "self-mobilization" became an important theme in pro-movement discourses in Hong Kong. The notion of self-mobilization connotes the idea that protesters are citizens capable of critical thinking and making independent judgment on whether to participate in an action or not. Self-mobilization can also be integrated with other themes to generate more elaborate imageries of "high quality protesters." For instance, political scientist Wilson Wong wrote in a commentary:

> Different from the participants in the handover anniversary celebration activities in the morning, participants in the July 1 protest in the afternoon were mostly self-mobilized; their participation was not the result of a top-down, tightly structured process of organizational mobilization. While there were many children among the participants in the handover celebration, the protesters included a lot of middle-class citizens and professionals. While the participants in the handover celebration could enjoy the charade and other entertainment programs, the protesters had to face the scorching sun and unreasonable obstructions by the police.[13]

Wong thus constructed an image of the independent, educated, and persistent July 1 protester. The passage pitted the July 1 protesters against the participants of pro-government rallies. It constructed a set of binary oppositions in which organizational mobilization is tied to the image of the ignorant, leisurely, and comfort-seeking pro-government rally participants.

In more academic accounts, the notion of self-mobilization is used to explain how large-scale protests can arise despite the weak mobilizing power of movement organizations in Hong Kong. In our own study, we found that only 6.4% of the 2003 July 1 protesters were active members of social or political groups. The percentages in the 2004, 2005, and 2007 July 1 protests were only slightly higher at 9.0%, 9.7% and 7.6%, respectively. Besides, fewer than 5% of the protesters in each of the four surveyed July 1 protests reported that they were participating with the groups they belonged to (Lee & Chan, 2011, pp. 145–164).

In addition, the July 1 protesters did not see the calls to actions issued by political figures and social organizations as important to their participation decision. Comparatively, they were somewhat more likely to recognize the calls from the media or from their friends and relatives as influential. Combining the findings, we argued that the mobilization process behind the July 1 protests mainly involved common people not associated with social and political groups sharing information and messages they derived from the news media with each other and calling upon each other to act (Lee & Chan, 2011, p. 200).

However, the July 1 protests were after all organized by movement and political groups. The Civil Human Rights Front (CHRF), a coalition of social groups, movement organizations, and political parties, planned the protest, announced it through the news, negotiated with the police, and mobilized people to participate through their own networks. Our argument was that the CHRF did not have substantial mobilizing power. Hence their role was largely restricted to being the organizer who set up the event in the first place; the most important mobilizing agents were the citizens themselves.

In comparison to the July 1 protests, self-mobilization can be regarded as having taken up new forms and meanings in Hong Kong in subsequent years. Table 2.1 has shown an increase in number of protests organized by "ordinary citizens." Certainly, protests organized by ordinary individuals are not new. Residents come together to protest against development projects in their district; students join hands to protest against school policies; consumers cheated by a company fight for their rights. All of these are conceivable. Sometimes social organizations get involved, sometimes not. Either way, these examples of possible citizen self-initiated protests typically involve a relatively small group of people making claims on a matter that directly affects them; the matter is of little concern to the wider public. In contrast, what is notable as a new development is the capability and willingness of individual citizens to initiate and mobilize for protest actions addressing society-wide issues or events.

The capability of individual citizens to initiate protests is significantly enhanced by the Internet. In February 2008, during a controversy surrounding the leaking of sex photos involving several local celebrities, a group of netizens called for a protest against the police's "selective execution of law." About 400 to 500 people turned up.[14] This was probably the first Internet-based, citizen self-initiated protest in Hong Kong. Another prominent example occurred in January 2012. After security personnel of a Dolce & Gabbana shop in a main shopping area forbade people on the street from taking photos of the shop windows, netizens called for a "photo-taking outing" to protest against the shop's attempt to regulate public space. About 1,000 people joined the action, forcing the company to issue a formal apology.

Admittedly, Internet-based citizen self-initiated protests did not occur frequently. The majority of protests in Hong Kong remain organized by social and political groups. Besides, the two cases recounted above were singular protests. They did not constitute movements or extended campaigns. But the capability of citizens to initiate protests by themselves through the Internet did introduce new possible dynamics into the social movement arena.

Lee (2015c) provided an analysis of the relationship between citizen self-initiated actions and existing movement organizations through two environmental campaigns. Framed within a resource mobilization perspective, that study argued that loosely organized citizens can often react to new issues more quickly and flexibly than formal organizations. This is because the latter are often constrained by their existing agenda, planned allocation of resources, operational routines, and sometimes ties with other organizations. But on the other hand, movement organizations still have significant advantages over self-mobilizing citizens in terms of resources, including not only human and financial resources but also trust and connections with stakeholders; professional knowledge about the issue at hand; experiences about how to handle the news media; and credibility as spokespersons on public affairs.

Lee's (2015c) analysis did not argue for the superiority of one form of mobilization. Rather, it aimed at illustrating how citizen self-mobilization and movement organizations can complement each other in generating and sustaining protest campaigns. The Protect Lung-mei Beach campaign, which was a campaign against the government's plan to create a man-made beach that could damage the ecology of the selected site, is particularly illustrative. The campaign was initiated by a group of disparate individuals from an online wildlife discussion forum. They were mostly unassociated with formal organizations and did not even know each other beforehand. But some of them did have their own social and cultural capital (e.g., advanced degrees in the biological sciences and/or friends in environmental organizations). They thus pooled together their individual-level resources to kick-start the action.

The initiators had enlisted the support and advices from environmental groups from the very early stages. Support and resources from formal organizations became even more important as the campaign intensified, gained media attention, and attracted the participation of large number of citizens. When the campaign evolved and turned to the legal tactic of applying for judicial review, movement organizations and experienced activists took over the leadership, partly because the original initiators found it difficult to sustain long-term intensive involvement, and partly because movement organizations and experienced activists had the know-how to deal with the court system.

In terms of the relationship between the self-mobilizing citizens and formal movement organizations, the Protect Lung-mei Beach campaign is not idiosyncratic. Instead, some of the most prominent protests in Hong Kong in the immediate years before the Umbrella Movement involved a similar cooperation between citizens inexperienced in the organizing of social movements and more formal and resourceful organizations.

The anti–national education movement in summer 2012 is a case in point. The movement aimed at overturning the government's decision to turn national education into a core subject for primary schools due to the fear that the state would "brainwash" the young generation. After a period of intensive mobilization, the movement ended with a week of rallies in front of the Government Headquarters in which tens of thousands of citizens participated, successfully forcing the government to shelve the plan. The movement was led mainly by Scholarism and the Parents Concern Group. The former is a student activist group formed in 2011 by a group of high school students; the latter was formed by a group of parents partly through an online forum. The leaders of these two groups were not experienced activists at the time of the campaign, but many of the core activists in the Parents Concern Group were veteran journalists, university teachers, NGO staff members, and the like. They were therefore capable of initiating actions through pooling together their individual-level social and cultural capital. As the campaign intensified, resources from more-formal social groups and political parties were indispensable, but the latter organizations largely remained backstage. Scholarism and the Parents Concern Group were therefore the public face of the movement throughout.

We can only speculate about the reasons behind the emergence of this form of citizen-movement collaboration. The prominent discourse of "citizen self-mobilization" may have inadvertently reinforced people's distrust toward politicians and formal organizations. Having leaders without formal organizational background may help portray the movement as untainted by vested interests. It may also help the movement to unite and garner support from a wider range of organizations that may have complicated relationships with each other.

In any case, the form of citizen-movement collaboration in the Protect Lung-mei Beach campaign and the anti–national education movement is worth discussing because it was also the form the Occupy Central campaign originally took. The campaign was initiated and led by two university professors and a pastor. The Trio had little or no experience in organizing and leading social movements, but they had relevant cultural and social capital in hand. Benny Tai, a law professor, is well-versed on the concepts of the rule of law and civil disobedience. Chan Kin-man is a renowned academic expert on civil society in China and Hong Kong. Chu Yiu-ming has been active in social movements for more than two decades and is a well-known and respected figure in the Christian churches in Hong Kong. All three persons have widespread interpersonal connections in the social movement sector, the formal political arena, and the media. These resources at the individual level made the initiation of the campaign possible, while formal organizations and political parties could provide additional support and resources when the needs arose.

Generational Differences and the Post-material Turn

Some academics have identified changes in cultural values as one of the main factors behind the rise of social mobilization in Hong Kong (Ma, 2011). The notion of post-materialism, in particular, has entered into public discourses in the city since 2010. A discussion of the "post-material turn" among the city's young people could provide the background for understanding certain occurrences during the Umbrella Movement.

Interests in post-materialism arose in the city largely in association with the anti-express rail protests in late 2009. The protests were against the government's plan to connect Hong Kong to China's express railway system. While some critiques of the government's plan focused on the unreasonably large budget, another main critique ventured by the protesters was the government's neglect of the interests of the rural villagers who would be affected by the construction work. The protesters' discourses were therefore articulated with themes such as the importance of rural areas to the city, the value of agriculture, and alternative lifestyles. Underlying the protests is a critique of a one-dimensional emphasis on economic development without regard for other societal goals and values (L. Y. Ma, 2014).

The protests thus expressed a strong post-material orientation. As the protesters were seemingly mostly young people, commentators began to make sense of generational differences in Hong Kong in terms of the post-material turn of the "post-80s" (i.e., people born in the 1980s). For instance, a newspaper columnist wrote: "the environment within which the 'post-80s' lived was an environment with material affluence. . . . The material needs of the 'post-80s' were already satisfied. Therefore they naturally go after values beyond materialistic satisfaction, such as green economy and social justice."[15]

The above statements can be regarded as a straightforward application of Inglehart's (1977, 1990) theory of post-materialism to Hong Kong. Briefly put, Inglehart's thesis is built upon what he called the scarcity hypothesis and the socialization hypothesis. The scarcity hypothesis posits that people would strive for things and values that are scarce. Drawing upon Maslow's hierarchy of needs, Inglehart posits that people would choose to satisfy the basic needs of physical security before striving for more spiritual and intellectual goals. The socialization hypothesis posits that the value orientation of a person is largely determined by formative experiences, that is, how he or she grows up. Taken together, the theory postulates that value change in a society is largely a result of generational displacement. In advanced industrialized societies, the younger generations growing up with higher levels of formative security would exhibit stronger orientations toward post-material goals.

Interestingly, academic research in Hong Kong in the 1990s and early 2000s largely failed to discover any significant cohort differences in value orientation (Cheung & Leung, 2004; Ho & Leung, 1995, 1997; Ting & Chiu, 2000).[16] However, survey data in the early 2010s did show substantial generational differences in post-material orientation. More complete discussions of the findings and their implications are available in Lee and Tang (2013). Here, the purpose is to present the most important findings in order to provide the relevant context for understanding certain aspects of the Umbrella Movement.

The two surveys, conducted in summer 2012 and 2014, contain a set of questions addressing people's material vs. post-material orientation. Adopting a format utilized in the World Values Survey, each question states four possible goals for the future development of Hong Kong.[17] Two are material goals and two are post-material goals. The respondents were asked to pick what they personally regarded as the most and the second most important goals. For example, the first question asked the respondents to choose among "high levels of economic development," "development of infrastructure," "allowing citizens to have more say at work and in community affairs," and "making the city and rural areas more beautiful." In this case, the first two are material goals, and the last two are post-material. In the 2012 survey, 46.0% of the respondents selected "economic development" as one of the two more important goals, while 49.9% selected "development of infrastructure."

"Having more say" was chosen by 54.6% of the respondents, whereas "beautiful city" was chosen by 41.8%.

For simplicity, a post-material orientation index was created. A respondent got 1 point whenever he or she chose a post-material goal. Hence a respondent could have a score from 0 to 2 from one question and a score from 0 to 10 when all five questions are added together. For presentational clarity, the respondents were differentiated into three groups. Those who scored 0 to 3 were the materialists; those who scored 4 to 6 were grouped as "mixed"; and those who scored 7 to 10 were the post-materialists.[18]

Table 2.5 summarizes the percentages of respondents falling into the three categories. In 2012, 26.8% of the respondents were classified as materialists, whereas 16.7% were post-materialists. In 2014, the proportion of materialists remained virtually the same (26.9%), but there was an apparent increase in the proportion of post-materialists—from 16.7% to 22.8%.

Table 2.5 **Proportions of materialists and post-materialists in Hong Kong, 2012 and 2014**

	Materialists	*Mixed*	*Post-materialists*
Overall			
2012	26.8%	56.5%	16.7%
2014	26.9%	50.3%	22.8%
By age: 2012 (χ^2=50.70, p < .001)			
18–29	10.9%	54.7%	34.4%
30–44	25.9%	57.6%	16.5%
45–59	28.8%	57.3%	13.9%
60 and above	35.7%	55.7%	8.6%
By age: 2014 (χ^2=67.95, p < .001)			
18–29	7.0%	48.2%	44.7%
30–44	18.8%	55.9%	25.3%
45–59	34.9%	45.5%	19.5%
60 and above	33.6%	52.8%	13.6%

Notes: The three groups were differentiated based on the respondents' scores on a 0–10 index: 0–3 = materialists; 4–6 = mixed; 7–10 = post-materialists. N = 806 and 800 for 2012 and 2014, respectively.

The important point here is not the overall proportion of post-materialists and materialists in Hong Kong. The crucial findings are the generational differences. In 2012, only 10.9% of the respondents between 18 and 29 years old were materialists, whereas more than one-third of these youth were post-materialists. In sharp contrast, more than one-third of the respondents aged 60 or above were materialists. Only 8.6% of these senior citizens were post-materialists.

The relationship between age and post-material orientation is not linear. The proportion of post-materialists increases by 8% when one moves from the "60 or above" group to the 30–44 group, but the proportion increases by 18% when one moves from the 30–44 group to the 18–29 group. In other words, there are no strong differences in value orientation among the several older groups. The youngest group—those born between 1983 and 1993—stood out as exceptionally inclined toward post-materialism.[19] The 2014 survey findings replicated the pattern: while the percentage of post-materialists became higher within each age group, the youngest group stood out as exceptionally inclined toward post-materialism.

Why would a post-material turn appear among people born during and after the 1980s but not more conspicuously in earlier generations? Lee and Tang (2013) argued that the post-material turn in Hong Kong was "postponed" by a dominant discourse in the society emphasizing the presence of abundant opportunities and the possibility of individuals achieving upward mobility through diligence and competence. This dominant discourse began to face serious challenges only when the Asian financial turmoil in the late 1990s led to the first serious and persistent economic downturn of the city after its economic miracle (Ku, 2001). These were also the formative years for the "post-80s." In other words, the post-80s grew up within a context where the myth of continual social and economic progress was debunked and the presence of fair opportunities in Hong Kong started to be questioned.

Although the economic downturn ended in 2003 and 2004, social developments since then—persistently high levels of income inequality[20] and skyrocketing property prices, etc.—only deepened (young) people's suspicion toward the dominant discourses. In 2009, a former employee of a major property developer published a book titled *The Property Hegemony*, and the phrase "property hegemony" quickly became the catchphrase for people to articulate a set of criticisms of the Hong Kong society. On the whole, the increasing conspicuousness of serious social and economic inequalities in the context of an affluent society had triggered the youngest generation's post-material turn.

While the validity of this argument needs to be further substantiated, for the present purpose, suffice it to illustrate young people's attitudes toward the traditional discourse of equal and abundant opportunities and the emerging discourse of property hegemony or, to generalize the term, corporate hegemony. The 2012 and 2014 surveys asked the respondents if they would agree with four statements representing the discourse of opportunities: (1) all people have equal opportunities in the Hong Kong society; (2) there are many chances of upward social mobility in Hong Kong; (3) in Hong Kong, individual hard work and competence are the most important determinants of success; and (4) the social system of Hong Kong is, overall speaking, fair. Respondents answered with a five-point Likert scale (1 = strongly disagree and 5 = strongly agree). An index of agreement with the discourse of opportunities was created by averaging the answers. In addition, three statements were used in the questionnaire to represent the discourse of corporate hegemony: (1) the Hong Kong society is controlled by big corporations; (2) many Hong Kong people cannot share the fruits of prosperity; and (3) the distribution of wealth is very unreasonable in Hong Kong. An index of agreement with the discourse was similarly created by averaging the answers.

As Table 2.6 shows, in 2012, the youngest group was indeed the least likely to agree with the discourse of opportunities and the most likely to agree with the discourse of corporate hegemony. In addition, from 2012 to 2014, the youngest group's mean score on the index of discourse of opportunities decreased. They became even less receptive to the idea of Hong Kong being a place with equal and abundant opportunities. At the same time, their mean score on the discourse of corporate

Table 2.6 **Perceptions of Hong Kong society among different age groups**

	Discourse of opportunities	*Discourse of corporate hegemony*
2012		
18–29	3.23	3.88
30–44	3.36	3.77
45–59	3.41	3.65
60 or above	3.32	3.30
F-value	2.74*	20.71***
2014		
18–29	3.03	4.04
30–44	3.31	3.80
45–59	3.46	3.56
60 and above	3.51	3.47
F-value	12.00***	13.11***

Notes: Entries are mean scores on a five-point Likert scale (1 = strongly disagree to 5 = strongly agree). Significance of differences among age groups was tested by one-way ANOVA. * $p < .05$; *** $p < .001$. $N = 806$ and 800 for 2012 and 2014, respectively.

hegemony index increased, that is, they had become even more receptive toward the idea that the social and economic system is unfair.

Notably, only the youngest group exhibited this pattern of changes—that is, increasing disagreement with the discourse of opportunities *and* increasing agreement with the discourse of corporate hegemony—in the most clear-cut manner. For the 30–44 group and the 45–59 group, the mean scores on the two indices obtained in the two surveys were virtually the same. For people aged 60 or above, agreement with the two discourses increased at the same time. Between the two surveys, only the youngest group exhibited a clear and consistent trend toward being increasingly critical about the society.

Behind the Call for Democracy

This chapter has discussed certain social and cultural changes in Hong Kong since the beginning of the 2000s, focusing mainly on the rise of protest politics, mutation of citizen self-mobilization, and the emergence of generational differences in value orientation and perceptions of the society. The purpose of the discussion is to delineate the contexts and precedents for the Occupy Central campaign and the subsequent Umbrella Movement. The Umbrella Movement did not arise out of a vacuum; the growth of social mobilization in Hong Kong since the early 2000s set the conditions for the rise of a large-scale and radicalized protest campaign on the issue of democratization. The decentralized and self-mobilized character of the Umbrella Movement may seem to exhibit some of the characteristics of new forms of social movements emerging around the world. But from a historical perspective, the formation of the Umbrella Movement could and probably should also be understood as yet another reconfiguration of citizen self-mobilization, which has long been an important feature of protest politics in Hong Kong.

The discussion of citizens' value orientation and perceptions of the society, in particular, suggests that underlying people's call for democracy are grievances generated from perceived injustices of the social and economic system. The stated demand of the Umbrella Movement centered on the institutionalization of genuine popular election of the Chief Executive of the SAR government, but the movement was not only about the development of democratic institutions; underlying the demand was the more fundamental concern of social justice.

In fact, liberal democracy is not an idea deeply rooted in the city's political history and culture. In the 1980s, the pro-democracy movement in Hong Kong did not garner huge public support. The largest rallies throughout the decade were participated in by no more than 8,000 citizens (Sing, 2000). Public support for democracy surged only after the 1989 Tiananmen incident (A. So, 1999). By early 2000s, some local political scientists still opined that the conservative political culture in Hong Kong constituted an internal constraint of the city's democratization process (Sing,

2004). A significant proportion of Hong Kong people used to understand democracy as a government willing to consult public opinion (Lau & Kuan, 1988). The question, then, is what can facilitate a process of cognitive liberation (McAdam, 1982) through which people come to see the institutionalization of democratic elections of their leaders as pertinent to their lives and crucial to the well-being of the society.

There was probably no single event leading to widespread cognitive liberation among all. Rather, each social crisis, policy mistake, and political controversy might have led some citizens to question the fairness of the society and realize the relevance of democratization. In our study of the July 1 protests, some citizens opined that the reelection of the highly unpopular Chief Executive Tung Chee-hwa in 2002 led them to realize the central significance of political institutional arrangements (Lee & Chan, 2011). Other participants picked other moments of "awakening." In large-scale protests since 2003, it is not uncommon for the news media to highlight the presence of citizens who were joining a protest for the first time. As protests in the city have addressed a wide range of issues over the years, they have brought different groups of people into the broadly defined pro-democracy movement.

3

Contesting the Idea of Civil Disobedience

On January 16, 2013, Hong Kong University law professor Benny Tai published the article "The most lethal weapon of civil disobedience" in the daily newspaper *Hong Kong Economic Journal*.[1] He criticized the SAR government's lack of commitment to genuine democratic reform. He also doubted the efficacy of previous movement's tactics "because Beijing's intention not to allow Hong Kong to have genuine popular election may be too strong. . . . Therefore, to fight for the realization of genuine democracy in Hong Kong, [we] may need to prepare a more 'lethal' weapon—Occupy Central."

Occupy Central was conceived as an act of civil disobedience: "Participants illegally occupy the main roads in Central for long periods of time in order to paralyze the political and economic center of Hong Kong, forcing Beijing to change its stand." Tai listed eight requirements for Occupy Central to produce the desired effects: a large number of participants, participation by societal opinion leaders, the principle of non-violence, sustainability of the action, participants' willingness to bear the legal consequences, timing of the action, pre-announcement, and having genuine popular election as its goal. Tai further stated:

> Participants need to include societal opinion leaders, especially those who have never broken the law, or those political leaders, ex-government officials, religious leaders, and academics who do not belong to the radical faction. Their participation would signify that the controversy is reaching the critical moment. Even these opinion leaders are forced to express their views through civil disobedience—it could become a powerful moral inspiration for the whole society.

Tai himself fit this profile—an academic who did not belong to the radical faction. The fact that a proposal of civil disobedience was initiated by a person such as Tai is probably one of the reasons behind the high levels of interest and attention the proposal aroused. As Chan Kin-man, who quickly joined Tai as one of the initiators of the Occupy Central campaign, wrote in a newspaper article, "When Tai proposed the occupation action, we were all surprised. Why do even scholars become so radical?"[2] Some commentators took this as a signal of widespread frustration among the middle class in Hong Kong. For example, an editorial in *Ming Pao* on March 2, 2013, stated:

> Whether [Occupy Central] is over-idealistic and operable are subjects for further discussions, but no matter how the situation evolves, the pro-democracy movement in Hong Kong has developed to a point of having the proposal of "Occupy Central," and it was proposed by legal scholar Benny Tai, who had long held moderate views. This reflects his frustration about the progress of democratization. But he is definitely not the only one with such emotions. It is believed that many Hong Kong people who, in the 1980s, supported the idea of democratic return of Hong Kong to the motherland, and who have now joined the ranks of the middle-class, are having such feelings.

Occupy Central, therefore, did not signify the radicalization of a small section of the social movement sector. It was not radicalization as a result of increasing resource competition among movement groups, in which case the moderates and the radicals would have diverged from each other in the process of differentiation. Instead, Occupy Central signified the radicalization of the moderates and so was also taken as signifying the radicalization of a large group of people who supposedly belong to the mainstream society.

Certainly, Occupy Central would not be immediately understood and accepted by all simply because it was initiated by a hitherto politically moderate law professor. The idea attracted immediate criticisms not only from the conservative side, who predictably lambasted the open call for people to break the law, but also from part of the radical faction of social movements, who argued that Tai's discourses and proposed tactics remained overly conservative. Even sympathetic commentators, activists, and politicians raised various questions about the principles guiding the planned action, the proper timing of the action, and the practicalities involved.

What followed the publication of Tai's original article was therefore a "critical discourse moment" (Gamson & Hertog, 1999; Gamson & Modigliani, 1989) in which the concept of civil disobedience was intensively debated. A search on Wise News showed that there were 125 articles in the Hong Kong news sections in eight local newspapers[3] mentioning the term "civil disobedience" in year 2000. The number of articles mentioning the term dropped to between 17 and 90 from 2001 to 2012, but it jumped to 774 in 2013 and 1,507 in 2014.[4]

Civil disobedience was not new to the city, and a campaign called "Occupy Central" had actually occurred in 2011 and 2012, albeit in a somewhat different form as the local movement sector's response to Occupy Wall Street.[5] But civil disobedience remained relatively rare and by no means a well-established item in the city's repertoire of contentious actions. Intended, pre-announced, and long-term occupation of main roads in the urban center also constituted a new movement tactic in the city. As social movement scholars pointed out, protest actions are "learned cultural creations" (Tilly, 1995, p. 42), and people in different societies and at different times may tend to undertake certain forms of actions rather than others (e.g., Allam, 2014; De Fazio, 2012; Ekiert & Kubik, 1998; Wada, 2012). New movement tactics would need to establish their feasibility, legitimacy, and effectiveness. Hence social movements need to engage in discursive work to promote the new tactics among their supporters and members of the public (Biggs, 2013; Hayes, 2006). The intensive discussion surrounding civil disobedience in 2013 and 2014 thus involved the discursive work carried out by the proponents and supporters aiming at articulating the principles underlying the proposed action and defending it against the critics. The discursive work was important in establishing certain principles that would continue to shape the occupation campaign even after the campaign's transformation into the Umbrella Movement. It was also important in facilitating and enhancing public understanding of civil disobedience, paving the way for more widespread participation.

This chapter discusses the Occupy Central campaign ("OC campaign" hereafter)—referring here to the range of discursive and other preparatory works for Occupy Central conducted between early 2013 and late September 2014. It begins by continuing the previous chapter's discussion of the development of protest politics in Hong Kong. Specifically, it points out that the OC campaign was embedded in a context where an enduring emphasis on "social order" in the public culture coexisted with a trend toward radicalization of social movements. The chapter then overviews the discourses surrounding civil disobedience during the campaign. It illustrates how Occupy Central, through the discursive contestation in the public arena, took the form of radicalization with self-restraint.

Then, drawing upon two population surveys conducted in September 2013 and October 2014, respectively, this chapter illustrates the extent to which the Hong Kong public understood the idea of civil disobedience and whether public understanding of the concept increased during the OC campaign. We also examine whether and how media and communication factors predict understanding of civil disobedience, and this begins our analysis of the impact of media and communication on the Umbrella Movement.

Persistent Emphasis on Public Order vs. the Urge of Radicalization

Conceptually speaking, the notion of radicalism or radicalization can refer to several interrelated yet distinguishable aspects of a social movement. As Mueller

(1999) pointed out, when discussing radicalization, one may focus on the forms of actions being undertaken, the collective identities involved in the movement, or the substantive claims being advanced. Generally, radicalization of tactics can be defined as the adoption of more confrontational forms of actions that violate prevailing norms of how movement claims should be expressed and processed, whereas radicalization of substantive claims can be defined as the adoption of claims that ask for a larger extent of redistribution of resources and power and/or for changes at a more fundamental and systemic level (Beach, 1977). In this sense, the proposal of Occupy Central does involve a radicalization in form of actions, but it does not involve the radicalization of claims in an obvious and clear-cut sense.[6] Our discussion in this section thus centers on radicalism/radicalization in terms of protest tactics.

While the previous chapter has presented evidence of increasing public acceptance of the general idea of social movements, it does not entail acceptance of all specific movements and forms of protests. A person supporting social movements in general may still oppose a specific movement if the latter makes claims or adopts actions that violate the norms and values of a society. For example, during the anti–express rail movement in early 2010, the protesters adopted a number of innovative actions, including the trekking protest in which the protesters marched slowly and bowed to the ground every 26th step.[7] At the peak of the movement, thousands of protesters surrounded the Legislative Council, aiming to prevent the legislators from leaving the building after meetings. The 2010 survey introduced in Chapter 2 (from where data about generalized action potential were derived) asked the respondents whether or not they found four actions during the anti–express rail protests acceptable. With answers expressed through a five-point Likert scale ranging from 1 = highly unacceptable to 5 = highly acceptable, only "protest marches" obtained a mean score higher than the midpoint of the scale (3.07). The trekking protest had a mean score of 2.86, slightly below the midpoint, whereas surrounding the legislature and charging the police defense obtained mean scores of 2.38 and 1.95, respectively, indicating strong public disapproval.

The low mean scores partly reflected the negative attitude held by many citizens toward the anti–express rail movement as a whole. Even "protest marches" thus obtained a mean score just above the midpoint of the scale. But the finding that the trekking protests obtained a mean score below the midpoint of the scale and lower than that of protest marches also illustrates the public's suspicion toward unfamiliar forms of protest actions. Although the trekking protest was nonviolent and arguably even less disruptive to social lives than protest marches, it was still accepted by the public to a lesser extent.

To gauge public opinion toward forms of protest actions detached from specific issues and campaigns, the 2012 and 2014 surveys asked the respondents to indicate, by means of the same five-point Likert scale, whether they found "charging the

Table 3.1 **Public attitude toward forms of protest actions**

	Whole sample	By education		By age group		
		Non-college	College	18–29	30–49	50+
2012 survey						
Charging police	1.96	1.97	1.94	1.94	1.93	2.00
Protest marches	3.62	**3.45**	**3.93**	**3.89**	**3.77**	**3.34**
Labor strike	3.22	**3.14**	**3.34**	**3.18**	**3.31**	**3.15**
Sit-in rallies	3.87	**3.73**	**4.13**	**4.03**	**3.96**	**3.71**
Slow driving	2.88	**2.79**	**3.05**	**2.92**	**3.06**	**2.68**
2014 survey						
Charging police	1.85	**1.77**	**1.97**	**2.28**	**1.85**	**1.68**
Protest marches	3.59	**3.34**	**3.95**	**4.12**	**3.77**	**3.22**
Labor strike	3.14	**3.02**	**3.30**	**3.46**	**3.18**	**2.95**
Sit-in rallies	3.85	**3.70**	**4.05**	**4.10**	**3.95**	**3.66**
Slow driving	2.89	**2.76**	**3.06**	**3.14**	**2.99**	**2.68**

Notes: Entries are mean scores on five-point Likert scales (1 = very unacceptable, 5 = very acceptable). Statistical significance of differences between mean scores by educational level was examined by independent samples' t-tests, while significance of differences among mean scores by age groups was examined by one-way ANOVA. Significant differences ($p < .05$) are indicated by figures in boldface. N = 806 and 800 for 2012 and 2014, respectively.

police defense," "protest marches," "labor strike," "sit-in rallies," and "slow driving" as acceptable. Table 3.1 summarizes the findings.

The 2012 survey found that, once forms of actions are detached from specific campaigns, sit-in rallies and protest marches were generally accepted by the public. The mean scores are substantially higher than the midpoint of the scale. Meanwhile, labor strike and slow driving obtained mean scores that are relatively closer to the midpoint of the scale. Labor strike was accepted by the public to a somewhat larger extent when compared to slow driving. One plausible interpretation of the findings is that they show the impact of perceived disruptiveness of the forms of actions on public acceptability. Both labor strike and slow driving can be considered more disruptive to social life when compared to protest marches and sit-ins. At the same time, slow driving is arguably more disruptive to the everyday lives of citizens, since it inevitably obstructs traffic. Labor strike, in contrast, may not have direct implications on citizens' everyday lives (depending on the industries involved). Hence slow driving was accepted to a lesser extent when compared to labor strike.

More important, detaching "charging the police defense" from specific protest campaigns did not result in higher levels of acceptability. The mean score 1.96 is virtually the same as the score obtained in the 2010 survey. It shows a high level of general disapproval of the action of directly confronting the police. In addition, in 2012, disapproval against charging the police defense was shared by all groups of people defined by age and educational levels. For the four forms of actions other than charging the police defense, perceived acceptability was higher among more-educated and younger citizens. But there were no significant differences among people with different levels of education or different age groups on the acceptability of charging the police defense. It shows that the unacceptability of the action was a near social consensus in 2012. In fact, only 7.1% of all respondents of the 2012 survey regarded the action as acceptable.

The finding regarding the unacceptability of charging the police defense is perhaps not surprising given the emphasis on social order in Hong Kong's political culture. In two studies on public discourses surrounding a civil disobedience campaign in year 2000, Ku (2004, 2007) found that media discourses were initially supportive toward the movement, but they "quickly yielded to the rationality of institutional order" (pp. 193–194). Ku (2007) concluded that a hegemonic framework of "order versus chaos" had underlined public discourses in Hong Kong. Similarly, Lee's (2008) analysis of local media coverage of the anti-WTO protests in the city in December 2005 showed that, although the liberal and/or professional-oriented newspapers covered the protests by the Korean farmers relatively positively in the first few days of the WTO meeting, media discourses turned against the Korean protesters when the latter escalated their actions and turned violent (even though the violence employed remained largely "symbolic" as they were not targeted at human bodies).

The "order imagery" was not only the basis of criticisms against "unruly protesters" in public discourses; it also underlined positive portrayals of protest actions in the city. After the July 1 protest in 2003, media discourses converged to praise the protesters for "being peaceful and rational" (Lee & Chan, 2011). The emphasis on "peacefulness and rationality" helped legitimize protest actions in the city. Yet it also reinforced the emphasis on order. The persistence of the order imagery can help explain the low level of acceptability among the Hong Kong public of charging the police defense as a form of protest actions.

The bottom half of Table 3.1 shows that levels of acceptability of the five forms of actions did not change substantially in 2014. There was a slight decline in acceptability of charging the police defense. This finding suggests the persistence of the order imagery and seems to contradict the argument of a trend toward radicalization. However, some considerations should be kept in mind. While radicalization may be a phenomenon led by and/or affecting a significant portion of the public, it does not necessarily affect all people. Besides, radicalization is likely to lead to acceptance of forms of actions that were "marginally unacceptable" before. If a form of action is regarded as severely violating some deep-rooted social norms, acceptability is unlikely to change substantially in a short period.

Furthermore, a closer look at the findings would show some subtle changes in public opinion. Specifically, in 2014, education and age became significantly related to acceptability of charging the police defense. More-educated people and younger citizens were more likely to see the action as relatively less unacceptable. If we compare the 2012 and 2014 figures in a different way, we can say that acceptability of charging the police defense declined only among less-educated citizens and senior citizens. Among the college-educated, acceptability of charging the police defense increased nominally (from 1.94 to 1.97); among people aged between 18 and 29, acceptability of charging the police defense increased statistically significantly (from 1.94 to 2.28). These findings by themselves are not definitive evidences of radicalization, but they are consistent with an argument of a process of radicalization affecting members of specific social groups (e.g., young people) with non-negligible sizes and influences.

In fact, the finding that acceptance of more radical forms of actions had increased among young people is consistent with happenings in the political scene. It should be noted that major signals of the rise of radicalism in the political arena in contemporary Hong Kong had appeared at least since 2004, when veteran social activist Leung Kwok-hung won in the Legislative Council election. Leung was portrayed by the news media as particularly popular among young voters (Lee, 2006b). In subsequent years, political groups adopting relatively radical platforms and action repertoire, such as People Power and Civic Passion, continued to grow. In addition, an informal "localist faction" emerged. Centering on established groups such as Civic Passion and several prominent societal opinion leaders who are often very active on social media, the localists exhibit a strong anti-China sentiment and are arguably radical in both their preferred action repertoire and views on political matters (e.g., a complete rejection of the Chinese identity and even a call for independence of Hong Kong).

The presence of the radical groups and activists in social protests is conspicuous by their actions. For example, some localists carried the colonial Hong Kong flag to the July 1 protests and other large-scale collective actions. The action was seen by the Chinese government as an indisputable sign of pro-independence sentiment in the city. In the July 1 protest of 2011, around 4,000 supporters of the radical groups left the marching route and occupied roads in the Wanchai district, while another 500 protesters confronted the police in another area, resulting in the police using pepper spray to disperse the crowd.

Some commentators and pro-democracy politicians criticized the radicals' actions for "hijacking" that year's July 1 protest. They argued that most protest participants would not approve the radicals' actions. But from the perspective of the radicals, their action was driven by the dissatisfaction with the routinized form of the July 1 protest. As Kursk, a prominent blogger-commentator, explained:

> Hong Kong people often take pride in the "peacefulness and rationality" of the 2003 July 1 protest. The so-called "peacefulness and rationality" means not only that the protest march needs to be orderly, but also that everything ends after the march, and people can go home to wait for the good news.[8]

Borrowing from another public affairs commentator, Kursk described the protests of Hong Kong people as "karaoke-style"—"go to the street, shout a few slogans, raise a few banners, feeling good after venting the anger; no one cares if any outcome is achieved in the end." In his opinion, "after experiencing many years of futile karaoke-style resistance, some people continue to feel good, but there are also more and more dissatisfied people."[9]

Putting aside whether the karaoke analogy is entirely fair, it was undoubtedly true that more people have started to feel dissatisfied with routinized marching and have become concerned about the seeming loss of power of "peaceful and rational" protests. Certainly, the character of an established series of protests cannot be easily changed, especially with the persistence of the society's emphasis on order. In subsequent years, the radical faction compromised by taking their actions mainly after the end of the protest march. The main July 1 protest march and the subsequent actions by the radical faction were in one sense linked by contiguity in time, but in another sense differentiated by time-space separation.

Nevertheless, debates surrounding forms of protests continued, especially in certain online forums and social media sites where many young people with a localist orientation were active. To mock the moderates' insistence on "peacefulness, rationality, non-violence, and no foul language,"[10] the term *wo-lei-fei-fei* was created by netizens by putting together the first Chinese word of each of the four terms (*wo-ping, lei-sing, fei-bou-lik, fei-cou-hau*). The abbreviation was used in a pejorative sense to sustain the criticism against "peaceful and rational" protests. For instance, Lewis Loud, another prominent blogger, wrote in a newspaper article comparing peaceful protests in Hong Kong to student protests during the May 4 Movement in 1919 in China:

> In May 4, the patriotism of Chinese people was for real. They did not adopt the model of "*wo-lei-fei-fei*" still embraced by Hong Kong people these days; they were not interested in "occupying the Tiananmen Square peacefully." ... The government [during the May 4 movement] detained the students, but they had to let them go in the face of the crowd's anger. And the government dared not take action against those who burnt buildings and

beat people, because the students' valor had gained people's respect.... So-called toleration, respect, and *wo-lei-fei-fei* are only the cowards' somnilo-quy in an evil world.[11]

In place of rational and peaceful protests, the radical and the localists prefer what they call "valiant resistance" (*jung-mou kong-zaang*).[12] In response, defenders of the conventional movement repertoire argued that, if the conventional forms of protest actions often failed to achieve results, it is difficult to see how the use of violence or any form of "valiant resistance" can achieve results either. Some criticized the supporters of the radical faction in the online arena for being "key-board warriors," calling upon others to engage in risky actions without engaging in the actions themselves. More important, some commentators emphasized the necessity of nonviolence for a movement to gain public support. A prominent activist wrote:

> "peacefulness, rationality and non-violence" should not be seen as chains on a movement's legs; instead, they could protect a movement by helping it gain people's recognition of its moral legitimacy. Just like the anti–national education movement, the almost obsessive *"wo-lei-fei"* was undeniably a main reason for its ability to gain widespread support from the society.[13]

In sum, Occupy Central was proposed within a context combining an enduring emphasis on social order in the public culture and an urge for social movements to shed the constraint of "peacefulness and rationality" because of a perceived ineffi-cacy of existing tactics. In fact, Benny Tai had acknowledged the probable inefficacy of existing tactics in his January 2013 piece, and his talk of "lethal weapon" can be considered a rhetorical response to the urge of radicalization. But Occupy Central was still planned to be rational, peaceful, and nonviolent. The tension between the insistence on order and the urge to radicalize would persist throughout the OC campaign and the Umbrella Movement.

Debating Civil Disobedience

As noted earlier, the January 16, 2013, article by Benny Tai attracted a lot of atten-tion as well as criticisms. Among the questions raised is why the action was not executed immediately. Critics argued that Tai—and later the Trio—were scholars after all, spending all the time to deliberate without taking action. For the Trio, the question was partly a matter of finding the appropriate time to act, and partly a mat-ter of the need for a long period of deliberation in order to accumulate public sup-port. As Tai stated, Occupy Central "adopts a new paradigm of social movement organizing. One point is that it does not follow the conventional social movement model to heat up public sentiment quickly and then let it explode; rather, it aims at accumulating supporters through a relatively long period of preparatory work."[14]

The OC campaign, in other words, was conceived as a combination of actual preparation for the civil disobedience action and discursive work aiming at influencing public opinion. By mid-2013, Tai would talk about Occupy Central as a campaign to influence not only the electoral arrangement in 2017 but also the city's political culture:

> The success of "OC" [*zim-zung*] resides not only in changing the political system but also in changing the political culture that sustains the political system. "OC" is no longer just to occupy Central; it includes the belief of civil disobedience and the preparatory work of democratic deliberation and civil referendum. Therefore, "OC" also became a goal in itself, because the belief of civil disobedience and the democratic procedure of democratic deliberation and civil referendum are valuable in themselves.[15]

Indeed, a significant aspect of the discursive work of the OC campaign resided in the articulation and justification of civil disobedience. Between January 2013 and September 2014, Tai and Chan engaged in public dialogues—both actual dialogues in public forums and virtual dialogues through writing—with supporters, opponents, and neutral commentators on a wide range of questions about what civil disobedience means, when civil disobedience is justifiable, and in what sense Occupy Central can be justified in terms of civil disobedience.

For instance, one criticism ventured by conservative critics in the early stage of the debate is that Occupy Central deviated from historical cases of civil disobedience because the action does not seem to have an existing "unjust law" as its target. As articulated by an author in an article on April 13, 2013, the public-order laws that the occupation action would directly violate cannot be regarded as unjust, and the law regarding the arrangement of the 2017 elections has not even been proposed. Nor did the Trio regarded the Basic Law as a whole as unjust. It was unclear what unjust laws there were.[16] Tai responded on April 17, arguing that, both historically and conceptually, not all acts of civil disobedience violate the laws that are actually considered evil. Further, the unjust electoral rule in Hong Kong is already in place and will continue to be in place if a new set of genuinely democratic procedures cannot be institutionalized. Moreover, Occupy Central would not be conducted immediately. It would involve a process of public deliberation to determine what kinds of electoral arrangements would be regarded as normatively justifiable. The action would be undertaken only when the government's proposed electoral arrangement failed to meet the standard.[17]

As the exchange illustrates, between criticisms and defenses, questions and answers, and suspicions and explications, various principles and concepts associated with the notion of civil disobedience were elaborated in the public arena. For another example, in face of criticisms from the conservatives that Occupy Central would damage the rule of law, Tai set out his view of the four layers of meanings of the rule of law. He argued that critics of Occupy Central defined the rule of law merely in terms of the need to follow the law, neglecting that the ultimate goal of the rule of law is "achieving justice through law."[18] Besides, in various writings, Tai repeatedly emphasized that the participants of Occupy Central need to bear the legal consequences of their actions. Breaking the law does not entail damaging the rule of law (Erni, 2015).

There is no need for us to cover how the proponents of Occupy Central responded to all specific issues and questions posed by others. But related to the discussion in the previous section, it is worth noting how Tai and his colleagues addressed the questions of violence and disruption. On the question of violence, Occupy Central faced two different criticisms from opposite sides of the political spectrum. Activists and commentators with more-radical orientations questioned the necessity of nonviolence. For instance, a commentator wrote:

> According to the author's understanding, all social movements in Hong Kong after the 1967 [riots] were non-violent. Non-violence and no use of force are two different things. . . . [In today's society], there should not be any taboo on the use of reasonable force to fight against the application of unreasonable force by the authorities.[19]

The crux of the response from the OC campaign was quite straightforward: non-violence is necessary to maintain the moral legitimacy of the movement. But the discursive work conducted also helped deepen the discussion of what nonviolence means and where its significance resides. In a dialogue between Benny Tai and veteran social activist Leung Kwok-hung, both Tai and Leung agreed that the principle of nonviolence is not a guarantee of the absence of violence, since violence can be exercised by the other side. In fact, the importance of nonviolence on the protesters' part resides in how it can create a contrast between the nonviolent protesters and the violent state.[20] This idea was further developed by Tai in another article, in which he argued that, when the participants of civil disobedience behave in a selfless and peaceful manner, a strong contrast will appear when the police exercise violence. "But if the protesters have used force during the action, then the contrast will become weaker. . . . The higher the level of force used by the protesters, the easier it would be [for the opponents] to rationalize the police's use of higher levels of force."[21]

In the context of the discursive contestation surrounding civil disobedience, the emphasis on nonviolence was crucial in the campaign's defense against the conservatives, who criticized Occupy Central for promoting violent protests. The criticism did not disappear even with the Trio's repeated emphasis on nonviolence and the titling of the campaign as "Occupy Central with Love and Peace." Some conservative politicians either neglected the promise by the Trio and continued to criticize Occupy Central as violent resistance, or argued that the Trio did not have any method to control the crowd and guarantee that violence would not occur. The latter criticism was probably a main reason leading the Trio to emphasize "iron-like discipline" in the action. Specifically, on September 23, 2014, the Trio announced that Occupy Central would take place on October 1. They issued a Manual of Disobedience in which eight "rules for non-violent protest" were stated, including, among others:

- Insist on the use of non-violent means. In the face of law enforcers and [counter-protesters], never hurt anyone physically or mentally, or damage any properties.
- Do not bring any weapons or anything that can be used as weapons.
- When facing arrest, form a human chain and lie down to show our non-cooperation. Do not struggle hard so as to avoid injury.
- Respect the decisions of OCLP. Any disagreements should only be reviewed after the operation. Avoid any action that may disrupt the operation.[22]

The OC campaign, in other words, not only insisted on nonviolence but also moved toward an emphasis on "discipline" under the fear that violence during the occupation would cost the movement its moral legitimacy and public support. Concomitant to the emphasis on discipline is the emphasis on centralized decision making and standardization of action.

The Trio's articulation might have convinced neither the radicals nor the conservatives, but they proposed a set of more or less coherent arguments justifying the relatively simple principle of absolute (or near absolute) nonviolence. In comparison, the question of disruption caused by Occupy Central is arguably more complicated. Benny Tai's original explication in the January 16, 2013, article did talk about paralyzing the political and economic center of Hong Kong. In some of his other writings in early 2013, Tai also used the metaphor of "nuclear blast" to describe the impact of Occupy Central. Although Tai certainly did not mean that the action would create physical damage to properties and human lives, the language of "paralyzing the city" and "nuclear blasts" became the critics' ammunition. For instance, a conservative politician wrote:

For Benny Tai, it is not enough to trigger the nuclear blast in Central. He is going further, the "destructive power" produced by the "nuclear blast" would not end at the moment of "explosion." Various kinds of non-cooperation movements will continue, and only that can truly paralyze Hong Kong. . . . Benny Tai had abandoned the disguise of "love and peace." His talk of nuclear blasts is extremely irresponsible. It is an attempt to destroy the rule of law, which will have long-term devastating consequences to Hong Kong. It is already deviating from the principle of Rawls' "non-violent resistance" and Martin Luther King's "civil disobedience."[23]

The passage illustrates the conservatives' tendency to over-interpret or misinterpret the Trio's rhetoric, picking up hyperbolic elements in the latter's discourses to construct a threatening image of Occupy Central. But still, Tai did use the lexicons quoted in the passage. The criticism cannot be regarded as completely groundless, and in fact it points to an important characteristic of the idea of Occupy Central as it was originally expressed in early 2013: it involves, in the terminologies of political philosophy, a combination of persuasive and coercive civil disobedience (Chaim, 1992; Falcon y Tella, 2004; Quill, 2009). That is, on the one hand, Tai talked about the necessity of nonviolence and willingness to bear the legal consequences so as to appeal to the conscience of the public. This is typical of persuasive civil disobedience. But on the other hand, the original idea of Occupy Central also involved an important coercive element: paralyzing Central through occupying roads in order to force the government to concede.

One line of criticism from the conservatives centers on the proposal's coercive element. Interestingly, this kind of criticism often presumes the justifiability of persuasive civil disobedience and evokes, as in the above-quoted passage, Gandhi, King, and Rawls approvingly. The evocation of Rawls is particularly telling: the name appeared in nine OC-related articles published by the pro-Communist newspaper *Wen Wei Po* between January 1, 2013, and September 28, 2014, whereas it appeared in only three articles in the same period in the professional and somewhat liberal-oriented *Ming Pao* and two articles in the strongly pro-democracy *Apple Daily*. The conservatives' favorite line from Rawls, quoted in several *Wen Wei Po* articles, is: "there is a limit on the extent to which civil disobedience can be engaged in without leading to a breakdown in the respect for law and the constitution thereby setting in motion consequences unfortunate for all" (Rawls, 1973, p. 374).

For our purpose, it is unimportant to discuss the justifiability of coercive civil disobedience or the Rawlsian view on the matter.[24] The notable point is that the Trio soon began to downplay the coercive elements in the original proposal. As Chan Kin-man wrote in early March 2013, "The crucial point of the action is not to paralyze Central, the important point is to, through self-sacrifice, call upon various sectors to resist the current unjust political institution, and to express deep concerns about the future of this city."[25]

However, as long as the plan was to occupy the main roads in Central, paralyzing the financial district could remain the actual outcome. Conservatives thus continued to criticize Occupy Central for affecting people's work and everyday lives. Some argued that the action was irresponsible because the economic losses it caused would be borne by the whole citizenry. The question phrased by James Tien, then chairperson of the pro-business Liberal Party, highlights the crux of this line of criticism: "As the saying goes, rancor has its target and debt has its owner, you clearly say that the target is the government, but then the true victims are the common people, what kind of logic is that?"[26]

The question was answered in several somewhat different ways by the Trio in various writings. But one of the most systematic replies came in an article on August 30, 2013, in which Tai argued that the justifiability of the disruption caused by Occupy Central needed to be considered in terms of proportionality. Discussing the proportionality of the action, in turn, needed to consider the nature of the rights being pursued, the identity of the true culprit of the disruptions, the futility of institutional means to strive for the rights, and the degree of damage as compared to the gain that can be obtained if the action is successful. Tai concluded after his analysis based on the framework: "compared to the nature of the rights and the amount of losses of those who may suffer from the action of Occupy Central, the positive consequences and social benefits of civil disobedience, if successful, should be proportional to the possible losses caused, hence [the action] should be reasonable."[27]

No matter whether one agrees with Tai's analysis and conclusion, by emphasizing proportionality, the disruption caused by the action was no longer seen as the source of its power; it was seen almost as a kind of unwanted and yet inevitable "collateral damage" that needed to be justified by weighing it against the benefits of the action. Given that the calculation of losses and benefits can be highly subjective, the logic of proportionality would compel the proponents to reduce the disruption caused by the action to the extent that is possible, since the smaller the amount of disruption caused, the more easily justifiable the action would be. In fact, in September 2014, the Trio would be talking in terms of beginning the action on a day that would help "minimize" the economic impact of Occupy Central.[28] October 1, the first day of a two-day holiday, was finally picked.[29]

The above analysis thus shows how the radical edges of the idea of Occupy Central were smoothed. The idea of civil disobedience was widely discussed. In the end, not only was the principle of nonviolence retained, there was also an emerging emphasis on discipline. The coercive element of the original idea was downplayed. The role of disruption was turned upside down—from being the source of the power of a "lethal weapon" to being unwanted consequences to be minimized.

While we see Occupy Central as the response from the moderates in the pro-democracy camp to the radical faction's urge to escalate forms of protest actions, the campaign ended up as radicalization with severe self-restraint. On the one hand, the development toward self-restraint is understandable given the persistence of certain conservative elements in Hong Kong's political culture. Throughout 2013 and early 2014, various opinion polls have shown that about 25% to 30% of the Hong Kong public supported Occupy Central. By mid-September 2014, a university-conducted poll found that public support for Occupy Central stood at 31%, while 45% of the public were against the action.[30] No one could know what the level of public support would have been if the Trio had adopted more radical rhetoric and plans. Yet one cannot ignore the need for Occupy Central to gain wider public support. On the other hand, the self-restrained character of Occupy Central alienated people with more radical orientations. Discontent against the Trio was already conspicuous in the online arena before the beginning of the action on September 28, 2014. It would be even more openly expressed during the Umbrella Movement.

Public Understanding of Civil Disobedience

Regardless of the final shape taken by Occupy Central, the debates surrounding the concept of civil disobedience could have had an educational impact on the society, that is, through the discussions generated by the campaign, the general public might have gained an understanding of the concept of civil disobedience. If the goal of the OC campaign was to prepare the public to understand and accept an innovative form of action justified by the concept of civil disobedience, one could evaluate the OC campaign by analyzing whether the educational impact existed.

Two points should be noted at the outset. First, we are examining citizens' knowledge about, instead of attitude toward, civil disobedience. This choice of focus is due to our interests in the more long-term impact of the campaign. We are therefore concerned with cognitions and attitudes that have more long-term relevance. Logically, we could have examined people's attitude toward the generalized idea of civil disobedience. However, it might have been very difficult for citizens to differentiate between the abstract idea of civil disobedience and Occupy Central as a concrete instantiation at the time of the OC campaign. Understanding or knowledge of civil disobedience is less subjected to this kind of conflation.

Second, the relatively in-depth and elaborated discussions reviewed in the previous section existed mainly in the opinion pages of the print media. We certainly do not expect the majority of citizens to have read the opinion pages on a regular basis. Nevertheless, the discourses are important because they have driven a much wider public debate occurring on a wider range of platforms, including the Internet. In one sense, the discourses in the opinion pages can be considered the most systematic and coherent expressions of the much more fragmented debates occurring throughout the society. Consistent with our theoretical emphasis on the integrated media environment, a plausible scenario is that individual themes related to civil disobedience have diffused across the society through an information loop formed by various media platforms. In fact, Benny Tai himself stated:

> "Occupy Central" could take shape and develop . . . because of the power of the civil society of Hong Kong. When the *Hong Kong Economic Journal* first published the article, it aroused little interests. But *Inmedia* [an online alternative media outlet] published an interview of me on the Internet afterward. It spread the idea of "Occupy Central" through the web and then the mainstream media.[31]

In addition, it is worth noting that understanding of civil disobedience constitutes a specific type of political knowledge, namely oppositional political knowledge. Researchers interested in examining citizens' levels of political knowledge have typically adopted measures focusing on citizens' grasp of certain basic facts about the established political institutions and their leaders (e.g., Bourdreau & Lupia, 2011; Delli Carpini & Keeter, 1996; Fraile, 2013; Ostman, 2012). But some scholars have noted the possibility that citizens' political knowledge can be domain-specific (Iyengar, 1990; Kim, 2009), that is, people may be knowledgeable about certain areas of public affairs but not others. Moreover, different types of political knowledge may have different antecedents and consequences (Johann, 2012; Kaufhold, Valenzuela, & Gil de Zuniga, 2010). It follows that general political knowledge focusing on the established institutions may not be the best predictor of people's attitudes toward and participation in social movements. Lee (2015b) thus put forward the notion of oppositional political knowledge, defined as knowledge about facts and concepts that are instrumental in the formation of critical attitudes toward dominant power and generating support for or actual participation in oppositional actions, as a conception of political knowledge more pertinent to movement-related attitudes and behavior.

The concept of oppositional knowledge captures the idea that people fail to challenge the existing political system or specific policies often because they are uninformed or misinformed (Lewis, 2001). It also captures the idea that certain types of knowledge—e.g., knowledge about social injustices, about oppositional groups, about movement tactics, etc.—can be instrumental in the formation of what Mansbridge (2001) called "oppositional consciousness"—"an empowering mental state that prepares members of an oppressed group to undermine, reform, or overthrow a dominant system" (pp. 4–5).

Lee (2015b) further differentiated among three types of oppositional knowledge, including factual information about oppositional groups and figures, negative considerations about the dominant political and economic power, and understanding of concepts that are central to oppositional discourses and/or contentious political actions. Understanding of civil disobedience was used as an example of the third type of oppositional knowledge. The empirical analysis in that article, which was based on the September 2013 survey to be analyzed below, found that education, age, external efficacy, interpersonal discussion, support for democratization, and usage of online alternative media were among the most important predictors of oppositional knowledge. At the same time, oppositional knowledge mediates the influence of support for democratization, external efficacy, and usage of online alternative media on protest participation and support for Occupy Central.

The following analysis is an extension of Lee (2015b). It draws upon both the September 2013 survey and a survey conducted in October 2014, just two weeks after the beginning of the occupation action on September 28.[32] This allows an examination of whether public understanding of civil disobedience had risen over the year.

To measure citizens' understanding of civil disobedience, both surveys asked the respondents if they had heard of the term "civil disobedience." Nearly two-thirds (64.2%) of the respondents said "yes" in September 2013. The percentage rose to 82.0% in October 2014. The respondents who replied affirmatively were asked if they understood the term. Answers included "not at all," "a little," "quite well," and "very well." In September 2013, 24.1% of the respondents who had heard of the term said they did not understand it, while 28.5% of those who had heard of the term replied they understood it "quite well" or "very well." In October 2014, only 17.4% of those who had heard of the term said they did not understand it, while 43.0% replied they understood the term "quite well" or "very well." In other words, self-perceived understanding of civil disobedience had increased over the year.

Of course, a person who claimed that he or she understood the term might not really understand it. Therefore, those who said they understood civil disobedience at least "a little" were further asked to name up to two differences between "civil disobedience" and "typical law-breaking behavior." A 0–2 index of understanding of civil disobedience was produced. Those who had not heard of the term, did not understand the term, or could not name any valid differences between civil disobedience and typical law-breaking behavior scored zero. Others scored 1 or 2 based on whether they were able to name one or two valid differences.

Obviously, what constitutes a valid difference between civil disobedience and law-breaking can be a matter of judgment. In his various public writings, Benny Tai emphasized three characteristics of civil disobedience most prominently and frequently: (1) it aims at achieving social justice instead of personal gains; (2) it takes peaceful and nonviolent forms; and (3) participants are willing to bear the legal consequences. But it would be unreasonable to treat only these as correct answers, especially because respondents provided a range of other largely valid answers, for example, "civil disobedience aims at winning the support of the majority of the public," "civil disobedience is a form of conscientious actions," etc.

Moreover, the validity of some answers could be debatable. An example is "civil disobedience is consistent with the moral value of the majority in a society." The goal espoused by a civil disobedience campaign may not in fact be what the majority is already supporting. But still, civil disobedience (and social movements in general) typically appeals to the fundamental cultural codes of a society in order to gain support (Alexander, 2005). Hence there is a sense in which civil disobedience is—or has to be—consistent with certain moral values of the majority in the society.

Meanwhile, some answers are definitely incorrect, such as, "civil disobedience is legal." In addition, several respondents simply claimed that there is no difference between civil disobedience and typical law-breaking behavior. This answer probably came mostly from opponents of Occupy Central. While respondents can hold this belief, it does not constitute a valid answer to the survey question, which was asking for differences between the two.

To minimize the impact of subjective judgments on the findings, two indices were created. The first can be called "activists' understanding" of civil disobedience. A respondent scored 1 or 2 on the index if he or she could name 1 or 2 of the three points emphasized by the OC campaign listed above. The second index can be called "broad understanding" of civil disobedience: a respondent got a score of 1 or 2 if he or she could name 1 or 2 differences that are at least arguably correct (i.e., answers falling into the "gray area" were also counted).

Table 3.2 summarizes the respondents' levels of understanding of civil disobedience in the two surveys. In September 2013, Hong Kong citizens could name on average 0.21 of the three differences between civil disobedience and law-breaking pinpointed by the proponents of Occupy Central, and they could name on average 0.39 differences that are at least arguably correct. Citizens' understanding of civil disobedience substantially improved by October 2014. Focusing only on respondents aged between 18 and 69 (in order to make the findings most comparable since the 2013 survey included respondents only between 18 and 70), the mean scores of the two indices are 0.39 and 0.51, respectively.

The bottom parts of the table provide information about levels of understanding of civil disobedience for different age and educational groups. Levels of "activists' understanding" increased significantly between the two surveys for all groups. Levels of "broad understanding" also increased nominally for all groups, though the increase was statistically significant only for the youngest group and for people with medium levels of education. The increase in understanding is most conspicuous among young people. Reorganizing the figures in Table 3.2, levels of understanding of civil disobedience of the three age groups did not differ significantly in September 2013 no matter which index is concerned.[33] But in October 2014, there were significant differences among the three age groups,[34] with the youngest group exhibiting the highest level of understanding of civil disobedience. This finding is particularly interesting because research has typically found a positive relationship between age and general political knowledge (Delli Carpini & Keeter, 1996). Yet the finding here is consistent with the idea that young people in Hong Kong are increasingly supportive toward social movements and even the more radical forms of political actions.

Admittedly, with only surveys in September 2013 and October 2014, we cannot precisely trace the development of citizens' understanding of civil disobedience

Table 3.2 **Public understanding of civil disobedience, September 2013 and October 2014**

	Activists' understanding	Broad understanding
Total		
September 2013	0.21	0.39
October 2014 (only 18–69)	0.39	0.51
t-value	5.94***	2.91**
October 2014 (full sample)	0.39	0.52
By age		
Young		
September 2013	0.26	0.49
October 2014	0.48	0.72
t-value	3.28**	2.54*
Middle-age		
September 2013	0.22	0.37
October 2014	0.36	0.45
t-value	3.07**	1.46
Senior		
September 2013	0.20	0.41
October 2014	0.37	0.48
t-value	3.92***	1.24
By education		
Low		
September 2013	0.12	0.22
October 2014	0.24	0.28
t-value	2.43*	1.03
Medium		
September 2013	0.17	0.32
October 2014	0.33	0.46
t-value	3.73***	2.43*
High		
September 2013	0.34	0.62
October 2014	0.52	0.69
t-value	3.64***	1.16

Notes: Entries are mean scores on a 0–2 index. When comparing the two surveys, only respondents aged between 18 and 69 in the 2013 survey were included so as to make the two samples as comparable as possible. Young: 18–30 for 2013 and 18–29 for 2014; Middle-age: 31–50 for 2013 and 30–49 for 2014; Senior 51–70 for 2013 and 50–69 for 2014. *** $p < .001$; ** $p < .01$; * $p < .05$. $N = 782$ and 802 for 2013 and 2014, respectively.

over the period. We do not know how citizens would have responded to the question before the debate surrounding Occupy Central started in January 2013, and we do not know the exact degree of citizen knowledge about civil disobedience on the eve of the Umbrella Movement. But the finding does clearly illustrate an increase in understanding of the concept in the 13-month period between the two surveys and thus the public education function of the OC campaign.

Explaining Understanding of Civil Disobedience at the Individual Level

While the previous section shows an increase in understanding of civil disobedience among Hong Kong people, this section examines the factors that can explain variations in understanding of civil disobedience. We are particularly interested in the impact of media and communication. The analysis focuses on the October 2014 data,[35] examining the predictors of understanding of civil disobedience after the occupation had just begun.

The extant literature pinpointed motivation, ability, and opportunity as the main factors behind political learning (Delli Carpini & Keeter, 1996; Luskin, 1990). It should not be surprising if education (an indicator of ability and possibly opportunity) and political interests (an indicator of motivation) would explain understanding of civil disobedience. The analysis here is not aimed at testing a general model for political knowledge though. Instead, we set up several hypotheses to illustrate the specificity of understanding of civil disobedience as a kind of oppositional political knowledge. Specifically, it is expected that support for and participation in the occupation could explain understanding of civil disobedience (*hypotheses H3.1 and H3.2*). This is because those who understood the concept were more likely to support and participate in the occupation. Besides, attitudinal support can provide the motivation to learn, while actual participation in the occupation can provide the opportunities to learn.[36]

Media use and interpersonal discussion have long been established as predictors of political knowledge (Delli Carpini & Keeter, 1996; Eveland, 2004; Norris, 2000). But Lee (2015b) has found that mainstream media consumption did not contribute to a range of oppositional knowledge. In the earlier article, Lee (2015b) argued from a more general theoretical perspective: the mainstream media, embedded in the dominant political economic structure of the society, may not contain much oppositional knowledge. For the analysis here, another point to consider is that, although there were many discussions of civil disobedience in the opinion pages of newspapers between 2013 and 2014, the texts might have been read only by a very small group of the most educated readers. Therefore, we do not expect mainstream news consumption to relate to understanding of civil disobedience.

Instead, as mentioned earlier, the proponents of Occupy Central themselves have noticed the role of new media as platforms for the transmission of ideas first expressed in the mainstream media. Thus we expect that, at the individual level, political usage of social media is related to understanding of civil disobedience (H3.3).

We further expect a relationship to exist between understanding of civil disobedience and interpersonal political discussion. However, our analysis does not expect frequency of discussion by itself to generate understanding of civil disobedience. Rather, it is through debating with disagreeing others that citizens may come to understand civil disobedience better. We thus posit a positive relationship between discussion with disagreeing others and understanding of civil disobedience (H3.4). This is because disagreeable discussion can force people to defend, clarify, and elaborate on their thoughts and ideas. This process can help people develop a more articulate and elaborate understanding of abstract concepts. This argument is consistent with research on the importance of exposure to disagreement in generating political knowledge and understanding of different political perspectives (Mutz, 2006; Schaefer, 2015).

Operationally, *support for the occupation* was measured by the question: "An occupy movement has occurred in Hong Kong recently. Do you personally support this movement?" The term "occupy movement" was used because it was still the more commonly used label in everyday discourse at the time of the survey. Answers were registered by a five-point Likert scale ranging from 1 = very unsupportive to 5 = very supportive ($M = 3.06$, S.D. = 1.47). Those who were very supportive, supportive, or "so-so" toward the movement were then asked if they had gone to the occupied areas to support the movement. The answers include "1 = no," "2 = have gone there one day," "3 = have gone there two to three days," and "4 = have gone there more than three days." Those who were unsupportive toward the movement were presumed not to have gone to the occupied areas to support the movement and thus scored 1. The survey found that 8.5%, 8.4% and 5.7% of the respondents had gone to the occupied areas one day, two to three days, and more than three days, respectively ($M = 1.42$, S.D. = 0.87). This item represents respondents' *participation in the occupation*.

Two questions asked the respondents to report with a six-point scale (1 = none; 6 = more than an hour) how much time they spent daily (1) reading newspapers and (2) watching TV news in the previous three weeks. The answers were averaged for an index of *mainstream news media exposure* ($M = 4.12$, S.D. = 1.37, $r = .29$). Respondents were also asked which newspaper they read the most frequently. During at least the early stages of the movement, *Apple Daily* and *Ming Pao* stood out as being relatively (or even strongly) supportive toward the movement. A dummy variable of *reading pro-movement newspapers* was created, with *Apple* and *Ming Pao* readers coded as 1 (43.4%).

Respondents were also asked to indicate, using a scale from 1 = not using at all to 5 = more than 180 minutes per day, how much time they spent daily on "Facebook, Twitter, or other social networking sites" in the previous three weeks (M = 2.04, $S.D.$ = 1.20). This item represents *time spent on social media*. Time spent on social media, however, may not affect political attitudes and behavior because of variations in purposes of use (Baumgartner & Morris, 2010; Gil de Zúñiga, Jung, & Valenzuela, 2012). Social media users were asked how frequently they (1) obtained political and public affairs information; (2) expressed views on politics and public affairs; (3) joined groups about public affairs; and (4) paid attention to the actions of parties, movements, and news commentators via social media. They were also asked (5) how many of their social media "friends" were political party members, movement activists, or news commentators. The answers, registered with a five-point scale (1 = not at all to 5 = very frequently/large number), were averaged for an index of *political use of social media*, with non-users of social media scoring 1 (a = 0.70, M = 1.75, $S.D.$ = 0.84).

Regarding political discussion, respondents were asked if they had discussed the occupation movement with their family or friends, with answers ranging from 1 = not at all to 5 = very frequently. They were also asked if they had disputes with "family or relatives" and "friends" about the movement (either "yes" or "no"). Based on the two latter questions, each respondent scored 0, 1, or 2 for the frequencies of disputes they had. *Disagreeable discussion* is the product of frequency of discussion and frequency of disputes (M = 1.18, $S.D.$ = 2.24). Control variables include four demographics (sex, age, income, and education), interests in politics, internal efficacy, collective efficacy, external efficacy, and past protest participation.

Table 3.3 summarizes a multiple regression analysis predicting understanding of civil disobedience. The regression model can explain about 22% to 25% of the variance of the two dependent variables. Supporting H3.1 and H3.2, both attitudinal support and actual participation in the movement significantly predict understanding of civil disobedience.

The findings also support H3.3. Political use of social media is strongly positively related to both dependent variables, illustrating that social media constituted a channel through which many citizens encountered ideas related to the concept of civil disobedience. Interestingly, time spent on social media related to understanding of civil disobedience significantly negatively. In line with extant research, usage frequency does not necessarily generate knowledge and political understanding because people use social media for various purposes. After controlling for political use of social media, sheer usage frequency may come to represent primarily non-political uses. This could explain the negative relationship between time spent on social media and understanding of civil disobedience.

Table 3.3 **Predictors of understanding of civil disobedience**

	Activists' understanding	Broad understanding
Demographics		
Sex	−.04	−.03
Age	.07	.05
Education	.06	.10*
Family income	.03	.01
Political orientation and behavior		
Political interest	.08*	.07
Internal efficacy	.09*	.11**
Collective efficacy	.05	.06
External efficacy	−.12**	−.13**
Past protest participation	.08*	.04
Movement support	.13**	.13**
Movement participation	.11**	.09*
Media and communication		
News exposure	.02	.03
Reading pro-movement papers	−.04	−.03
Time spent on social media	−.12**	−.10*
Political use of social media	.16**	.20***
Disagreeable discussion	.09*	.09**
Adjusted R^2	0.227***	0.246***

Notes: Entries are standardized regression coefficients. Missing values were replaced by means. $N = 802$. *** $p < .001$; ** $p < .01$; * $p < .05$.

Unlike political usage of social media, neither news exposure nor reading of pro-movement newspapers significantly predicts the dependent variables. People who consumed the mainstream media to larger extents did not exhibit a higher level of understanding of civil disobedience. But consistent with H3.4, disagreeable discussion had a significant impact on understanding of civil disobedience. On the whole, we see that the two more interactive kinds of communication activities—use of social media for political information and discussing with disagreeing others—are significantly related to better understanding of the concept of civil disobedience even after controlling for a range of attitudinal and behavior factors.

Summary

This chapter has analyzed the Occupy Central campaign that preceded the Umbrella Movement, with the emphasis on the discursive work carried out by the campaign. It is argued that the campaign was situated within a context where a strong emphasis on social order within the mainstream society coexisted with an urge to develop novel and more radical forms of protests in the movement arena. The tension created between these two tendencies significantly shaped the discursive contestation surrounding Occupy Central and the concept of civil disobedience. While Occupy Central was originally proposed as a way to force the government to make concessions through disrupting social and economic lives in Hong Kong, the coercive element was downplayed in the proponents' discourses later in the campaign, resulting in a form of self-restrained radicalization.

Nevertheless, no matter how one judges the desirability of the Trio's final version of Occupy Central, one important consequence of the campaign is the higher level of understanding of civil disobedience among the public. As stated at the chapter's beginning, while movement organizations can adopt new action tactics through exercising their creativity, through borrowing from the action repertoire of other societies, or sometimes simply by accident, more widespread acceptance or adoption of the new action tactics require legitimization and justification in the public arena (Biggs, 2013; Hayes, 2006). Understanding is an important step before acceptance, and our analysis shows that more citizens obtained some understanding of the concept by the time the occupation began. The educational function of the OC campaign arguably justified the proponents' emphasis of having a prolonged period of deliberation.

The analysis shows that political use of social media, instead of conventional mass media exposure, relates significantly to understanding of civil disobedience. It does not mean that the mainstream media were unimportant—throughout the OC campaign, the mainstream media remained the key platform for the proponents of Occupy Central to explicate their views and debate with the critics. What the survey findings suggest is that, in contemporary societies, intensive discussions in the mainstream media may diffuse throughout the society and reach individuals mainly through political communications via digital media. The significance of digital media in the communication of oppositional knowledge is partly grounded in the rise of online alternative media in Hong Kong (Leung, 2015; Leung & Lee, 2014; Yung & Leung, 2014). At the same time, interactive digital media platforms can be particularly important for people to gain an understanding of abstract concepts such as civil disobedience because people can ask for elaborations and missing background information when they interact. In any case, the findings confirm the importance to consider mass media institutions and digital media platforms as forming an integrative media environment for information circulation (Chadwick, 2013).

The 2014 survey found that 82% of the public had heard of civil disobedience, 35.6% could name at least one arguably valid difference between civil disobedience and typical law-breaking behavior, and 30.0% could name one of the three main characteristics of civil disobedience emphasized by the proponents of Occupy Central. The latter percentages are not large. But it should be noted that survey research in other countries has often discovered low levels of basic political knowledge among the citizenry (e.g., Delli Carpini & Keeter, 1996). In fact, the September 2013 survey also contained several factual knowledge questions. For example, only 25.6% of the respondents could correctly name the Secretary for Transport and Housing of the Hong Kong Government. Only 11.5% could name the official title of Ko Wing-man, another government bureau chief. In other words, even in 2013, Hong Kong citizens' understanding of civil disobedience was apparently not worse than their ability to identify key government officials.

One may also argue that citing a simplistic point such as "civil disobedience is aimed at social justice" does not reflect any sophisticated understanding of the concept. Of course it does not. But political scientists have long discovered that rationality of public opinion is not reliant on complete and in-depth information (Popkin, 1991; Sneiderman, Brady, & Tetlock, 1991). Theorists have long argued that the ideal of the fully informed citizen is unrealistic and misguided (Lippmann, 1922; Schudson, 1998). It is often adequate for people to have some valid ideas and information to reason with. Therefore, it is significant that a substantial proportion of Hong Kong people have obtained some ideas about civil disobedience.

Although the disciplined and minimally disruptive form of action imagined by the Trio did not materialize, it does not mean that the discursive work done during the OC campaign did not influence later happenings. The emphasis on nonviolence and willingness to bear the legal consequences, in particular, persisted and continued to be at the core of the movement's self-understanding even after its later transformation. It is also notable that the Umbrella Movement, after all, ended largely according to the "script" drafted by the Trio—non-resistance when the police took action to evict the occupied areas. These are the reasons we emphasize the significance of putting the Umbrella Movement into its historical context, including the more long-term context elaborated in Chapter 2 and the more immediate context of the Occupy Central campaign. But the OC Campaign did not totally determine what happened afterwards. How Occupy Central evolved into the substantially different configuration of the Umbrella Movement will be analyzed in later chapters.

Photo 1 The police fired the first tear gas to disperse the crowds taking over the highways in Admiralty on September 28, 2014. Courtesy Wu King Hei, *Ming Pao*

Photo 2 The umbrella, tear gas, pepper spray, batons, and shields were the major "weapons" used at the confrontations between the protestors and the police. Courtesy Yip Ka Ho, *Ming Pao*

Photo 3 Protesters running away from tear gas near the City Hall. Courtesy Kwok Hing Fai, *Ming Pao*

Photo 4 The highways adjacent to the Government Headquarters were taken by tens of thousands of protesters during the early days of the occupation. The photo was taken in the evening when many protesters were off from work. Courtesy Joseph M. Chan

Photo 5 Thousands gathered to sit in at the cross section of the thoroughfares in the busy Mongkok District in Kowloon. Courtesy Joseph M. Chan

Photo 6 Clashes between protesters and police were common scenes on television news. Courtesy Joseph M. Chan

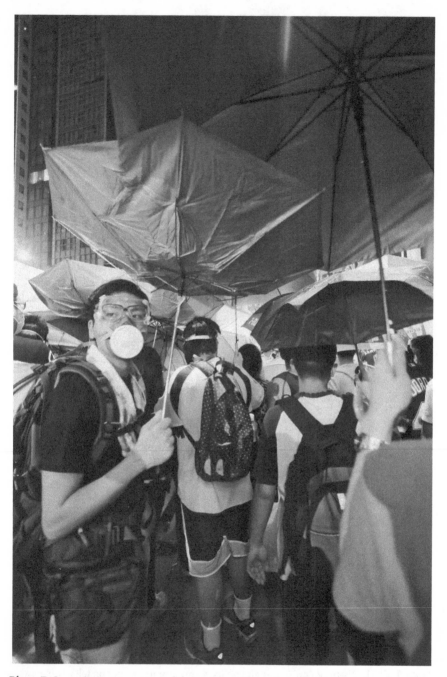

Photo 7 Some protesters protected themselves with masks and umbrellas when they challenged the police, who often responded with pepper spray and batons. Courtesy Joseph M. Chan

Photo 8 A wall of the Government Headquarters was turned into a Lennon Wall where protesters expressed their personal views and wishes. Supportive email messages from all over the world were projected onto the wall above the stairway. Courtesy Joseph M. Chan

Photo 9 Young protesters wrote on the Lennon Wall with Post-it notes. Courtesy Joseph M. Chan

Photo 10 Some protesters chose to sleep at the sites of occupation throughout the night. The photo was taken in Mongkok. Courtesy Joseph M. Chan

Photo 11 Traffic came to halt as the highways in Admiralty were occupied. The photo was taken during the day when many protesters had to work. Courtesy Joseph M. Chan

Photo 12 Tents went up in the highways in Admiralty as protesters realized that the occupation might go on for an extended period. Courtesy Joseph M. Chan

Photo 13 The Umbrella Movement witnessed the quick development of arts promoting its cause. This photo shows an installation art made of broken umbrellas stitched together and hung from above. Courtesy Joseph M. Chan

4

Media, Participation, and Public Opinion toward the Movement

As Chapter 3 explained, from early 2013 to September 2014, the idea of Occupy Central moved toward the direction of self-restraint. In fact, as the Trio acknowledged after the end of the Umbrella Movement, they did not expect the occupation to last for more than a few days. But the Trio could not prevent the events from deviating from their script. After a week of class boycotts and protests in front of the Government Headquarters, in the late evening of September 26, student protesters rushed into the "Civic Square," the enclosed space in front of the East Wing of the Government Headquarters that used to be an open space where social groups could stage rallies. Several student leaders and protesters were arrested.[1] The news led even more young people to join the protest. The Trio also arrived at the scene on September 27. Facing calls to kick-start the occupation campaign earlier, the Trio announced the beginning of OC in the early morning hours of September 28.

The occupation campaign thus deviated from the original plan in several ways right from the start. The occupiers were not in Central, but only the nearby district of Admiralty. They were not exactly "occupying" the main roads of the Hong Kong Islands, but the areas in front of the East Wing of the Government Headquarters. There was no immediate rush of people to the Government Headquarters to support the occupiers. Instead, television news showed that many young student protesters were leaving the Government Headquarters because they were not prepared to participate in civil disobedience (and bear the legal consequences). Some young protesters even accused the Trio of "hijacking" the student protests when some of the arrested student leaders were not yet released. Veteran activist Leung Kwok Hung famously knelt down on the street, imploring people not to go away. Within the first 12 hours after the Trio's announcement, there was no sign of a sustainable, large-scale occupation to come.

Large numbers of supporters started to arrive at Admiralty only around noon of September 28. The police force blocked off the entrance to the area in front of the Government Headquarters, however. It forced thousands of citizens to stay on the overcrowded pedestrian way along Harcourt Road and Connaught Road Central, the main roads in the Admiralty area just outside the Government Headquarters. But as more and more people arrived, the congestion on the pedestrian way became more and more serious. At around 3 p.m., some protesters breached the police's defense and charged into Harcourt Road and Connaught Road Central, thus inadvertently starting the occupation of the roads.

Nevertheless, as the police still blocked off the entrance to the space in front of the Government Headquarters, the tens of thousands of supporters on the street were separated from the leaders of the occupation. There was no way for the movement groups in front of the Government Headquarters to direct and coordinate the actions outside. Some protesters in the front line on Connaught Road Central repeatedly charged the police defense line in an attempt to reach the East Wing of the Government Headquarters. The police used pepper spray to attack the protesters who charged the police, whereas the protesters protected themselves with umbrellas and plastic wrap. At around 6 p.m., the police fired tear gas into the protesting throng. But even the tear gas failed to disperse the crowd. The protesters just receded and then moved forward again. A prominent ex-journalist and blogger, who was in the "protest frontline" on the day, described the scenario in one of his blog articles published on September 30:

> For the first can of tear gas, people screamed and ran.
> For the second can of tear gas, people receded again and rearranged their gears.
> For the third can of tear gas, people moved back a few steps, took the place again after the smoke dispersed, and had their combat capacity risen to another level.
> Every can of tear gas is a training in courage. Took a breath, the fear disappeared, and confidence rose. Everyone wore the goggles, put up the plastic wrap, came forward to witness, reported live; you shoot tear gas, people can choose to stay firm, can choose to let flowers blossom all over the place.
> For the tear gas that came afterwards, people asked: That's it?[2]

The firing of the tear gas continued into the evening and late night. In the end, a total of 87 cans of tear gas were fired. Some protesters decided to start occupation in other districts so as to prevent a complete and immediate police eviction of the occupation. By the morning of September 29, occupation had started in Causeway Bay, Mong Kok, and Tsim Sha Tsui. When the dust settled, the occupation had taken a totally unpredicted shape.

The above were the event contingencies that facilitated the transformation of Occupy Central into the Umbrella Movement. These event contingencies have two major implications on how we may understand the role of media and communication in the mobilization and formation of the occupation campaign. First, the afternoon protests on September 28 were live broadcast by all major television stations in the city. Besides, the police also intriguingly started to fire tear gas into the protesting crowd just half an hour before the major evening newscast of TVB, the most important free-to-air television broadcaster of Hong Kong. Thus, while many commentators and observers agreed that the tear gas backfired, galvanized people's resolve, and led more people to go to the street, it might be argued that it was more precisely the *mediated images* of the tear gas (and police violence in general) that led to the quick scaling up of the protests. It thus points to the continual significance of the basic surveillance function of the mass media institutions, even though, as we emphasize throughout, the contemporary mass media institutions play their roles and exercise their power within an integrated media environment.

Second, as the events unfolded in a way that deviated more and more from the original "script" of the protest organizers, and the protesters occupying the main road in the afternoon of September 28 were cut off from the protest organizers in front of the Government Headquarters, the protesters were left to improvise their responses and coordinate among themselves on their own. This opened the window of opportunity for the rise of connective actions coordinated through digital and social media.

We will discuss the emergence of connective actions and the implications of the protesters' digital and social media use on the formation and dynamics of the movement in the next chapter. This chapter focuses on the first implication noted above. We will provide empirical evidence demonstrating the impact of the mediated images of tear gas on the scaling up of the occupation campaign. But more important, we treat the impact of the mediated images of tear gas as one of the instances during the Umbrella Movement when the public monitor function of the media system was most conspicuous. That is, we do not see the happenings on September 28 as exhibiting some type of media impact that is unique at the conceptual level. Rather, it was illustrative of a general role of the media system in a large-scale protest campaign. We contend that the Hong Kong media—comprising both mass media institutions and digital media platforms—can be considered as a *partially censored public monitor* that has a complicated and mixed impact on large-scale protests.

This chapter will therefore begin by explicating the concept of a partially censored public monitor. We will then draw upon the population survey conducted in October to illustrate how demographics, social and political attitudes, and media and communication variables explain citizens' attitudes toward the Umbrella Movement. We will demonstrate part of the political impact of the partially censored public monitor through this analysis. We then turn to the October protest onsite survey to illustrate how the rise of mass participation in the occupation action in late September can be understood in relation to the instant provocation resulting from televised images of tear gas fired by the police. The chapter then further illustrates the mixed impact of the media on public opinion during the Umbrella Movement through analyzing a "double scandal" involving police violence and media self-censorship that occurred in mid-October. This chapter ends with a brief discussion of how political actors responded to the presence of the partially censored public monitor.

Media as the Partially Censored Public Monitor

In their study of the symbolic violence exercised by the anti-WTO protesters in Seattle in 1999, DeLuca and Peeples (2002) developed the concept of public screen in an attempt to reconstruct the basis for critical evaluation of public communication in contemporary societies. Writing at a time when the Habermasian notion of the public sphere and theories of deliberative democracy dominated the discourses of many media and political theorists, they argued against Habermas's emphasis on rational argumentation and consensus seeking. "For a cultural critic, the key response to the structural transformations of our moment is neither to adopt a moral pose nor to express yearnings for a mythical past, but to explore what is happening and what is possible under current conditions" (p. 133).

Given the premise, the concept of the public screen was put forward as a metaphor that can help characterize the "current conditions" for public communication. The word "screen" partly refers to the dominance of television in the mediascape, but the public screen does not refer merely to television itself. Rather, DeLuca and Peeples's (2002) argument is that the visual language of television has become so dominant that all media, as well as social and political actors, have to seriously consider how to speak to the public through the discourse of images—"even newspapers can do no better than imitate TV, moving to shorter stories and color graphics" (p. 133). Therefore, the public screen does not refer to a single media technology. It should be understood as "a constant current of images and words, a ceaseless circulation abetted by the technologies of television, film, photography, and the Internet. These technologies' speed, stream of images, and global reach create an ahistorical, contextless flow of jarring juxtapositions" (p. 115).

The two authors were mainly interested in how, under the condition of the public screen, protest groups can communicate with the general public through the staging of image events (DeLuca, 2005). Image events are "dense surfaces meant to provoke in an instant the shock of the familiar made strange" (p. 144). Using the 1999 anti-WTO protests as the case study, they argued that the protesters' symbolic violence and the uncivil disobedience succeeded in gaining the attention of the news media. The media's focus on the images and the symbolic violence did not entail a lack of attention to the protesters' substantive messages. Instead, the symbolic violence enabled the message to be reported more extensively and in greater depth than it would have been. Media coverage "was not a zero-sum game. Uncivil disobedience and the anarchists' actions expanded the totality of coverage" (p. 144).

With its emphasis on images, the concept of public screen is highly pertinent to the analysis of the Umbrella Movement. In fact, the name "Umbrella Movement" would not have arisen without the iconic images of people opening their umbrellas in face of pepper spray and tear gas—images captured by television cameras and photojournalists that then appeared repeatedly on magazine covers, newspaper front pages, television newscasts, and the Internet. To Hong Kong people, the war-like picture of tear gas flying over Connaught Road Central certainly produced "the shock of the familiar made strange" and probably created a kind of "mediated instant grievances" (Tang, 2015) that drove many citizens onto the streets.

However, the concept of public screen also has its limitations. Cottle (2006) criticized studies of public screen for remaining "conspicuously silent about the role of production dynamics as well as strategic claims making and struggles over definition that are often at the center of protests and demonstrations" (p. 53). In simpler words, the problem is that publicity does not entail positive coverage. Koopmans (2004) treated visibility and legitimacy as two separate dimensions of social movements' media appearance, while Gamson and Wolfsfeld (1993) distinguished between standing, preferred framing, and sympathy. Standing or visibility by itself does not guarantee sympathy or legitimacy, and protesters often have little control of exactly how they would appear on the public screen (Cammaerts, 2012).

In fact, the observation that spectacular images could help protest movements to gain media attention is neither new nor surprising. But many social movement scholars tended to see protest movements as being caught in a dilemma. If they produce spectacular images, they could gain media visibility but would have their substantive messages ignored. Alternatively, they could focus on communicating their messages, but they might not gain any media visibility (Bennett et al., 2004). As McHendry (2012) noted, "the formation . . . of the public screen as a way of reading social movement rhetoric posits at its core that any publicity is good publicity" (p. 153). Yet this could be a highly controversial presumption.

Empirically, it is certainly possible that media attention on images and coverage of substantive messages do not contradict each other in *some* individual cases. The question is how frequently this can happen. Batziou's (2015) study of the Greek protests in December 2008, for instance, challenged DeLuca and Peeples's (2002) conclusion by showing that the Greek media emphasized the protesters' violence while largely ignoring the substantive issues involved. Batziou concluded that, in the case he analyzed, "as the public screen presents its own interpretation of the events, it is rather the elites speaking to the public than the protesters speaking to the elites" (p. 38).

While we share DeLuca and Peeples's (2002) recognition of the significance of visuals and images, we do not adopt the strong presumption that any publicity is good publicity for social movements. Besides, while the concept of public screen is used to characterize the general condition for public communication in the society at large, we are more interested in developing a concept that can characterize the role of the media and make sense of its impact in large-scale protests. We therefore develop the notion of the partially censored public monitor. We use the word "monitor" to replace "screen" because the former has several interrelated meanings that are simultaneously relevant to our current concern. First, monitor does refer to a type of device that displays visual images, so the emphasis on images is retained. Second, according to the online *Oxford English Dictionary*, monitor carries the meaning of a person or device that "observes a process of activity to check that it is carried out fairly or correctly, especially in an official capacity."[3] Third and related to the second, the word monitor is closely tied to the watchdog role of the news media, that is, the idea that one of the most important professional roles of journalism in a democratic society is to prevent and expose the abuse of power.

Because of the second and third meanings, the word monitor calls our attention to the fact that, while social movements need to strive for visibility in the media arena, they also need to ensure that they appear in the media in the "right way." Moreover, the word monitor calls our attention to the point that the power holders also have their own "visibility problem": while gaining access to the mainstream media is not difficult for them, power holders do have the need to prevent unwanted media visibility. As Thompson (1995) argued, an important consequence of the development of the media system is the increased visibility of the actions of public figures. Public figures and powerful institutions are finding it more and more difficult to maintain privacy and secrecy. Instead of creating a panopticon in which the few watches the many, the modern media constitute a synopticon where the many continually watch the few (Bauman, 1999). An indication of this trend is the proliferation of political scandals in the contemporary world (Thompson, 2000).

The term "public monitor," then, highlights the point that the power of the media is exercised not only through what they show on their screens, but also through how their presence can prevent people and groups from acting in certain ways because of the need to avoid unwanted visibility (and hence certain images would *not* appear). For instance, one important impact of the mass media—Al Jazeera in particular— during the Egyptian uprising noted by researchers is that their presence arguably prevented the government from using military force (Howard & Hussain, 2013).

The term monitor also points to a specific role of the watching public. Schudson (1998) has coined the term "monitorial citizen" to describe what citizens in contemporary democracies can be realistically expected to do. Ordinary citizens may not be able to get themselves fully informed about all kinds of public affairs and actively participate in the political process all the time. But similar to parents beside a swimming pool keeping an eye on their children, citizens in front of the public monitor are expected to be monitoring the society, evaluating the words and deeds of political actors, and taking actions when needed. In the context of a large-scale and extended protest campaign, the media may also allow people to become "monitorial participants," that is, people may not be able to participate all the time, but the media connect them to the protest scene. They can monitor the situation and take action when needed.

As noted earlier, DeLuca and Peeples's (2002) concept of the public screen does not refer merely to the conventional mass media. Digital media also constitute part of the public screen. In a more recent article, DeLuca, Lawson, and Sun (2012) talked about the public screens of social media and the public screens of the mass media: "Originally anchored to traditional mass media such as television, with the advent of smartphones and social media, public screens are now mobile and everywhere" (p. 488).

Indeed, the ubiquity of photo-taking and video-recording technologies via mobile phones has further enlarged the possibility of visibility and shrunk the realm of privacy and secrecy for public figures and institutions (Thompson, 2005). Even without the presence of professional journalists, a public figure would be monitored once he or she gets into public space, and flattering or unflattering images can be circulated by people via digital media platforms. In this sense, digital media have simply constituted part of the public monitor. But more directly pertinent to this chapter, digital media have also strengthened the public monitor function of the mainstream mass media. Images related to public figures or public institutions circulated on the Internet can be picked up by the mainstream media, which would signify the presumed importance of the images, further widen their circulation, and thereby amplify their impact. At the same time, images originating from the mass media can reach a larger audience through being shared on digital media platforms.

Up to this point, we have only explicated the conceptual meanings associated with the term "monitor." But as the conceptual label suggests, the public monitor in Hong Kong is partially censored. Even before the transfer of sovereignty, the Chinese government started to co-opt the news media owners in the city. As pointed out in Chapter 2, most media owners in Hong Kong are business people with vast interests in the mainland, and many of them hold formal political titles in the Chinese political system, such as being members of the Chinese People's Political Consultative Conference (Ma, 2007). As a result, media ownership is largely concentrated not so much in the hands of a few companies but in the hands of a group of people sharing the same kind of ties with China (Fung, 2007). Meanwhile, the Chinese and Hong Kong government attempted to influence the media via other informal means, including not only typical public relations strategies but also occasional criticisms toward specific media outlets, direct contact with the top-level newsroom managers, and frontline operational harassment (Lee, 2015a).

Many of the strategies adopted by the government are aimed at inducing self-censorship, and professional journalists do regard self-censorship as a serious problem. In a survey of professional journalists conducted in 2011, 39.0% of the respondents regarded self-censorship as "existing and serious," while 40.9% regarded self-censorship as "existing, though not very serious." Only 1.5% claimed that there is no media self-censorship at all.[4] The general public also recognizes the problem. People are particularly critical toward the two free television broadcasters TVB (Television Broadcasting Ltd.) and ATV (Asia Television Ltd.).[5] On the

Internet, the two stations are often nicknamed CCTVB and CCATV (CCTV is the official abbreviation of Chinese Central Television, the state broadcaster in mainland China).

Nonetheless, the public monitor is only *partially* censored. As Chan and Lee (2007) explicated, there are counteracting forces that prevent the Hong Kong media from totally succumbing to political power. Journalists largely subscribe to a liberal model of journalistic professionalism, which emphasizes journalistic autonomy and sees the news media as playing important roles in disseminating information and monitoring the society (So & Chan, 2007). Besides, most media organizations in Hong Kong are commercial operations. They cannot completely ignore their credibility in the market. Moreover, the presence of a few critical news outlets, especially *Apple Daily*, helped maintain the width of the range of public discourses available in the mainstream media. With the critical news outlets testing the boundary of acceptable discourses, political pressure on other media outlets can be alleviated. When a sensitive story is already broken by someone else, the media outlets that follow up on the story should be facing lesser pressure as they are not the primary "troublemakers." There is also the pressure on the other media outlets not to self-censor too conspicuously because what they fail to report will still be available through other channels.

Therefore, the Hong Kong media rarely self-censor too unscrupulously. In the 2011 journalist survey, 35.6% of the respondents claimed that "toning down negative news about the Chinese government" occurred frequently, but only 18.4% claimed that "omitting negative news about the Chinese government" occurred frequently. This is not difficult to understand: adjusting the tone of coverage may be couched in terms of editorial judgment, but outright omission is much less defensible and therefore much less frequently done.

Indeed, self-censorship often involves intra-organizational dynamics in which suspicious orders are couched in vague, technical, or professional terminologies, and experienced frontline journalists may find ways to resist (Lee & Chan, 2009a). Production routines can also affect the likelihood and extent of self-censorship. Particularly pertinent to the Umbrella Movement, television stations can hardly self-censor when live reporting is concerned. Frontline journalists—and especially the camera operators—did have a significant degree of operational autonomy because only they were on the site witnessing the events. Newsroom managers have more options if they want to self-censor a news story for a newscast because judgments and decisions can come into play throughout the editing process. But the options for a self-censoring newsroom manager are very limited during live reporting.

Therefore, what the partially censored public monitor offers is a mix of censored and uncensored content. This is why the mainstream media may have complicated or even contradictory impact on public opinion. To the extent that the daily news output is biased toward the government, frequent news exposure can have a negative impact on people's attitude toward and participation in the Umbrella Movement.

But to the extent that the mainstream media retain the public monitor function, they have the potential to become the conveyors of images that could generate support for the movement and outburst against the government. This potential impact of mediated visibility means that both government and movement actors would need to adjust their strategies in the presence of the public monitor.

Examining Public Opinion toward and Participation in the Umbrella Movement

After the above conceptual explication, we can now begin the empirical analysis of this chapter. We first provide an analysis of the social psychological factors shaping public attitudes toward and participation in the Umbrella Movement by drawing upon the October population survey introduced in Chapter 3. Besides providing additional information about the individual-level driving forces of participation, the findings will illustrate part of the impact of the media as the partially censored public monitor.

For simplicity, we utilize basically the same explanatory model for both attitude toward and participation in the movement. The model includes three blocks of factors. The first block includes the four basic demographics of sex, age, education, and family income. The second block consists of a number of social and political attitudes that can potentially explain protest participation. They include general political interests, which is the average of respondents' agreement with "you are very interested in political issues" and "you are very interested in general news and public affairs." One may expect people interested in politics to be more likely to participate in political activities, including protests.

Efficacy is widely recognized as one of the core determinants of protest behavior (Finkel & Muller, 1998; Klandermans, 1997; Opp & Roehl, 1990; Seligson, 1980). Hence the second block also includes internal, collective, and external efficacy. The operationalization follows past research in Hong Kong, that is, adopting the statements shown in Table 2.4. Feelings of internal and collective efficacy are likely to relate positively to protest participation (Lee, 2006a, 2010), whereas external efficacy—the belief in the responsiveness of the political system—should relate negatively to participation. Moreover, people may become more likely to participate in protests when protest participation has become a norm or even a habit (Opp, 2004). Therefore, participation in past protests is included and expected to relate positively to both attitude toward and participation in the Umbrella Movement.[6]

Agreement with the goal of a movement is certainly a main factor driving support and participation. The Umbrella Movement strived for genuine democracy. But given the fact that the government also claimed to be advancing democracy by pushing political reform forward, a general and abstract measure of support for democracy may not reflect the extent to which people agree with the movement's goal. Instead, since the actual debate surrounded whether the 2017 election would be "genuinely democratic," the measure used is one asking people whether they thought the legislature should vote down the government's proposal if the latter failed to guarantee fairness and people's right to stand as candidates in the election.

While the stated goal of the movement was genuine popular election in 2017, the movement was also arguably driven by a broader sense of social injustice. This was discussed toward the end of Chapter 2. Hong Kong people, especially the youngest generation, have become less likely to believe in the idea that Hong Kong is a society with equal and ample opportunities and more likely to believe that the society is dominated by big businesses. Therefore, respondents' belief in the discourse of equal and abundant opportunities and their perceptions of corporate hegemony are included in the second block. Operationalization was based on six of the seven statements listed in Chapter 2. We expect people who regarded corporate hegemony as a problem and those who rejected the discourse of opportunities to be more positive toward the Umbrella Movement and more likely to participate.

The third block of factors includes the media and communication variables. Chapter 3's analysis of the predictors of understanding of civil disobedience (Table 3.3) included news exposure, reading of pro-movement papers, time spent on social media, political communication via social media, and amount of disagreeable discussions. Reading of pro-movement papers, political use of social media, and time spent on social media are here retained. Television news watching and newspaper reading are treated as separate variables. Additionally, while constructing a single variable of disagreeable discussion is useful when analyzing the understanding of complex concepts, frequency of political discussions and exposure to discordant views are treated as separate variables here.

The performance of the news exposure variables is most pertinent to the focus of this chapter. If the news content proffered by the mainstream media were indeed biased toward the establishment, one may see a negative relationship between general frequencies of news consumption and attitude toward and participation in the movement. But the mass media also constitute sources of movement-related and mobilizing information (Lemert, 1981) for the public. To the extent that the mainstream media have retained its public monitor function and remained a provider of mobilizing information, a positive relationship between general news exposure and attitude toward and participation in the movement is also conceivable. Certainly, reading of pro-movement newspapers is likely to be associated positively with attitude toward and participation in the movement. Finally, following past research (Tang & Lee, 2013; Tufecki & Wilson, 2012; Valenzuela, Arriagada, & Scherman, 2012), political use of digital media, but not sheer time spent on social media, is likely to relate positively to protest participation.

Table 4.1 summarizes the findings of the analysis on citizens' opinions toward the occupation. When only demographics are included, attitude toward the movement

Table 4.1 **Factors affecting citizens' attitudes toward the Umbrella Movement**

	Demographics only	*Attitudes added*	*Full model*
Demographics			
Sex	−.01	.03	.04
Age	−.28***	−.10***	−.05
Education	.02	−.08*	−.08*
Family income	−.04	−.03	−.03
Change in R^2	0.077***		
Political attitudes			
Political interests		.02	.03
Internal efficacy		−.00	.01
Collective efficacy		.14***	.14***
External efficacy		−.31***	−.28***
Past protest participation		.13***	.11***
Insistence on genuine election		.31***	.28***
Discourse of opportunities		−.10**	−.11***
Discourse of corporate hegemony		.09**	.07**
Change in R^2		0.446***	
Media and communication			
Newspaper exposure			.05*
TV news exposure			−.09**
Pro-movement papers			.12***
Social media: time spent			.06
Social media: political use			−.01
Discussion			−.06*
Disagreement			−.01
Change in R^2			0.024***
Adjusted R^2	0.073***	0.516***	0.536***

Notes: Entries are standardized regression coefficients. Missing values were replaced by mean scores of the variables. $N = 802$. *** $p < .001$; ** $p < .01$; * $p < .05$.

does not relate to sex, education, and family income, but younger participants were much more supportive toward the occupation. When social and political attitudes are added, the explanatory power of the model increases tremendously. People with higher levels of collective efficacy held more positive attitudes toward the movement. Even more strongly related to movement support is external efficacy: people who regarded the political system as responsive to public opinion were more negative toward the movement. In addition, people who had participated more in past protests and people who had a stronger insistence on the establishment of genuine popular election in 2017 were more positive toward the occupation.

Even after controlling for the other attitudinal factors, perceptions related to social and economic inequalities are still significantly related to attitude toward the movement: People who perceived corporate hegemony as a serious problem and people who rejected the discourse of opportunities were more supportive. These findings support the argument that the social and political attitudes underlying the Umbrella Movement went beyond a narrow concern with institutionalization of popular elections. But at the same time, the regression coefficients of the two variables are substantially smaller than that of insistence on genuine popular election in 2017. Among the public at large, the issue of democratic reform remained more central to the occupation.

Adding the media and communication factors does not affect the impact of the social and political attitudes. This is understandable because political attitudes and judgments such as efficacy feelings and beliefs about the society are formed over the long haul based on lived experiences and interpersonal communications in addition to mediated communications, and these attitudes and perceptions constitute the most important bases for people's opinions toward current events and issues. But given this consideration, it is remarkable that some of the media and communication variables still exhibit significant relationships with attitude toward the Umbrella Movement even after a large set of social and political attitudes is controlled. Besides, the relationship between age and attitude toward the movement becomes statistically insignificant in the full model. It suggests that young people's tendency to hold more positive attitudes toward the Umbrella Movement are completely mediated by some of their social and political attitudes and media and communication behavior. That is, young people were more positive toward the Umbrella Movement because they were more active in pro-movement communication activities and they were more likely to hold the set of social and political attitudes related to support for the movement.

Regarding the individual media and communication variables, readers of pro-movement newspapers were more supportive toward the movement. Frequency of political discussion relates significantly, though only weakly, with attitude toward the movement. Neither of the two social media variables relates significantly to attitude toward the movement. This is understandable because the opponents of the occupation were also active online. Hence a person who was active in political communication online could have been an opponent of the movement, and his or her online political communication might only have reinforced his or her negative attitude toward the occupation. Another possibility is that the impact of political communication via social media on attitude toward the Umbrella Movement was completely channeled through the other social and psychological factors already existing in the model.

Most interesting, there is a significant negative relationship between television news watching and attitude toward the movement. Given TVB's status as the overwhelmingly dominant information source for local citizens,[7] the finding is consistent with widespread criticisms against the station's pro-government bias. In fact, a study of TVB's performance during the Umbrella Movement has found that the station has "banned or not recommended" its journalists to use a range of terminologies that could be regarded as supportive toward the movement. Journalists were instructed to use "police waving the baton to disperse" instead of "police beating with baton," "Occupy Action" instead of "Occupy Movement," "clearance of blockages by the police" instead of "clearance of the site by the police," etc. (Au, 2016). Many of these differences in wordings are subtle, but combined together they suggest a careful attempt not to legitimize the Umbrella Movement. The negative relationship between television news exposure and attitude toward the movement thus points to how regular exposure to the biased content of the partially censored media was related to more pro-government and anti-movement attitudes.

We can now turn to the factors explaining participation in the Umbrella Movement. The dependent variable is the four-point scale item on whether the respondents had gone to the occupied areas to support the movement (1 = no to 4 = for more than three days). The regression model is the same as that in Table 4.1, only with the addition of attitude toward the Umbrella Movement as an independent variable in the second block.

Table 4.2 summarizes the findings. When only demographics were included, younger people, more educated people, and males were more likely to have participated in the movement. The impact of education becomes statistically insignificant in the second column, showing that the impact of education on participation was completely mediated through the set of social and political attitudes included in the second block. However, only three variables in the second block obtain a significant coefficient. This is probably because of the inclusion of movement support as an independent variable. Attitude toward the movement itself of course would constitute a powerful predictor of participation. Taking into account the findings in Table 4.1, attitude toward the movement could be considered as a mediator of the impact of other social psychological factors on participation.

Collective efficacy and past protest participation are significantly positively related to participation even after controlling for attitude toward the movement. In other words, among people with the same level of support for the Umbrella Movement, those with stronger beliefs in the capability of the public as a collective

Table 4.2 Factors affecting citizens' participation in the Umbrella Movement

	Demographics only	Attitudes added	Full model
Demographics			
Sex	−.12**	−.09**	−.09**
Age	−.22***	−.09**	−.02
Education	.12**	.03	.02
Family income	.03	.03	.03
Change in R^2	0.116***		
Political attitudes			
Political interests		−.02	−.07*
Internal efficacy		.00	−.02
Collective efficacy		.07*	.07*
External efficacy		−.06	−.04
Past protest participation		.33***	.25***
Insistence on genuine election		.00	.01
Discourse of opportunities		−.04	−.05
Corporate hegemony		−.01	−.03
Support for the movement		.26***	.25***
Change in R^2		0.271***	
Media and communication			
Newspaper exposure			.08**
TV exposure			−.01
Pro-movement papers			−.00
Social media: time spent			−.12**
Social media: political use			.31***
Discussion			.03
Disagreement			.05
Change in R^2			0.051***
Adjusted R^2	0.111***	0.376***	0.423***

Notes: Entries are standardized regression coefficients. Missing values were replaced by mean scores of the variables. $N = 802$. *** $p < .001$; ** $p < .01$; * $p < .05$.

actor to effect social change and those who had more experiences participating in protests were more likely to participate in the occupation. These two factors are capable of generating action given the presence of attitudinal support.

Similar to Table 4.1, age ceases to have a significant relationship with the dependent variable in the full model. The relationship between age and participation in the Umbrella Movement is completely mediated through the attitudinal and communication variables. Regarding the individual media and communication variables, reading of pro-movement newspapers does not relate to participation significantly and is therefore similar to some of the attitudinal factors in the second block. It could be considered as having an indirect impact on participation through attitude toward the movement, but it does not directly enhance participation after attitude toward the movement is controlled.

Television news exposure does not have a significant direct relationship with participation. Yet newspaper exposure has a positive relationship with participation. It suggests that newspaper readers were more likely than nonreaders to have participated in the movement given the same level of attitudinal support for the movement. A plausible explanation is that the more detailed coverage and in-depth discourses proffered by newspapers were more likely to contain the triggers for actions among those who supported the movement.

There is a strong relationship between political use of social media and participation. Although both supporters and opponents of the movement could be active on the Internet, for movement opponents, political communication via social media would not affect their participation because they would not participate in the movement no matter whether they engaged in any form of political communication or not. In contrast, among movement supporters, political communication via social media might provide the final trigger for participation, e.g., a call to action issued by a friend or a provocative image that went viral. Hence political communication via social media could have an overall strongly positive relationship with participation without being a factor affecting attitude toward the movement.

Finally, sheer time spent on social media has a negative impact on protest participation. This negative relationship should also be understood in relation to the fact that other factors are controlled in the full model. In fact, at the bivariate level, time spent on social media relates to participation in the movement positively and significantly ($r = 0.31$, $p < .001$). Yet the correlation would immediately become negative when political communication via social media is controlled ($r = -0.11$, $p < .001$). Conceptually, when political communication via social media is controlled, the time spent on social media variable should represent primarily nonpolitical use of social media (e.g., entertainment). The negative relationship, in the context of the regression model, thus suggests that people who spent more time on social media for nonpolitical purposes were less likely to have participated in the movement.

A note about the notion of media and communication effects should be added here. The analyses in Tables 4.1 and 4.2 are based on a cross-sectional survey, and there is no guarantee that media and communication activities are the "causes" of pro- or anti-movement attitudes and participation. In reality, communication activities and attitudes probably mutually influence each other. But Tables 4.1 and 4.2 at least show that there are systematic relationships between communication activities and attitudes and behavior related to the movement. Moreover, the notion of media effects could provide more sensible interpretations of some of the specific findings. For instance, newspaper reading, but not reading of pro-movement papers, is related to participation. If participation is actually the cause of communication activities, it is difficult to understand why reading of pro-movement papers would not relate to participation.

More important, Tables 4.1 and 4.2 only provide an analysis of "media effects" at the individual level. The presumption in such analysis is that media effects are manifested in the differences between media users and non-users (or between heavy and light users). However, the impact of media and communication on the Umbrella Movement is by no means restricted to the effects of individual level media use. There are other ways to make sense of and document media influence on the movement, as shown in the following sections.

Tear Gas on the Public Monitor and Instant Provocation

Tables 4.1 and 4.2 do not show any evidence regarding the mobilizing power of televised images on people, as television news exposure does not relate positively to participation: it even relates negatively to attitudinal support toward the movement. However, Tables 4.1 and 4.2, as just noted, follow a conventional approach of survey-based media effects research by positing amount of exposure to a news medium as the independent variable. Underlying this approach is the presumption that amount of exposure is related to likelihood of message or information reception (Price & Zaller, 1993). That is, the news media are considered as providers of certain types of information and messages that might persuade people to adopt certain cognitions or attitudes, and the larger amount of time people spend on the news media (or, in some studies, the higher levels of attention people pay to the news), the more likely they are to receive the information or message and have their cognitions or attitudes influenced. In relation to Table 4.1, one may argue that television news provided a steady stream of overall speaking negative coverage about the movement. The more time people spent watching television news, the more likely they would develop negative impressions about the movement.

The conventional approach to media effects analysis is useful for many purposes. In the current context, the findings in Table 4.1 provide some empirical support to the argument that mainstream television news in Hong Kong was biased against the movement. But the conventional approach may fail to capture certain types of media effects that are not dependent on *amount* of exposure. Specifically, while the mobilizing power of the public monitor may be realized through the dissemination of shocking images that generate moral indignation, the reception of the shocking images may not depend on whether a person is a frequent television news watcher or not. First, if the shocking images are conveyed through live reporting, then any person who happens to be among the television audience when the shocking images are conveyed could be influenced. In times of highly significant events, even people who normally do not pay attention to the news may monitor the media closely. Thus exposure to the shocking images is not related to the usual amount of time people spend on the news. Second, the shocking media images associated with highly significant events are likely to enter into a media loop and get quickly and extensively circulated via all kinds of media channels and platforms. The images can become diffused throughout the society such that reception of the images is actually a "constant" instead of a variable, i.e., almost everyone has seen it, even though not everyone necessarily reacts to the images in exactly the same way.

The latter scenario was arguably what happened surrounding a double scandal of police violence to be discussed in the next section, whereas the former arguably happened on September 28. As noted earlier, not only were the images of tear gas live broadcast through 24-hour news channels, the use of tear gas began only about half an hour before TVB's main evening newscast at 6:30 p.m. The timing ensured a huge audience. The live broadcast of the images resulted in an instant provocation among the public, created what Tang (2015) labelled mediated instant grievances, and contributed to mass participation in the movement.

We can document the instant provocation and the role of the media, especially television, in producing it through the October protest onsite survey.[8] The survey, which was conducted in the first weekend (October 4 and 5) after the movement formally began on September 28, asked the respondents the time they decided to participate in the occupation. Only 3.2% of the respondents claimed that they decided to join the occupation even before the National People's Congress's (NPC) decision regarding democratic reform in Hong Kong on August 31, and only 4.6% decided to join the occupation right after the NPC decision. Another 10.2% of the respondents said they decided to participate during the week of class boycott organized by the HKFS between September 22 and 26. In other words, not more than 20% of the respondents said they had decided to join the movement before the end of the one-week class boycott, and less than 10% had decided before the class boycott.

At the other end of the answering scale, only 4.0% reported that they decided to join the movement "today or yesterday," and 10.4% of the respondents did not give a valid answer to the question. A further 17.5% of the respondents claimed that they decided to join the movement on September 27, when students were protesting in front of the Government Headquarters and the police arrested several prominent student leaders. Most remarkably, 49.9% of the respondents claimed that they decided to participate in the movement on September 28.

The distribution of time of participation decision is very different from those in other large-scale protests in Hong Kong. In the July 1 protest in year 2003, time of participation decision was roughly evenly spread throughout the weeks prior to the protest. The pattern suggests a gradual snowballing process as a result of continual social mobilization. In subsequent July 1 protests and the annual June 4 commemoration rallies, time of participation decision was heavily skewed toward "early decisions": many participants claimed to have decided to join the action more than one month prior. This is because participation in those "ritualistic protests" has become routinized or even a matter of habits for some (Lee & Chan, 2011). But in the Umbrella Movement, time of participation decision was heavily skewed toward "late decisions." The pattern suggests that a very substantial portion of the participants was provoked into actions almost instantly after they saw the televised images of tear gas.

Table 4.3 provides more direct evidence about the effect of tear gas through examining the relationship between time of participation decision and reason for participation. For simplicity, participants who decided to join the movement during the week of class boycott or before were grouped together, whereas people who did not give a valid answer and those who decided to join only "yesterday or today" were also grouped together into a residual category "others." The finding shows that those who decided to participate on September 28 were somewhat less likely to recognize fighting for a filter-less election and fighting for civil nomination as very important to their participation decision when compared to the early deciders. More important, the extent to which the police's use of tear gas was recognized as an important reason for participation varies substantially according to time of participation decision. Among the early deciders, among participants who decided to join the movement on September 27, and among participants who decided to join the movement later than September 28, 46.5%, 52.1%, and 60.2%, respectively, recognized the police's use of tear gas as a very important reason for their participation. The corresponding percentage reaches 70% for participants who decided to join the movement on September 28.

The September 28 deciders were also more likely than the early deciders to recognize protecting the students as important to their decision, though the difference is statistically insignificant. Of course, even among the September 28 deciders, fighting for a filter-less election, fighting for civil nomination, and protecting Hong Kong's liberty were still the relatively more important reasons for participation. One would be unlikely to be provoked into joining a protest unless one agrees with the values of the protest in the first place.

It is worth noting that the OC Trio announced the beginning of the occupation also on September 28. But Table 4.3 shows that the September 28 deciders (and the September 27 deciders) were less likely than the early deciders to acknowledge

Table 4.3 **Reasons to participate for people who made the decision at different time points**

Reasons for participation	Time of participation decision			
	Before September 27	September 27	September 28	Others
Fight for election without filter[a]	93.6	91.0	85.0	82.1
Fight for civil nomination	82.2	79.5	77.0	70.7
Protect Hong Kong's liberty	88.4	91.6	91.6	89.9
The use of tear gas by the police[a]	46.5	52.1	70.2	61.3
Support and protect students[a]	68.0	70.7	74.1	80.6
Empower the movement	40.4	37.7	35.8	41.6
Experience mass protests	9.9	8.9	13.5	16.4
Mobilized by friends[a]	4.1	3.6	3.1	8.9
Mobilized by family/relatives[a]	3.0	1.8	2.6	8.0
Call from HKFS[a]	15.8	10.7	10.5	22.1
Call from Scholarism	14.6	12.5	10.8	20.6
Call from OC Trio[a]	10.1	4.2	4.4	11.2
Call from other organizations	9.3	3.7	4.1	9.1

Notes: Entries are percentages of respondents who regarded a reason as "very important." When a variable is marked with superscript "a," significant differences (at $p < .05$ in a Chi-square test) among the four groups of respondents exist on perceived importance of the reason. $N = 969$ for the whole survey.

the importance of the call to action by the OC Trio. They were also nominally less likely to acknowledge the influence of the two student groups. The pattern is reasonable. Given the lengthy period of advance planning and discursive contestation surrounding Occupy Central, those who heeded the call of the central organizers would not have waited until September 27 or 28 to decide to participate.

Presumably, the media, especially television, should have been the more important mobilizing agent for participants who decided to join the movement on September 28. The onsite survey included a set of questions about the perceived importance of media platforms as sources of information about the Umbrella Movement. As Table 4.4 summarizes, two digital media platforms—Facebook and the mobile chat application WhatsApp—were widely recognized by movement participants as important sources of information, while other digital media

Table 4.4 **Perceived importance of media platforms and credibility of mass media channels**

	Very important/ important	Very unimportant/ unimportant	Mean score
Perceived importance of			
WhatsApp	73.1	6.0	4.15
Firechat	13.8	40.4	2.41
Other mobile chat apps	17.8	33.6	2.66
Facebook	89.8	2.7	4.63
Twitter	10.6	46.4	2.20
Other social media sites	23.4	35.1	2.72
TV live reporting	72.1	9.3	4.02
TV news reporting	66.3	12.7	3.87
Newspapers (and their websites)	67.7	9.1	3.95
Radio stations (and their websites)	43.2	21.8	3.33
	Very credible/ credible	*Very not credible/ not credible*	*Mean score*
Perceived credibility of			
TVB	4.9	76.7	1.77
Cable TV	50.5	6.2	3.65
Sing Tao Daily	9.3	30.1	2.52
Ming Pao	37.5	9.8	3.41
Apple Daily	63.9	3.3	3.78

Notes: Entries in the first two columns are percentages, and entries in the last column are mean scores on a five-point Likert scale. $N = 969$ for the whole survey.

platforms were regarded as important to a much lesser extent. But the prominence of WhatsApp and Facebook does not suggest insignificance of the mass media. More than 70% of the respondents acknowledged that TV live reporting was an important source of movement information, while 66.3% and 67.7% recognized TV news reporting and newspapers, respectively, as important sources of movement information. Even radio was recognized by more than 40% of the respondents as an important source of movement information.

In their analysis of the participants in the July 1 protest series, Lee and Chan (2011) noted that protesters in Hong Kong are often attentive analysts of public affairs and media performance. They are highly aware of the political predilections of media organizations and critical toward suspected self-censorship. The bottom of Table 4.4 shows that the Umbrella Movement participants were highly critical toward TVB, the dominant free television broadcaster in Hong Kong. Among television stations, they were more positive toward the pay television service provider Cable TV. Among newspapers, the strongly pro-democracy newspaper *Apple Daily* and the professional-oriented *Ming Pao* (i.e., the two "pro-movement newspapers" in our earlier analysis) were regarded generally positively, though to different extents, by the movement participants. In contrast, the middle-class and pro-government newspaper *Sing Tao Daily* was evaluated generally negatively. Nevertheless, perceived credibility may not be a crucial condition for television and the mainstream media in general to carry out their public monitor function, especially when live reporting is concerned because of the absence of editing. Shocking live images can be powerful no matter which station is showing them.

In fact, the September 28 deciders did not necessarily see the specific media organizations as more or less credible. As the bottom of Table 4.5 shows, although the four groups of participants differed significantly in perceptions of credibility of TVB and *Sing Tao Daily*, the main difference resides only in that between respondents belonging to the residual category and the first three groups.

There is a significant relationship between time of participation decision and perceived importance of WhatsApp. Of the early deciders, 87.2% saw WhatsApp as an important source of movement information, whereas only 72.1% of the September 28 deciders saw WhatsApp as important. Since WhatsApp is a mobile application for interpersonal communication among acquaintances, the finding suggests that the early deciders were relatively more likely to be embedded in social networks of other movement supporters and participants.

More important, the September 28 deciders were the most likely to see various mainstream media as important sources of movement information. Among this group, 73.5% saw television news reporting as important, whereas only 59.4% of the early deciders and 56.2% of those who decided to participate on September 27 saw television news reports as important. The differences among the groups of participants were statistically significant. Further, 76.3% of the September 28 deciders saw television live reporting as an important source of movement information, whereas only 70.0% and 66.7%, respectively, of the September 27 deciders and the early deciders saw television live reporting as important, even though the differences among the percentages are not statistically significant in this case.

In sum, the October onsite survey shows that nearly half of the movement participants decided to take action only on September 28. These participants were more likely than the others to name the police's firing of tear gas as an important reason for their participation. They were more likely than other participants to regard

Table 4.5 **Perceived importance and credibility of media platforms and time of decision**

	Before September 27	September 27	September 28	Others
Perceived importance of				
WhatsApp[a]	87.2	75.0	72.1	68.7
Firechat	20.3	15.9	17.7	12.6
Other mobile chat apps	23.4	18.2	23.0	18.3
Facebook[a]	90.0	94.6	93.6	84.6
Twitter	15.5	12.5	12.5	12.4
Other social media sites[a]	22.4	21.8	30.9	29.3
TV live reporting	70.0	66.7	76.3	75.9
TV news reporting[a]	59.4	56.2	73.5	68.9
Newspapers (and their websites)	67.8	62.2	72.3	71.3
Radio (and their websites)	38.6	39.5	46.9	57.1
Perceived credibility of				
TVB[a]	4.1	0.6	5.5	10.2
Cable TV	65.3	63.7	61.6	51.9
Sing Tao Daily[a]	11.2	9.3	14.2	18.1
Ming Pao	50.0	50.3	42.3	50.9
Apple Daily	67.7	68.0	64.7	63.2

Notes: Entries are percentages of respondents who regarded a media platform or channel as "important/credible" or "very important/very credible" (i.e., scoring 4 or 5 on the five-point Likert scale). When a variable is marked with superscript "a," significant differences (at $p < .05$ in a Chi-square test) among the four groups of respondents exist on the item. $N = 969$ for the whole survey.

the mainstream media platforms as important sources of information related to the Umbrella Movement. Taken together, these evidences point to how televisual images of tear gas flying over the urban landscape of the city had shocked the public and provoked many of them into action. Conceptually, we may also argue that the initial participation decision of many supporters of the movement exhibited the character of monitorial participation, in that they were concerned citizens monitoring the situation through the public monitor and decided to act when they saw something that compelled them to act.

The Police under the Public Monitor

The police force has the important task of maintaining basic order in the sites of protests. In the Umbrella Movement, the presence of the police around the occupied areas was crucial to preventing the conflicts between the protesters and the counter-protesters from getting out of control. However, the police was also, in one sense, the "representatives" of the state at the sites of protests. They could potentially become the agents of state violence. This was how the movement participants and supporters viewed the police after the latter's use of tear gas on September 28. Even some pro-government politicians were seemingly confused by the police's decision. Member of the Executive Council of the SAR government Fanny Law stated in a radio interview on September 29 that the police force needed to explain to the Executive Council the reasons for using tear gas, even though she quickly changed her expression and followed closely the "official line" a day later after reports surfaced that the police force were outraged by her remarks.

It should be noted that police-protester conflicts had seemingly been on the rise in Hong Kong in the few years before the Umbrella Movement. This can be indicated by the increased discussions of "police-citizen conflicts" in association with protests and rallies in the news. A keyword search in Wise News found that, from year 2001 to 2005, there were only 32 articles in the "Hong Kong news" section of six newspapers mentioning both the term "police-citizen conflict" (*ging-man cung-dat*) and either march (*jau-hang*) or rally (*zap-wui*).[9] The number doubled to 66 in the five-year period between year 2006 and 2010. It then rose further to 84 between January 2011 and August 2014.

The growth of police-protester conflicts is arguably partly attributable to the radicalization of movement actions. But from the perspective of movement supporters and activists, the government and the police were the ones to blame, because the latter were perceived to have tried to curtail citizens' freedom of expression through various "tricks." For instance, during the July 1 protests in the few years before the Umbrella Movement, the police typically allowed the protesters to use only three of the six lanes of the main roads along the marching route. The police's rationale was that the protests should not affect traffic too severely, and there is the need to allow the movement of emergency vehicles. However, critics can easily point to the fact that the government was willing to seal off a larger number of roads and lanes for the Chinese New Year Parade and Christmas Eve celebrations. In any case, the result of the police's decision not to open all six lanes for the march was that many protesters often found themselves stuck for hours at the starting point of the marching route due to the huge number of participants involved. Some protesters even believed that the police was intentionally making the protest march difficult so as to undermine citizens' intention to participate. While this conspiracy theory cannot be easily proven, the police decision had, as a matter of fact, contributed to heightened tension between the police and the protesters even in the largely peaceful July 1 protests.

Accompanying the rise of police-protester conflict was the decline in public trust toward the police in recent years. It should be noted that the Hong Kong police force, despite a history of corruption before the establishment of the Independent Commission Against Corruption in 1973 (Ip, 2014), had gained very positive media representations and public evaluations since the early 1980s. The positive evaluation persisted into the early years after the handover. According to the tracking survey conducted by the Public Opinion Programme at the Hong Kong University,[10] 71.2% of the Hong Kong public were satisfied with the performance of the police force in the latter half of year 1997. Public attitude toward the police remained highly positive even as evaluation of the government declined sharply between 1997 and 2003. In 2003, amid the national security legislation debate, the severe acute respiratory syndrome outbreak, and the historic July 1 protest, more than 75% of Hong Kong people remained satisfied with the police. But by the first half of year 2012, the percentage feeling satisfied with the police had gone down to 54.5%. The percentage stood at 55.6% in the first half of 2014.

The action of the police was therefore closely monitored by the media even before September 28. In the morning of September 27, for instance, television images of a young female protester being dragged by a police officer on the ground during a police-protester confrontation in front of the Government Headquarters were widely shared via social media. After the tear gas visuals on September 28 and within the first week of the movement, the occupied areas—especially Mong Kok—was repeatedly "under attack" by counter-protesters and even suspected gangsters. The police was criticized by the protesters for being lukewarm when dealing with the violence exercised by the counter-protesters. Such accusations, when shared via social media, were typically accompanied by TV news footage or the protesters' own video clips taken on site showing the alleged police malpractice.

There were even some movement supporters accusing the police of collaborating with triad societies, and the term "black police" (hak-ging)[11] was coined and used widely by movement supporters in the online arena to refer to police who were connected to gangsters or behaved like gangsters. On the other side of the political divide, the counter-protesters rallied to express their support for the police to "execute the law." In the online arena, many movement opponents changed their profile picture into a blue ribbon with the line "support the police's execution of the law." Among the articles widely shared by movement opponents online were those written by police officers or their family members arguing that the police were only doing their job; they were facing harsh situations in the frontline, and the behaviors of some protesters were far from being unquestionable.

In response, some movement participants and supporters adopted a less negative and dismissive stance toward the police as a whole. These protesters argued that not all frontline police officers were "bad," and video clips of friendly interactions between police officers and protesters in the occupied areas were sometimes widely shared. This group of protesters singled out top-level decision-making as the root of the problem. They thus strongly urged the government and the top-level decision makers in the police force not to turn the frontline officers into political tools exercising political missions.

Against the above backdrop, the double scandal of the so-called dark corner incident occurred in the early morning of October 15. A group of protesters tried to occupy a road outside the South Wing of the Government Headquarters, which was part of an attempt to block off various entrances to the government building. Confrontations ensued when the police tried to push the protesters back to the Tamar Park, an open area nearby. In the process, TVB journalists captured the scenes in which seven police officers were clearly seen to be carrying a protester to a "dark corner" under a building where they beat the protester as the latter was lying on the ground.

The news came out on the 24-hour news channel TVB in the early morning hours, but it quickly became a scandal of not only police violence but also media self-censorship. When the news story was aired for the first time, the reporter's voiceover described the scene with the phrase *kyun-daa goek-tek*, which literally means beating with fists and kicking with legs. But the phrase and its associated sentence disappeared from the story—though the visuals were unchanged—starting from around 7 a.m.; that is, the story was re-edited so that the verbal accusation against the police was removed. Around noon, another version of the story came out in which a sentence about "suspected use of violence by the police" was added.

TVB's treatment of the story created not only public outcry. More than 50 TVB journalists issued a public letter in the afternoon of October 15 to express their concerns with the management's handling of the story. The letter defended the original version of the story:

> We reiterate that the deleted narration did not involve the reporter's personal stance or emotion. It was objective reporting based on facts. The reaction of the viewers, such as whether they would feel dissatisfied with the police's treatment [of the protester] or they would sympathize with the difficulty of the police's frontline operation, would be the result of public debates. Journalists should not and need not consider them.[12]

This passage does not defend the story through explicitly invoking the media's role in exposing the abuse of power, but it can be considered a defense of the public monitor function of the press exercised through factual and objective reporting. The number of co-signing TVB journalists would increase to about 100. In Hong Kong, this was the first instance of collective public expression of discontent by television journalists against their own news organization on issues related to press freedom since the early 1990s.

Of course, there was also public outcry against the police. The Centre for Communication and Public Opinion Survey at the Chinese University of Hong Kong happened to be conducting the October population survey from the 8th to the 15th. On the question of trust toward the police force, while the mean score of respondents interviewed between October 8 and 14 was 5.60 on a 0–10 scale, the mean score of respondents interviewed on October 15 was significantly and substantially lower, at 4.96.[13] Admittedly, the decline was mainly registered among the movement supporters. Trust toward the police among movement supporters who were interviewed on or before October 14 was at 3.77, and the figure dropped to 2.30 on October 15. The drop is highly statistically significant.[14] Among non-supporters of the movement, the change in trust toward the police on October 15 was statistically insignificant, but the mean score also declined nominally from 6.86 to 6.52.

We further analyzed the data through regression analysis. The control variables include demographics, past protest participation, political interest, the three dimensions of political efficacy, whether the respondents were a supporter of the democrats or the pro-establishment faction (as two separate dummy variables), attitude toward the Umbrella Movement, and the respondents' opinion toward how the police handled the movement in its first two weeks (average of respondents' answers to two statements). Media and communication variables include mainstream newspaper reading, TV news exposure, reading pro-movement newspapers, interpersonal discussion, time spent on social media, and political communication via social media. A dichotomous variable of date of interview (October 15 = 1, October 8 to 14 = 0) was also included, and this should indicate whether the "dark corner incident" had any impact on public opinion after controlling for all other factors.

As Table 4.6 shows, the dichotomous date of interview variable retains a significant negative relationship with trust toward the police. Interestingly, there is also a significant positive relationship between TV news exposure and trust toward the police. Newspaper reading frequency does not relate significantly with attitude toward the police, but the coefficient is also positive in sign.[15] In other words, similar to attitude toward the Umbrella Movement at large, the impact of the media on public opinion toward the police was mixed. On the one hand, regular exposure to the conventional news media, especially television, was related to higher levels of trust in the police, that is, a more pro-government attitude. But on the other hand, the televisual images of police violence on October 15 generated a rise in distrust toward the police.

The "dark corner incident" thus constitutes another instance where the public monitor function of the media was conspicuously displayed. It also illustrates the paradox that can be generated by the partially censored public monitor: the media organization that captured the shocking images was none other than the one most

Table 4.6 **Regression on trust toward the police**

	Model 1	Media variables added
Demographics and basic controls		
Sex	.02	.03
Age	.04	−.02
Education	.11***	.11**
Family income	.04	.05
Political interests	.03	.03
Internal efficacy	−.06*	−.06
Collective efficacy	−.01	.00
External efficacy	.18***	.16***
Past protest experience	−.07*	−.04
Change in R^2	0.362***	
Political attitudes		
Support Democrats	.02	.01
Support Pro-establishment	.02	.01
Support for the Umbrella M.	−.20***	−.20***
Opinion toward police's handling of protests before	.43***	.45***
Change in R^2	0.187***	
Media and communications		
Newspaper reading		.03
TV news exposure		.06*
Read pro-movement papers		.00
Social media: time spent		.03
Social media: political use		−.11**
Political discussion		−.05
Interview date (Oct 15 = 2)		−.09***
Change in R^2		0.017***
Adjusted R^2	0.542***	0.556***

Notes: Entries are standardized regression coefficients. Missing values were replaced by mean scores of the variables. $N = 802$. *** $p < .001$; ** $p < .01$; * $p < .05$.

distrusted by the protesters. The organization did seemingly attempt to exercise self-censorship, but exactly because of the suspected self-censorship behavior, the case also shows the *partial* character of the censoring of the public monitor. The images of police violence could not be totally suppressed, partly because of commercial considerations, and partly because of a professional bottom line that cannot be crossed. The images were not manipulated; only the verbal narrative was adjusted. Similar to many cases of suspected self-censorship in the Hong Kong media in the past, the director of the news department of TVB defended the editing of the story by referring to the norm of objectivity: his argument was that the phrase *kyun-dat goek-tek* carries subjective judgment. Putting aside the viability of this defense, the point to note is that the news director still had to refer to professional norms when he tried to defend his decision. More broadly, objectivity remains an important discursive reference point for people debating about media performance during the Umbrella Movement (Chan, 2015).

Another noteworthy point about the incident is that the news came out in the early morning hours, and the story was first aired through newscasts on the 24-hour news channel. Without going too much into the operational routines of 24-hour news channels in Hong Kong, one basic implication of the presence of 24-hour news channels is the shrinking of the interval of time between the collection of the raw materials and the airing of the news story. Professional journalists around the world often lament about how the increased speed of news reporting has deprived newsrooms the time to process news information properly, such as taking the time to verify the information (Kovach & Rosenstiel, 1999). But in the present case, the constant search for the newest information and images on the 24-hour news channel also "deprived" the newsroom managers the time and the chance to "negotiate" with the journalists about the treatment of the story. It is quite probable that, without the 24-hour news channel, the re-edited version of the story would have been the only publicly aired version.

Moreover, the case illustrates the role digital media platforms can play in the exercise of the public monitor function. Since the news story was first aired in the early morning hours, very few citizens could have seen the original version of the story through television. Even the first re-edited version of the story aired around 7 a.m. could not have been seen by many people directly. Instead, the majority of citizens probably saw the images of police violence via a digital media platform. For movement supporters, their Facebook accounts could have been "page-washed" on October 15 with stories about the double scandal.[16] On YouTube, the early "pre-censored" version of the story was uploaded by many citizens. Some of the clips attracted hundreds of thousands of views.[17] The dark corner incident was a case of the mainstream media professional carrying out the public monitor function, but the circulation of the images was highly reliant on digital media platforms.

Summary

This chapter puts forward the concept of the partially censored public monitor as a way to understand the complicated and potentially contradictory impact of the media on the Umbrella Movement. The empirical analysis illustrates such contradictory impact, especially of television. Analysis of the population survey data shows a negative relationship between television news exposure and attitude toward the Umbrella Movement. This finding corresponds to widespread perception of biases in the news content offered by the dominant free television broadcaster in the city. However, through conveying the images of tear gas flying over the urban landscape, television provoked people into action and contributed to the scale of the movement. The happenings of September 28 and the impact of mediated images of tear gas illustrate how the media allow monitorial participation on the part of monitorial citizens (Schudson, 1998). Similarly, the police was under the public monitor throughout the movement. Survey data analysis shows a positive relationship between mainstream news media exposure and trust toward the police. But in the "dark corner incident," images of inexcusable police violence led to an immediate rise in distrust toward the police.

The concept of partially censored public monitor helps us make sense of such mixed impact of the media. Similar to DeLuca and Peeples's (2002) concept of the public screen, we emphasize the power of television images to generate shock and moral indignation that are conducive to movement mobilization. But at the same time, the concept retains an emphasis on the implications of the probable pro-establishment bias exhibited by the mainstream media.

Although the analysis in this chapter has put relatively more emphasis on the mainstream media's impact, it also illustrates the influence of digital media. The analysis of the population survey shows that political communication via social media was quite strongly positively related to participation in the Umbrella Movement even after controlling for all other variables. The finding points to social media's support activation function: political communications among citizens via social media are likely to contain the triggers that can turn attitudinal support into action. Besides, digital media enhanced the public monitor function of the mainstream media. This enhancement function of digital media can be realized when influential citizen-produced images are taken up by the mainstream media, as well as when powerful images conveyed by the mainstream media are further circulated via digital media. The latter occurred regularly throughout the Umbrella Movement and was particularly crucial in the "dark corner incident."

More broadly speaking, the "dark corner incident" is a good example of how conventional mass media's impact needs to be understood within an integrated media environment composed of a mix of technologies and platforms. At issue here is not only digital media; the presence of 24-hour news channels is also a crucial component without which the "dark corner incident" might not have had its impact. The dichotomy of digital media and conventional mass media can be problematic not only because it may lead to the overlooking of the intertwinement of the two, but also because it may lead to the overlooking of certain media phenomena, such as 24-hour news channels, that are neither prototypically digital nor prototypically conventional.

As pointed out in the process of conceptual explication, the impact of the public monitor does not reside only in how the images conveyed may influence attitudes and behavior. The public monitor's effect also resides in how its sheer presence may affect the strategic calculations of relevant actors, and as a result shaping the dynamics of an ongoing movement. In the Umbrella Movement, after the dark corner incident, the Hong Kong government and the police had seemingly taken the presence of the public monitor more seriously. There would be no more images of one-sided police violence against the protesters. While the use of force by the police was shown at the later stages of the movement, it was in cases when the protesters escalated their actions. Public attitude toward the police also improved after mid-October. The survey conducted by the Centre for Communication and Public Opinion Survey at the Chinese University of Hong Kong in early November found that public trust toward the police had risen from 5.49 back to 6.25.[18]

If the use of tear gas on September 28 signified the government's intention to "kill off" the movement immediately and decisively, the government had changed its strategy since mid-October. The media also widely reported that the Central Government had ordered the Hong Kong government to follow the principle of "no compromise and no bloodshed." The news was not officially confirmed, but it did correspond to the unfolding of events. The insistence on "no bloodshed" is arguably partly the consequence of the presence of the public monitor. Throughout the Umbrella Movement, the Chinese government was adamant on the point that the events in Hong Kong were internal affairs within China about which foreign governments had no rights to intervene or even comment on. But in reality, the Chinese government could not totally ignore international opinion on the matter and the possible repercussions that images of bloodshed conveyed through the public monitor might create.

Under such conditions, the Hong Kong government started to play the game of attrition (Yuen & Cheng, 2017), while at the same time attempting to invoke opposition to the movement by the general public through a number of discursive and counter-mobilization strategies. We will further discuss in Chapter 6 the government's approach to handling the protests and public opinion toward the occupation in the later stages of the Umbrella Movement. But before that, we will first further analyze the role of digital media in the Umbrella Movement, especially how they contributed to the emergence of connective actions and accentuated the tendency of decentralization of the movement.

5

Digital Media Activities and Connective Actions

PARTICIPANT A: Denise Ho is a popular singer in Hong Kong. She is among a minority of celebrities in the local entertainment industry who is willing to express views on social and political affairs. After becoming the first female artist in the city to publicly acknowledge her homosexual orientation in November 2012, Ho cofounded the Big Love Alliance with a number of other prominent public figures to "advocate and protest basic equal rights for the LGBTQ community."[1] On September 27, 2014, she appeared in the protest in front of the Government Headquarters and spoke on stage to support the arrested student leaders. She was one of the first artists from the entertainment industry to speak out. After the beginning of the Umbrella Movement, she helped liaise with other artists and songwriters and produced the song "Upholding the Umbrella," which would become one of the songs frequently played and sung in rallies during the movement. Ho also co-convened, with a group of people from the entertainment and cultural industries, the "Hong Kong Shield," an informal action group aiming at monitoring police's use of force and violence surrounding the occupied areas in general. Ho stayed in Admiralty until the end of the movement and was one of the participants arrested on December 11 in the police eviction.

PARTICIPANT B: Allan Au is a famous veteran television journalist who had worked for TVB for 20 years. He left the news organization to pursue a PhD in 2010, researching journalistic professionalism and media self-censorship. But Au remained prominent in the public arena after shedding his identity as a professional journalist. He guest-hosted several television programs and Radio Television Hong Kong's main early evening public affairs radio phone-in talk show on weekdays. More important for his "post–TV journalist career," Au became an influential public affairs blogger in the city. After the Umbrella Movement began, Au could be seen in the occupied areas almost every day. He published blog articles about the movement almost daily. His articles were widely shared by movement supporters and participants via social media. After the Umbrella Movement, Au's relevant articles were grouped together and published as a book titled *Umbrella Together*.

PARTICIPANT C: Sampson Wong is, to quote his self-description, "an artist, independent curator, academic and urbanist from Hong Kong."[2] He received a PhD in Urban Studies and Geography from the University of Manchester and was a cofounder of the Hong Kong Urban Laboratory, which was active in promoting urban studies, participatory art projects, and related exhibitions and conferences. During the Umbrella Movement, Wong co-initiated the project "Stand by You: Add Oil Machine for OCLP (Occupy Central with Love and Peace)." Add Oil was conceived as a mobile media-based art installation. It invited people from all over the world to send supportive messages to the movement and then projected the messages onto the sides of high-rise buildings in Admiralty. Add Oil later won the FFF Award for the contribution of arts to the realization of human rights conferred by Switzerland's Freedom Flowers Foundation in February 2015. Toward the end of the Umbrella Movement, Wong convened the Umbrella Movement Visual Archives & Research Collective, aiming at keeping a comprehensive record and archive of the public arts within the occupied areas.

We begin this chapter with these three participants to highlight several interrelated points about the Umbrella Movement (and for this purpose, the choice of Ho, Au, and Wong is arbitrary; other figures could have been evoked to highlight the same points). First, besides the main organizers (HKFS, Scholarism, and the Trio), the movement had a range of individuals who exerted significant influences on the mass of participants. These individuals' influences were not only exercised by the songs, writings, and art works they produced; in the online arena, many of them shaped the flow of materials among movement supporters, because what they shared would be read, "liked," and further shared. They are similar to what Tufekci (2013) has called "network microcelebrities" in contemporary social movements, even though they cannot take their "online followership" for granted. There is no guarantee that all movement participants would always "like" what they produce. But they do constitute an important aspect of the structuration of contemporary networked social movements.

Analyzing the role played by such influential individuals is beyond the scope of this book. Second, and more directly pertinent to this chapter's analysis, the three cases are illustrative of the possibilities of personalized and small group–based actions within the Umbrella Movement. When taken individually, any one of these actions cannot be said to have been crucial to the character and perpetuation of the movement as a whole. But these actions can still be regarded as central to the movement in the sense that the Umbrella Movement can be considered to have been made up of all of these personalized and small group–based actions, in addition to the actions of the main organizers and other more well-established groups.

Certainly, few individuals' actions could attain the prominence and influence of Denise Ho, Allan Au, or Sampson Wong. The influence of these individuals was largely based on the amount of social, cultural, and symbolic capital they held: talent, knowledge, experiences, social connections both within the movement and in the society, established fame, formal titles, etc. But there were also cases of highly influential acts or creative products by individuals from a relatively ordinary background, such as the hanging of the huge "I Want Genuine Popular Election" banner on the hillside under the Lion Rock, or the production of a parodic music video "Shopping Everyday" by Mocking Jer,[3] a group formed by several graduates of the Hong Kong Academy for Performing Arts. While the Umbrella Movement, similar to other contentious collective actions, produced opportunities for more or less standardized actions for the participants, such as attending the evening rallies held in the Admiralty occupied area, it also offered the space for citizens to experiment with their own ways of participation. Occasionally, the creative acts by some individual participants could capture the attention and imagination of numerous others. These personalized or small group–based actions, to borrow Johnston's (2014, p. 23) articulation, "are the multitudinous building blocks of a movement's structure and its ideations. . . . It is where movement culture is created and confirmed."

This brings us to the concept of connective action. While collective action connotes the image of a large group of co-present individuals engaging in the same act, connective action generates the picture of numerous personalized and small group–based actions that are nonetheless connected with each other to constitute a single movement. In contemporary large-scale movements extending over space and time, collective and connective actions are intertwined. Moreover, part of the tasks crucial for the organization and perpetuation of collective actions that were originally taken up by movement organizations can nowadays be coordinated by disparate groups and individuals. The Umbrella Movement is a case in point. The setup and defense of the road blockades that carved out and protected the occupied areas, for instance, was often done by self-coordinating citizens. While Occupy Central had its own team of marshals, the maintenance of order within the occupied areas and the handling of counter-protesters were often reliant on initiatives by individual participants. This was especially true in the unplanned occupation in Mong Kok.

As Bennett and Segerberg (2013) emphasized, digital media technologies are crucial to the emergence of connective actions. Of course, Denise Ho could have liaised with other artists and produced Upholding the Umbrella with or without digital media.[4] Allan Au could have visited the occupied area every day and published his writings as newspaper column articles, and Sampson Wong could have devised similar public art installations even if only "low technologies" were available. But Upholding the Umbrella would not have had its reach without YouTube, Au's influence as a writer was grounded in the blogosphere, and digital media were central to the global character of the Add Oil Machine. Digital media were not a necessary condition for personalized and small group–based actions, but it was a condition for their proliferation, influence, and interconnectedness. Digital media were probably even more important when the coordination of actions that are more central to or constitutive of the occupation is concerned, such as setting up road blockades and confronting the counter-protesters, as mentioned above.

This chapter addresses the implications of digital media activities and connective actions on the Umbrella Movement. We put forward and attempt to verify three main contentions. First, digital media activities and connective actions empowered the movement. Theoretically, the logic of connective action allowed participants to join the movement in their own ways. It offered participants the space to express themselves within the movement. Digital media activities and connective actions were therefore likely to deepen the participants' psychological and actual involvement in the movement.

Second, digital media activities and connective actions contributed to the "decentralization" of the movement. The emergence of the Mong Kok and Causeway Bay occupation sites was dependent on the participants' ability to coordinate among themselves in real time. During the movement, participants shared among themselves not only supportive messages toward the movement and its central organizers; many of them also shared their critical views toward the main organizers, declared their "independence" from them, called for the disbanding of the team of marshals and the dismantling of the "big stage," etc. As participants became more involved through engagement in connective actions and digital media activities, they may have become less likely to see themselves merely as "followers" who acted according to what the "leaders" suggest.

Third, and despite the second point, digital media communications and activities do not create the "problem of decentralization" by themselves; that is, depending on its degree and its connections with other factors, decentralization is not necessarily a problem. In fact, with or without digital media, a movement can have its own bases of internal divisions and dissension. The Umbrella Movement involved the participation of groups holding a variety of ideologies and views regarding proper movement strategies. The different groups then tended to congregate at different occupied areas. What digital media communications may do is to become tied to and in the process reinforce such internal divisions.

The following pages will present evidence for the three contentions. We will first draw upon the protest onsite survey to present a picture of the frequencies of the movement participants' engagement in a range of digital media–based activities. We will then examine the relationships among digital media activities, perceived importance of digital media, degree of involvement in the movement, willingness to retreat, and willingness to consider the views of the main organizers at the individual level. The chapter then turns to an analysis of the contents of and interconnections among participant-initiated Facebook pages related to the movement. The Facebook page analysis will further illustrate the range of social media activities generated from the bottom up within the movement, as well as how these social media activities relate to the three central organizing groups. The last analysis section examines the interconnections among occupation areas, ideological beliefs, group affiliations, and digital media communications.

Participants' Digital Media Activities and Their Implications

PREVALENCE OF DIFFERENT TYPES OF DIGITAL MEDIA ACTIVITIES

Chapter 4 has shown that, in early October, many movement participants perceived WhatsApp, Facebook, and various conventional mass media as important channels of information about the Umbrella Movement. Table 5.1 presents the findings from an extended set of questions included in the November onsite survey. Similar to the findings from October, Facebook was perceived as by far the most important information source by the participants. WhatsApp also obtained a relatively high mean score among the channels and platforms, despite a significant decline in its perceived importance from October to November.

Among the online information sources that movement participants could turn to were online forums and online alternative media sites. We added related questions in November. As Table 5.1 shows, online forums were not rated particularly highly as information sources by the participants, though *Golden Forum*, a prominent online forum among young people in the city, was rated quite positively by participants in Mong Kok.

In contrast, the movement participants perceived the online alternative media sites as very important sources of movement information. *Inmedia*, which was established in 2005 and was closely related to a range of protest movements about heritage protection, rural development, and urban redevelopment in the previous decade, was rated as the second most important source of information by participants in both occupied areas. *Passion Times*, an online media site connected with the political group Civic Passion, was also highly rated. Interestingly, even the residual category "other online alternative media sites" was regarded as very important by the participants. It suggests that a range of online alternative media sites had played an important role in information and message dissemination throughout the movement. The significance of the online alternative media sites should also be understood in relation to the importance of Facebook, since what movement supporters and participants shared via Facebook were often articles and materials from the online alternative media.

While perceived importance of most of the digital media platforms had remained generally stable between October and November, perceived importance of television had conspicuously declined from October to November. While TV live

Table 5.1 **Participants' perceptions of importance of various media platforms**

Perceived importance of:	October Admiralty	November Admiralty	November Mong Kok
Mobile chat applications			
WhatsApp[a]	4.15	3.85	3.74
Firechat	2.41	2.27	2.46
Other mobile chat apps	2.66	2.76	2.86
Social media sites			
Facebook	4.63	4.54	4.40
Twitter	2.20	2.27	2.31
Other social media sites	2.72	2.70	2.70
Online forums			
Golden Forum[b]		2.92	3.29
Other public forums		2.57	2.74
Online alternative media sites			
InMedia		4.00	3.84
Passion Times		3.64	3.78
Other alternative media sites		3.69	3.76
Mainstream media platforms			
TV live reporting[a/b]	4.02	3.68	3.39
TV news[a/b]	3.87	3.55	3.25
Newspapers[b]	3.95	3.99	3.52
Radio[b]	3.33	3.34	2.96

Notes: Entries are mean scores on a five-point Likert scale. When a variable is marked with superscript "a," the mean scores derived from the Admiralty surveys in the two months differ from each other significantly at $p < .05$ in an independent samples t-test. When a variable is marked with "b," the mean scores derived from the two occupied areas in November differ from each other significantly at $p < .05$ in an independent samples t-test. $N = 969$ in the October Admiralty survey, 273 in the November Admiralty survey, and 296 in the November Mong Kok survey.

reporting had a mean score of 4.02 in the October Admiralty survey, its mean score declined to 3.68 in the November Admiralty survey. The mean score for TV news reports similarly declined, from 3.87 to 3.55. A plausible explanation is that the televised images of tear gas had heightened people's perceptions of the importance of television in early October. Also, during the first week of the movement, there were huge anxieties about how the Chinese and Hong Kong government would respond, including the possibility of military suppression. Live broadcasting and 24-hour news channels played extremely important roles in providing live updates. After the first two weeks, the movement "settled down" into a prolonged occupation. The government largely refrained from drastic actions. The need for live updates went down, and so did the perceived importance of television.

Nonetheless, television was still regarded by many as an important source of information. Moreover, not all mainstream media had their perceived importance showing a decline. The perceived importance of newspapers remained virtually exactly the same in the two surveys. It shows that the relatively detailed coverage and in-depth commentaries provided by newspapers had remained important to many participants.

Further, Table 5.1 shows that the Mong Kok participants rated the various mainstream media platforms significantly less positively than the Admiralty respondents did. In fact, our onsite survey finds that the Mong Kok participants were more likely to be supporters of radical groups, more likely to have engaged in confrontational actions, and held more positive views toward the idea of self-mobilization. We will return to the Admiralty–Mong Kok distinction toward the end of this chapter. Here, suffice it to say that the Mong Kok participants could be described as relatively distant from various "centers": both the "center" of the mainstream society and the "center" of the movement itself.

Throughout the study, we did not attempt to ask the participants about the amount of time they spent on various media platforms and channels because time spent would be very difficult to assess and could be misleading for some of the digital media platforms. For example, time spent on WhatsApp may not make very good sense when what a person actually does is to read and respond to WhatsApp messages intermittently throughout the day. Hence we developed a set of questions about perceived importance and asked a series of questions about specific types of digital communication and participation activities.

Table 5.2 summarizes the findings. In the October survey, which was only a week after the movement began, we included seven items in the questionnaire, and the answering scale was a simple yes-no dichotomy. Notably, a large number of rumors had greeted the beginning of the Umbrella Movement. In the evening of September 28, for instance, many Hong Kong citizens would have seen an image of a military vehicle crossing one of the major tunnels in the city. In the first week of the movement, there was also a rumor about an upcoming police and military crackdown and chaotic scenes in the occupation sites. There were faked stories about how traffic jams caused by the occupation had led to tragic consequences for other citizens. As Table 5.2 shows, 98% of the respondents in the October survey had encountered rumors about the movement on the Internet. The percentage of participants who encountered rumors is also around 95% in both occupied areas in November, and

Table 5.2 **Participants' engagement in movement-related online communications and activities**

	October Admiralty	November Admiralty	November Mong Kok
Online communication and activities:			
Exposed to rumor about the Movement	(97.5)	55.4 (95.5)	54.6 (94.5)
Try to refute rumor about the Movement	(69.9)	28.4 (82.3)	34.9 (79.5)
Exposed to anti-occupation views from acquaintances[a]	(86.2)	41.5 (93.7)	42.3 (85.3)
Exposed to anti-occupation views from strangers	(80.5)	39.1 (84.9)	42.3 (87.0)
Respond to anti-occupation views of acquaintances	(60.6)	27.3 (79.3)	31.7 (75.8)
Respond to anti-occupation views of strangers [a]	(24.5)	8.1 (44.8)	19.7 (59.2)
Unfriend people with different views	(17.1)	4.0 (25.4)	7.8 (32.8)
Change one's profile picture to show support		59.0 (71.6)	53.4 (69.5)
Show pictures and videos taken in the occupied areas [a]		43.8 (83.8)	38.2 (72.7)
Show pictures made by oneself (including "re-creation")		9.6 (25.8)	12.6 (28.0)
Publish commentaries about the movement		16.6 (52.4)	18.8 (57.0)
Publish brief personal reflections about the movement		30.6 (82.3)	31.6 (79.6)
Forward news and commentaries from mass media		46.5 (84.5)	45.6 (84.0)
Forward online commentaries about the movement		40.8 (81.2)	39.8 (79.3)
Forward photos, pictures, and videos made by friends		31.0 (72.7)	29.9 (70.7)

(continued)

Table 5.2 **(Continued)**

	October Admiralty	*November Admiralty*	*November Mong Kok*
Forward articles written by friends about the movement		24.0 (64.9)	27.3 (64.2)
Explain to foreign friends about the movement and the situation of HK		17.3 (61.3)	17.1 (53.8)
Explain to mainland friends about the movement and the situation of HK		12.2 (39.3)	10.2 (42.0)
Forward information about the movement via mobile phones		38.1 (82.2)	35.6 (80.1)
Discuss the movement with friends via mobile phones		43.8 (85.3)	33.9 (81.5)
Set up mobile chat groups to discuss the movement		19.9 (48.2)	18.8 (44.5)

Notes: The bracketed numbers in the first column are percentages who answered yes in the October survey. Entries in the second and third columns are percentages answering "yes and frequently" in the November survey, while the bracketed numbers refer to the total percentages of people who answered "yes" (i.e., "yes and frequently" plus "yes but not frequently"). The differences between the Admiralty surveys in October and November were not tested for statistical significance. When a variable is marked with superscript "a," the percentage distributions in the two occupied areas differ from each other at $p < .05$ in a Chi-square test. $N = 969$ in the October Admiralty survey, 273 in the November Admiralty survey, and 296 in the November Mong Kok survey.

more than half reported encountering rumors frequently. In the later survey, a three-point scale was adopted so that respondents would report whether they engaged in the activity frequently or not. About 55% in both areas reported encountering rumors frequently.

Nevertheless, the scenario also triggered the movement supporters' collective efforts to dispel rumors. Facebook pages such as "Occupy Central Myth Killer"[5] and "Myth Terminator"[6] were established to collect rumor-dispelling information. Former journalists wrote articles about how to differentiate between rumors and facts. With some participants leading the way, others could help dispel rumors simply by forwarding the clarifying information and/or the rumor deconstruction do-it-yourself articles. In the October survey, 70% of the participants reported that they had tried to refute rumors about the movement. In November, about 80% in both occupied areas had tried to refute rumors, with about 30% doing it frequently.

Right from the beginning of the movement, digital media also became a platform for fervent and often unpleasant debates among friends and acquaintances about the merits and demerits of the movement. In the October survey, 86% of the respondents had encountered online anti-occupation views sent by people they knew, while 81% had encountered such views from strangers. Not everyone felt comfortable to engage in debates, but there were still 61% of the respondents in October who had responded to anti-occupation views from people they knew, while about one in four had responded to anti-occupation views from strangers.

Into November, about 90% of the respondents had encountered anti-occupation views from acquaintances, and more than 40% even encountered such opinions frequently. The percentages of respondents exposed to anti-occupation views from strangers are similar. Nearly 70% of the respondents had tried to respond to anti-occupation views from acquaintances. About 30% did that frequently. Meanwhile, about half the respondents had responded to anti-occupation views from strangers, with the Mong Kok participants being significantly more active in doing so.

The widespread occurrence of heated debates among friends led to talks about "unfriending" people via social media (cf. Zhu, Skoric, & Shen, 2017). Yet the proportion of participants who had actually unfriended people was not large. In the October survey, only 17.1% of the respondents reported having done so. The percentages in November were 25% and 33% among the Admiralty and Mong Kok participants, respectively. Only about 5% said they had unfriended people "frequently."

No matter whether people debated with others, social media are first and foremost spaces for expression. On Facebook, people can signal their attitude by changing their profile pictures, first to a "student photo"—usually a photo of themselves in primary or secondary school uniforms—during the week of the class boycott organized by the HKFS in order to support the students, then to a yellow ribbon or a yellow umbrella after the beginning of the Umbrella Movement, and then to a wider range of symbols such as the Lion Rock with the "I Want Genuine Popular Election" banner. (Movement opponents could also signal their attitude through changing their profile pictures into a blue ribbon.) The relevant survey item existed only in the November survey. About 70% of the respondents had changed one's profile picture to show support for the movement.

Moreover, people could publish their thoughts, feelings, observations, and comments in various ways, ranging from a simple status update or a single photograph taken in the occupied site to a lengthy commentary piece or a carefully edited video. As Table 5.2 shows, most respondents had engaged in these expressive activities. About 75% of the respondents had shown pictures or videos taken in the occupied areas through digital media. Nearly 40% had done that frequently. About 80% published brief personal reflections about the movement, and around 30% had done that frequently. The percentages of people engaging in more elaborate forms of expression are understandably smaller, but still more than half of the respondents had published commentaries about the movement online. About 25% of the respondents had shown self-made pictures or graphics online.

While many scholars have commented on the rise of the "prosumer" or "produser" (Bruns, 2008), some scholars have noted that most people would not actually engage in original content production (van Dijck, 2009). What many people would do is to forward messages produced by others, thus playing a role in distributing and recommending materials for their friends (Messing & Westwood, 2014). Many of the materials forwarded by people online actually came from conventional mass media. The findings from our November survey are consistent with this pattern. More than 80% of the respondents in both occupied areas had forwarded news and commentaries from the mass media, and 45% had done so frequently. Although Table 5.1 has shown that the Mong Kok occupiers perceived the mainstream media as less important, they were equally likely to have shared materials from the mainstream media.

About 80% of the respondents also forwarded online commentaries about the movement, many of which probably came from online alternative media sites. About 70% had forwarded photos, pictures, and videos made by friends. About 60% had forwarded articles written by friends about the movement.

The Umbrella Movement had attracted much attention of the international media. But within each individual foreign country, the amount of relevant information could still be relatively limited. According to Sparks (2015), even in the United Kingdom, the former colonizer of Hong Kong, reports about the movement in the much more widely circulated tabloid press were cursory. Among the elite press, only the *Financial Times* and the *Guardian* provided systematic coverage and analysis of the issues involved. Meanwhile, information about the Umbrella Movement was largely blocked in China. The official media could not report on the movement freely. Online communication related to the movement was also censored, even though the more technically sophisticated, internationally connected, and motivated Internet users were able to obtain relevant information from the outside world by "crossing the firewall" (Yang & Liu, 2014). In this context, what movement participants could do is to help explain to people outside the city the background, aims, and development of the movement. More than half of the respondents in both occupied areas had explained the movement and the situation in Hong Kong to friends in foreign countries. About 40% had done the same for friends in mainland China.

Lastly, the survey included three questions referring to the use of mobile phones to communicate about the movement. More than 80% of the respondents in both occupied areas had forwarded information about the movement via mobile phones, and more than one-third had done so frequently. The percentages of respondents having discussed the movement with friends via mobile phones were largely the same. More than 40% of the respondents had set up mobile chat groups for discussing the movement. Generally speaking, consistent with the finding about the perceived importance of WhatsApp as a source of movement information, movement participants were active in communicating about the movement via mobile phones.

The respondents in the two areas did not differ substantially in the degree of digital media activities. Significant differences exist in only three of the 21 items, and even those statistically significant differences are not large in size.

DIGITAL MEDIA ACTIVITIES AND MOVEMENT INVOLVEMENT

In a large-scale movement that extends over time and space, participation can take up various meanings. Some participants might have spent huge amounts of time every day in the occupied areas, whereas others might have visited the occupied sites only once in a while. People could vary in how actively they had participated in a wide range of activities within the occupied areas, as well as whether they had tried to persuade others to join the movement. In short, there are variations in the mode of participation among the participants. The onsite survey included questions related to five dimensions of the participants' mode of participation: time spent in the occupied areas, spatial location and coverage, companionship, participation leadership, and specific actions undertaken (see the Appendix for descriptive statistics regarding these dimensions). Three of these dimensions are related to the participants' degree of involvement in the movement, defined as actual involvement in the act of occupation that is central to the campaign. Participants who spent more time in the occupied areas, those who tried to mobilize others, and those who had participated in a wider range of activities could be regarded as more deeply involved.

We can therefore examine the idea that digital media activities empowered the movement through analyzing whether participants more involved in the movement were also more actively engaging in digital media activities. It is impossible for us to disentangle the causal direction here; in other words, whether digital media activities led to deeper involvement or the other way round. The most plausible scenario is that the two reinforced each other as the participants constructed the hybrid space of autonomy (Castells, 2012) for themselves. But in any case, an overall positive association between involvement and digital media activities could be suggestive of the role digital media played in strengthening the movement.

Participation leadership is represented by a single question of whether people had tried to persuade others to join the movement. For time spent in the occupied areas, the survey contains three relevant questions: number of days visiting the occupied areas, average amount of time spent per visit, and whether one had stayed in the occupied areas overnight. An index was created by averaging the respondents' standardized scores on the three variables.[7]

The survey contains nine relevant items about actions undertaken. The nine items were subjected to an exploratory factor analysis. A clean two-factor structure emerged, suggesting that there is an empirical basis to differentiate the nine items into two sets. The factor structure makes conceptual sense. "Discussing movement direction and strategies," "delivering materials or maintaining order," "setting up

blockades," "handling the anti-occupation protesters," and "protecting the occupation areas when police took actions" belong to one factor. This factor can be labeled
"frontline activism," because most items refer to activities occurring in the "frontline" that required real-time coordination. "Attending civic lectures or seminars,"
"donating materials to the movement or participants," "donating money to the
movement," and "doing something outside the occupied areas to support the movement" form another factor. This can be labeled "support provision," since most of
the items refer to the provision of moral or material support. Respondents' scores
on the two variables were the sum of their scores on the items (yes = 1; no = 0)
belonging to the indices.[8]

Similarly, an exploratory factor analysis was conducted on the 21 digital media
activities items in Table 5.2. A relatively clean four-factor structure emerged. The
first factor can be labeled "online expressions." Eight items are relatively heavily
loaded on this factor[9]: "changing one's profile picture to express support for the
movement," "publishing pictures or videos taken on the site," "publishing commentaries on aspects of the movement," "publishing brief personal reflections about the
movement," "forwarding news and commentaries from the mass media," "forwarding online commentaries about the movement," "forwarding photos, videos, or re-
created pictures produced by friends," and "forwarding articles on the movement
written by friends."

The second factor consists of the first six items in Table 5.2, that is, exposing and
responding to rumors and anti-occupation opinions shared by friends or strangers.[10]
The factor is labeled "online debates" because the items involve people's exposure
and responses to messages against the movement. The third factor is composed of
"publishing pictures or graphics produced by oneself," "explaining to foreign friends
about the movement and the situation in Hong Kong," "explaining to friends in the
mainland about the movement and the situation in Hong Kong," and "unfriending
people who have views different from oneself." The two items about explaining the
movement to people outside Hong Kong have the highest loadings. Therefore, the
factor is called "online explanatory activities." The last factor consists of the three
items about usage of mobile phones; hence it is labeled "mobile communication."

Based on the factor analysis, four indices about digital media activities were created by averaging the items belonging to each of the factors.[11] Moreover, indices
for perceived importance of digital media and perceived importance of mass media
were created based on the items in Table 5.1. They were simply the average of the
digital media items and the average of the mass media items, respectively.[12]

Multiple regression was conducted to examine the relationship between digital
media activities and the variables representing involvement in the movement. The
independent variables include the four basic demographics and the area where the
participants were interviewed, plus the digital media activities indices and perceived
importance of media platforms indices. When predicting participation leadership,
frontline activism, and support provision, time spent in the occupied area was also

included as an independent variable because spending much time in the occupied area is likely to be a precondition of persuading others to participate and engaging in frontline activism. It should be noted that the four indices of digital media activities are rather substantially correlated to each other.[13] In the regression context, their high correlations may introduce multicollinearity that affects the performance of each factor. We therefore also present bivariate correlations for illustrative purposes.

Table 5.3 summarizes the findings. All four digital media activities indices and perceived importance of digital media are related positively and significantly to time spent in the occupied areas at the bivariate level, whereas perceived importance of mass media relates to time spent in the occupied areas significantly negatively. In the multivariate analysis, education is the only demographic factor relating significantly to time spent in the occupied areas, with respondents having higher levels of education spending less time. The negative relationship between perceived importance of mass media and time spent in occupied areas remain significant. However, among the digital media activities indices, only mobile communication retains a significant relationship. People who spent more time in the occupied areas were more likely to be active in mobile communication related to the movement.

The four digital media activities and perceived importance of digital media are also all significantly positively related to participation leadership at the bivariate level. Those who have called upon others to participate were also those more active in digital media communications and activities related to the movement. In the multivariate analysis, young people and those who have spent more time in the occupied areas were significantly more likely to have tried to persuade others to join the occupation. Two of the four digital media activities indices are significantly related to the dependent variable. Participants who engaged in mobile communication related to the movement to larger extents and those who engaged in online debates more frequently were more likely to have tried to persuade others to join.

The bottom of Table 5.3 shows the results regarding participation in frontline activism and support provision activities. Again, all four digital media activities and perceived importance of digital media are significantly related to both frontline activism and support provision activities at the bivariate level. Interestingly, perceived importance of mass media also relates to participation in support provision activities positively at the bivariate level. In the regression analysis, women were less likely to have participated in frontline activism, and there is a very strong relationship between time spent in the occupied areas and engagement in frontline activism. But even after controlling for time spent, three digital media–related variables are still significantly positively connected with frontline activism. Respondents more active in frontline actions perceived digital media as more important and engaged in online explanatory activities and mobile communication to larger extents.

Nevertheless, mass media were not always unrelated or negatively related to involvement. The last column of Table 5.3 shows that perceived importance of the mass media was positively and significantly related to participation in support

Table 5.3 **Predicting involvement by digital media activities and perceived importance of media**

	DV: Time spent in area		DV: Participation leadership	
	Bivariate correlations	*Regression*	*Bivariate correlations*	*Regression*
Sex		−.08		.07
Age		−.04		−.20***
Education		−.15***		−.01
Income		−.07		−.01
Area (MK = 2)		.08		.03
Time spent				.10**
Online expressions	.21***	.05	.27***	.08
Online debates	.15***	−.00	.27***	.11*
Online explanatory activities	.16***	.07	.19***	.05
Mobile communications	.26***	.21***	.30***	.12*
Importance of new media	.08*	.01	.13**	.00
Importance of mass media	−.11**	−.11*	.01	.04
Adjusted R^2		0.112***		0.487***

	DV: Frontline activism		DV: Support provision	
	Bivariate correlations	*Regression*	*Bivariate correlations*	*Regression*
Sex		−.13***		−.03
Age		−.00		−.03
Education		.01		.04
Income		−.04		.01
Area (MK = 2)		.06		−.10*
Time spent		.56***		.22***
Online expressions	.26***	−.03	.27***	.07
Online debates	.23***	.02	.30***	.16***

(continued)

Table 5.3 **(Continued)**

	DV: Frontline activism		DV: Support provision	
	Bivariate correlations	Regression	Bivariate correlations	Regression
Mobile communications	.35***	.25***	.27***	.07
Importance of new media	.22***	.11**	.12**	−.04
Importance of mass media	−.08	−.03	.12**	.15***
Adjusted R^2		0.487***		0.178***

Notes: Entries in the first of each pair of columns are Pearson correlation coefficients, and entries in the second of each pair of columns are standardized regression coefficients. Missing values were replaced by mean scores of the variables in the multiple regression analysis. $N = 569$ for the regression analysis. *** $p < .001$; ** $p < .01$; * $p < .05$.

provision activities. Since support provision involved actions not only within but also outside the occupied areas, the finding suggests that the mass media have retained a role for participants to connect with the society at large. Meanwhile, two types of digital media activities obtain significant positive relationships with the dependent variable in the full model. People who engaged in online explanatory activities and online debates more frequently were more likely to have participated in support provision.

Notably, the different types of digital media activities seem to relate to the pro- testers' mode of participation somewhat differently. Mobile communication is related particularly significantly to time spent in the occupied areas and frontline activism. This is understandable. Frontline activism in the Umbrella Movement often relied on real-time coordination and sometimes involved improvisatory acts. Mobile communication was particularly suitable for the purpose of coor- dinating such real-time actions. In addition, it is possible that participants who spent huge amounts of time in the occupied areas were reliant on mobile com- munication to stay in touch with others and to gain immediate knowledge about ongoing happenings. This finding is consistent with Haciyakupoglu and Zhang's (2015) study of the Gezi protests in Turkey, which found that participants relied particularly on WhatsApp for circulating messages among friends when they were in the field.

Different from mobile communication, engagement in online debate was more strongly related to participation leadership and support provision. This pattern also makes conceptual sense. Online debate requires participants to engage discursively with disagreeing others. Participation leadership, similarly, requires participants to engage discursively with people who are not necessarily movement supporters. When one tries to mobilize others, one may need to try to convince others about the legitimacy of the movement, and people who often debate with movement opponents should be better prepared to do so. Similarly, one important item in the support provision index is support activities outside the occupied areas (and this is the item most strongly related to online debate when the four items belonging to the index were treated separately). Once the participants go outside the occupied areas, they may need to be prepared to engage discursively with people holding different views. Support provision thus also partly draws upon a willingness and ability to engage discursively with others.

The findings also suggest that not all types of digital media activities are equally powerfully tied to involvement in the movement. Online expression does not relate significantly to any of the four dependent variables in the regression analysis. Online expression, when compared to online debates and explanatory activities, requires the least mental efforts. This is not to say that online expression cannot involve significant mental efforts; it is only to say that simple expressive activities, such as a simple status update or sharing a commentary article, do not *require* much effort.

The above interpretations suggest the possibility for individual participants to selectively engage in different types of digital media activities in order to construct their own distinctive forms of participation in the movement. But for this chapter, the most important overall finding is that all kinds of digital media activities and perceived importance of digital media were related consistently to involvement at the bivariate level. The findings thus provide strong support for our first contention: there is a systematic linkage between digital media activities and involvement in the movement, which is a sign showing that digital media and the emergence of connective actions have empowered the movement.

WILLINGNESS TO RETREAT AND TAKE INTO ACCOUNT THE CENTRAL ORGANIZERS' VIEWS

After examining the relationship between digital media activities and involvement in the movement, we turn to examine the implications of the decentralization tendency of digital media activities and connective actions. Specifically, we use the respondents' opinions related to the question of retreat as an entry point to tackle the issue. Calls for the movement to consider retreating from the occupied areas were issued by not only the pro-establishment camp but also figures from the pro-democracy camp within two weeks after the beginning of the occupation. Most notably, the former Catholic Bishop Cardinal Joseph Zen, who was together with the Trio on September 28 when the movement began, publicly suggested on October 10 that the students should leave the occupied areas in order to retain the movement's energy. For those who favored a retreat, the movement should first take a step back and further negotiate with the government. There was also the concern that the disruption of everyday life caused by continual occupation would alienate the general public. But the call for retreat was rejected by HKFS and Scholarism.

Many participants were highly critical toward any call for what they regarded as premature retreat before any concrete outcomes were achieved.

On October 21, five representatives of the HKFS engaged in a televised public meeting with Chief Secretary of the Hong Kong government Carrie Lam and four other top-level government officials. In the meeting, Carrie Lam promised that the government could: (1) submit a "public sentiment report" to the Hong Kong and Macau Affairs Office (HKMO) of the State Council of China; (2) try to maximize the democratic character of the nomination committee within the constraints set by the NPC; and (3) establish a multi-party platform to discuss further reform of the electoral system. But these "concessions" fell far short of the movement's demands.[14]

Nevertheless, the government did at least claim to have made some concessions. In the morning after the televised meeting, Chief Executive C. Y. Leung also mentioned in an interview with foreign media the possibility of changing the corporate votes to individual votes in the formation of the nomination committee.[15] The movement organizers proposed to conduct a referendum within the occupied areas to gauge the participants' views about the government's newest promises. But many participants criticized the idea of referendum, partly because of technical difficulties such as how to ensure that all votes would be cast by real movement supporters, and partly because of the suspicion that the organizers were trying to use the vote as a prelude to retreat. The organizers ultimately called off the referendum.

We have no intention to discuss the desirability of various movement strategies and whether the protesters should really have retreated at some points. The above only serves to offer the background for understanding the debate within the movement about retreating. The following analysis will focus on the participants' opinions on questions related to the issue.

The top half of Table 5.4 shows the onsite survey findings regarding the participants' willingness to retreat. Relevant questions were asked only in November, because the question of retreat was not yet raised when the October survey was conducted. The findings show that very few participants were willing to retreat given only what the government promised in the televised meeting with HKFS. Interestingly, the percentage of Mong Kok respondents who replied "definitely will retreat" or "likely to retreat" was even slightly higher than the percentage of Admiralty respondents replying in the same way. Yet it should be noted that the percentage of Mong Kok respondents stating that they "definitely will not retreat" or "[were] unlikely to retreat" was also higher (78% vs. 74%). On the whole, the Mong Kok occupiers were not more or less likely to retreat if no further concessions were made; they were just more likely than the Admiralty respondents to have made up their mind on the matter.

However, many more participants were willing to retreat from the occupied areas if the government could make some more substantive concessions. If the government agreed to submit a supplementary report to the NPC, 22% of the Admiralty

Table 5.4 **Willingness to consider others' opinions on movement strategies**

	Admiralty	Mong Kok
Willingness to retreat if		
There is no more new responses from the government[a]	5.4	8.2
The government agrees to submit a supplementary report to the NPC[a]	22.0	14.5
The government promises to eliminate functional constituencies in 10 years[a]	36.6	31.3
The government promises to eliminate corporate votes in the nomination committee[a]	33.8	29.6
Willingness to consider the opinions of the following groups/people on questions of the direction and strategies of the movement		
HKFS[a]	75.7	57.1
Scholarism[a]	69.3	54.8
The Occupy Central Trio[a]	42.5	25.1
The party or organization one supports	37.2	31.2
University presidents	29.9	21.0
Friends	41.8	44.5
Family members	28.7	25.2
Public opinion as reflected in opinion polls	48.7	40.2
Newspaper editorials[a]	35.5	26.6
Online commentaries by movement supporters[a]	51.0	48.9
Online commentaries by movement opponents[a]	17.8	16.1

Notes: Entries are percentages answering 4 or 5 on the respective five-point Likert scales. When a variable is marked with superscript "a," the percentage distributions (on the original five-point Likert scales) obtained from the two occupied areas differ from each other significantly at $p < .05$ in a Chi-square test. $N = 273$ in the Admiralty survey and 296 in the Mong Kok survey.

respondents were likely to retreat. The percentage rises further to 37% and 34%, respectively, if the government promised to eliminate functional constituencies of the legislature within 10 years and if the government promised to eliminate corporate votes in the selection committee.

Of course, substantial proportions of the participants claimed that they would be unmoved even with such concessions. Moreover, the Mong Kok occupiers were significantly less willing to retreat. Interestingly, if we analyze the four items by mean scores, we can see that the mean scores of the first item obtained from the two occupied areas did not differ from each other significantly. But the mean scores from the two occupied areas on the remaining three items all differ from each other significantly, with the Mong Kok participants less likely to retreat even if further concessions were made. The findings suggest that the Admiralty participants were relatively more ready than the Mong Kok participants to compromise and take the provisional gains if the latter were offered.

Besides the participants' willingness to retreat, another important issue to consider when the decentralization tendency of the movement is concerned is whether the movement participants were willing to follow the views of the central organizers on questions of movement strategies. The bottom of Table 5.4 shows the participants' degree of willingness to consider the views of various organizations, groups, and individuals on the question of movement directions and strategies. It should be noted that the question adopts the word *ting-ceoi*, which can be translated as "take into account." The phrase does not entail a deferral of one's judgment to others.

The word choice thus partly explains the high percentages on the items for the three central organizers. More than three-fourths of the Admiralty respondents were willing to take into account the views of HKFS on matters of movement direction and strategies, and nearly 70% were willing to take into account the views of Scholarism. Only 43% of the Admiralty respondents were willing to take into account the views of the Trio, but the percentage is still higher than the political party or organization that one supports (37%).

Besides the main organizers, the Admiralty respondents were also relatively more willing to take into account the views of friends (42%), online commentaries by movement supporters (51%), and public opinion as reflected in opinion polls (49%). The Admiralty respondents were least willing to take into account the views of online commentaries by movement opponents (18%), family members (29%), and university presidents (30%). This is understandable because these three latter categories did not form part of the movement.

The Mong Kok participants were less willing to take into account the views of others on the question of movement direction and strategies. The percentages in the second column in the bottom half of Table 5.4 are consistently lower than those in the first column, with "friends" as the only exception. More important, the Mong Kok participants were significantly less willing to take into account the views of the main organizers, even though the percentages still stood at 57% and 55% for HKFS and Scholarism, respectively. Slightly more than 30% of the Mong Kok respondents were willing to take into account the views of the political party or organization one supports, whereas only 25% of the Mong Kok participants were willing to take into account the views of the Trio.

The Mong Kok respondents were not significantly less willing than the Admiralty respondents to take into account the views of university presidents, family members, and poll results. Consistent with Table 5.1's finding that the Mong Kok participants perceived the mass media as less important, they were significantly less willing to take into account the views of newspaper editorials. Interestingly, the Mong Kok participants were also less willing to take into account the views expressed in online commentaries.

We can now examine how digital media activities and perceived importance of digital media relate to willingness to retreat and willingness to take into account the views of organizers and other agents. Regression analyses were conducted for that purpose. For simplicity, willingness to retreat was represented by a single index, which was the average of the four items in Table 5.4. Willingness to take into account the views of the main organizers was the average of the items for HKFS, Scholarism, and the Trio, whereas willingness to take into account the views of others was the average of all other items.[16]

Besides basic demographics, the dichotomous "occupied area" variable, digital media activities, and perceived importance of media, also included as independent variables in the model are time spent in the occupied areas, perceived likelihood of positive and negative outcomes, and perceived advantages and disadvantages of self-mobilization. Time spent in the occupied areas, as an indicator of involvement, can be expected to relate negatively to willingness to retreat, while it would be interesting to see if the more involved participants were more or less willing to take into account the views of the main organizers.

Perceived outcome likelihoods and perceptions of self-mobilization are included as plausible predictors of the dependent variables. Scholars have found perceptions of outcome likelihoods to influence whether protesters would persist or not (Corrigall-Brown, 2012; Einwohner, 2002). In the present case, participants who regarded positive outcomes as more likely can be expected to be less willing to retreat. Meanwhile, people with a more positive attitude toward the idea of self-mobilization might be less willing to take into account the views of the main organizers. Perceived positive outcome is the average of the respondents' answers to three questions, whereas perceived negative outcome is the average of the respondents' answers to another three items.[17] Perceived advantage of self-mobilization is the average of respondents' agreement with two statements, whereas perceived disadvantage of self-mobilization is likewise the average of respondents' agreement with another two statements (see Appendix A for the items).[18] We treat perceived positive and negative outcomes, as well as perceived advantages and disadvantages of self-mobilization, as separate variables because political psychologists have shown that people can be ambivalent toward political ideas, that is, they can hold positive and negative thoughts about a political object at the same time (Feldman & Zaller, 1992; Lavine, 2001; Lee & Chan, 2009b).[19]

Hence positive and negative thoughts or feelings can have independent effects on other variables.

Table 5.5 summarizes the results of the analysis. The Mong Kok participants were less willing to retreat when compared to the Admiralty participants even after all variables are controlled. As expected, participants who were more involved—those who spent more time in the occupied areas—and those who were more optimistic about the likelihood of positive outcomes were less willing to retreat. Participants who viewed self-mobilization more positively were less willing to retreat, whereas those who acknowledged the disadvantage of self-mobilization were more willing to retreat.

Table 5.5 **Predicting willingness to retreat and consider others' views on movement strategies**

	Willingness to retreat	Willing to take organizers' views	Willing to take others' views
Sex	.00	.09*	.06
Age	−.03	.22***	−.14**
Education	.03	.01	−.01
Income	.07	.01	.02
Area (Mong Kok = 2)	−.10*	−.12**	−.03
Time spent in the occupied areas	−.16***	−.11**	−.16***
Positive outcomes of movement	−.10*	.03	−.06
Negative outcomes of movement	−.04	−.03	.06
Advantage of self-mobilization	−.12**	−.05	−.05
Disadvantage of self-mobilization	.17***	.01	.08*
Online expressions	−.10	.07	.01
Online debates	.00	−.03	−.04
Online explanatory activities	.13**	.04	.12**
Mobile communication	−.05	−.02	.13*
Importance of new media	.06	.11*	.04
Importance of mass media	.08	.19***	.21***
Adjusted R^2	0.136***	0.152***	0.151***

Notes: Entries are standardized regression coefficients. Missing values were replaced by mean scores of the variables. $N = 569$. *** $p < .001$; ** $p < .01$; * $p < .05$.

In the full model, only online explanatory activities was related to willingness to retreat. Those who engaged in such activities more frequently were more willing to retreat. One possible reason is that people who explained the situation in Hong Kong to friends in foreign countries and mainland China might be prone to put the movement within a national or even global context. They might be more aware of the high probability that China was not going to bulge and the struggle for democracy requires long-term strategies and continual struggles, thus justifying retreat as a temporary move. In any case, the findings show that not all kinds of digital media activities would lead to lower levels of willingness to retreat.

The second column shows the predictors of participants' willingness to take into account the main organizers' views when considering movement direction and strategies. Older citizens, females, and participants in Admiralty were significantly more likely to do so. Participants who spent more time in the occupied areas were nonetheless less willing to listen to the organizers. This might be considered a result related to the logic of connective action. In conventional protests organized by movement organizations, the most involved participants are likely to be those most closely connected to the organizers. We may expect them to be more willing to consider the views of the organizers. But in the Umbrella Movement, degree of involvement was not tied to connections with the main organizing groups. As participation was to a certain extent personalized, the more involved a participant was, the more the participant might insist on his or her autonomy. Thus the participant could also become less willing to take into account the organizers' views on movement strategies.

None of the digital media activities variables was related to the dependent variable significantly. Yet both perceived importance of digital media and perceived importance of mass media were significantly related to willingness to take into account the organizers' views. This is probably partly because people who regarded various information sources as important tended to be people who were willing to listen to others. Putting it another way, people who are unwilling to listen to others may simply treat all kinds of information sources as less important. In fact, the last column of Table 5.5, which can be used for comparative purposes, shows that the two perceived importance of media variables are also positively related to willingness to take into account the views of others (though only perceived importance of mass media has a highly significant coefficient).

While young people were less willing to take into account the organizers' views on movement direction and strategies, they were more willing to take into account the views of others. Besides, people who have spent more time in the occupied areas were less willing to listen to not only the main organizers but also a full range of other groups and people. In addition, two digital media activities variables have positive relationships with the dependent variable. Participants who engaged in mobile communication and online explanatory activities were more willing to listen to the views of other groups and people. This is not difficult to understand, as both mobile communications and the act of explaining the situation to foreign and mainland friends heavily involve listening to one's own friends and acquaintances. These people are likely to take the views of acquaintances more seriously.

In sum, Table 5.5 shows that there was little direct connection between digital media activities and willingness to retreat or willingness to listen to the central organizers. The finding is reasonable, though, since movement participants supportive toward the central organizers also needed to rely on digital media to know about the views and actions of the organizers. But at the same time, the analysis also shows that the more deeply involved participants were less willing to retreat and less willing to listen to the central organizers.

The previous section has shown that digital media activities were related significantly to degree of involvement. To the extent that digital media activities had strengthened people's involvement, we could argue that digital media activities did have an indirect negative impact on participants' willingness to retreat and listen to the central organizers. This interpretation is consistent with the contention of the decentralizing tendency of digital media activities.

Emerging Social Media Activities

PARTICIPANT-INITIATED FACEBOOK PAGES SURROUNDING THE UMBRELLA MOVEMENT

Confirmed by the onsite survey data, Facebook and WhatsApp constituted the two most important social networking tools that supporters of the Umbrella Movement utilized to obtain information and communicate with others about the movement. While it is impossible for us to access the content and flows of communications via WhatsApp and the private Facebook accounts of citizens, many citizens and activists set up Facebook public pages throughout the occupation campaign, sometimes in association with specific projects and/or informal groups the movement participants had organized offline. These are public pages created in particular for and about the movement. The setting up of these pages is one of the most conspicuous indicators of the rise of dispersed, small-group based actions during the occupation campaign. An examination of these pages should provide us with additional insights into the characteristics of digital media activities and connective actions in the Umbrella Movement.

We did not have access to data-crawling systems at the time of the Umbrella Movement. We attempted to recover relevant public pages and materials from Facebook in December 2015. The time lag can create several issues. For instance, there are signs showing that a few Facebook pages have deleted many of their posts published during the occupation campaign, a point to which we will return below. The numbers of shares and likes for the pages and posts also did not precisely represent the numbers of shares and likes at the time of the movement. Hence the time lag needs to be kept in mind when interpreting the findings. But overall speaking, on the analytical issues to be addressed, we believe that the time lag does not create problems that would distort the substantive conclusions.

Methodologically, we also did not use computerized techniques to look for relevant pages in late 2015. This is partly because of the belief that the total number of such pages should not be bigger than what a "manual approach" can handle. More important, in order to judge whether a page was created in direct connection to the movement, we take into account the characteristics of the profile picture and cover photo of the page. Typical data-crawling techniques might not be more effective than a manual search when visuals have to be considered and the total number of pages is not huge. Specifically, a Facebook page created in direct connection to the Umbrella Movement is operationalized as one that:

1) has published or shared contents related to the Umbrella Movement, though not necessarily focusing only on the movement, and
2) fulfills one of the following two self-identification criteria: a) its name includes one of the several major labels referring to the movement, including *zim-ling* (occupy), *zim-zung* (occupy Central), *jyu-saan* or simply *saan* (umbrella), and *ze-daa* (a Cantonese-based Chinese phrase literally meaning using the umbrella to fight), or b) its cover photo or profile picture uses either one of the three core symbols of the Umbrella Movement (i.e., a yellow umbrella, a yellow ribbon, or the "I Want Genuine Popular Election" banner) or a picture clearly identifiable as one of the occupied sites (no matter whether it was taken at Admiralty, Causeway Bay, or Mong Kok).

The Facebook pages of the three major organizers of the movement were included in the data set, even though they did not meet the above criteria.

A research assistant searched for relevant Facebook pages by starting with a number of prominent pages established during the Umbrella Movement as well as the pages of the three main organizers. Additional pages were identified through the pages "liked" by these "starting pages." In other words, relevant Facebook pages were identified through moving along the linkages created by the "page likes." This procedure could have missed relevant Facebook pages that were not "liked" by anyone else. Put differently, the Facebook pages included have all achieved a very minimal degree of recognition by others belonging to the movement. It implies that the sample may underestimate how idiosyncratic and disconnected the individualized movement-related social media activities could have been.

It should also be noted that the pages derived from the search do not include the Facebook public pages of political parties, civic associations, online alternative media groups, influential individual public figures, and other entities that could have been highly instrumental in the communication of movement information during the occupation campaign. But they are not included because, given the underlying concern with the notion of connective action, our analytical interest in this part of the analysis is restricted to whether and how the pages created specifically in relation to the Umbrella Movement by ordinary participants were connected with each other and to the main organizers.

A total of 181 Facebook public pages, including the three pages of the three main organizers, were identified through the above procedure. For each page, we registered the number of likes the page itself got, the range of other pages it liked, timing of the first post (which is used as an indicator of the time of establishment of the page), and timing of the most recent post. Some of these 181 pages were created before the beginning of the Umbrella Movement. Examples include Christians in Support for Democratic Reform (created in November 2013), OCLP Toronto (created in October 2013), and 2014 July 1 Occupy Central Support Group (created in late June 2014). As their titles suggest, these pages were responses to the original Occupy Central campaign.

On the other side, some of the 181 pages were created after the end of the Umbrella Movement. Examples are Umbrella Relief Fund and Alliance of Umbrella Movement Arrestees, created in February and June 2015, respectively. These two pages (and the informal groups behind them) were set up to provide various kinds of support for participants in the aftermath of the movement.

Since we are primarily interested in social media communications and connective actions during the Umbrella Movement, the following analysis includes only those pages created between September 28 and December 15, 2014. We also include the pages of the three main organizers, though, because we are interested in whether and how they were connected to the pages created during the Umbrella Movement. The delimited data set includes 141 public pages, inclusive of the three main organizers. In other words, excluding the three main organizers, 138 of the 178 (77.5%) public pages in the larger data set were created during the Umbrella Movement.

The public prominence of the Facebook pages varies substantially. The page of HKFS was liked by more than 140,000 people by the time of data collection, whereas the corresponding figures for Scholarism and OCLP were more than 310,000 and more than 90,000, respectively. The figures for HKFS and Scholarism, of course, do not necessarily represent the amount of support they received as organizers of the Umbrella Movement. They merely reflect the general social media prominence of the two groups. Among the other 138 Facebook pages, the more prominent ones include 926 Ordinary Citizens at the Government Headquarters, which was liked by more than 130,000 people at the time of data collection, and LIVE: Verified Updates, which was liked by more than 100,000 people. In other words, the number of likes obtained by them was even higher than that for OCLP and comparable to that for HKFS. This hints at the point that the central movement organizers were not necessarily the most central in the social media communications surrounding the movement.

Admittedly, 926 Ordinary Citizens at the Government Headquarters and LIVE: Verified Updates, both created at the very beginning of the Umbrella

Movement and that mainly served as sites for "live information" from the protest sites, were exceptional in the amount of attention they attracted. Their prominence was probably because events evolved quickly and unpredictably at the very early stage of the movement, and people were craving for constant updates amid a very high degree of uncertainty and anxiety. In fact, another Facebook page titled Information from Mong Kok Occupy Site, which was created on September 29, also attracted more than 40,000 likes.

As the movement settled down and became a long-term occupation campaign, other pages created later during the movement received relatively less online public attention and approval. The number of likes obtained by the pages registered in the data set and the date of their first recoverable post, when turned into a variable ranging from September 28 = 1 to December 15 = 79, are significantly, though only mildly, negatively correlated ($r = -.17$, $p < .05$).[20] Nevertheless, several Facebook pages created after the first three weeks of the movement still obtained substantial amounts of social media attention and approval.

Table 5.6 provides a list of the Facebook pages (not including the three main organizers) that registered more than 10,000 likes. It includes the Hong Kong Shield mentioned at the beginning of this chapter, which was organized by numerous figures in the entertainment and cultural industries aiming at monitoring police violence. The list also includes Occupy Central Myth Killer, mentioned earlier in the analysis, which was devoted to dispelling movement-related rumors. Umbrella Movement Visual Archive was the project initiated and coordinated by Sampson Wong, whose background was briefly introduced at the beginning of this chapter. Mr & Ms HK People was devoted to produce and distribute cartoon-like graphics, "in the hope that people can use their own ways to explain to children what is happening in Hong Kong and the world" (from the "About" section of the page).

What Table 5.6 helps illustrate is that, as the movement continued, participants started working on projects with more sharply defined focuses. Occupation Night Shift was a Facebook page devoted to providing immediate updates of happenings within the occupied areas during nighttime. Civil Servants Demanding Genuine Election was a page for government workers to express their support for the movement. A typical photo uploaded onto the page would show the staff identity card of the uploader, with the name of the government department clearly shown and the name of the uploader concealed by a yellow ribbon or a message supportive toward the movement. Umbrella Parents was a group established to provide counseling for parents and students involved in the movement. The "About" section of the page suggests that the group would construct a network of social workers, lawyers, medical professionals, and teachers to provide informational and other kinds of support to affected people.[21] Occupy Supports Small Shops is one of a number of Facebook pages addressing the issue of the survival of small shops in Hong Kong, which is tied to the critique of corporate hegemony. Some of these pages encourage movement supporters to consume at small shops that explicitly support the Umbrella Movement.

Table 5.6 **Examples of relatively prominent Facebook pages about the Umbrella Movement**

Page names	No. of likes	1st post
1. 926 平民在政總現場 [926 Ordinary Citizens at the Government Headquarters]	139,426	October 4
2. LIVE: Verified Updates已證實消息發放專頁	107,708	September 28
3. Mr & Ms HK People	76,644	October 20
4. 旺角佔領現場資訊 [Information from Mong Kok Occupied Site]	41,937	September 29
5. Hong Kong Democracy Now	40,171	September 28
6. 遮打革命Umbrella Revolution	28,644	September 29
7. 公務員要真普選 [Civil Servants Demanding Genuine Election]	25,177	October 21
8. 文化界監察暴力行動組/Hong Kong Shield	22,489	October 10
9. OCMK 佔中謠言追追追/Occupy Central Myth Killer	18,405	September 30
10. 佔領撐小店 [Occupy Supports Small Shops]	18,019	October 1
11. 佔領夜更 [Occupation Night Shift]	15,600	September 30
12. 傘下爸媽 [Umbrella Parents]	12,833	November 6
13. 雨傘運動視覺庫存 Umbrella Movement Visual Archive	11,580	October 19
14. 旺角社區團結－旺角佔領直擊 [Community Solidarity in Mong Kok]	10,518	October 9

Notes: English names in square brackets are the authors' own translation. Some pages have "official" English names (those following a slash). Some pages have titles including both English and Chinese.

Through these pages and the projects they represent, citizens participated in extending the actions and enriching the meanings of the Umbrella Movement.

THE INTERCONNECTIONS AMONG THE FACEBOOK PUBLIC PAGES

Beside the general significance of the Facebook pages, one important question is how these Facebook pages are interconnected to each other, and how the main organizers of the Umbrella Movement are related to these pages. Here, we may consider the pages *as if* they constituted a network. We emphasized "as if" here because, in reality, they might not be well-connected with each other, and they might belong to other networks involving other kinds of pages. But we focus on the 138 pages here just because they were the participant-initiated pages that formed a core characteristic of a connective action campaign, and treating them as a network is simply the way to tackle questions regarding their interconnections.

More precisely, we can differentiate between two analytical questions. First, if the three main organizers' pages and the other 138 pages are taken together as constituting a network, are the three main organizers' pages located centrally in it? Second, if the 138 Facebook pages themselves are considered as forming a network, would the pages located centrally in it tend to be those connected with the main organizers? If the answer to the first question is affirmative, it would mean that the main organizers embedded themselves at the center of the network of emerging connective actions in the movement; if the answer to the first question is negative and yet the answer to the second question is affirmative, it would mean that the three main organizers, though not having embedded themselves into the network of emerging connective actions, had nonetheless retained their symbolic status as movement leaders so that those groups connected to them were more likely to gain centrality in the network of emerging connective actions.

Tackling the first question requires us to analyze the 141 Facebook pages together as a network. Methodologically, we can reconstruct the interconnections among the pages in two different ways. The first is to rely on page like, that is, whether one Facebook page has liked another and vice versa. The second is to rely on the extent of content sharing. Conceptually, page like signifies basic recognition and approval, but it does not entail actual interaction and/or flow of communication. The latter could be indicated by content sharing. Two matrices were therefore created. The matrix regarding page like could be created based on information derived from the Facebook page coding. For the matrix on content sharing, a research assistant downloaded all the recoverable posts published by the pages between September 28 and December 15, 2014, and then used a search function that would allow one to derive the relevant numbers of instances of content sharing.[22]

As noted, some of the Facebook pages may have deleted some of their posts during the Umbrella Movement. A few pages have ostensibly systematically deleted their posts due to the possibility that the posts might become evidence in potential court proceedings. Hence there could be errors in the counts of number of times of content sharing. But there are no signs that the systematic deletion of posts was a widespread phenomenon. In any case, if the results based on the two matrices are similar, the conclusions should be robust.

The matrices were analyzed through UCINET 6 for Windows to derive several key indicators of centrality of the Facebook pages in the online network: betweenness centrality scores, in-degree scores, and out-degree scores. In network analysis, "betweenness centrality" refers to the extent to which a page falls on the geodesic paths between other pairs of pages in the network. It is a common measure of centrality. An actor with a high score is viewed as being in a favored position that can influence the group by information transmission (Freeman, 2008; Hanneman & Riddle, 2005). "In-degree" and "out-degree" scores, meanwhile, refer to the extent to which a page is linked by others and the extent to which a page is linking to others, respectively. In social network analysis, in-degree is typically a measure of a node's importance—an actor with a high score is seen as being in a focal point of communication in the network (Hanneman & Riddle, 2005; McCulloh, Armstrong, & Johnson, 2013). Out-degree can be considered a measure of the degree to which a node has attempted to reach out to others. It is related to the possibility for the actor to acquire resources or information.

The first column of the top half of Table 5.7 shows that, when the network created by page likes is concerned, the top three pages in terms of normalized betweenness centrality are Umbrella Parents, Umbrella Revolution Archive, and Umbrella United. None of the three main organizers entered the column of top ten Facebook pages in terms of betweenness centrality. Among the three main organizers, HKFS had the highest betweenness centrality score (0.192), but it ranks only 30 among the 141 Facebook pages. Scholarism and OCLP even scored zero on betweenness centrality based on page likes.

One characteristic of betweenness centrality is that a high score would appear only when a node is both being linked to by many other nodes and actively linking to many other nodes. A page would score zero if either its in-degree or out-degree score is zero because when no one links themselves to a node or the node does not reach out to anyone else, movement between other nodes in the network would never need to go through the node concerned. The reason for Scholarism and OCLP to score zero on betweenness centrality is that they score zero on out-degree, that is, they did not "like" any other pages in the sample, which also means they did not actively reach out to the emerging Facebook pages. In contrast, some of the pages in the sample actively linked themselves to other pages. As shown in the second column of the top half of Table 5.7, Telling Stories through the Umbrella and Umbrella Revolution Art from Hong Kong had liked 28 other pages in the sample.

We can see some indication of the three main organizers' status only when paying attention to the third column, which shows the in-degree scores of the pages. Both HKFS's and Scholarism's Facebook pages were liked by 10 other pages in the sample, while OCLP's page was liked by seven others. All three of them made the top ten list, that is, they were among the most recognized and approved Facebook pages in the set of 141 pages. But even here, the main organizers did not substantially outscore some of the more prominent Facebook pages related to the Umbrella Movement. Umbrella Parents and Umbrella Movement Visual Archive also got an in-degree score of 10. Mr & Ms HK People was liked by nine other pages in the sample. As a result, OCLP ranked only eighth on the list.

Table 5.7 **Top ten Facebook pages in terms of centrality to online network**

	Based on page likes				
Betweenness centrality		*Out-degree*		*In-degree*	
1. Umbrella Parents	10.87	1. Umbrella Rev. Art from HK	28.0	**1. HKFS**	**10.0**
2. Umbrella Revolution Archive	4.39	1. Telling Stories through the Umbrella	28.0	**1. Scholarism**	**10.0**
3. Umbrella United	4.37	3. Umbrella Parents	23.0	1. Umbrella Move. Visual Archive	10.0
4. Telling Stories through the Umbrella	4.01	4. Umbrella Move. Tents Pop. Census	20.0	1. Umbrella Parents	10.0
5. Umbrella Move. Tents Pop. Census	3.88	5. Umbrella Gallery	15.0	5. Mr & Ms HK People	9.0
6. Small Shops Support Occupy	3.55	5. Creative Ze-daa	15.0	6. Umbrella Unity	8.0
7. Umbrella Unity	3.46	7. Umbrella United	14.0	6. Umbrella Neighborhood	8.0
8. Umbrella Rev. Art from HK	3.40	8. Umbrella Movement Archive	10.0	**8. OCLP**	**7.0**
9. Occupy Supports Small Shops	2.46	8. HK UR Political Art Movement	10.0	9. Lennon Wall Hong Kong	6.0^
10. Hong Kong Shield	1.83	10. Umbrella Creation Laboratory	8.0*	9. Umbrella Move. Art Preservation	6.0^

(*continued*)

Table 5.7 **(Continued)**

	Based on content sharing				
Betweenness centrality		*Out-degree*		*In-degree*	
1. 926 Ordinary Citizens at GH	1.55	1. Occupy Night Shift	81.0	**1. HKFS**	**121.0**
2. Causeway Bay Occupation Record	1.52	2. *Ze-daa* Move. Integrated Info.	67.0	2. 926 Ordinary Citizens at GH	83.0
3. Umbrella Creation Laboratory	1.35	3. Umbrella Revolution	54.0#	2. Hong Kong Democracy Now	83.0
4. Occupy Supports Small Shops	1.30	4. List of Occupy Suffering Shops	36.0	**4. Scholarism**	**70.0**
5. Hui Sir at 7 o'clock	1.11	5. Hui Sir at 7 o'clock	33.0	5. Occupy Supports Small Shops	35.0
6. Umbrella Rev. Art from Hong Kong	1.01	6. Shop Local for Umbrella Resistance	32.0	6. Info. from MK Occupy Site	25.0
7. Pad Printing in Support for Umbrella	0.95	7. Umbrella Revolution	27.0#	7. I Want Genuine Popular Election	22.0
8. Hong Kong Democracy Now	0.70	8. Umbrella Revolution	23.0#	**8. OCLP**	**21.0**
9. Occupy Night Shift	0.69	8. HK's True Demo. Newsfeed	23.0	8. Buy at Affected Shops	21.0
10. Small Shops Support Occupy	0.54	10. USC for Demo. In Hong Kong	22.0	10. Mr & Ms HK People	20.0

Notes: Bolded ones are the main leaders of the occupation campaign. * several other Facebook pages also had an out-degree score of 8.0 when page likes are concerned; ^ several other Facebook pages also had an in-degree score of 6.0 when page likes are concerned; # there are several Facebook pages with the title "Umbrella Revolution."

A similar pattern of findings appears in the bottom half of Table 5.7. In fact, the amount of interaction through content sharing among the pages was not huge. Only 31 Facebook pages have a non-zero betweenness centrality score based on content sharing. HKFS, Scholarism, and OCLP all scored zero, because they did not share the contents of the other Facebook pages (i.e., they have an out-degree score of zero). The status of the three main organizers is reflected by their relatively high in-degree scores. HKFS, in particular, has an in-degree score much higher than the other pages in the sample. But similar to the top half of the table, some other pages have also obtained an in-degree score comparable to or even higher than those of Scholarism and OCLP. After all, the actions of the main organizers were core to the movement dynamics. A number of other Facebook pages would thus pay attention to them and share their content. But some of the pages also had their contents relatively frequently shared by others. For example, many supporters had paid close attention at the beginning of the movement to a few pages providing live updates. Table 5.7 shows that the contents of 926 Ordinary Citizens at the Government Headquarters and Information from Mong Kok Occupy Sites were relatively more frequently shared by other Facebook pages.

On the whole, the three main organizers' Facebook pages were not central to the online network constituted by all 141 public pages, mainly because the main organizers did not proactively reach out to the others. When only in-degree scores are concerned, there are signs suggesting that the three main organizers attracted relatively more attention. But even in terms of in-degree scores, there are several other Facebook pages that were also liked by numerous others and had their contents relatively widely shared. Notably, the matrix based on page likes and the matrix based on content sharing are significantly positively correlated with each other (Pearson $r = .095, p < .001$).[23] It means that when a Facebook page has liked another page, it is also more likely to share the other page's content. The correlation is not strong, suggesting that basic recognition by no means entail frequent interaction. But the similarity of the results in the two halves of Table 5.7 and the positive relationship between the two matrices should confirm the robustness of the above interpretations of the analysis.

While the three main organizers did not embed themselves in the network constituted by the emerging Facebook pages, we calculated the betweenness centrality and in-degree and out-degree scores for the 138 Facebook pages, again based on the matrices constituted by page likes and content sharing among only these 138 pages (i.e., taking the three main organizers away). Understandably, removing only the central organizers would not change the relative centrality of the other 138 pages. For instance, the top 10 pages in terms of betweenness centrality based on page likes remain exactly the same as shown in Table 5.7.

Our second analytical question for this section asks whether the public pages central to the online network would tend to be the ones connecting themselves with the main organizers. In other words, we intend to explore the relations between the pages' centrality status and their connection with the main organizers. To answer this question, we conducted a set of multiple regression analysis to examine whether the degree of centrality of a Facebook page would relate to a number of characteristics, most notably the extent to which the pages were linked to different types of other Facebook pages through liking or content sharing.

Table 5.8 summarizes the results. The top half of the table shows that, among the 138 Facebook pages, those that have liked HKFS's Facebook page tend to have higher betweenness centrality scores and out-degree scores. Besides, the more Facebook pages of civic associations or political parties and the more "other

Table 5.8 **Predicting the centrality of Facebook pages in the online network**

	Page likes		
	Betweenness	*Out-degree*	*In-degree*
Time of setup	.02	−.02	−.01
No. of likes by people	.04	−.02	.30***
Like OCLP	.07	−.07	−.07
Like HKFS	.19*	.24***	.01
Like Scholarism	.05	.00	.07
Like legacy media	−.20**	−.17**	−.19
Like online media	.17	−.02	.12
Like civic/parties	.33***	.23**	.10
Like all others	.36***	.72***	.22*
Adjusted R^2	0.565***	0.710***	0.120**

	Content sharing		
	Betweenness	*Out-degree*	*In-degree*
Time of setup	−.06	−.13	−.08
No. of likes by people	.06	−.05	.65***
Share OCLP	−.06	.01	−.06
Share HKFS	−.02	.03	.10
Share Scholarism	.48*	.52**	−.14
Share legacy media	−.11	.02	.22
Share online media	−.09	.07	−.14
Adjusted R^2	0.066*	0.397***	0.446***

Notes: Entries are standardized regression coefficients. $N = 138$. *** $p < .001$; ** $p < .01$; * $p < .05$.

Facebook pages" that a Facebook page had liked,[24] the higher its betweenness centrality score and out-degree score tend to be.

In one sense, these findings simply illustrate the point that those Facebook pages that have actively liked a range of other pages were also more likely to have liked other Facebook pages created in relation to the Umbrella Movement. They would therefore have higher out-degree and betweenness centrality scores (because actively linking themselves to the other Facebook pages in the sample is a condition for a high betweenness centrality score). But understood this way, it is notable that whether a Facebook page has liked Scholarism's page or not and whether it has liked OCLP's page or not have no relationship with the page's centrality in the online network. Interestingly, Facebook pages that have liked a large number of Facebook pages of conventional mass media organizations even tended to have lower betweenness centrality, out-degree, and in-degree scores. It suggests that the pages at the periphery of the network constituted by the 138 pages in the current sample might yet be embedded in other online networks involving mass media organizations.

On the whole, when the movement-related pages are regarded as a network, those central to the network were more likely to have linked themselves to a range of Facebook pages of civic associations, political parties, and so on, including the Facebook page of one—but only one—of the three main organizers. The findings do not provide strong evidence for any "special status" enjoyed by the three main organizers from the perspective of the participant-initiated Facebook pages.

The bottom half of Table 5.8 shows the findings based on content sharing. Facebook pages that are more central to the network of content sharing tended to have shared the contents from Scholarism to larger extents. But there is no connection between network centrality and whether a page has shared contents from HKFS, OCLP, and the Facebook pages of both conventional and online alternative media. Our data did not contain information about the extent to which the Facebook pages have shared contents from civic associations and political parties. But the two halves of Table 5.8 are consistent with each other on one point: the Facebook pages more central to the online network constituted by the Umbrella Movement–related pages are more closely linked to only one of the three main organizers. This again suggests that the three organizers did not occupy a significant and central position in the networks of connective actions in the social media arena.

DECENTRALIZATION OVER TIME?

One limitation of the above analysis is that it does not involve examination of the transformation of the online network over time. We do not know when the pages liked each other, and the data regarding content sharing did not include the timing of the acts of sharing. It is worth noting that centrality of the Facebook pages to the online network is unrelated to the timing of their establishment: among the 138 pages (i.e., excluding the three main organizers), the "date of first post" variable is not significantly related to any of the three network centrality measures. In any case, we cannot judge from the Facebook page-level data whether there was a process of decentralization over time during the Umbrella Movement.

Nevertheless, some evidence regarding whether the main organizers had become "decentered" over time can be derived from a content analysis of the posts. Two assistants helped code a number of basic characteristics of the posts published by the Facebook pages between September 28 and December 15. We coded all the posts related to the Umbrella Movement published by the three main organizers' Facebook pages in the period. But to render the rest of the analysis feasible, sampling was involved for the other Facebook pages with large numbers of posts. Specifically, a sample of about 80 to 120 posts would be derived for a Facebook page through systematic sampling if the total number of posts published by the page in the period is above 150. In the end, a total of 8,350 posts were coded.[25]

A series of regression analysis was conducted to predict the numbers of likes, shares, and comments received by individual posts. The independent variables include: (1) inclusion of videos; (2) inclusion of photos; (3) inclusion of graphics; (4) time of publication (September 28 = 1 and December 15 = 79); (5) number of likes received by the Facebook page that published the post (in thousands); (6) post by the main organizers or not; and (7) an interaction term between time of publication and whether the post was by the main organizers. The interaction term is the central concern here. While the impact of the "main organizer" variable would indicate whether the posts posted by the three main organizers would get more likes, shares, and comments, the interaction term would signify whether the differences between main organizers and the other pages would increase or decrease over time.

Table 5.9 summarizes the results. The first column shows that, when other variables are controlled, posts involving videos and photos were liked by fewer people. Instead, posts involving graphics were liked by a significantly larger number of people. Not surprisingly, posts published by pages having more page likes would also receive more likes. But even after controlling for page likes, the main organizer variable still obtains a significant positive coefficient. Posts published by the three main organizers received more likes even after discounting their advantages on page likes. This points toward the status of HKFS, Scholarism, and OCLP as the central organizers of the movement.

However, the interaction term between "main organizer" and "time" is statistically significant and negative in sign. It means that the difference between the posts by the main organizers and the posts from the other pages diminished over time (after taking away the advantage the main organizers had due to their larger numbers of page likes).

The second column provides a similar pattern of findings. Again, while the main organizers' posts received on average significantly more shares when compared to posts from other pages, the difference between the main organizers and the other

Table 5.9 **Predicting numbers of likes, shares, and comments received by posts**

	Likes	*Shares*	*Comments*
Videos (Y = 1)	–65.81*	38.89**	2.13
	(32.69)	(13.96)	(1.56)
Photos (Y = 1)	–44.28*	–11.71	–0.28
	(18.05)	(7.71)	(0.86)
Graphics (Y = 1)	168.21***	34.60***	4.57***
	(17.52)	(7.48)	(0.84)
Page likes	7.20***	0.57***	0.17***
(in thousands)	(0.26)	(0.11)	(0.01)
Time (Sept 28 = 1)	0.62	–0.05	0.01
	(0.35)	(0.15)	(0.02)
Main organizer (Y = 1)	117.29*	341.89***	38.76***
	(57.63)	(24.61)	(2.75)
Time X main organizer	–8.40***	–5.90***	0.02
	(1.30)	(0.55)	(0.06)
Adjusted R^2	0.218***	0.064***	0.250***

Notes: Entries are unstandardized regression coefficients. Bracketed numbers are standard errors. $N = 8,350$. *** $p < .001$; ** $p < .01$; * $p < .05$.

pages diminished over time, as suggested by the significant and negative coefficient of the interaction term. Nevertheless, there is no significant interaction effect between time and the main organizer variable in the regression analysis on the number of comments received. Posts on the Facebook pages of the three main organizers were commented on by significantly larger numbers of people throughout the entire movement.

On the whole, the findings in Table 5.9 suggest a process of gradual decentering of the three main organizers in social media–based communications and activities surrounding the movement. The three main organizers did have a degree of centrality in that their contents received larger amounts of attention, approval, and reaction on social media. But their advantages over the other emerging Facebook pages had diminished somewhat over the period of the occupation campaign.

Digital Media and the Admiralty–Mong Kok Divide

The analyses in the previous sections have provided some empirical support to the first two contentions stated earlier in this chapter. On the one hand, digital media

activities empowered the movement by allowing people to construct their own specific ways of participating in the movement. Digital media allowed people to stay
connected with the movement even when they were not in the occupied areas,
but digital media activities did not displace frontline actions. Instead, those who
were more engaged in digital media activities were also more deeply involved in the
actual occupation in the physical sites.

The more deeply involved participants were also the ones less likely to listen to
the views of the central organizers on issues of movement strategies and directions.
The Facebook page analysis shows that the central organizers were by no means at
the center of the emerging network of connective actions online. There was also evidence suggesting that online attention and reactions became relatively less focused
on the main organizers' Facebook pages over the course of the occupation. These
findings are consistent with the argument that digital media activities contributed
to the trend of decentralization of the movement.

Nevertheless, we do not intend to argue that digital media communications and
connective actions were the only or prime cause of the trend toward decentralization in the Umbrella Movement. After all, decentralization is not necessarily unde-
sirable. One may argue that a certain degree of decentralization is conducive to or
even necessary for the continual vibrancy of the occupation. Decentralization could
become problematic mainly when it couples with other factors to generate a significant degree of internal dissension and even conflicts. In the Umbrella Movement,
decentralization and internal dissension have their ideological, spatial, and organizational bases. Ultimately, the role of digital media in the decentralization of the
movement can best be understood in terms of how it allowed the various divisions
within the movement to be manifested, foregrounded, and reinforced.

It is beyond the current study's capacity to fully capture the complex configura-
tions of internal division within the Umbrella Movement. But we can try to illustrate the connections between digital media communications and the various lines
of divisions based on ideologies, space, and organization. We may start by referring
to an analysis by a team of researchers at the Journalism and Media Studies Centre
at Hong Kong University, who mapped the networks of communications about
Occupy Central/Umbrella Movement among Facebook public pages in Hong
Kong since July 1, 2014.

According to Chan and Fu's (2014) analysis of the content sharing networks
among 885 Facebook pages during the Umbrella Movement, the pro-movement
and anti-movement communications were not only differentiable from each other,
the pro-movement pages could also be differentiated into what they called "the
mainstream sector," "the social movement sector," and "the localist sector." In line
with our analysis in the previous section, while the Facebook pages of the three main
movement leaders were among the relatively more prominent ones in the online
arena, they were not by far the most central ones in the communication networks.
Rather, when measured by betweenness centrality, *Inmedia* was the most central to

the communication network of the "social movement sector." Degree of centrality of Scholarism in "the mainstream sector" was matched by influential opinion leader Kin-Ng, *Apple Daily*, and the online media site *Polymer. Passion Times* was the most central to the communication network of the "localist sector."

Chan and Fu's (2014) analysis confirms the commonly perceived distinction between the liberal-leftists (i.e., the social movement sector and part of the mainstream sector) and the localists in Hong Kong. Put in a brief and simplified manner, while the liberal-leftists strive for democratization through emphasizing the significance of democracy, social justice, and equality as universal values, the localists emphasize the priority of the interests of Hong Kong vis-à-vis China. The more radical localists would emphasize the distinctiveness of the "Hong Kong nation" and would even call for Hong Kong independence. Historically, the liberal-leftists constituted the mainstream of the pro-democracy movement in Hong Kong, whereas the rise of localist groups was one of the indicators of the radicalization of the social movement sector in more recent years. The localists were critical not only toward the Chinese and Hong Kong government. They were also highly critical toward the liberal-leftists and other mainstream democrats for being too moderate and willing to compromise.

While the analysis by Chan and Fu (2014) illustrated the demarcation among the factions in the online arena, during the Umbrella Movement, the localist vs. leftist divide also became physically spatial. It was widely observed that more localist groups and supporters were stationed in Mong Kok, whereas Admiralty was seen as the "big stage"—a term used pejoratively by the localist—of the three main organizers and other groups in the mainstream pro-democracy camp. During the movement, the central organizers were often booed by some of the occupiers when they visited the Mong Kok occupation and tried to speak to the occupiers there. One could see posters with the slogan "beware of the leftards"[26] when one walked around the Mong Kok occupation.

Our protest onsite survey in November also provides some evidence of the distinction between Admiralty and Mong Kok. In the survey, we asked the respondents the degree to which they regarded "local interest," "universal values," and "democratization of China" as the "foundational beliefs" of the Umbrella Movement. As Table 5.10 shows, the Mong Kok occupiers were significantly more likely than the Admiralty occupiers to see local interest as the movement's foundational belief.

Besides, the survey asked the respondents to indicate their views toward the idea of self-mobilization. Table 5.10 shows that the Mong Kok occupiers agreed with the two positive statements about self-mobilization to larger extents, and they disagreed with the two negative statements about self-mobilization to larger extents. That is, the Mong Kok occupiers were consistently more positive toward the idea of self-mobilization. These findings signified the Mong Kok occupiers' distrust toward the "big stage" in Admiralty. They are consistent with the findings

Table 5.10 **Differences between the Admiralty and Mong Kok occupiers**

By survey time-points	November Admiralty	November Mong Kok
Perceived foundational beliefs		
Local interest[a]	4.27	4.57
Universal values	4.34	4.46
Democratization of China	3.35	3.25
Views on self-mobilization		
S-M movements are purer[a]	3.89	4.18
S-M can prevent hijacking[a]	3.74	4.09
S-M leads to loss of focus[a]	2.99	2.61
S-M leads to loss of leadership[a]	3.22	2.99
Support for political parties/groups		
Democratic Party	3.7	3.1
ADPL	1.1	1.0
Civic Party[a]	17.6	10.5
Confed. of Trade Union	1.5	2.4
Labor Party[a]	6.6	3.7
League of Social Democrats	9.6	11.2
People Power	8.8	11.9
Civic Passion[a]	4.8	12.9

Notes: Entries are mean scores on five-point Likert scales for perceived foundational beliefs and views on self-mobilization, and entries are percentages for support for political parties. When a variable is marked with superscript "a," the mean scores or percentage distributions obtained from the two occupied areas in November differ from each other significantly at $p < .05$ in an independent samples t-test or a Chi-square test.

in Table 5.4 that the Mong Kok occupiers were less willing to consider the opinions of the three central leaders of the movement on questions of movement strategies and direction.

Moreover, the survey asked the respondents whether there were any political groups or parties that they supported in particular. Respondents were allowed to indicate more than one political group or party. As the bottom of Table 5.10 shows, the Mong Kok occupiers were significantly more likely to be supporters of the localist group Civic Passion when compared to the Admiralty occupiers, whereas the

Admiralty occupiers were significantly more likely to be supporters of the Civic Party and the Labor Party, two political parties belonging to the more mainstream and liberal-leftist faction of the pro-democracy movement.

Certainly, one should not oversimplify or exaggerate the Admiralty–Mong Kok division. The significant differences between the occupiers in the two places shown in Table 5.10 are not always substantial. The two groups of occupiers did not differ from each other significantly on emphasis on universal values and democratization of China. In addition, the Mong Kok occupiers were also slightly (though not significantly) more likely to be supporters of People Power and League of Social Democrats. The two latter political parties were considered as relatively radical but still belonged to the liberal-leftist instead of the localist faction. After all, both occupations included a mix of participants holding different ideological positions. The division between the two places was therefore not clear-cut.[27]

Nevertheless, for the present discussion, the important point is that there were some systematic connections among ideologies, occupied areas, and support for specific political groups. Digital media communications could also be part of these systematic connections. In fact, Table 5.1 has shown that the Mong Kok occupiers were significantly more likely than the Admiralty occupiers to perceive the *Golden Forum* as an important information source. The Mong Kok occupiers also seemed to be slightly more likely to see *Passion Times*, which was central to the localist's social media network, as an important information source and slightly less likely to see *Inmedia*, which was central to the liberal-leftists' communication network, as important. Although these latter differences were statistically insignificant, the directions of the apparent differences are consistent with the idea that the Mong Kok occupiers, overall speaking, had a relatively stronger localist orientation.

To see whether and how the perceived importance of *Golden Forum*, *Passion Times*, and *Inmedia* related to the occupiers' ideological orientation, spatial location, and support for political groups, a series of multiple regression analysis was conducted with perceived importance of the three sites as the dependent variables in turn. The independent variables include demographics, occupation area, perceived importance of the three foundational beliefs of the Umbrella Movement, attitude toward self-mobilization, and support for a number of political parties— Civic Passion, People Power, League of Social Democrats, and the mainstream pro-democracy parties combined together.[28]

Table 5.11 summarizes the findings. Perceived importance of the *Golden Forum* was significantly associated with a stronger emphasis on local interest as the foundational belief of the Umbrella Movement. But since the *Golden Forum* was not associated specifically with a political group, perception of its importance was not associated with support for any political parties. Instead, it was associated with a stronger emphasis on the positive aspect of self-mobilization. Perceived importance of *Passion Times*, meanwhile, was also related to a stronger emphasis on local

Table 5.11 **Predicting perceived importance of specific websites**

	Perceived importance of		
	Golden Forum	Passion Times	Inmedia
Gender	−.03	.10*	.11*
Education	−.06	−.04	.00
Age	−.16***	−.12**	−.13**
SES	−.00	−.01	−.03
Area (MK = 2)	.08	.04	−.05
Foundational beliefs			
Local interest	.10*	.10*	.02
Universal values	.04	−.00	.09^
Democratization of China	−.06	−.10*	.02
Group support			
Support People Power	.07	.01	.02
Support Civic Passion	.00	.15***	.04
Support LSD	−.00	−.09*	−.00
Support mainstream democrats	.02	−.05	.00
Views toward self-mobilization			
Self-mobilization: Positive	.11*	.02	−.06
Self-mobilization: Negative	.01	.04	.07
Adjusted R^2	0.056***	0.072***	0.032**

Notes: Entries are standardized regression coefficients. Missing values were replaced by means. $N = 569$. *** $p < .001$; ** $p < .01$; * $p < .05$; ^ $p < .06$.

interest. It was also associated with a weaker emphasis on democratization of China. Not surprisingly, supporters of Civic Passion saw *Passion Times* as more important, while supporters of the League of Social Democrats were less likely to see *Passion Times* as an important information source.

Among the attitudinal and group support variables, only perceived importance of universal values is marginally significantly and positively related to perceived importance of *Inmedia*. Perceived importance of *Inmedia* also seems to be related negatively to attitude toward self-mobilization: while the two self-mobilization variables in Table 5.11 do not obtain significant coefficients, a single attitude toward self-mobilization variable (created by positive views toward self-mobilization minus the negative views toward self-mobilization) would relate significantly negative to perceived importance of *Inmedia* ($\beta = -.09, p < .04$).

Again, the relationships among the variables are not strong and clear-cut. But when taken together, the pattern of findings in Table 5.11 do correspond to the characteristics of the three sites—a localist site not affiliated with specific political groups (*Golden Forum*), a localist site associated with a specific political group (*Passion Times*), and a site belonging to the liberal-leftist faction and closer to the main organizers of the movement (*Inmedia*). Digital media communications are not only decentralized; they were connected systematically with the internal divisions within the movement based on ideology, organizational affiliation, and spatial setup of the occupation.

Summary

This chapter focuses on digital media activities and connective actions within the Umbrella Movement. Bennett and Segerberg (2013) argued that connective actions can maximize the chances of people participating in a movement. This is because it allows the space for people to express themselves in their own ways and determine which actions to and not to adopt. Part of the empirical findings of this chapter supports this claim. However, the findings also support the contention that connective actions introduced forces of decentralization into the Umbrella Movement. The most deeply involved participants, who were also the most active digitally, were less likely to listen to the main organizers on issues of movement strategies. The central movement leaders were also not particularly central to the networks of digital communications and connective actions that emerged during the movement. Nevertheless, we argue that digital media communications did not create the problem of internal division by themselves. They were tied to the organizational, spatial, and ideological divisions already existing in the movement. Admittedly, the empirical findings do not directly demonstrate the effects of digital media communication and activities on reinforcing the internal dissensions, but such a division-reinforcement influence of digital media is highly likely given the pattern of findings presented.

These findings provide us with some insights, from a communication perspective, into the strategic impasse that the movement had seemingly run into after the televised meeting between HKFS and government officials on October 21. For most movement participants, the concessions made by the government during the meeting were purely symbolic (if those were regarded as concessions at all). But what could be the next step? Of course, there were many factors behind the difficulties of the movement organizers in devising coherent and effective strategies, including the basic fact that there was no institutional means through which the movement and its allies could more effectively pressurize the Hong Kong government. The

movement involved the participation of a range of political groups and their supporters, and these groups were holding different ideologies, judgments regarding
the political reality, and thus vastly different views on key questions of movement
strategies. But digital media activities and the logic of connective actions have arguably aggravated the difficulties by reinforcing the dissension, providing platforms
for the expression and circulation of disagreement, producing a more fragmented
communication space in the online arena, as well as by strengthening individual
participants' sense of "ownership" and "independence." It makes the achievement of
anything close to a consensus extremely difficult. Similar conclusions were drawn
by Cheng and Chan's (2016) analysis of the Umbrella Movement, who argued that
protesters and the leaders were influenced by both online opinions and onsite ecology. Although online opinion leaders and their supporters "might have lacked decision-making authority, they possessed *veto power*" (p. 15).

The emphasis on the ideological, organizational, and spatial bases of internal
dissension in the last analysis section of this chapter implies that digital media and
connective actions did not create the problem of decentralization in the Umbrella
Movement out of whole cloth. It was exacerbating certain tendencies already existing
within the movement. Here, we may further consider Tarrow's (2013) view about the
limitation of electronic communication for social mobilization. He acknowledged
that electronic communication travels fast, spreads far, and is condensed, but what is
lacking is "interpersonal trust that can come only from intense and sustained interaction, such as occurs in the course of a strike, a school occupation, or the experience of
working together during a boycott" (p. 209). Of course, electronic communication
does not destroy trust either. Nor does it preclude or displace face-to-face interactions. But as long as trust cannot be easily produced through online communication
alone, the presence or absence of social trust can be considered as an existing condition that shapes what electronic communication can and cannot do.

In relation to Tarrow's (2013) comments, it is worth noting that there is arguably
a "culture of distrust" in the social movement scene in Hong Kong, signified by the
frequent appearances of code words such as "hijack" and "advantage-taking" (*cau-
seoi*) in public discourses surrounding social movements. When political groups
take the stage and proclaim their support for a movement, they are often criticized
for trying to take advantage. In the Umbrella Movement, when the Trio announced
the beginning of Occupy Central on September 28, there were opinions among the
student protesters criticizing the Trio for hijacking the student protests. This culture
of distrust can be subjected to much more in-depth analysis beyond the focus of this
book. The point here is that, within the Umbrella Movement, there did not seem
to be high levels of trust existing between the young participants ("represented" by
the HKFS and Scholarism) and the adult participants ("represented" by the Trio),
between the central organizers and the mass of individual participants, between
the middle-class and the grassroots participants, and between the "leftists" and the
"localists."

Introducing and reinforcing the forces of decentralization of a movement may not be a problematic impact of connective actions if the movement is non-programmatic, so that there is no need for the movement to engage in strategic interactions with the target, and thus no need for the movement to come up with strategic decisions that all participants are willing to follow. But the Umbrella Movement is not non-programmatic. Its strategic impasse means that it cannot effectively negotiate with the government when it needs or has the opportunity to. As already noted earlier, after HKFS met with top government officials on October 21, the main organizers of the occupation put forward the plan of having a referendum within the occupation area in order to gauge the participants' views toward the government's responses. The idea of a referendum was heavily criticized by some participating groups and individuals. Facing strong opposition, the central organizers had to abandon the plan of a referendum.

Throughout the occupation campaign, it was publicized that there were disagreements on various matters among the main organizing groups. This is not surprising. Internal dissension among movement leaders is not rare in large-scale social movements around the world. There could be various reasons and factors behind the emergence of internal dissension. Observers and analysts who focus on the "inside operation" of the movement may address issues such as the interaction dynamics among the core leaders, the success or failure of establishing effective decision-making mechanisms, etc. For this book's analysis, the crucial point is that the intervention of connective actions and the resulting decentralized formation of the movement contributed to the difficulties of resolving internal tensions and disagreements among the movement leaders as well as between the movement leaders and the participants at large.

This has arguably strengthened the hands of the government in the strategic interaction. The next chapter will focus on the government's strategies to handle the movement after the initial attempts of decisive actions failed, as well as how an anti-movement public opinion was produced and constructed in the public arena toward the later stages of the movement. These are core aspects of the dynamics that paved the way for police eviction in the end.

6

Counter-Movement Discourses and Governmental Responses

Public opinion constitutes a major battlefield throughout the Occupy Central campaign and the Umbrella Movement. As Chapter 3 illustrated, the ideas of Occupy Central and civil disobedience were fervently debated in the mainstream media since early 2013. In addition to the discursive contestations, both sides organized collective opinion expressions in order to showcase the public support on their side. OCLP conducted a civil referendum in June 2014. It allowed citizens to vote on the electoral arrangement proposal that the OCLP should submit to the government and on what the Legislative Council should do if the government's electoral reform proposal did not meet the international standard of universal suffrage. The referendum claimed to have registered a total of 792,808 votes, with 88% indicating that the legislature should vote down the government's proposal if it fails to meet the standard of genuine popular election.

On the other side, a group of pro-establishment public figures established the group Silent Majority for Hong Kong in August 2013 with the explicit goal of opposing Occupy Central. The group organized an Anti–Occupy Central petition campaign in July and August 2014, and claimed to have collected more than 1.8 million signatures. Then, the group and other pro-establishment forces organized an anti-occupation rally on August 17, 2014. The organizers claimed that 190,000 citizens had participated.[1]

Meanwhile, various public opinion polls conducted in year 2013 and 2014 showed that only around 25% to 30% of Hong Kong citizens were in favor of Occupy Central.[2] These figures are understandable given the relative novelty and radicalness of occupation as a form of collective action and the emphasis on social order in the political culture of Hong Kong. In mid-September 2014, after the NPC decision and the Trio's announcement that Occupy Central would go ahead, a poll conducted by the Centre for Communication and Public Opinion Survey (CCPOS) at the Chinese University of Hong Kong showed that 31.1% of citizens were supportive toward Occupy Central, whereas 46.3% were opposed to the planned occupation campaign.[3]

Public support for the occupation grew after the campaign started and transformed into the Umbrella Movement. The CCPOS poll in October showed that 37.8% of citizens were supportive toward the occupation, whereas the percentage of opposing citizens declined to 35.5%. Nevertheless, there was no continual increase in public support for the movement. The CCPOS survey in November found that 33.9% of citizens were supportive toward the movement, four percentage points lower than the October figure, while the percentage of opposing citizens rose to 43.5%. Level of public support for the movement then stabilized. In the December CCPOS poll, the percentages of citizens supporting and opposing the movement were 33.9% and 42.3%, respectively.[4]

In one sense, the Umbrella Movement did not lose any public support by the end of the occupation. The level of public support for the movement registered in the December poll is still nominally higher than the level of public support registered in September. But the Umbrella Movement did not succeed in gaining sustainable public support either. The anti-occupation public opinion was equally stable and robust.

Moreover, by November and December, there was a seemingly strong public opinion in favor of a retreat by the occupiers. In the November CCPOS poll, 67.4% of the respondents said that the occupiers should or "exceedingly should" evacuate all the occupied areas immediately, whereas only 13.9% said the occupiers should not evacuate. The percentage of citizens opposing evacuation was smaller than the percentage of citizens supporting the movement, indicating that a significant proportion of the movement supporters were also in favor of evacuation by November. Into December, more than 75% of Hong Kong citizens thought the occupiers should evacuate the occupied areas immediately; only 6.5% of citizens thought the opposite. The pro-retreat public opinion was one of the major factors that allowed the police to evict the occupied areas and thus ended the Umbrella Movement without much controversy.

The formation and mobilization of the anti-occupation public opinion is therefore a crucial aspect of the dynamics of the Umbrella Movement. This chapter focuses on how the anti-occupation camp—the party-state of China, the Hong Kong SAR government, the pro-establishment groups, and the pro-establishment mainstream media outlets—attempted to delegitimize the Umbrella Movement. We use the notion of framing to organize our analysis. We begin by examining a number of counter-movement frames articulated and propagated by the anti-occupation camp, mainly through the pro-establishment media. However, a focus on framing does not mean that the government and pro-establishment forces engaged only in discursive work. Our contention is that the major counter-mobilization strategies adopted by the government actually involved a combination of discursive work and concrete practices. The aim of the analysis below, therefore, is not only to highlight the presence of certain counter-movement frames, but also to discuss how some of those frames were coupled with the counter-mobilization strategies and practices of the government and pro-establishment groups.

After discussing the major counter-movement frames and their associated counter-mobilization strategies, the chapter will analyze how the counter-movement frames and discourses circulated through the pro-government enclaves on social media. We then further analyze how images of public opinion were constructed in the mainstream media in the latter stages of the movement, paving the way for the end of the occupation.

Counter-framing the Movement

Similar to other large-scale protest actions, the Umbrella Movement sparked off a discursive battle among the contesting parties. For the anti-occupation camp, the aim of their discursive efforts was to delegitimize the Umbrella Movement in order to undermine its public support and to justify governmental actions. Based on our observations of mainstream media discourses during the Umbrella Movement, we identified three major counter-frames utilized by the anti-occupation camp: the foreign intervention frame, the rule of law frame, and the public nuisance frame. Two of these three counter-movement frames were closely related to the concrete counter-mobilization strategies and practices adopted by the government and the pro-establishment forces.

Generally speaking, we follow Gamson and Modigliani (1987, 1989) in treating a frame as an ideological package including a central idea, a set of discursive devices for discussing the matters at hand, ways of portraying the actors involved, a set of claims about the causes and consequences of a situation, and thus a set of claims about the preferred resolutions. The three counter-frames to be explicated may or may not have been developed into complete and systematic ideological packages with all such specific components. But they could be considered as frames to the extent that they have some of the features of an ideological package and constitute a distinctive way to talk about the Umbrella Movement.

To reconstruct the three counter-frames utilized by the anti-occupation camp, we conducted a textual analysis of newspaper editorials published during the Umbrella Movement. We focus on newspaper editorials because editorials are constituted by argumentative discourses through which the ideological predilections of news organizations are most clearly and systematically exhibited (Le, 2004; Lee & Lin, 2006). Hence they should be one of the sites where the ideological packages are most readily discernible. We conducted keyword searches through the electronic news archive Wise News to identify relevant editorials from nine Hong Kong newspapers: the three Communist-sponsored newspapers (*Ta Kung Pao, Wen Wei Po, and Hong Kong Commercial Daily*), three pro-government newspapers (*Hong Kong Economic Times, Sing Tao Daily, Oriental Daily*), the relatively centrist *Hong Kong*

Economic Journal, the professional and somewhat liberal oriented *Ming Pao*, and the pro-democracy *Apple Daily*.

For the foreign intervention frame, we identified editorials that included the phrase "foreign force" (*ngoi-gwok sai-lik*) or "external force" (*ngoi-bou sai-lik*) plus one of the labels of the Umbrella Movement, such as *jyu-saan* (umbrella), *zim-zung* (Occupy Central), or *zim-ling* (occupation). Ninety-five editorials were derived from the period of September 1 to December 15, 2014.[5] For the rule of law frame, we identified editorials that included the phrase "damaging the rule of law" (*po-waai faat-zi*), "destroying the rule of law" (*ceoi-wai faat-zi*), or "challenging the rule of law" (*cung-gik faat-zi*), plus one of the movement labels. A total of 103 editorials were derived from the period. For the public nuisance frame, we identified editorials that included the phrase "affecting people's livelihood" (*jing-hoeng man-saang*), "affecting the citizens" (*jing-hoeng si-man*), or "harassing the people" (*jiu-man*), plus one of the movement labels. Sixty-nine such editorials were found.

THE FOREIGN INTERVENTION FRAME

In a social upheaval, it is not unusual for contestants to debate its causes and consequences. The Umbrella Movement is no exception. Indeed, the first major counter-frame propagated by the pro-government press was to attribute the uprising to foreign intervention. The movement organizers were portrayed to be linked ideologically, organizationally, and even financially to the Western powers, which aimed at advancing their hegemonic power around the world. China is known for holding strongly on to nationalism and anti-foreignism as a means to sustain the legitimacy of the current Communist regime (Wang, 2012; Zhao, 2004). In this political culture, labeling an action a result of foreign influence is often adequate to render it condemnable. The externalization of causes thus serves two purposes: to delegitimize an action by defining it as something that is dubious and alien, and to render any crackdown on the action legitimate.

As Table 6.1 indicates, *Oriental Daily* was the most active in invoking the notion of foreign intervention, as it accounted for 38 of the 95 editorials derived from the keyword search. The three Communist-sponsored newspapers combined to contribute 28 editorials to the corpus. The other conservative newspapers did not invoke the theme frequently, nor did *Hong Kong Economic Journal* or *Ming Pao*. Interestingly, *Apple Daily* contributed 13 editorials to the corpus, indicating that the pro-democracy newspaper was quite active in contesting this counter-frame.

The discursive tactics used in referring to foreign powers vary by newspapers. *Oriental Daily*, *Ta Kung Pao*, and *Wen Wei Po* were the three newspapers most likely to have named the Western powers explicitly. By foreign powers, they referred primarily to the United States and the United Kingdom. This was readily comprehensible because the United States is the world hegemonic power and has been advocating for liberal democracy as a universal value. Besides, the U.S. Congress had been

Table 6.1 **Number of editorials and commentaries mentioning foreign intervention**

	Oriental Daily (N=38)	Ta Kung Pao (N=14)	Apple Daily (N=13)	Ming Pao (N=5)	Sing Tao Daily (N=3)
UK	7	3	0	0	0
USA	19	8	0	0	2
Japan	0	0	0	0	0
Not specific/not agents	18	4	13	5	1

	HK Econ. Times (N=4)	HK Econ. Journal (N=4)	HK Com. Daily (N=4)	Wen Wei Po (N=10)	Total
UK	1	0	0	2	13
USA	0	0	0	3	32
Japan	0	0	0	1	1
Not specific/not agents	3	4	4	5	57

Notes: Entries are numbers of articles. The total in the last column of the table is more than 95 because one piece of editorial can simultaneously name the United States and the United Kingdom as the instigator.

publishing periodic reports on the state of democracy and freedom in Hong Kong. The United Kingdom, as the former colonizer, presumably had a role to oversee the continual development of the city. And as an ally of the United States in international politics, the United Kingdom was sometimes lumped together with the United States into the "British-American forces" by the newspapers. While it is difficult to pinpoint the operation of foreign powers in Hong Kong, some editorials singled out the funding support offered to Hong Kong NGOs by some U.S.-based governmental agencies or foundation. The editorials equated these activities with "American influence." For instance, *Oriental's* editorial on October 7, 2014, stated:

> The American State Council supported and funded the occupation action through the National Endowment for Democracy (NED) and the National Democratic Institute (NDI). The organizer of Occupy Central Benny Tai, as well as Jimmy Lai, Martin Lee, Joseph Zen, Audrey Eu and Joshua Wong all have close ties with these organizations. Most intriguingly, when Martin Lee and Anson Chan visited the U.S. this April . . ., they had meetings with the NED and NDI, introducing in details the idea, demand, and number

of participants of the occupation action. In the hour-long meeting, the two acted obsequiously and betrayed their country for personal gain.

As this passage illustrates, an important part of the foreign intervention frame is a highly negative portrayal of the proponents of Occupy Central and the prominent politicians and public figures of the pro-democracy camp—these people were cast as shameless betrayers of the Chinese nation. A range of lexicons was invoked in the editorials for the purpose: the pro-democracy figures were labeled "slaves of the Westerners" (*joeng-nou*), "traitors of the Han race" (*hon-gaan*), "political puppets," and "chess pieces" in the foreign power's master game plan. They were "political tools" at the service of foreign powers. The relationship between the foreign powers and the local democrats was therefore portrayed as one between the "country behind the scene" and their local agents serving as the "instigators" of or "black hands" behind the Umbrella Movement. With the involvement of foreign powers, the Umbrella Movement thus constituted "a conspiracy" (*Sing Tao Daily*, October 6, 2014) and a "vicious attempt" to subvert Hong Kong and China (*Wen Wei Po*, October 11, 2014). The instigators of the Umbrella Movement were described as "inviting a wolf into one's own room" (*Hong Kong Commercial Daily*, September 1, 2014) and "dancing to the tune of an evil pipe" (*Oriental Daily*, October 30, 2014).

The most direct way of substantiating a frame is to provide relevant evidence. The pro-establishment newspapers' editorial discourses mainly invoked two kinds of evidence to substantiate their claim about foreign influence in the Umbrella Movement. The first, as noted above, was funding support provided by foreign agencies to the Occupy Central campaign and the pro-democracy political parties and groups in general. The second was the interactions and meetings between the movement proponents and foreign politicians. For instance, *Oriental*'s editorial on October 5, 2014, described the relationship between Occupy Central and pro-independence politicians in Taiwan as follows:

Besides the support from external forces, Occupy Central is also closely intertwined with pro-Taiwan independence forces. As [Fan Ke-qin, a Taiwan politician] revealed, Occupy Central was planned single-handedly by the Chairman of Next Media Ltd. Jimmy Lai. Lai sought advices about Occupy Central from [pro-Taiwan independence politicians] Fan Ke-qin and Shi Ming-de more than a year ago. Shi Ming-de taught [Lai] everything, suggesting that Occupy Central should involve more young people, especially students, young girls, and women carrying babies so as to gain the sympathy and support from the media, the public, and the international community.

The passage stays "politically correct" by not treating Taiwan politicians as "foreign forces" (since Taiwan is considered a part of China). But the description of the interactions follows the same logic of portraying the movement as affected by forces outside Hong Kong. On the one hand, claims about political groups and civic associations in Hong Kong getting funding and advice from "foreign forces" are not entirely fabricated. But on the other hand, having groups and parties getting such support from organizations and individuals in the international arena is arguably entirely normal for an international city such as Hong Kong. Treating them as evidence of foreign infiltration into the Umbrella Movement involved a strained and far-fetched interpretation of what happened. In the end, factual evidence produced by the pro-establishment camp regarding foreign infiltration into the Umbrella Movement was scanty at best.[6]

Without more solid evidence, the pro-establishment media tried to bridge the veracity gap by other discursive tactics. One specific approach was to establish coherence and plausibility through the construction of analogy. The Color Revolutions, in particular, constituted a frequently used referent by the pro-establishment press. *Oriental's* editorial on September 29, for instance, stated that the Umbrella Movement was a "Hong Kong–style Color Revolution" that took place as the United States had chosen to "return to the Asia-Pacific." In this perspective, the Umbrella Movement was seen as the foreign forces' tactic of "containing China by the Chinese" and "using Hong Kong as a subversive base against China." The same newspaper's editorial on September 30 argued that the Western powers wanted to overthrow the Chinese government with a color revolution in the mainland. But as they failed to achieve that, disrupting the social order in Hong Kong became their second best option, a stepping stone for triggering a political reconfiguration in mainland China.

By invoking the Color Revolution as an analogy, the Umbrella Movement was raised to the level of being a matter of "the imperative of nationalism" (*man-zuk daai-ji*) and a threat to "national security," with "Hong Kong's survival being at stake." The pro-establishment press thus went further to call upon the readers to fight against foreign intervention as such.

For the pro-establishment press, the decision-making power over democratic reform in Hong Kong rests with Beijing. In framing the Umbrella Movement as instigated from outside, the newspapers cited a range of Chinese officials and representatives. References to Chinese officials served to strengthen the validity of the claim of foreign intervention; the officials were treated as authoritative definers of social reality, and their claims regarding the presence of foreign intervention were themselves taken as evidence. Further, the invocation of the Chinese officials was often associated with the assertion of the ultimate futility of the foreign power's conspiracy. *Wen Wei Po's* editorial on October 14 stated:

> As State Council's Vice-premier Wang Yang pointed out during his visit to Russia, . . . [Occupy Central aims] to overthrow the Hong Kong SAR government, acquire ruling power, and then use Hong Kong as the bridgehead

for subverting the socialist system in the mainland. But Hong Kong is after all a special administrative region of China. With the strong support from the Central Government, Hong Kong will not change. "OC" is destined to fail miserably.

In essence, the frame of foreign intervention was articulated through sheer accusation, treating international interactions as evidence of foreign influence, decontextualized connection with historical events such as the Color Revolutions, and recontextualized connection with Chinese nationalism. It is impossible for us to judge only through media content the extent to which the general public believed in the idea of foreign intervention. But what should be noted is that even the conservative newspapers did not always embrace the idea of foreign intervention unreservedly. *Sing Tao Daily* did not invoke the idea of foreign intervention frequently in its editorials. When it did, foreign intervention was treated more as a perception of the Chinese government than as a proven fact. The *Hong Kong Economic Times*, for another example, wrote in its editorial on October 11:

> ... there are opinions saying that there are foreign forces intervening into [the Umbrella Movement]. . . . This worry is not groundless. Hong Kong has been a British colony for more than a century. The influences of foreign powers such as the U.S. and the U.K. are convoluted in Hong Kong. . . .
>
> But the occupation action has one character that cannot be ignored, that is its loose organization, lack of clear leaders, and not to say [lack of] systematic engineering by foreign forces. The absolute majority of the students may be impetuous, but they are going to the street spontaneously based on their love for Hong Kong.

The passage acknowledges foreign intervention as a reasonable "worry," and by describing the protesting students as impetuous, the editorial remains against the Umbrella Movement. Nevertheless, the editorial also emphasizes the implausibility of foreign intervention by pointing to the decentralized character of the movement and the idea that the students were participating spontaneously. It is arguable that the idea of foreign intervention, while being a prominent notion in Chinese political discourse, is not a widely accepted theme in Hong Kong's political culture. Without hard evidence, local pro-establishment groups did not rely too much on the foreign intervention frame when criticizing the movement.

THE RULE OF LAW FRAME

The Umbrella Movement is an unexpected spinoff of Occupy Central. The proponents of Occupy Central took it as an act of civil disobedience in the fashion of what Gandhi and Martin Luther King did in their political struggles. It was by definition illegal behavior because the breaching of the law was an integral part of the scheme. Indeed, Benny Tai asserted that no protester in his or her honesty could deny the illegality of civil disobedience. However, for Tai and other proponents of Occupy Central, breaking the law does not entail breaching the rule of law. This is because abiding by the law itself is not the ultimate meaning of the rule of law. Instead, one can choose to break the law if one is to realize the higher goal of social justice through the illegal act. Besides, the act of civil disobedience shall not damage the rule of law if the protagonists are willing to accept the legal consequences of their actions. An important part of the original plan of Occupy Central, therefore, is that the occupiers shall surrender themselves to the police and subject themselves to potential legal penalties after the end of the occupation.

Nevertheless, the sophisticated account of civil disobedience and its relation to the rule of law offered by OCLP was definitely rejected by the pro-establishment camp. Despite nearly two years of elaborations and discussions, it probably remained difficult for all common citizens to fully understand abstract ideas such as "achieving justice through the law" and nuanced distinctions such as that between breaking the law and breaching the rule of law. As Chinese legal scholars have pointed out, rule of law and rule by law were often conflated in China (Fang & Forges, 2008; Li, 2007). Part of the reason is that both are expressed by the same Chinese phrase, *faat-zhi*. After all, the importance of abiding by the law is the much simpler and straight-forward idea that ordinary people can readily understand and agree with. Hence it is not surprising that, when the Umbrella Movement began, the anti-occupation camp would invoke the value of the rule of law to condemn it.

As noted above, we identified a total of 103 relevant editorials that included one of the identifying labels of the Umbrella Movement plus the phrase "damaging the rule of law," "destroying the rule of law," or "challenging the rule of law." This does not necessarily capture all editorials that invoked the theme. If we changed the keyword search into an identifying label of the movement plus the phrase "the rule of law" only, the total number of relevant editorials in the period would go up to 360. It is plausible that some of the additional editorials had also criticized the Umbrella Movement for breaching the rule of law without using the exact phrases utilized in the current keyword search. In any case, the rule of law frame appeared in the pro-establishment press's editorial discourse more frequently than the for-eign intervention frame did. In the current corpus of 103 editorials, 66 came from the three Communist-sponsored papers *Wen Wei Po, Ta Kung Pao*, and *Hong Kong Commercial Daily. Oriental* and *Sing Tao Daily* contributed 15 and 11 editorials to the corpus, respectively, while *Hong Kong Economic Journal* also accounted for eight editorials. *Ming Pao, Apple Daily*, and *Hong Kong Economic Times* contributed a total of only six editorials to the corpus.

The rule of law was often invoked in the editorials as the city's "core value" (*hat-sam gaa-gik*). The latter phrase appears in 32 editorials in the corpus. In public dis-course of Hong Kong, the notion of "core value" was first promoted by a group of liberal progressive intellectuals in 2004 in an attempt to counteract the rhetoric of patriotism promoted by China at the time (Lee & Chan, 2011, p. 114; Ng, 2008). The rule of law, together with liberty, democracy, human rights, fairness, and social justice, etc., was identified as the "core values" of the city. In other words, the liberal intellectuals invoked a cluster of liberal democratic values and treated them as both universal and already rooted in the local political culture. But in the Umbrella Movement, the notion of core value was appropriated by the conservative forces. For instance, *Wen Wei Po*'s editorial on October 23 claimed that "respecting the rule of law is Hong Kong's most important core value; it is the cornerstone of Hong Kong's prosperity and stability." The paper's editorial on November 17 stated: "respecting the rule of law is Hong Kong's core value. It is also the most important competitive advantage of Hong Kong. Without the rule of law, the competitive advantage of Hong Kong will disappear."

What is remarkable about these statements is that, instead of being associated with other liberal values, the rule of law was invoked in association with prosperity, social stability, and economic development, notions with highly conservative overtones in the local political context. Through such selective association, the value of the rule of law in restricting the exercise of political power was backgrounded; what was foregrounded was the connection between the rule of law and social order.

Regarding the portrayal of actors, the discourses surrounding the rule of law separate the protectors of the law from its violators. In the pro-establishment media, the protectors of law include the central authorities and the state apparatus, the Hong Kong SAR government, the Chief Executive C. Y. Leung, the police force, the High Court, the bailiffs, etc. The violators include the Trio, Next Media's owner Jimmy Lai, the Western powers, Scholarism, the HKFS, the pro-democracy legislators, and the "radicals." Interestingly, the pro-establishment press was sometimes careful not to criticize the huge group of citizen-protesters. *Wen Wei Po*'s editorial on October 6 claimed that people "should distinguish the organizers and the violent protesters from the majority of peaceful participants." Nonetheless, exonerating the huge group of citizen-protesters was also a way to construct more serious accusations toward the main organizers and the so-called radicals. For instance, *Hong Kong Commercial Daily*'s editorial on October 21 argued:

> The transformation of Occupy Central from petitioning by students to riots was a result of "hijacking." . . . The continuation of Occupy Central had destroyed the right of millions of citizens to a normal life. Its damage to the rule of law, the economy, and people's livelihood had cumulated to a highly dangerous level. Most citizens and students who were once misled had refused to continue to join the occupation after witnessing the truth of how Occupy Central is damaging Hong Kong. The remaining hardcore occupiers are members of radical groups who had received illegal money.

When compared to the foreign intervention frame, the rule of law discourse was more closely connected to the actual strategies used by the government and the anti-occupation camp in handling the movement. Specifically, a minibus company and the owner of the CITIC Tower, which was located just opposite to the East Wing of the Government Headquarters, applied for court injunctions against the occupation in mid-October. In other words, the anti-movement groups attempted to make the court intervene and declare the illegality of the occupation. On October 20, the High Court issued the first injunction against occupation at the CITIC Tower and certain roads in the Mong Kok occupied area. The rule of law frame had provided the discursive support for the legal approach the anti-occupation camp undertook. At the same time, the court injunction further heightened the relevance of the rule of law frame. In fact, 79 of the 103 editorials in the corpus were published after October 20.

The occupiers largely disregarded the court injunction. But the issuing of the court injunction did bring a new challenge to the theory of civil disobedience articulated by Benny Tai because the injunction introduced a new question: would one be damaging the rule of law when one refuses to abide by an existing court order? Even the Hong Kong Bar Association, which had earlier publicly criticized the NPC's decision on August 31 as imposing unreasonable constraints on the 2017 elections, issued a five-page public statement on October 28, stating that the Association "views with dismay recent calls for open defiance of injunctions granted by the Court in relation to the occupation of certain areas in Mongkok and Admiralty."[7] It further wrote:

> When deliberate defiance of a court order is committed *en masse* as a combined effort, a direct affront to the Rule of Law will inevitably result. For the same reason, open calls to the public to disobey a court order applicable to them would undoubtedly constitute an erosion of the Rule of Law.

Not surprisingly, the pro-establishment press invoked the Bar Association's arguments and embedded them in stronger rhetoric to criticize the movement. *Wen Wei Po*'s editorial on October 31, three days after the Bar Association's public statement, stated:

> The court order requesting the return of the roads to the public was neglected. The occupiers openly disregarded the court. The legislators and barristers of the opposition faction instigated the occupiers to fight the injunction. "Occupy Central" has done unprecedented damage to the spirit of the rule of law. . . . The Bar Association could not bear watching the scenario and therefore issued a strongly worded statement, lambasting "Occupy Central" for slandering the spirit of the rule of law. It even

described the rule of law in Hong Kong as "an egg very much at risk of being broken."

Moreover, the court injunction provided the discursive node through which the law enforcement is brought into the rule of law frame. Since the injunction was applied by private companies, some movement leaders and supporters questioned whether the police had a role in helping the enforcement of the injunction. In this regard, *Wen Wei Po*'s editorial on November 12 observed that the court order to clear the blockades in the occupied areas would probably be met with strong resistance. Without the help of the police, the injunctions would just become empty words. Hence the police needed to get prepared to help enforce the injunctions. Similarly, *Ta Kung Pao*'s editorial on November 29 noted:

> Therefore, we can say without hesitation that the police actions in Mong Kok in recent days, which included a certain degree of force, was completely a response to the situation that the roads in Mong Kok have already been illegally occupied for two months and that the occupiers had refused to follow the court "injunctions." [The use of force] was carried out in face of violent resistance by the occupiers. . . . Without the use of force, there would be no method to control the situation, and it would be impossible to attain the demand of the court "injunctions."

The frontline work of the police was treated as essential for the realization of the rule of law. In the above passage, the necessity of police enforcement was even tied to an attempt to justify the police's use of force. By the end of the movement, the rule of law frame was not only a way to criticize the occupation campaign. It was directly and explicitly articulated with the legitimacy of police eviction of the occupied areas. Therefore, what we see throughout the movement is that the rule of law frame was integrated with actual practices ranging from application for court injunction to police actions to form one major counter-movement strategy employed by the government and its allies.

THE PUBLIC NUISANCE FRAME

The Umbrella Movement lasted for 79 days, during which three strategic traffic arteries of Hong Kong were blocked. Detours as well as makeshift measures had to be devised. Buses and minibuses had to change their routes. Shops operating in the occupied areas were directly affected. The blockades also affected the transportation plans of those, including students and workers, who had to travel across the occupied areas. The adverse impact of the occupation on people's everyday lives thus constituted a general concern of the public and the media. The Chinese phrase summarizing this discursive package is *jiu-man*, literally meaning harassing the people. This is the third major counter-frame promulgated by the anti-occupation camp.

We identified only 69 editorials through Wise News that mentioned an identifying label of the occupation campaign plus one of three relevant phrases: affecting people's livelihood, affecting citizens, and harassing the people. But the keyword search probably missed numerous other articles that invoked the idea of public nuisance—the various adverse impact of the occupation on people's everyday lives could have been described concretely without invoking general phrases such as "affecting people's livelihood." In any case, *Hong Kong Commercial Daily* and *Wen Wei Po* accounted for about half of the articles derived from the search (32 out of 63). Interestingly, *Ta Kung Pao*, the other Communist-sponsored newspaper, did not publish editorials using those keywords at all. *Sing Tao Daily* and *Oriental Daily* contributed a total of 14 articles. Meanwhile, *Apple Daily* and *Ming Pao* also had a total of 15 editorials including the keywords. As will be discussed later, the two papers' attitude toward the notion of public nuisance had changed over the course of the movement.

Compared to the foreign intervention and rule of law frames, the idea of public nuisance appeared in the pro-establishment press conspicuously only after the actual beginning of the Umbrella Movement, and especially after mid-October. This was reasonable because the adverse consequences would accumulate and become more serious as the occupation continued. It was not difficult for the pro-establishment press to come up with concrete illustrations of the inconveniences and nuisances caused by the occupation. Yet some of the claims made by the pro-establishment press were highly questionable, if not simply absurd. For instance, *Hong Kong Commercial Daily's* editorial on October 10 noted:

> Occupy Central . . . caused severe traffic jams. Car queues in various districts are longer than 20 kilometers. . . . Citizens going to work, students going to school, shops' operation, and public services are all seriously affected. Public transportation bears the brunt, with revenue going down by 20% to 40%. . . . The transportation industry point out that tens of thousands of drivers have their livelihood affected. They have to work longer hours and yet have less income and have to pay more for oil. Residents at the Mid-Level complain that a trip to work or to school that normally takes only a few minutes now takes two hours.

It is difficult to verify some of the cited figures and to debate whether something has indeed been "seriously" affected. But at least two claims in the above passage are utterly implausible. First, car queues of more than 20 kilometers are hardly imaginable in Hong Kong, because 20 kilometers would be equivalent to the length of the route across the whole Hong Kong Island from the East side to the West side. Second, the distance that usually can be covered by a car in a few minutes can probably be covered by walking in an hour or less. It does not make sense at all to claim that the trip would need two hours no matter how bad the traffic is. While such rebuttals may sound like quibbling about the details, it should be noted that the anti-occupation camp did have the tendency of exaggerating the negative impact of the movement. In one of the most notorious cases, a pro-establishment economist claimed that, based on stock market performance a few days after the beginning of the occupation, the movement had caused the Hong Kong economy a loss of HK$350 billion.

The public nuisance frame pitted the protesters against "ordinary citizens." In the pro-establishment press, this opposition was represented by the conflicts between the protesters and counter-protesters in the occupied areas. *Sing Tao Daily's* editorial on October 4 is typical of how the pro-establishment press wrote about protester-counter-protester conflicts:

> The Occupy Central movement . . . severely affected people's livelihood and thus caused disgust from more and more citizens. Yesterday, there was finally the outburst of large-scale conflicts in Mong Kok. Some occupiers were attacked by angry people; the police needed to separate the groups and maintain the order.

Since early October, there were citizens and groups organizing counter-protests, sometimes resulting in violent conflicts. The above passage stopped short of defending the counter-protesters explicitly. But by contextualizing the conflict against the background of the occupation's negative impact on people's everyday lives, the passage implicitly treated the "angry people's" reaction as understandable. In some cases, the "affected citizens" would be portrayed as deserving sympathy, as in this editorial published in *Sing Tao Daily* on October 5:

> It can be seen from many television reports and online video clips that the public is getting increasingly disgruntled about how Occupy Central severely affects people's livelihood and breaks their rice bowls. Just like how an old granny and a woman pointed toward the protesters and said, they only wanted the occupiers to "give [them] a road to walk on," "give [them] a bowl of rice." The requests are humble. These complaints represent what millions of citizens hold in their hearts. The grievance of the silent majority is on the rise with the continuation of Occupy Central, and it is reaching the critical point of outbursts.

The passage implicitly treats the majority of Hong Kong people as concerned first and foremost with their "rice bowls." It positions the counter-protesters as representing the "majority" of millions of citizens. At the same time, it uses "an old granny and a woman," figures of "the weak," to represent the counter-protesters. The phrase "give [them] a road to walk on" (*bei tiu lou hang*) has a strong connotation of one begging for mercy. The portrayal thus positions the protesters as the powerful bullies. This portrayal of the relationship between the protesters and counter-protesters contrasts sharply with that provided by the pro-movement press. *Apple Daily*'s editorial on October 3, for instance, criticized the pro-establishment camp for "mobilizing their forces, making use of the inconveniences caused by Occupy Central to create conflicts, and thus trying to arouse the dissatisfaction of the affected citizens." In other words, the counter-protesters were seen by the pro-movement newspaper as people organized and mobilized by a political force to achieve a political purpose.

It is difficult to collect systematic and definitive evidence regarding how many of the counter-protesters were mobilized by conservative groups to act. Throughout the movement, there were even rumors about the government and conservative groups linking with gangsters, with the latter responsible for organizing counter-protests and "causing troubles" in the occupied areas. Regardless of whether gangsters were indeed involved and how, mobilizing counter-protests was apparently an important strategy by the anti-movement camp to showcase anti-movement sentiments in the society, and creating conflicts around the occupied areas could also undermine the occupation's claim to be peaceful and nonviolent. Nonetheless, the discourse of public nuisance was important to the strategy of organizing counter-protests because it sustains the claim that the counter-protests were also the result of "self-mobilization" by ordinary people whose everyday lives were affected.

It is notable that, while the pro-movement newspapers tended to deny the factuality of foreign intervention in the movement and the breaching of the rule of law by the occupation, they did not—probably because they could not—contest the factuality of nuisances and inconveniences caused by the occupation. The editorial of *Ming Pao* on October 1 spent two full paragraphs outlining the various negative impact of the occupation on people's everyday lives and Hong Kong's economy. But rather than criticizing the occupation, the point of the article is to urge the occupiers to beware of alienating the public. The editorial also suggested that the Chief Executive C. Y. Leung should not make use of the negative impact of occupation as ammunitions to attack the movement. *Apple Daily*'s editorial on October 15 is titled "There is no social movement in this world that does not interfere with people's lives." It pointed out that many social movements do not have the support of the majority of the public. "Causing nuisances to many people and leading many citizens to feel disgruntled is a common scenario for social movements around the world." But when people are fighting for justice and equality instead of personal gains, people would need to insist even when they are opposed by the majority.

Nevertheless, as the movement continued, the inconveniences and nuisances inevitably accumulated. Toward the end of the movement, even the pro-movement newspapers began to invoke the theme of public nuisance and called upon the protesters to consider retreating. By November 22, *Apple Daily*'s editorial would state that, "under the current scenario, even escalating the action could not force the dominant power to make concessions, while insisting on occupying roads would affect the normal lives of citizens, perhaps it is time to show that the occupiers have the ability to retreat." *Ming Pao*'s editorial on December 12, in the midst of the police eviction in the various occupied areas, stated approvingly: "in fact, many social figures have long called for the end of the occupation, so that the life of the affected citizens can return to normalcy. Although the day arrives rather late, it illustrates the capability of the Hong Kong society to self-adjust." In other words, public nuisance turned out to be the theme that even movement supporters found difficult to dismiss. It became the justification for the end of occupation that was accepted by various actors across the political divide.

Anti-Movement Communication in Social Media

While the previous section has reconstructed three major counter-frames articulated by the pro-establishment camp through analyzing mainstream media discourses, the ideas and themes associated with the counter-frames could be expected to have been diffused through interpersonal communication and a wide range of digital media platforms. Studies of the political impact of digital and social media in Hong Kong have usually emphasized how such new media platforms constitute an online counter-public sphere or insurgent public sphere (e.g., Lee, 2015b; Lee, So, & Leung, 2015; Leung & Lee, 2014). The analysis in Chapter 4 has also shown that, among Hong Kong citizens, political communication via social media during the Umbrella Movement was positively associated with more positive attitudes toward the movement and higher levels of likelihood of having participated in it. However, it does not mean that the anti-occupation camp and their supporters did not utilize social media to communicate and promote their views.

In fact, various scholars have noted that authoritarian governments around the world have devised sophisticated methods of controlling and censoring the Internet (Hussain & Howard, 2013; MacKinnon, 2013; Pearce & Kendzior, 2012). An important aspect of Internet control in many contemporary authoritarian systems is that the governments do not merely suppress expressions and censor content in a reactive manner; they also proactively mobilize their own supporters to engage in online expressions so as to manipulate the online opinion climate. The presence of the so-called fifty-cents—people reportedly paid by the government to post pro-regime messages online—is a well-known phenomenon in mainland China (Han, 2015; Yang, 2016). The "fifty-cents" phenomenon was also emerging in Hong Kong at the time of the Umbrella Movement. Although there is a lack of systematic documentation, one can often see a significant number of pro-establishment messages, sometimes couched in inflammatory rhetoric, when reading the comments under the news stories on the websites of mainstream news media.

In the Umbrella Movement, one important set of anti-movement communications through digital media was constituted by online rumors, as Chapter 5 mentioned. It is hardly possible to trace how the rumors were produced. Some simplistic rumors, such as a claim that a high school girl was sexually harassed in the occupied area, could conceivably be a result of unintentional miscommunication among anxious citizens. But some more elaborate rumors were obviously intentionally produced and deliberately crafted. One notorious example is an audio clip broadcast by a radio station on September 30 and then circulated widely through WhatsApp among citizens. In the clip, an old woman tells the story, in a sorrowful tone, of how a four-hour traffic jam caused by the occupation prevented her and her family to go to the hospital in time to see her daughter-in-law, who was dying of cancer. Many citizens pointed out on the Internet that there were no traffic jams on the night and at the places mentioned in the story. That is, the story was fabricated and "professionally performed." It strongly hints at the organized production of anti-movement rumors.

Certainly, parts of the counter-movement communications in the digital arena can be much less elusive, ominous, and morally questionable. While the pro-movement citizens and groups set up many Facebook public pages for the production, collection, and sharing of pro-movement information and messages, the anti-occupation forces could do the same. Specifically, a number of pro-government citizen-groups were established in the few years before the Umbrella Movement. These groups often appeared in the news media as they were active in organizing counter-protests against the pro-democracy camp. They also set up their Facebook public pages or sites. For example, Caring Hong Kong Power operates a "public forum" on Facebook, which had more than 9,000 members as of early 2016. Justice Alliance started operating a Facebook public page in 2013, though its Facebook activities were much less frequent and hence had attracted only about 800 likes by early 2016.

Two of the most prominent Facebook public pages belonging to the anti-occupation camp are the page of the aforementioned Silent Majority for Hong Kong (Silent Majority) and Speak Out Hong Kong (Speak Out). The former had more than 114,000 likes by early 2016. The latter is an online information hub founded in early January 2013 by the Hong Kong United Foundation Limited, which had close connections with Chief Executive C. Y. Leung. Hence the page was widely regarded as an extension of the public relations arm of the Chief Executive Office. As of early 2016, the page had more than 220,000 likes.[8]

The numbers of page likes attracted by the two pages are thus comparable to that obtained by the public pages of OCLP and HKFS. It needs to be pointed out that some pro-democracy citizens have "liked" these pages so as to monitor the messages shared by them. This is especially the case for Speak Out due to the supposed connection between the page and the government. But this does not negate the fact that the anti-occupation camp does have their substantial following in the social media arena.

Speak Out published 287 recoverable posts about the Umbrella Movement between September 28 and December 15, whereas Silent Majority published 386 posts in the period. The posts attracted an average of 5,352 likes, 663 shares, and 679 comments. These figures are substantially larger than those obtained by the posts published by the three main organizers of the movement (which are 1,203 likes, 257 shares, and 71 comments for the three groups combined), as well as those obtained by the most prominent pro-movement Facebook public pages created during the movement. One possible interpretation is that pro-movement discourses and communications were much more dispersed across a much larger number of outlets in the social media arena. Hence the attention attracted by any specific platform would be diluted. In contrast, anti-movement discourses in social media were seemingly much more concentrated into a few sites.

There are subtle differences in the content of the posts on Speak Out and Silent Majority. As Silent Majority represents a group established with the specific aim of opposing Occupy Central, the posts on its Facebook page were relatively more likely to be based on original content. Some of the posts were about the activities of the group itself. The posts of Silent Majority were also more likely to target at the Trio. After the movement began on September 28, several posts questioned the Trio for manipulating the students and pushing them onto the frontline. Even after it was clear that the movement had been transformed, the Trio was still largely treated as the ones pulling strings behind. It remained the case until the Trio declared to leave the occupied area in late October. In contrast, Speak Out relied much more on materials from the mainstream press and other social media channels. Its posts focused relatively more on highlighting the anti-movement views expressed by social and political elites, such as celebrities in the entertainment industry, who are widely recognized by the general public and yet usually not known for their political views.

Moreover, Silent Majority was willing to "go further" than Speak Out in offering their anti-movement interpretations of ongoing events and images from the occupied scene. Most illustrative was how Silent Majority "reported" about the tear gas on September 28 and the "dark corner incident" on October 15, which was discussed in Chapter 5. Regarding the former, Speak Out refrained from showing any images of tear gas in their posts. In contrast, several posts of Silent Majority showed images of tear gases separating the protesters and the police. One post was published with the note: "Mr Tai has always said that they would call off Occupy Central once violence appears or control is lost. So it turns out that, for the occupiers, these scenes are not violent." The statement thus disregarded who was perpetrating the violence and merely pointed to the presence of violence at the protest site and criticized the Trio for not keeping their promise.

Regarding the dark corner incident, the immediate response from Speak Out was to highlight the police's official statement that they would investigate and handle the matter seriously and fairly. Afterward, the page published a post quoting TV news reports and online information that the social worker who was later attacked by the police had thrown "unknown liquid" onto the police during the earlier protest. In comparison, Silent Majority was more adamant in treating the police violence in the dark corner incident as merely the reaction to earlier provocation. A couple of posts claimed that the liquid thrown by the social worker was mixed with excrement. One post of Silent Majority also offered explicit support for TVB on its treatment of the news story.

Consistent with its approach of dealing with the dark corner incident, Speak Out seemingly attempted to construct an image of the anti-occupation citizens as reasonable and civilized. As mentioned in Chapter 5, there were discussions of people unfriending each other on Facebook due to political differences after the movement began. Speak Out published a post on September 30, quoting a letter written by an ordinary citizen saying her friend had "unfriended" her because of her belief that the police were not to blame. In response, the letter writer stated, "friend, I see you as a friend for my whole life." Another post on October 22 criticized the "wave of unfriending people" as "unlike Hong Kong." These messages evoked a picture in which the Umbrella Movement supporters were the only ones who had unfriended others, whereas the movement opponents were always open-minded and remained loyal to their friends even when they were treated badly. Similarly, after the televised meeting between the representatives of the HKFS and top government officials on October 21, Speak Out published a few posts quoting public figures and social elites who said that it was time for reasoned dialogue. These posts posited the anti-occupation camp as the "reasonable party" in the conflict, thus implicitly positing the occupiers as unreasonable.

Certainly, behind the differences, the communications through the two anti-occupation Facebook pages had the same functions of offering a continual stream of anti-movement narration of the ongoing happenings; enlarging the circulation of information that would put the movement under negative light; expressing support for the government and the police; foregrounding the support the anti-movement camp had across various social sectors; portraying the protesters and the movement leaders as deviant, ignorant, and/or evil; and, in relation to the analysis in the previous section, perpetuating and reciting the major counter-movement frames already articulated in the mainstream media.

We conducted a simple coding of the posts to examine if they contained ideas related to the foreign intervention frame (e.g., highlighting the financial support offered to the occupation movement by foreign agencies), the rule of law frame (e.g., criticizing the occupiers for not following the court injunctions), and the public nuisance frame (e.g., highlighting various impact of the occupation on citizens' everyday lives). The results showed that only 4.2% of the posts from the two public pages invoked the idea of foreign intervention, but 34.6% invoked the idea of the rule of law, and 42.9% invoked the idea of public nuisance. This is consistent with the argument made in the previous section that the foreign intervention frame was more difficult to sustain by hard evidence and relatively "alien" to the local political culture. The posts related to foreign intervention mainly quoted the coverage of pro-establishment media about the connections between the movement leaders and various kinds of "foreign agents." Comparatively, the ideas of the rule of law and public nuisance were invoked much more frequently because they were often embedded in the anti-movement comments expressed by public figures and quoted in the Facebook pages. On the whole, the three frames could be regarded as quite dominant, as nearly 66% of the posts contained ideas related to at least one of the three major counter-frames.

The prominence of the three counter-frames did not vary significantly between the two Facebook pages. But their relative prominence varied over the course of the movement. Consistent with the pattern observable from mainstream media discourses, the foreign intervention frame was more prominent in the earlier stage of the movement: 6.4% of the posts published in September and October invoked the idea of foreign intervention, whereas only 1.3% of the posts in November and December did so ($\chi^2 = 10.6$, $p < .01$). The rule of law frame, in contrast, became more prominent in the later stages of the movement: 27.1% of the posts in September and October invoked the idea of the rule of law, whereas 44.1% of the posts in November and December did so ($\chi^2 = 21.1$, $p < .001$). The public nuisance frame became somewhat less prominent over time (46.0% in September and October vs. 39.1% in November and December), but the decline is not statistically significant ($\chi^2 = 3.3$, $p = .07$). Posts with and without invoking ideas related to the three major counter-frames did not differ from each other in terms of the number of likes, shares, and comments attracted.

In sum, anti-movement discourses were not unlike the pro-movement discourses in how they were circulating in an integrated media environment comprising both mass media outlets and digital media platforms. Compared to the pro-democracy camp, the anti-movement camp's presence in social media was less well established, probably because of the perception that supporters of the anti-movement camp are generally older and hence relatively less likely to be avid users of social media. But Tsui (2015) has commented that the government and the pro-establishment groups in Hong Kong are catching up quickly in their digital media tactics. This above analysis should have suggested why the social media activities of the pro-establishment forces should not be neglected.

Discursive Construction of Public Opinion in the News

As indicated at the beginning of this chapter, public opinion toward the Umbrella Movement was monitored by the polling industry throughout the occupation campaign. On the one hand, opinion polls could be considered as providing facts about where the public stood regarding the movement. But on the other hand, poll findings can be subjected to various treatments and interpretations. Hence polls can also be considered as merely providing the raw materials for the construction of images of public opinion (Herbst, 1993; Lewis, 2001; Stephens, 2012). Therefore, an analysis of how the mainstream media reported and interpreted the poll findings throughout the Umbrella Movement can help us further understand the shifting opinion climate surrounding the movement and the dynamics in public discourses that preceded the end of the occupation.

We derived a corpus of relevant newspaper articles for analysis from Wise News. The keywords set used was one of the identifying labels of the movement plus either "man-ji diu caa" (opinion polling) or its abbreviation "man-diu." The search was restricted to five newspapers, including the Communist-sponsored Wen Wei Po and Ta Kung Pao, the pro-government Sing Tao Daily, the professional and somewhat liberal-oriented Ming Pao, and the pro-democracy Apple Daily. The search resulted in a total of 543 articles published between September 28 and December 15. They include news reports, editorials, and commentary pieces.[9]

THE SELECTIVE REPORTING OF POLL FINDINGS

The first poll directly addressing the occupation was reported by newspapers on October 1. Conducted by the Center for Social Policy Study (CSPS) at the Hong Kong Polytechnic University, the poll found that 59.8% of the respondents disagreed with the way the police handled the protest, whereas only 26% agreed; 46.3% believed that the Chief Executive C. Y. Leung and his subordinates bore the greatest responsibility for the situation, whereas 27.9% believed that the OC Trio bore the greatest responsibility.

Despite the timeliness of the survey, the poll was reported only by Ming Pao, Apple, and Sing Tao Daily. In the case of the pro-government Sing Tao Daily, the poll was reported in only two paragraphs at the end of an article mainly about pro-establishment politicians' criticisms against the movement. Ming Pao and Apple, in contrast, gave the survey full article treatment. A basic aspect of the politics of polling, therefore, was whether certain poll findings would be reported at all. While ignoring the first CSPS survey, conservative papers reported the surveys conducted by organizations with pro-establishment background more extensively. For instance, a survey conducted by the Hong Kong Research Association (HKRA) in mid-October found that 56% and 61% of the respondents, respectively, found the way the government and the police handled the protests acceptable. Wen Wei Po and Ta Kung Pao reported this survey prominently, whereas Apple and Ming Pao neglected it.

Certainly, there were numerous occasions when the same poll was reported by newspapers with differing political predilections. The university polls, in particular, were difficult to completely ignore given the conductors' presumed credibility. Yet newspapers could adopt several reporting and discursive strategies to construct their preferred image of public opinion. These strategies include the choice of headlines, subtle lexical choices, construction of the immediate context for the poll findings, and the use of quotations from sources. Take *Sing Tao Daily*'s and *Apple*'s reports on October 6, which are about another survey conducted by Hong Kong Polytechnic University' CSPS, as the example:

> [*Apple*] Opinion poll: CY the most responsible for violence[10]
> Amidst disturbances in the occupied areas created by triad societies and the frequent occurrence of violent attacks and harassment of protesters, [CSPS] conducted a survey on the evening of October 4, that is, after days of riots in the Mong Kok occupied area. The largest number of respondents believed that Chief Executive C. Y. Leung, the Hong Kong government, and government officials were the most responsible for the occurrence of the "occupation movement" and the violent attacks in recent days.

> [*STD*] Forty percent of respondents trusted the police force
> A survey by [CSPS] shows that nearly 30 percent of citizens believed that Chief Executive C. Y. Leung and the Hong Kong SAR Government are most responsible for the violent attacks targeting the occupy movement in recent days. About 13 percent believed that the Occupy Central Trio were the most responsible. The citizens were split on their views toward the trustworthiness of the police, as the scores zero and 10 were each given by 10 percent of people.

Both lead paragraphs focus on the same findings. But several notable differences between the two newspapers exist. First, *Apple* highlighted the finding unfavorable toward the government in the headline. Second, *Apple* emphasized explicitly that the Chief Executive and the government were considered as "the most responsible" party. In contrast, *Sing Tao Daily* only stated the percentages; it did not state explicitly which party was considered by the public as a whole as more responsible. Third, *Apple* contextualized the poll findings by foregrounding the violent attacks committed by triad societies in the occupied areas. This posited the occupiers as deserving support. Fourth, the *Sing Tao Daily* article included the finding of citizens' trust toward the police in the lead, and public opinion toward the police was described as being "split." The image *Sing Tao Daily* constructed, therefore, was a public without a clear majority. The images of public opinion created in the two articles differed as a result of selective emphasis and accentuation of the poll findings.

The possibility and significance of selective emphasis and accentuation reside in the fact that a single poll often presents "mixed results": some findings are apparently favorable to the movement, whereas others are apparently favorable to the government. Another case in point is the October poll by Chinese University's CCPOS mentioned at the beginning of this chapter. It registered nominally more citizens supporting than opposing the movement. Yet the same poll also found that the proportion of citizens supporting the legislature to pass the political reform under the framework laid down by the NPC had increased, a finding favorable toward the government. Furthermore, more than half of the respondents supported passing the political reform plan if the nomination committee were to further democratize.

Most newspapers reported the survey. The Communist-sponsored *Wen Wei Po* highlighted the finding most favorable toward the government in the headline, which reads "55% support political reform if the nomination committee becomes more democratic." The article is brief. Levels of support for and opposition toward the occupation were described as "similar to each other." *Sing Tao Daily* also published only a 241-word article recounting the survey findings straightforwardly. In contrast, *Apple* published an 835-word report headlined "The spirit of sacrifice and resistance has moved Hong Kong people; more people support than oppose the movement." The lead paragraph emphasized the magnitude of changes in public opinion after the beginning of the occupation through repeatedly using the phrase "increase (or decrease) substantially." The end of the lead paragraph repeated the explanation: "some legislators believe that the sincerity and the spirit of sacrifice exhibited by the occupiers have moved Hong Kong people." The pro-democracy legislators' view would appear a third time in the last paragraph of the article. It thus becomes the "anchor" for the whole article, fixing its overall tone and theme.

CONVERGENCE OF POLL FINDINGS AND THE "MAINSTREAM PUBLIC"

As discussed in previous chapters, the police's use of tear gas on September 28 led to "mediated instant grievances" (Tang, 2015) among the watching public and mobilized people to join the occupation. But as the government was unwilling to make quick concessions, there were calls from prominent pro-movement figures for a strategic retreat as early as around mid-October. Researchers aiming at capturing public reactions toward the newest developments thus started to ask questions about whether the movement should retreat. Polytechnic University's CSPS was again the first to ask the question. We can compare *Apple*'s and *Ta Kung Pao*'s report on November 5:

> *Apple*: The occupation action has persisted for over a month, [CSPS] announced the third round of its "occupation movement" survey yesterday. The results showed that as high as 73.2% of the respondents tended to agree to retreat, whereas 26.8% disagreed.
> *Ta Kung Pao*: The "Occupy Central" action has damaged Hong Kong for nearly 40 days. The mainstream public opinion has become clearer and clearer– the occupiers should immediately retreat. Polytechnic University announced yesterday the newest round of survey results regarding Hong Kong citizens' views on the development of "Occupy Central." More than

70% of the respondents agreed that the occupiers should retreat. Among these people, the largest number worried that the occupation action would affect the economy and people's livelihood.

The differences between the two reports are similar to the differences in the previous examples. One newspaper reported the poll relatively straightforwardly, juxtaposing the percentages of people holding contrary views without making an explicit statement of where the public as a whole stands. But since the key finding here is unfavorable to the movement, *Apple* is the newspaper adopting the style of simple factual reporting.

Ta Kung Pao described the "mainstream public opinion" as "becoming clearer and clearer." The presumption is that an anti-movement "mainstream public" has long existed. In fact, "mainstream public opinion" (*zyu-lau man-yi*) was a frequently utilized figure of speech in the Communist-sponsored press. A search in Wise News found that the term appeared in 128 *Wen Wei Po* articles and 88 *Ta Kung Pao* articles during the Umbrella Movement. In contrast, it appeared in only 30 *Ming Pao* articles and 5 *Apple* articles in the period.

The pro-establishment press's invocation of "mainstream public opinion" was supported by a seeming convergence of poll findings since late October. CCPOS also found that nearly 70% of respondents agreed that the movement should retreat. In addition, various opinion polls produced a range of other findings unfavorable toward the movement. CCPOS found that the proportion of movement supporters had gone down in November, while the proportion of movement opponents had gone up. The monthly survey by Hong Kong University's Public Opinion Programme found an increase in the approval rating of Chief Executive C. Y. Leung from October to November. These ratings have not included the results from polls conducted by pro-establishment parties and organizations. In the pro-establishment media, the poll findings not only became evidence for the presence of an anti-movement "mainstream public," they also became the basis for the construction of a moral critique of the movement. For instance, *Sing Tao Daily*'s editorial on November 9 wrote:

> The spirit of democracy is to respect the will of the majority. . . . But the representatives of the HKFS treated public opinion as worn out shoes and disregarded it on the question of whether to retreat or not. Recent public attitude is very clear. Polytechnic University's survey shows that more than 70 percent of people, including supporters of Occupy Central, thought that this should be the time to retreat. . . . However, in their recent speeches, representatives of the HKFS did not mention "the majority view" at all. The principle of democracy has quietly disappeared.

Similar invocation of the principle of majority rule appeared extensively in other pro-establishment newspapers. By invoking the principle, such discourses conclude that it is *morally* wrong for the movement to reject the call to retreat. The movement was therefore portrayed as selfish and stubborn. This argument, however, assumes that the principle of majority rule is pertinent to a social movement's decision-making. It disregarded the fact that social movements often represent the views, interests, and values of specific social groups—who are sometimes the minorities in the society—instead of the public at large, and movements do not make socially binding and authoritative decisions. Democratic principles such as majority rule may be pertinent to the internal operation of a movement, but a movement does not have a moral obligation to adopt the society's majority view. Rather, the aim of many social movements is exactly to change the society's majority view.

Besides the principle of majority rule, the "mainstream public opinion" was also articulated with the rule of law frame:

> Recent surveys . . . show that the proportion of people opposing the move-ment substantially surpasses the proportion of people supporting the movement. The rule of law is a core value of Hong Kong. . . . The opposi-tion faction publicly initiates law-breaking actions and hence completely violates Hong Kong people's values. How can it gain the support of the majority? (Chan Yung, November 22, *Ta Kung Pao*)

> . . . more than 90 percent of the respondents agreed that the rule of law is Hong Kong's core value. . . . It not only shows that respecting the rule of law is the mainstream public opinion in Hong Kong; it also shows that citizens are extremely worried about the law-violating "Occupy Central." (Editorial, October 31, *Wen Wei Po*)

Through such articulation, the "mainstream public" took up the desirable charac-ter of being a law-respecting and law-abiding public. The articulation strengthens the argument for the movement to follow the majority: not only because of the principle of majority rule in abstract procedural terms, but also because the current . "majority opinion" is rooted in the core values of the city.

REACTING TO THE "PUBLIC OPINION REVERSAL" IN THE PRO-MOVEMENT MEDIA

How did the pro-democracy media react to the survey results unfavorable toward the movement? We can first look at *Apple*'s coverage of CCPOS's survey on November 17:

> Reversal in public opinion: 43.5% of people do not support occupation
>   The occupation movement has entered the 51st day. A survey by the Chinese University shows that public opinion has reversed when compared

to one month ago. The proportion of people not supporting the occupation surpasses the proportion of supporters by nearly 10 percent. 67.4 percent of citizens thought that the occupiers should retreat completely, and only 13.9 percent opposed. There are also more than half of the respondents who thought that the government should make concrete concessions to resolve the current deadlock. Some occupiers stated that they still refuse to retreat and will stay until genuine popular election is successfully achieved.

Even in the face of largely unfavorable opinion, *Apple*'s pro-movement character is indicated by its highlighting of the finding that more than half of the respondents regarded the government as having the responsibility to make further concessions. Nevertheless, the most important characteristic of *Apple*'s coverage is its use of "reversal of public opinion" (*man-cing jik-zyun*) as the overarching description of the survey results.

One can talk about a reversal only if a value first rises and then falls (or vice versa). Hence the idea of reversal presumes the existence of more than two time points. Indeed, CCPOS conducted three surveys in September, October, and November. The proportion of citizens supporting the movement increased from 31.9% in September to 37.8% in October, and then fell back to 33.9% in November. Nevertheless, "reversal" is not the only possible interpretation here. It is also possible to argue that level of public support for the Umbrella Movement remained relatively stable, hovering between 30% and 40%. Alternatively, one might emphasize the fact that public support for the movement in November remained at a level slightly higher than that registered before the occupation began. In contrast, the idea of "reversal in public opinion" connoted the likelihood of continuing decline of public support for the movement.

In fact, poll results in December would find the proportion of movement supporters staying almost exactly the same as in November. But "reversal of public opinion" remained the preferred description utilized in the pro-movement newspapers and some of the centrist newspapers. The phrase "*man-yi jik-zyun*" or "*man-cing jik-zyun*" appeared in 15 *Apple Daily* articles and 32 *Ming Pao* articles in the period. It appeared in only 10 articles in *Ta Kung Pao, Wen Wei Po,* and *Hong Kong Commercial Daily* combined together. For the Communist-sponsored press, reversal of public opinion was not an appropriate description because "the mainstream public" was regarded as opposing the movement from the beginning.

For *Apple* and *Ming Pao*, adopting the notion of public opinion reversal was consistent with their preference for a retreat by the Umbrella Movement by November. The image of the reversed public opinion was invoked largely in connection with a strategic discourse about how the movement should move ahead. *Ming Pao*'s editorial on November 14 argued:

> As long as we look into the objective reality, everyone would know that the occupation movement has been degraded into a minority act. . . . Facing the reversal of public sentiments and the dissolution of public support, the

perpetuation of the movement's energy has become a problem. . . . The occupation movement is not going to achieve concrete results on the issue of democratic election. It is really unwise to insist on occupying roads and being the enemy of citizens.

This extract shows that *Ming Pao* had become critical toward the movement by mid-November. Phrases such as "degraded into a minority act" put the legitimacy of the movement into question. But *Ming Pao* did not claim that the movement was morally wrong to refuse to retreat. The judgment is primarily strategic: the movement would be "unwise" not to do so, as substantive achievement had become unlikely. In *Apple*, many authors similarly invoked public opinion to articulate arguments about proper strategies:

[the poll conductor] . . . interpreted the finding as suggesting that the marginal utility of the movement is declining . . . this kind of poll findings is a warning. How to avoid losing support and how to occupy more people's hearts have become an urgent task. (Lee Wai-ling, November 6, *Apple*)

If the occupation movement can retreat peacefully at this point, it could conserve the remaining public support for civil disobedience. If the occupation continues as the occupiers wish, it is difficult to guarantee that [violent events] would not happen again. It would only lead the occupation movement into the quagmire of oppositional public opinion. (Luk Yan-chi, November 24, *Apple*)

Both authors positioned themselves as writing from the perspective of the movement. The first author refrained from making concrete suggestions about what the movement should do. She only pointed toward the need to consider how to win public support. The second passage called for a retreat more explicitly. But regardless of the differences, the two extracts shared the same strategic mindset and argumentation in terms of cost-benefit calculation.

Considered together, the analysis here and in the previous subsection show that, by late November and early December, despite the differences in the logics and moral evaluations invoked, the mainstream media had converged to call for the end of occupation partly based on supposedly objective evidences from opinion polls. The movement, in other words, was portrayed to have lost the battle of public opinion.

The End of Occupation

This chapter has examined how the government and the anti-occupation camp in general responded to the Umbrella Movement, with a particular focus on three

counter-frames promulgated through the mainstream media and then further diffused and communicated via digital media platforms. There is no systematic evidence regarding to what extent the three specific frames had affected how people
thought about the Umbrella Movement. But overall speaking, the discursive efforts
on the part of the pro-establishment camp had seemingly solidified the view of the
anti-movement public and hence ensured that the movement would not win further public support. Besides, two of the three counter-frames were closely tied to
concrete actions undertaken by the government and the pro-establishment groups.
The frames thus also served to legitimize the main counter-movement strategies
utilized by the power holders, including the use of legal means to undermine the
movement and the mobilization of counter-protests.

Toward the later stages, the mainstream media even converged to portray public opinion as increasingly turning against the occupation. The image of public
opinion was constructed by the media in the sense that it was not the only possible interpretation of the available evidences at the time. But the mainstream
media did not construct images of public opinion out of nothing either. There
was indeed a substantial majority of citizens favoring the end of occupation since
early November.

The movement thus faced a strategic dilemma. They could decide to follow the
wish of the general public, withdraw from the occupied areas, and reconsider the
next step. But this could be equivalent to admitting defeat, since the movement had
yet to achieve any tangible outcomes in the form of meaningful concessions from
the government. Practically, a substantial proportion of the occupiers were likely to
defy any calls to retreat issued by the central organizers. In the latter scenario, the
central organizer might be further lambasted for leaving their supporters behind if
they decided to end the occupation by themselves.

Simply continuing the occupation was also not an attractive option. As already
pointed out in Chapter 1, the Umbrella Movement differs from Occupy Wall Street
and some other occupation movements around the world in that it had a clear policy goal that needed to be resolved within a given time frame. Moreover, since the
main roads in the urban districts in Hong Kong were occupied, continual occupation could indeed lead to the accumulation of adverse impact on people's everyday
lives, generating more and more public grievances. Meanwhile, there were concerns
about fatigue among the occupiers and the conditions on the street when the city
entered winter.

Hence, if the organizers did not want to retreat, they would need to develop
new strategies and actions. One possibility was to escalate the action to a new
level of disruptiveness, but this might entail the use of violence and thus would
deviate from the principle of nonviolence. In fact, there were calls from part of
the movement participants to abandon the principle of nonviolence. We would
not examine closely how the central organizers deliberated on the matter at the
time. Suffice it to note that the central organizers maintained the necessity of

the principle of nonviolence, and yet seemingly failed to come to an agreement among themselves on how to carry the movement forward. In late October, the Trio left the occupied area and returned to their work. Then, three core members of the HKFS tried to go to Beijing on November 15 to "express Hong Kong people's demands" to the Chinese government during the APEC meetings. But they were stopped by airline staffs at the Hong Kong Airport, saying that their Home Return Permits—the identification card that allows Hong Kong people to enter the mainland—were no longer valid.

The strategic stalemate also made it more difficult for the movement leaders to maintain control of the whole movement. In the night of November 19, a group of mask-wearing protesters charged the Legislative Council Building and crashed the glass windows and doors. Anti-riot police were dispatched. Physical confrontations between the police and the protesters ensued. The protesters' action was predictably condemned by the conservative media outlets. But even *Apple Daily* reported the incident with the headline "masked challengers damaged the occupation movement." As the action deviated from the proclaimed principle of nonviolence, the Trio, HKFS, Scholarism, and the major pro-democracy political parties all expressed their disapproval.

Nevertheless, Scholarism's leader Joshua Wong insisted that there was no need to "condemn" the action. Wong's careful and measured response illustrated his understanding of the tension within the movement at the time. As a matter of fact, calls for escalating the action did not stop. On November 30, Scholarism and HKFS finally decided to escalate the action through attempting to surround the whole Government Headquarters. About 5,000 protesters joined the action. The police used pepper spray, batons, and water cannons to drive the protesters away. The plan to surround the Government Headquarters failed, and the HKFS would later be heavily criticized by some movement participants for various mistakes in the execution of the escalation.

On December 1, three leading figures of Scholarism went on hunger strike, but the hunger strike ended after a few days for medical reasons. These various actions largely failed to generate new momentum for the movement. On December 3, when Scholarism's hunger strike was still ongoing, the Trio, together with other prominent participants of the occupation such as the former Catholic Bishop Joseph Żen and a number of pro-democracy legislators, surrendered themselves to the police in order to fulfill their promise of being willing to bear the legal consequences of the act of civil disobedience.

Earlier, on November 24, with the court injunction in hand, the legitimation by the rule of law discourse, and the support of a majority public opinion, the police had already evicted the Mong Kok occupied area. The police then evicted the Admiralty occupied area on December 11. In the Admiralty eviction, hundreds of movement participants stayed in the occupied area. They returned to the original script of Occupy Central: sitting down on the road, holding each other's arms at the elbow, and letting the police taking them away one-by-one without resistance. It took the police only about 13 hours to complete the eviction. Since Admiralty was the original and arguably the main occupied area throughout the movement, the Admiralty eviction could be taken as signifying the end of the movement, though the eviction of the final Causeway Bay occupied area occurred only on December 15.

7

Conclusion

The previous chapters have provided an account of the emergence, transformation, evolution, and ending of the Umbrella Movement. We put the Umbrella Movement into the long-term context of the rise of social mobilization in Hong Kong since the turn of the century as well as the medium-term context of the Occupy Central campaign since early 2013. We emphasized the contingent events that led to the transformation of Occupy Central into the Umbrella Movement. For the occupation itself, we focused particularly on the role of digital and mass media in shaping its dynamics. We also examined the counter-movement strategies of the government and its allies.

As explicated in Chapter 1, one of the main aims of the book is to use the Umbrella Movement as a case to shed light on various general theoretical issues in the study of media and social movements in the digital era. Therefore, the core parts of this chapter will discuss the theoretical implications of the findings. We will, specifically, discuss how we may explain and understand the origins of large-scale protest campaigns in the digital era, the power and limitations of digital media and connective actions, the continual significance of framing and its relation to the question of movement outcomes, and the relationship between mainstream and digital media. When discussing these issues, we will also compare the Umbrella Movement to what we know about other major occupation campaigns in other countries. Albeit informal, the comparisons can shed light on the scope and level of generalizability of specific phenomena in the Umbrella Movement.

Toward the end of the chapter, we will briefly discuss the happenings in Hong Kong after the end of the Umbrella Movement. It allows us to comment on the possible impact of the occupation campaign on the future of social mobilization and the politics of democratization in the city. We will also discuss the possible role of digital and social media in the further evolution of social movements in Hong Kong.

Origins of Connective Action

Social movement scholars have noted for many years that the growth of Internet technologies has allowed the emergence of protest actions not organized and coordinated by conventional social movement organizations (Buechler, 2011; Earl & Kimport, 2011). Against this background, Bennett and Segerberg's (2013) logic of connective action was an attempt to theorize how the emergence of large-scale protest campaigns is possible without centralized mobilization and coordination.

However, as noted in Chapter 1, the logic of connective action is largely about how, but not why, large-scale protest campaigns can arise and persist in the absence of movement organizations. It could provide an inspiring account of, for instance, how Occupy Wall Street could happen. But it could not, by itself, explain why a large-scale protest against financial capitalism emerged in a specific historical juncture and social context. One immediate implication of this argument is that conventional perspectives and theories about movement emergence could remain crucial when our question is why a protest campaign arises, whether or not the protest campaign is taking up the characteristics of certain new movement formations or action logics.

The current study attempts to make sense of the Umbrella Movement in relation to the evolution of the pro-democracy movement in Hong Kong. The underlying premise is the importance of understanding a social movement in terms of local dynamics. Following a theoretical perspective emphasizing historical trajectories, conditioned contingencies, and interactions among players, we emphasize that an urge to radicalize has emerged in the social movement sector in Hong Kong when earlier forms of "peaceful and rational" protests have become routinized, normalized, and apparently ineffective (cf. Lee & Chan, 2011). This was the context against which the idea of Occupy Central was proposed. Nonetheless, the conservativeness of the local public culture and the criticisms leveled by the government and the pro-establishment forces against Occupy Central had led to a form of self-restrained radicalization. By the time the occupation began, Occupy Central was scripted as highly disciplined and expected to last for only several days. Occupy Central was transformed into the Umbrella Movement only because of a series of unpredictable events on its first day (Cheng & Chan, 2017).

The contingent happenings on the first day of the occupation campaign created the window of opportunity for the participants to take charge and start rewriting the script through improvisation. This was also the window of opportunity for digital and social media to start playing a much bigger role than originally planned. If Occupy Central had gone on as scripted, the relationship between digital media and the protest could have been largely restricted to how political communication via digital and social media might help communicating ideas and information about the occupation and thus mobilize people to support and join the action. But as the protest transformed, digital media–based connective action arose and exerted more wide-ranging influences on the form and dynamics of the movement. In the terminologies of Earl and Kimport (2011), without the context and event contingencies, digital media could have had only supersize effects but not "theory 2.0 effects" on the Umbrella Movement; that is, it could have enhanced the effectiveness of mobilization and thus enlarged the movement, but not lead to a transformation toward new movement formations.

The rise of connective action in the Umbrella Movement therefore differed from both crowd-enabled connective action and organizationally enabled connective action as conceptualized by Bennett and Segerberg (2013). Different from crowd-enabled connective action, the rise of connective action in the Umbrella Movement "followed"—temporally but not organizationally—the centralized planning by social movement groups. The occupation would not have arisen without the previous plans. And even after the transformation, the planning and scripting by the Occupy Central campaign remained influential on certain aspects of the movement, such as its persistent emphasis on nonviolence and the largely non-conflictive ending. Meanwhile, different from organizationally enabled connective action, the dispersed, personalized, and networked actions on the part of the participants were not proactively facilitated by the central organizers. The co-presence of connective actions and central organizers was unintended. In fact, our analysis of social media content suggested that the central organizers were not particularly active in reaching out and connecting themselves with the participant-initiated actions.

We describe the situation as one in which connective actions had intervened into a planned collective action campaign. In this characterization, the term "connective action" does not constitute a description of the protest campaign as a whole; it refers to a set of specific elements and/or a certain "logic" of action and mobilization that might be found in a larger protest campaign. Judging by the case of the Umbrella Movement, connective actions can arise and intervene into a planned protest campaign particularly significantly when the original script of the collective action is disrupted *and* the central leaders are, at least temporarily, unable to maintain control and steer the direction of the protest. In this situation, the participants have the need to improvise by themselves, and the presence of digital media, especially mobile devices, facilitate forms of real-time improvisation and coordination. Once the participants have started rewriting the script, by the time the central organizers are ready to reassert a certain degree of leadership, the campaign as a whole has already been transformed substantially, constraining the choices and decisions of the organizers.

Certainly, digital media and connective actions would not always intervene and transform a planned collective action campaign. There are times when there is simply no collective action campaign planned by powerful central organizations. The prelude to the Egyptian Revolution in 2011, for instance, included the death of the youngster Khalid Saeed in June 2010, the establishment of the Facebook page "We Are All Khalid Saeed" by activist Wael Ghonim and the circulation of materials and discourses that generated outrage against the regime, the Tunisian Revolution starting in December 2010, and several self-immolation attempts by Egyptian citizens, etc. There was a distinctive lack of "coordinated planning" in this process. There were also no clear leaders in the onset of the opposition movement, even though some individual activists (such as Ghonim and Asmaa Mahfouz) were credited as having a huge influence through the online contents they produced and/or distributed. The mobilization process, in other words, was from the beginning "centerless." It was a process through which discontent spread and snowballed for months, mainly through the online arena, before multiple groups and actors took action simultaneously on a designated day. Largely the same could be said about Occupy Wall Street.

In other cases, digital media and connective actions can constitute a significant part of a movement without transforming its basic configuration and leadership. The Sunflower Movement in Taiwan in 2014 is a case in point. The movement involved a 24-day occupation of the Legislative Yuan by mainly college students in opposition to a cross-strait trade agreement by the Taiwan and mainland Chinese governments. It was led mainly by the Democratic Front against Cross-Strait Trade in Services Agreement and the Black Island Youth. The former was a coalition of more-established civil society associations, whereas the latter was an informal association led by college students. The groups had already been staging protest actions against the trade agreement from 2013 to early 2014 but with little effect. The occupation action was triggered by the "30 seconds incident" on March 17, 2014, when a KMT legislator used only 30 seconds to conclude a meeting and declared the completion of the second reading of the trade agreement with China. It created a huge outcry. Students stormed the legislature the next evening (Ho, 2015).

After the occupation was successfully mounted, the protest also took up some features of a connective action campaign. The main slogan of the movement— "save our country by ourselves"—can be considered the personal action frame that drove many people to act without first agreeing on the detailed diagnostic and prognostic framing of the issue. Digital and social media played various roles in the movement (Cheng & Chen, 2016). There were also internal tensions within the movement (Kuo, 2016; Rowen, 2015). But over time, the occupation did not become as decentralized as the Umbrella Movement. In the end, the Sunflower Movement succeeded in gaining some concessions from the government, and the occupiers retreated peacefully. Some of the contrasts between the Sunflower Movement and the Umbrella Movement will be further discussed in later sections in relation to other theoretical issues. For the discussion here, one important point to note is that, throughout the Sunflower Movement, there was no "window" similar to the situation on September 28, 2014, during the onset of the Umbrella Movement, namely, a "window" within which the leaders lost control of the situation and could not communicate with their supporters, leaving the supporters to improvise by themselves.

In any case, there are reasons to believe that the unintended co-presence of elements of connective actions and centrally organized collective actions could constitute the norm rather than the exception. The rise in the capability by ordinary citizens to organize contentious actions by themselves would not render social movement organizations obsolete, especially because, when broad, long-term social movements are concerned, formal organizations remain crucial in sustaining the movement, especially during periods of low levels of mobilization (Melucci, 1989; Taylor, 1989). One might even argue that what Bennett and Segerberg (2013) called organizationally brokered collective actions are likely to remain "the majority" where forms of protests are concerned (e.g., Anduiza, Cristancho, & Sabucedo, 2014). Yet, armed with digital media, the possibility for self-coordinating citizens to intervene into centrally organized protests should be far from negligible. The capacity of citizens to self-coordinate and mobilize would only increase over time as more people have accumulated relevant experiences and become more familiar with technological practices relevant to citizen self-mobilization and coordination in a society. What this study puts forward is the claim that event contingencies would shape the degree to which and the ways by which connective actions intervene into a protest campaign, thereby shaping the latter's dynamics and potentially its outcome. The more specific research implication is that researchers may try to identify cases of "connective action intervention" and examine its conditions of emergence, dynamics, and consequences.

The Power and Limitations of Digital Media and Connective Actions

Digital and social media empowered the Umbrella Movement in a number of ways. They were the tools with which the participants coordinated both their improvised actions and planned activities; they were the platforms through which mobilizing information and messages circulated, thus contributing to citizens' level of participation. They were also the platforms on which citizens executed some of their self-initiated actions, such as dispelling rumors and transmitting real-time images from the occupied areas.

The participants were very active in a wide range of digital media communications and activities. The presence of a range of options allowed movement supporters and participants to construct their own mode of participation based on their personal situations and interests. Those having many international connections could explain the local situation to their friends and acquaintances outside Hong Kong; those who were comfortable with or interested in debating with others could proactively respond to anti-occupation comments online, while the more reflective individuals could write lengthy commentaries. Beyond the digital media arena, the Umbrella Movement also involved a large number of action opportunities for the participants, ranging from confronting counter-protesters to attending seminars in mobile classrooms. There were numerous personalized and/or small group–based actions, which together constructed the physical environment and atmosphere of the occupy sites.

At the individual level, our data show that those who were active in digital media activities tended to have spent more time in the occupied areas, to have asked others to join the movement, and to have participated in frontline activism and support provision activities. Digital media activities, different from what some authors have argued (Gladwell, 2010), did not constitute "slacktivism"—people did not stop participating in the more effortful, "real world actions" after participating in online activities. Rather, online activities and offline actions were intertwined with each other and mutually reinforcing. The findings are more in line with Castells's (2012) claim about the construction of a space of autonomy through combining cyberspace and urban space. They are also consistent with Chen, Chang, and Huang's (2016) empirical analysis of the Sunflower Movement in Taiwan, which found that hours spent in the sit-in actions outside the Legislative Yuan were positively associated with being mobilized by netizens and reliance on social media for information.

An additional point worth noting is how digital media allowed supporters to engage in monitorial participation in the Umbrella Movement. The notion of monitorial participation was raised in Chapter 4 in relation to the media's role as the partially censored public monitor, to which we will return below. Schudson (1998) has argued that we could not expect citizens to keep themselves fully informed all the time; we could only realistically expect them to monitor the society through the news media and take action when needed. Analogously, in an extended protest campaign, we cannot expect all supporters to spend huge amounts of time participating in the action. Rather, we can expect supporters to pay attention to the situation through the media and take action when needed. The quick scaling-up of the protest on September 28 as a result of the police's firing of tear gas can actually be understood as a manifestation of monitorial participation. Throughout the movement, both mass media institutions and digital media platforms continued to perform this function of facilitating citizens' monitorial participation.

The same function of digital media was noted by Taiwan scholars in relation to the Sunflower Movement (Cheng & Chen, 2016), even though they did not employ the concept of monitorial participation. In a study of a protest campaign in Romania, Mercea (2014) coined the notion of "casual participants" to refer to a group of experienced protesters who have limited linkages with social movement organizations and yet have activist friends and would repeatedly participate in protests on their own. These casual participants tend to rely on social media for information about collective actions. The monitorial participant is similar to the casual participant in that he or she is not a "full-blown activist" embedded in the organizational networks constituting the social movement sector and not necessarily spending a huge amount of time and efforts on contentious politics. But he or she is an experienced protester who takes actions when needed. One major difference between the two notions, however, is that the idea of "monitorial participant" connotes a more active and attentive citizen than the word "casual" connotes.

Admittedly, the protest onsite survey data did not contain items that can directly demonstrate the mode of monitorial participation and how it was linked to digital media activities. But the concept should be highly relevant to analyses of future large-scale, extended protest campaigns. The concept usefully highlights the relationship between a movement and a large number of its supporters and potential participants. It helps explain why a protest campaign can sometimes scale up quickly—many would be participants are already monitoring the situation through the media, and any trigger could drive a large number of them to act simultaneously.

Nevertheless, the Umbrella Movement is also a case pointing toward several limitations of and challenges posed by digital media and the logic of connective action. Our analysis has emphasized the point that digital media and connective actions introduced forces of decentralization to the occupation campaign. At the individual level, digital media activities were associated with degree of involvement in the movement. Yet when participants became more involved, they were also less willing to consider the views of the central organizers on important questions regarding movement strategies. Meanwhile, the central organizers were by no means well connected to the participant-initiated groups and public pages in social media.

Decentralization is not necessarily a problem for all movements and protests. Castells (2012) even regarded decentralization as an advantage of networked social movement because it increases the difficulty for the state to suppress the movement: there is no center for the state to target, and the network can reform and reconfigure itself quickly in face of suppression (also see Boler, MacDonald, Nitsou, & Harris, 2014). This argument is valid and, in a sense, even applicable to the Umbrella Movement. The emergence of multiple occupation sites was itself motivated by an attempt to prevent an early eviction by the police. It would have been easier for the Hong Kong government to quickly put the movement to an end if Occupy Central was not transformed into the more spatially decentralized form of the Umbrella Movement.

However, the more dispersed formation would be a particularly significant advantage for a movement mainly when the movement is non-programmatic and not restricted by a definite time frame. For Castells (2012), in the ideal-typical networked social movement or the concrete cases of Occupy Wall Street and the Arab Spring, the protesters do not have clear and concrete goals. They express a general outrage on a matter, but do not aim at seizing the state apparatus to put forward a specific line of policies. Hence the movement does not need a schedule and a definite temporal endpoint. Rather, it lives in "timeless time" and aims at perpetuating itself indefinitely.

In contrast, the Umbrella Movement was not non-programmatic, and the issue of democratic reform in Hong Kong had an "institutional timetable." Perpetuating itself was an important goal only to the extent that persistence can bring about the concrete outcome of "genuine popular elections" or at least some significant concessions by the government. The movement had to consider questions of strategies, negotiations, and compromises in order to achieve the best possible result, especially given the closed political opportunity structure in Hong Kong regarding the issue of democratic reform. The debate surrounding whether the movement should retreat from the occupied areas after the televised meeting between the HKFS and the government officials was fundamentally such a strategic debate. There were clear signs showing that at least part of the central organizers were in favor of a retreat, and at least they were willing to hold a referendum within the occupied areas. Putting aside whether a retreat at that point would really have produced better outcomes, the canceling of the referendum showed the lack of control on the part of the central organizers. It made continual negotiation with the government extremely difficult.

Certainly, this type of challenge posed by networked publics was already identified previously by other scholars, including Bennett and Segerberg (2013). In the concluding chapter of their book, they pointed out that action logics can collide. They described one of the several plausible scenarios as follows:

> Formerly dominant conventional organizations, whether in brokered or more loosely enabling coalitions, may lose control of campaigns, as crowds join in unilaterally and continue the pressure even when lead organizations deem it time to stop. As a result, such organizations can lose effective negotiation standing and credibility with targets that expect pressure to be relieved if they comply with some demands. (p. 203)

A recent study by Gerbaudo (2017) about the operation of "social media teams" in several protest movements also highlighted the tension between the ideology of a networked social movement and the strategic need of movement management. His analysis of Occupy Wall Street, Indignados, and UK Uncut found a contradiction "between the techno-libertarian principles of openness, horizontality, and leaderlessness, adhered to by digital activists and the strategic needs of giving a coherent direction of collective action and maintaining forms of control over the content that is produced on social media accounts" (p. 199).

In one sense, the Umbrella Movement involved another instantiation of the scenario noted by Bennett and Segerberg (2013). To go a step further, the Umbrella Movement might also help suggest certain conditions under which the challenges posed by connective actions would become particularly intractable. Besides the presence of a concrete demand and a strict timetable, as already noted, we have emphasized that the digital media communication and activities were connected to the already existing internal divisions within the movement. Such internal divisions have their own organizational, ideological, and spatial bases, and the strength of these divisions could in turn be influenced by other factors and event contingencies. Here, another comparison between the Umbrella Movement and the Sunflower Movement would be useful. During the Sunflower Movement, a relatively more radical group of activists staged a sit-in on March 23, 2014, in front of the Executive

Yuan and later broke into the government building. Yet the police succeeded in retaking control. Although the images of police violence led to further public sympathy for the students, the police action also prevented the movement from being split into two sites led by different groups of activists. It allowed a command structure to be reestablished quickly, despite persistent tensions within the movement (Ho, 2015).

In contrast, while the Mong Kok occupation was originally mounted on September 28 to protect the Admiralty occupation, it evolved into its own site hosting a different set of social groups and activists. The spatial division allowed clearer manifestations of the organizational and ideological divisions within the movement. Digital media and connective actions did not create such internal divisions or distrust among movement participants by themselves, but neither did they help resolve the division or generate trust by themselves. Rather, digital media seemed to have provided the platforms for the expression and possibly reinforcement of the internal divisions and distrust. As a result, what was constructed in the Umbrella Movement was not a singular space of autonomy, but spaces of autonomy.

On Frames and Movement Outcomes

Another factor influencing the capability of a movement to negotiate with the target is whether the movement leaders could articulate and persuade the networked publics to accept a relatively coherent frame for action. In the Umbrella Movement, some people arguing for a strategic retreat might ground their conclusion on the following considerations: (1) the political opportunity structure is essentially closed, as the Chinese government, fearing that other cities in China would make similar demands, would definitely not allow Hong Kong to have genuine democratic elections immediately; (2) in the worst-case scenario, China would rather suppress the movement using military force; (3) therefore, the movement should be ready to compromise and take partial gains; (4) limited partial gains on the electoral setup in 2017 may create new dynamics in the political system that would be conducive to further democratization; and (5) in order to realize the biggest possible partial gains, a strategic retreat, or at least an expression of a willingness to retreat under specific conditions, would be needed.

This is not the only possible line of argument for a strategic retreat, and the point here is definitely not to say whether the above line of argument is valid or not. The point is just that a specific line of strategies and actions needs to be supported by a set of claims regarding the opportunity structure within which a movement is embedded, claims regarding the likely reactions of the targets in different situations, and claims regarding the consequences of accepting any "partial gains" on continual contention in the future.

Articulating a more or less coherent discourse that would support a line of action is, of course, one of the most important functions of collective action frames. The purpose of a frame is to help people make sense of the issue at hand, and a typical ideological package would involve both diagnostic and prognostic framing, that is, the identification of the causes of the current problems and the methods to address the problems (Gamson & Modigliani, 1987, 1989). In the theoretical discussion of networked social movements and connective actions, however, the emphasis is often put on how simple personal action frames can allow higher levels of participation among the general public because of their symbolic inclusiveness. The fact that a slogan such as "I demand genuine popular election" does not require people to commit to a specific theory of what constitutes "genuine popular election," a specific electoral setup for the 2017 elections, a specific collective identity, and/or a specific line of action, is taken as advantageous for the purpose of mobilization. Yet relatively less attention is paid to whether there are any mechanisms in connective actions that can take up the other roles and functions of collective action frames understood in the conventional sense.

Putting it somewhat differently, in conventional movement practices as well as theorization, a social movement could begin with a specific collective action frame that may not resonate with all in the society. But over time, the collective action frame can become more inclusive through processes of frame transformation and frame alignment (Snow & Benford, 1988; Snow, Rochford, Worden, & Benford, 1986). For connective actions, there may be a need to move in the opposite direction: if a connective action starts with an inclusive and simple personal action frame, there could be a need for the actors to develop relatively coherent and substantive frames in order to justify lines of actions. For a collective action campaign intervened by connective actions, whether the organizers can generate and maintain a collective action frame that the networked publics would find agreeable could be a factor in shaping the overall impact of connective actions on the movement. In the Umbrella Movement, the collective action frame that would support compromises and strategic retreat never achieved a dominant status, thus contributing to the strategic impasse.

The significance of collective action frames goes beyond whether a movement can persuade its participants to agree on a line of action. The lack of a powerful collective action frame during the Umbrella Movement also affected how the movement related to the general public. Specifically, one might contend that the lack of successful framing was part of the reason why the Umbrella Movement did not obtain support from larger proportions of Hong Kong citizens.

Persuading and gaining support from the general public is another function of collective action frames that simple personal action frames cannot carry out. In the theorization by Bennett and Segerberg (2013) as well as by Castells (2012), the emphasis was put on how networked communications and personal action frames can generate actions based on already existing and shared grievances. Personal action frames "require little in the way of persuasion, reason, or reframing to bridge differences in others' feelings about a common problem" (Bennett & Segerberg, 2013, p. 37). Connective action, in this conceptualization, does not arise because people are persuaded to support a cause. Rather, the starting point "is the self-motivated (though not necessarily self-centered) sharing of *already internalized or personalized* ideas, plans, images, and resources with others" (Bennett & Segerberg, 2012, p. 753, emphasis added).

In this case, how can a networked social movement or a connective action campaign gain the support from those people who have not already internalized or personalized its ideas, images, and plans? Of course, the problem of persuading the general public to support one's cause and action would not arise if the movement is already representing the views of the majority and is adopting a form of action that is not opposed by the majority. In the Arab Spring, for instance, there was widespread public discontent against the existing regimes due to years of political corruption, poverty, and human rights violations. In the case of Occupy Wall Street, various national opinion polls conducted by media organizations and research companies in late 2011 showed more Americans supporting than opposing the movement, even though the margin varied across surveys. In Taiwan's Sunflower Movement, opinion polls throughout late March 2014 have consistently shown that a majority of the public was supportive toward the occupation of the legislature (Ho, 2015, p. 89). The situation was different in Hong Kong, where opinion polls before and during the campaign generally showed more opponents than supporters of the occupation among the public, with a poll conducted in mid-October during the movement as the sole exception.

This is not to say that a connective action campaign can never go beyond preaching to the choir; the point is that, when one is not already representing the majority in the society, one would have the need to preach beyond the choir. For this purpose, the simple personal action frames are not enough. Moreover, as the analysis in Chapter 6 illustrates, a protest movement may also need to face the challenge of the targets' and opponents' counter-framing efforts. On the whole, beyond the initial mobilization, the articulation of collective action frames remains important to a protest movement for a number of reasons. It is not sure if networked publics by themselves can develop the collective action frames agreeable to most participants in the movement as well as persuasive to the general public, and it is even possible that the logic of connective action would make the articulation and promotion of collective action frames by movement organizations more difficult.

Another limitation of digital media–facilitated connective actions that have been commented on by numerous observers is whether they are capable of achieving concrete outcomes. Again, the nature of this question might differ somewhat depending on whether the protest campaign is programmatic or not. The Umbrella Movement seems to be an example that a skeptic about networked social movements and connective actions can refer to. After all, the Hong Kong and Chinese government did not make any concession during and after the Umbrella Movement. In early 2015, the Hong Kong government issued a formal proposal about the electoral setup in 2017 that followed completely the parameters set by the Chinese Central Government. In June 2015, the Legislative Council voted down the reform proposal. The practical result is that the Chief Executive election in Hong Kong in 2017 followed the setup and procedure of the election in 2012, namely, the Chief Executive was elected by only a 1,200-member election committee whose membership was largely in the control of China.

Certainly, no one has ever claimed that networked social movements or connective actions are all-powerful and can achieve their outcomes easily. Social movements usually can achieve outcomes only through long-term struggles, and factors such as political opportunities (Kolb, 2007) and the presence of a supportive public (Giugni, 2004) have to be considered. Take the Sunflower Movement as the reference point again. The movement ended with the KMT's Legislative Yuan speaker Wang Jin-pyng pledging that the trade agreement with China would not be passed without review and some kind of regulatory supervision mechanism enacted. Although Wang's offer still fell short of the movement's demand, it was substantive and appealing to the movement leaders. Yet one of the most important reasons the Sunflower Movement could achieve such results was the internal conflicts among the KMT elites, especially the rift between Legislative Yuan speaker Wang and President Ma Ying-jeou (Rowen, 2015). As just noted, the Sunflower Movement also had the support of the majority of the public. In contrast, in the case of Hong Kong, there is a lack of elite allies who can bring the demands and pressure from the protesting public into the Chinese political system, and China is extremely unlikely to make major concessions to Hong Kong when it has to consider possible repercussions on the mainland. In fact, local scholars have long argued that, on political matters, social movements in Hong Kong are much more capable of defending existing rights than gaining new rights (Lui, 2003; Ma, 2005). This claim probably remains valid today as the political structure has not changed.

Nevertheless, it is not the intention of the present authors to posit the political opportunity structure as determining. Rather, recognizing the significance of the political opportunity structure and general public opinion, the analytical question is how the relationship between connective actions and movement outcomes varies under different conditions and given the varying nature of the movement's goal. Based on the experience of the Umbrella Movement, we may hypothesize that connective actions when undermine the capability of a movement to achieve positive outcomes when the political opportunity structure itself is unfavorable, and hence only limited, partial outcomes may be achieved through strategic negotiations between the movement and the target. But this is not to dismiss the value of connective actions. It is also possible that, when "defensive movements" are concerned, for instance, when the movement is against the establishment of a new law instead of pushing for a new policy, decentralized connective actions may be more effective and powerful.

Digital and Mainstream Media

While many current studies of social movements in the digital era focus primarily on the role of new media technologies in the emergence and coordination of protests, this book emphasizes the continual significance of the mainstream media. This is partly because, at least at this particular moment in history, mainstream media institutions have retained significant degrees of information dissemination, message amplification, agenda-setting, and status conferral power in societies (Molaei, 2015). In the case of the Umbrella Movement, opinion surveys found that mainstream media, especially television, remained by far the most important channels of public affairs information for the general public (So, 2015).

This is also partly because, even in the foreseeable future, mainstream media institutions are likely to remain a significant player in public communication. The plausibility of this claim is grounded in the recognition that the term "digital media" actually refers primarily to platforms for communication and content transmission, whereas the term "mainstream media" refers primarily to institutions of content production. To elaborate, in the traditional communication environment dominated by mass media institutions, a medium often refers simultaneously to an institution in charge of producing content, a particular technology for reproducing or transmitting the content, and a technological object through which the content is received. There was a general correspondence among institutions, transmission technologies, and technological objects: "television" referred to both the institutions producing the audiovisual content as well as the television set in people's homes, and people had to watch television mostly through television sets. Against this background, one important impact of the advance of new media technologies is the dissociation among institutions, transmission technologies, and technological objects. In this scenario, the distinction between digital media and conventional mass media is misleading if it is taken to mean that the two are distinctive and separate communication platforms competing with each other. Rather, mass media institutions can operate on or have their content widely shared through digital media platforms.

Once the above is recognized, the question is no longer whether digital media will displace mainstream media. The question is whether, even as digital media platforms become the primary communication platforms for citizens in the society, the society and the citizenry still need resourceful and centralized institutions to produce professional content for general, mass consumption. It is beyond the scope of this book to discuss this question thoroughly, but our overall answer is a qualified yes. The production of certain types of content, ranging from investigative news stories to top-quality entertainment products, is likely to continue to rely on the pooling together of capital, knowledge, talents, and other kinds of resources by media organizations, even though these organizations may take up new forms and would certainly become *relatively* less powerful in public communication than they were in the past.

Therefore, we believe there is a need to understand the role of media in contemporary social movements by considering digital media platforms and mainstream media institutions together. In the case of the Umbrella Movement, Chapter 3 has shown that, while the most sophisticated and systematic debates surrounding the notion of civil disobedience had proceeded mainly through the commentary sections of mainstream media, the discourses of civil disobedience were also diffused through and further contested in the digital arena. The heated reactions generated by the notion of Occupy Central in the digital arena could then be taken by the mass media as a sign of the significance of the matter, thus encouraging the mass media to pay even more attention to it. In the end, at the individual level, consumption of conventional news media was not related to understanding of the concept of civil disobedience. Rather, people who engaged more actively in political communication via social media understood civil disobedience to larger extents.

In this scenario, rather than seeing digital media and conventional mass media as separate communication modalities having separate influences on people, it would be more appropriate to consider them as forming an integrated communication environment in which the circulation of information and images often constitute media loops or intertextual chains. Individual-level survey data analysis may show that political communication via digital media has a certain impact on people, but that impact cannot be properly understood without noting how the content circulating via digital media may often partly or even wholly originate from mass media outlets.

As a general principle, the claim about the importance of considering mass media and digital media as constituting a holistic system is not new (e.g., Chadwick, 2011, 2013). A few recent studies about the Arab Spring have also highlighted the significance of the interactions between social media and conventional mass media. Wolover (2016), through an analysis of Al Jazeera's and Western media's coverage of the Tunisian revolution, argued that there is a co-constitutive relationship between traditional news outlets and distributed online media. The two are reliant on one another for information and exposure. More concretely, "[V]ideos and photographs documenting protests can be quickly uploaded to social networking websites where they can be shared through 'friends' lists. Distributed media can act as an electronic clearinghouse of vetted information, which is easily accessible via a quick series of keystrokes in a search engine. Simultaneously, traditional media can add legitimacy to these sources while informing news consumers when publishing or airing stories containing information garnered from digital sources" (p. 197).

Similar emphasis on the social media–mainstream media interface existed in Ahy (2016) and AlSayyad and Guvenc (2015). The latter study, in particular, argued that once the Egyptian protests on January 25 started, broadcast TV played an important role in providing certain information that further fueled the protests. Al Jazeera's coverage of the Egyptian uprising was also credited by AlSayyad and Guvenc (2015) for having an especially important impact on the protests in Yemen.

There are some differences between the mainstream and digital media linkage in the Arab Spring and that in the Umbrella Movement, however. In the former case, scholars have mainly discussed how mobilizing messages, information, and images originating from and circulating via the Internet were sourced and thus amplified by mainstream media organizations, and the mainstream media were crucial in bringing the events to international attention. International attention was arguably an influential factor in the Arab Spring given the relationship between the political economic linkages between the Arab countries (especially Egypt) and Western powers. In the Umbrella Movement, the mainstream media's role was by no means restricted to being the amplifier of online information and messages. They were the platforms on which discursive contestations regarding the notion of civil disobedience were conducted. Broadcast images of the police's firing of tear gas led to mediated instant grievances and the quick scaling up of the action. On many occasions, communications through digital media amplified the information and images from mainstream media. Overall speaking, as the mainstream media in Hong Kong retain a degree of operational freedom and internal variety, mainstream media and digital media communications interacted with each other even more closely. Compared to the role of mainstream media outlets in the Arab Spring, one may say that mainstream media coverage constituted a much more integral part to the local dynamics of the Umbrella Movement.

At the conceptual level, Chapter 4 has put forward the notion of partially censored public monitor to summarize a range of possible functions and impact of the media system in a large-scale protest campaign. The notion of public monitor was inspired by DeLuca and Peeples's (2002) discussion of the public screen. While our concept of public monitor shares with the concept of public screen an emphasis on the power of images, the notion of public monitor also points to how the media allow various actors to keep track of the happenings of a movement and act or react accordingly. This function is crucial for the monitorial participants in the movement, as discussed earlier.

Equally important, because of its public monitor function, the media can affect the dynamics of a protest campaign through its sheer presence: the "threat" or "promise" of making things visible to the public and the world at large could lead people to take certain actions and refrain from others. The impact of media thus resides in not only what appears on the screen, but also what does *not* appear on the screen because of media monitoring. In the Arab Spring, this function of the media system was manifested in how the presence of Al Jazeera had arguably prevented military action by the Egyptian government (Howard & Hussain, 2013). In the Umbrella Movement, the power of the public monitor was manifested through the mobilizing impact of images of tear gas on the first day of occupation, the impact of images of excessive police violence on public opinion, and how these "lessons" arguably led the Hong Kong government to adopt a more "hands off" approach (Yuen & Cheng, 2017) in handling the movement after the first three weeks of the campaign.

Nevertheless, the public monitor function of the media system is not fully realized because of its partially censored character. While the Chinese state has attempted to co-opt the Hong Kong media through various means, the frontline journalists still uphold journalistic professionalism to a large extent. Many frontline Hong Kong journalists are liberal progressive in their personal political outlook, which further contributed to tensions within media organizations (Lee & Chan, 2009). As a result, the mainstream media has had a complicated and even contradictory impact on public opinion toward the Umbrella Movement. While the impact of the public monitor was manifested in specific occasions, citizens who consumed mainstream media more frequently tended to hold more negative attitudes toward the movement and more positive attitudes toward the police. In other words, the mainstream media exhibited an overall bias against the movement, but their performance was also punctuated by moments of manifestation of the power of the public monitor.

Although we articulated the idea of partial censorship mainly by referring to the situation of Hong Kong, where a lack of full democracy combines with a tradition of press freedom, the concept should be applicable to other democratic societies. The mainstream media in democracies are also embedded in the established political economic institutions and therefore cannot be fully independent from dominant power. The mainstream media should not be dismissed as merely agents of social control, but the structural and practical constrains placed upon them should be seriously considered (Cottle, 2006). The notion of partially censored public monitor, in other words, is capable of capturing simultaneously the possibility of the media system contributing to social mobilization *and* the role of the media as agents of social control. These two sides of the media coexist. An important question would be what factors and conditions can strengthen the public monitor function and limit the influence of partial censorship. Again, the development of media technologies itself can be a factor strengthening the public monitor function of the media system as a whole by widening the circulation of certain materials, helping specific content to circumvent efforts of censorship, and introducing certain dynamics of communication that cannot be easily controlled by dominant power holders.

Describing the media system as integrated does not entail the lack of any lines of demarcation in the system. But instead of a distinction between mass and digital media, when political issues and social movements are concerned, the line separating the two sides (or various sides) of a political debate is probably more significant. Studies on the role of digital media in social mobilization are sometimes tied to arguments about the emergence of online counter-publics (Cayli, 2013; Leung & Lee, 2014), but scholars have also noted how governments can try to control the Internet and proactively influence the online opinion climate (Hussain & Howard, 2013; Tsui, 2015). In the Umbrella Movement, while there was a pro-movement communication "network of networks" constituted by the few pro-democracy mainstream media organizations, a rising number of online alternative media sites, pro-movement groups' online communication platforms and networks, and the pro-movement citizens' own digital communication networks, there was also a similar anti-movement communication network of networks constituted by the large number of pro-government mainstream media organizations, the small number of pro-establishment online platforms and websites, pro-government groups' online networks, and the pro-government citizens' own digital communication networks.

Part of Chapter 6 illustrated the operation of part of this anti-occupation communication network in the Umbrella Movement. When compared to the pro-movement communication network, the anti-occupation communication network remained centered more on the mainstream media. Yet their new media presence was non-negligible and is growing continually. We will return to this point toward the end of the chapter. The general analytical point to note here is that analysis of the relationship between digital media and social movements should take into account the role and impact of both pro-movement and anti-movement communications simultaneously.

The Umbrella Movement as a Critical Event

No matter whether a large-scale protest movement can achieve its proclaimed goal, it can have an impact on the dynamics of contentious politics in the future. As Schudson (1992) explicated, important events have the power of contingency as they exert influence on the unfolding of reality and the happening of events afterwards. In Hong Kong, the July 1, 2003, demonstration, in which half a million citizens protested against national security legislation, constituted a "critical event" (Staggenborg, 1991) changing people's perceptions of reality and thus their actions (Lee & Chan, 2011). The July 1 protest led to the rise of social mobilization on the one hand, and led China to adopt a more interventionist approach in governing Hong Kong on the other. The change in China's approach to governing the city, in particular, is an important part of the political dynamics that led to heightened conflicts between the mainland and Hong Kong, which in turn constituted part of the background for the Umbrella Movement.

The Umbrella Movement is likely to become another critical event that will have profound implications on the pro-democracy movement in the city. It is certainly too early to make definite and substantive conclusions about the long-term impact of the Umbrella Movement. However, various happenings and events in the three years after the end of the occupation have already illustrated the Umbrella Movement's power of contingency. Two closely interrelated trends—further decentralization of the oppositional forces and further radicalization of both movement ideologies and tactics—can be discussed here in order to provide an update about the situation of Hong Kong and illustrate how a large-scale protest campaign may impinge on subsequent events.

It is not uncommon for a large-scale protest to produce "organizational spinoffs" in its aftermath. In Tarrow's (1988) conceptualization of the protest cycle, successful mobilization often brings about the proliferation of movement groups and associations. Indeed, the July 1 protest in 2003 in Hong Kong brought about the rise of online alternative radio sites and new civic groups (Leung, 2015a). However, many of these new groups did not survive for long, whereas the most important and long-lasting "spinoffs" took on conventional organizational forms, such as the political parties League of Social Democrats (established in 2006) and the Civic Party (established in 2005).

After the end of the Umbrella Movement, one also witnessed the proliferation of informal associations. It is extremely difficult to provide a comprehensive mapping of the new groups. But one might derive a sense of the emergence of new groups and political actors in the city through the District Council elections in 2015. The District Council is a local-level consultation body. In the 2015 elections, a total of 935 candidates competed for 431 seats. Throughout the campaign period, the term "umbrella soldiers" was coined and utilized in public discourses to refer to those candidates who were "political freshmen" and joined the election apparently due to the impact of the Umbrella Movement. "Umbrella soldiers" does not refer to one single group, however; it includes new and informal associations such as Youngspiration, individuals who belonged to various self-initiated groups emerging during the Umbrella Movement, and candidates who did not have any affiliation but were perceived to hold political views in line with the Umbrella Movement.

The label "umbrella soldier" is sometimes attributed to a candidate by the media instead of acknowledged by the candidate. Hence there could be debates about whether a specific candidate is an "umbrella soldier" or not, and there is no definitive count of their number. Yet according to media estimations, about 50 candidates and 7 to 9 winners could be counted as belonging to the category. Although these numbers are not large, most commentators regarded the results as impressive given the umbrella soldiers' resource disadvantages and lack of election experiences.

The election results thus illustrated a significant degree of public support for new political actors instead of conventional political parties after the Umbrella Movement. But the very loose, informal, and sometimes even tension-filled relationships among the "umbrella soldiers" and between the umbrella soldiers and the established pro-democracy groups also illustrated the increasingly decentralized or even fragmented character of the pro-democracy camp. The same can be said about the result of the Legislative Council election in September 2016. Among the winning candidates were two members of Youngspirations, the 23-year-old former HKFS leader Nathan Law, and Lau Siu-lai, a university lecturer who set up the "Siu-lai Democracy Classroom" in the Admiralty occupation area during the movement (all four of them were later "disqualified" to hold their offices in highly controversial circumstances). In any case, how the new legislators would cooperate with the "old guard" of the pro-democracy camp in the legislature remains to be observed.

Another series of significant events after the Umbrella Movement indicative of the continual decentralizing tendency in the movement sector was the withdrawal by several university student unions from the HKFS. The wave of withdrawal began in Hong Kong University when a group of students started a Facebook campaign in late December 2014 pushing the student union of the university to organize a public vote on the matter. The vote was held in February 2015, and the motion of withdrawing from the HKFS was passed by a margin of 41.4% vs. 37.4%. Similar ballots were later held by the student unions of four other universities, and the motion was passed in three cases. As of December 2016, only the student unions of four universities remained as members of the HKFS.

To briefly recount the background, by the end of the Umbrella Movement, the HKFS was already heavily criticized by many young participants for its "mistakes" during the failed attempt to escalate the action in the evening of November 30 (the attempt to surround the whole Government Headquarters). More generally, the HKFS has been active in the local movement sector for decades. It has long adopted a broadly speaking liberal leftist agenda (e.g., supporting democratization and press freedom, supporting labor rights, opposing neo-liberal policies, etc.) and an active interest in the democratization of China. The latter was criticized by the localists for being irrelevant to Hong Kong or even detrimental to the city's interests. The HKFS has also long emphasized the principle of nonviolence in contentious actions. As the Umbrella Movement did not bring about significant positive outcomes, many young people became even more frustrated about the political reality and the perceived futility of peaceful, nonviolent protests. Oppositional voices against the HKFS became ever louder.

There were also criticisms against the HKFS for being opaque in its operation, for administrative and financial mismanagement, and for its lack of internal democracy. Some of these criticisms might be legitimate to an extent. But what is notable is that anyone who disagreed with the existing agenda, ideological leaning, and/or administrative operation of the HKFS could have tried to seize the platform and reform the federation from within. Alternatively, the student unions that left the HKFS could have joined hands to establish a separate federation. However, instead of trying to reform the HKFS or establish an alternative, student unions of the individual universities simply withdrew from the Federation.

Therefore, the wave of withdrawal from the HKFS has to be understood as a continuation of the debates about the merits and demerits of having formal organizations at the center of social movements. Withdrawing from the HKFS signifies distrust toward not only the current federation but also any form of federation that might compromise the individual student unions' autonomy. In this context, the success on the withdrawal vote in four universities is illustrative of the sentiments among young people toward centralized organization in social movements. Certainly, it is unknown if the trend of preferring decentralization would continue.

But many signs are indicating that the centrifugal forces are stronger than the centripetal forces in the first two to three years after the Umbrella Movement.

Besides the trend toward an ever more decentralized formation, the Umbrella Movement was also followed by further radicalization of social movement. As discussed in Chapter 3, the Occupy Central campaign and the later Umbrella Movement constituted a form of radicalization with self-restraint. The perceived failure of the Umbrella Movement to achieve positive outcomes thus called into question the utility of self-restraint, leading some to adopt a more radical approach to its struggle for democracy and against China.

Mueller (1999) has distinguished among radicalization in terms of the substantive claims being put forward, the collective identities being taken up, and the form of actions undertaken. Combining substantive claims and collective identities together, we may distinguish between radicalization in ideology and in action. In the immediate aftermath of the Umbrella Movement, one could see the radicalization of both. In terms of ideology, the growth of "localism" continued, and more and more young people rejected their Chinese identity (Veg, 2017). Concretely, the occupation campaign in late 2014 exercised self-restraint by not going with the international media to call itself the Umbrella Revolution. By labeling itself the Umbrella Movement, the activists proclaimed their lack of intention to challenge the Chinese Communist regime or to seek secession. In contrast, after the Umbrella Movement, the idea of "Hong Kong independence" became more widely and openly discussed.[1]

Even without calling for Hong Kong independence, the claims put forward by other activists are also arguably more radical than before. For instance, China's promise of "no change [for Hong Kong] in 50 years" would end in 2047. Scholarism leader Joshua Wong and several other activists promoted the idea of amending the Basic Law and allowing Hong Kong to hold a referendum to extend the SAR's "high degree of autonomy" permanently. Although Wong's proposal did not ask for independence, the demand touched on the constitutional setup of the SAR and was phrased in terms of "self-determination." The latter might not differ too much from independence in the eyes of the Chinese government.

From 2015 to 2017, debates about Hong Kong independence continued to be fueled by both rhetoric and actual political events. In the 2016 Legislative Council election, the Hong Kong government first disqualified pro-independence young activist Edward Leung from standing as a candidate in the election. Two pro-independence Youngspiration candidates won in the election. But when the two staged a symbolic protest by not entirely following the oath, using demeaning lexicons to referring to China, and displaying a "Hong Kong is not China" banner when they were sworn in, they were disqualified through a combination of the Hong Kong government seeking judicial review by the court and the Chinese government exercising its power to "interpret" the Basic Law. China's interpretation of the Basic Law, in particular, was considered by opponents as setting up previously non-existing requirements regarding how public office holders should perform in oath-taking.

Then, in July 2017, four other pro-democracy legislators were disqualified due to their symbolic protests during the oath-taking. Although the four legislators were not, strictly speaking, pro-independence, at least two of them were vocal supporters of the aforementioned idea of "self-determination." Hence they were essentially treated as not different from pro-independence by the Chinese government.

The events indicated China's determination to use a hardline approach against pro-independence forces in Hong Kong. Nevertheless, it is also possible that China's actions would only further demonstrate to disgruntled citizens—especially the younger generations—in Hong Kong the impossibility of "one country, two systems," hence further strengthening pro-independence sentiments. As a matter of fact, a survey conducted by the Centre for Communication and Public Opinion Survey (CCPOS) at the Chinese University of Hong Kong in July 2016 found that 17% of the Hong Kong public were supportive of Hong Kong independence.[2] The figure did drop in June 2017, but there were still 11% of the public supportive of Hong Kong independence. In both surveys, respondents between 15 and 39 were more likely to support Hong Kong independence. Regarding radicalization of forms of action, an opinion poll conducted by the CCPOS in March 2015 asked the respondents whether they agreed that "activities demanding political reforms in Hong Kong must be peaceful and non-violent." More than 8 in 10 respondents (80.5%) replied "strongly agree" or "somewhat agree," while 6.1% replied "somewhat disagree" or "strongly disagree." Although the latter percentage is small, it is remarkable that more than 6% of the public would express disagreement toward the supposedly consensual principle of non-violence. Adding together respondents who replied "so-so" or did not give a valid answer, nearly 20% of citizens did not insist on the principle of nonviolence. The same question was repeated in another poll in July 2015, and the results were similar: 4.4% disagreed that activities demanding political reform must remain peaceful and nonviolent, 16.2% did not commit to one side, while 79.4% agreed with the necessity of nonviolence.[3]

Our interpretation of the findings is that they signify the presence of a substantial degree of ambivalence toward social movement violence among supporters of democratization in Hong Kong. Although the percentage of citizens explicitly acknowledging the possible need of violent actions remains very small, a nonnegligible proportion of the public no longer straightforwardly insists on the principle of nonviolence.

Meanwhile, radical groups have experimented with new action tactics. In 2015, some localist groups initiated a series of "reclaim action." The idea was that they needed to "reclaim Hong Kong" from the invasion by mainland tourists and parallel traders. They went to several districts in the New Territories where there were huge numbers of mainland visitors and tried to "drive away" the mainland tourists through directly scolding them on the street and/or disrupting businesses of retail shops. The activities remained largely nonviolent physically. But they were much more confrontational than the usual protest march since they involved direct conflicts between the protesters and the enraged tourists or the police.

Radicalization of action reached a new height in the late night of February 8, 2016, the first day of Chinese New Year, when chaotic scenes broke out in Mong Kok. A group of young protesters, led by the Hong Kong Indigenous (another new group formed after the Umbrella Movement), engaged in physical confrontations with the police as a result of an alleged attempt on the part of the police to crack down on street hawkers in the area. The protesters not only charged the police defense but also threw glass bottles, rubbish bins, and road bricks at them. During the confrontation, a police officer had to fire two warning shots into the air. The event resulted in numerous injuries. It was widely regarded as the most serious urban "riots" in Hong Kong in more than 30 years.

The Hong Kong government and the pro-establishment media branded the events in Mong Kok as a *"bou-dong,"* whereas some other media outlets used the term *"sou-lyun."* Although both phrases can be translated as "riot," *"bou-dong"* suggests something much more violent, malignant, and criminal. Many pro-democracy commentators argued that the government's hardline approach on political issues was the root cause of the Mong Kok clashes because it contributed to polarization of the society and forced the protesters to escalate their actions. There were even commentators arguing that the government was intentionally generating these conflicts in order to justify their own hardline approach.[4]

Radicalization is not an inevitable consequence of the Umbrella Movement; it resulted from how various actors reacted to the end and the aftermath of the occupation campaign. Radicalization is also not necessarily a linear trend. How the state responds to radicalism and violent protests can shape its further evolution. Between March and August 2017, the court convicted around 10 participants in the Mong Kok riots, and sentenced six of them to three years of imprisonment or longer for "rioting." In August, the court also sentenced 13 participants in an anti-rural development protest to eight to 13 months of jail for "unlawful assembly." In the same month, the court sentenced three student leaders of the Umbrella Movement, including Joshua Wong, HKFS leader Alex Chow, and Nathan Law, who had just been disqualified as a legislator months earlier, to six to eight months in jail. In the last case, the court's judgment was criticized by many observers for adopting a very low threshold of what constitutes "violent conduct" in protests.

As the authors finalized these pages in early October 2017, court cases surrounding the Umbrella Movement leaders were still continuing. The Trio had just appeared in court in late September over public nuisance charges. No matter how one judges the moral legitimacy of violent protests and the rightfulness of the court decisions, one could only speculate at this moment whether such clamping down on civil disobedience and (even arguably minimally) "violent" protests would really be able to suppress radical actions, or only sow the seeds for more radical ideas and actions in the future.

Media and the Future Development of Social Mobilization in Hong Kong

As mentioned above, in the months after the Umbrella Movement, digital and social media continued to be the places where informal groups were formed, ideas were promoted, campaigns were initiated, and tactics were discussed and debated. For instance, while the general public may have been shocked to see the 2016 Mong Kok protesters digging up bricks from pedestrian pathways and throwing them at the police, some commentators pointed out that supporters of radical groups had been discussing such tactics in the online arena for months.

The media system in Hong Kong will continue to provide the platforms and channels for communication, mobilization, and action coordination for people engaging in contentious politics. But three challenges might limit the degree to which the media system could facilitate or empower Hong Kong people in their search for political and social change. We end this concluding chapter with a brief discussion of these three challenges.

The first challenge is the impact of digital media on polarization and fragmentation within the pro-democracy movement. When analyzing the Umbrella Movement, we have already discussed the relationship between digital media and decentralization of the occupation campaign in terms of how digital media communications and activities were tied to the existing ideological and organizational divisions within the campaign. We also mentioned the practice of unfriending others holding different political views, which would lead to the formation of online echo chambers in which people are no longer exposed to contrasting opinions. The continual trend of movement radicalization after the Umbrella Movement led some commentators to continue to question whether digital and social media would lead to further polarization and fragmentation within the society. Some even argued that young people are becoming increasingly radical and extremist because they constitute the "Internet generation" or "social media generation."[5]

There is, of course, a long line of research and debate about the extent to which digital and social media would contribute to opinion polarization, extremism, or what Sunstein (2009, 2017) called cyber-balkanization (e.g., Colleoni, Rozza, & Adam, 2014; Harris, Morgan, & Gibbs, 2014; Suhay, Blackwell, Roche, & Bruggeman, 2014). While some argued that people have a tendency to talk to like-minded others and/or process information in ways that reinforce or protect existing views, others argued that social media may contribute to communication across differences due to a number of reasons: (1) social media are a platform for the maintenance of weak ties (Lee, Choi, Kim, & Kim, 2014); (2) people do not necessarily avoid counter-attitudinal information (Garrett, 2009); and (3) people are often exposed to political information and messages accidentally in social media (Kim, Chen, & Gil de Zúñiga, 2013). Hence political communications via social media are far from entirely homogeneous.

A recent article by the first author has re-examined the population survey data analyzed in Chapter 3 (i.e., surveys conducted in September 2013 and October 2014, respectively). Political communication via social media was found to be not associated with more extreme attitudes toward the Occupy Central campaign in 2013, but it was associated with more extreme attitudes toward the Umbrella Movement, the police, and the Hong Kong and Chinese government when the occupation was undergoing (Lee, 2016). Interestingly, during the Umbrella Movement, interpersonal political discussions and even conventional news media consumption were also associated with more extreme attitudes toward some of the aforementioned objects. The article argued that social media communications are not inherently polarizing; but when the society itself is moving toward polarization and fragmentation, social media communications—or even other kinds of political communication—could indeed exacerbate the trend.

Another recent publication by Chan and Fu (2017) created an cyberbalkanization index based on online communication among Facebook public pages in Hong Kong. They found that degree of cyberbalkanization indeed relates to and temporally precedes opinion polarization as reflected in polls. While the finding may apparently confirm the "polarization effect" of social media, it is noteworthy that, by creating a cyberbalkanization index that can go up and down, the study has implied the possibility that cyberbalkanization can decline under certain circumstances. Cyberbalkanization can lead to opinion polarization, but cyberbalkanization itself is not a necessary consequence of digital and social media communication.

More studies are needed to further interrogate into the dynamics of opinion polarization in Hong Kong. But the findings from the above studies suggest that, while we should not adopt a technological determinist view and see digital media as necessarily leading to one type of impact on public opinion, the worry of social media contributing to extremism and further fragmentation is valid given the political reality of contemporary Hong Kong.

The second challenge for the media system to play a more constructive role in the pro-democracy movement is the government's attempt to tame the Internet. When compared to mainland China, where Internet freedom has long been severely curtailed and has further worsened in recent years (Creemers, 2015), Hong Kong is still enjoying a by-and-large free and open Internet. But as Tsui (2015) discussed, the Hong Kong government is "catching up" in its "online tactics." When political control and censorship are concerned, emails of key leaders of the occupation movement have been hacked and leaked to the media. Although the identity of the hackers remains unknown, there was suspicion of involvement by agents related to the Chinese government.

In addition, the Hong Kong government had been using an existing law regarding "access to computer with criminal or dishonest intent" to arrest protesters. In one case during the Umbrella Movement, the law was invoked against a youth who, according to the description by the Hong Kong Government's Secretary of Security in a Legislative Council meeting, "incited others to join the unlawful assembly at Mong Kok and to storm the Police, suggesting protesters to paralyze the railway system by gathering on railway platforms in an attempt to create chaos, in case Mong Kok could not be successfully taken back."[6] In February 2016, after the Mong Kok clashes on the first day of the Chinese New Year, the police used the same law against "dishonest use of computers" and arrested a person who called upon others to join the Mong Kok "riots" via social media. The law against criminal and dishonest use of computers was originally set up to handle online fraud and other cybercrimes, but its broad and indefinite scope has led to worries about the government using the law as a weapon to suppress online expression and mobilization.

Besides what the government might do to curtail freedom of expression, the pro-establishment forces have continued to strengthen their online presence after the Umbrella Movement. The Facebook pages of Silent Majority for Hong Kong and Speak Out Hong Kong, which were analyzed in Chapter 6, continued to be active. In fact, during the controversy surrounding the disqualification of two pro-independence candidates after the Legislative Council election in 2016, an analysis of Facebook communication shows that the pro-government Facebook pages were the most successful in attracting "engagement"—liking, sharing, and commenting—through their posts related to the controversy.[7]

One might wonder if the controversy surrounding the disqualification of the pro-independence legislators was an exceptional event.[8] But given the government and the pro-establishment side's superior resources, their success in finding a foothold in the online arena is not surprising. There is hitherto no sign that the pro-government public communications on social media can influence public opinion at large, but it is likely able to at least establish a pro-government online enclave and thus "insulate" its supporters from the influence of the counter-public communications online.

The third challenge to the media's role in social mobilization centers on the mainstream media institutions. The mainstream news media in Hong Kong are, on the whole, only partially censored because of the impossibility for the state to exercise direct control of the press in Hong Kong, the presence of a few relatively daring outlets, the market orientation of the media corporations, and the continual significance of journalistic professionalism in the work of frontline journalists and in public discourse. But the state can attempt to further tighten its grip on the mainstream media. Most notably, the Chinese e-commerce corporation Alibaba acquired *South China Morning Post*, the most influential English-language newspaper in Hong Kong, in December 2015. While most media owners in Hong Kong are business people with vast interests in the mainland market, Alibaba's purchase of the *Post* signified "direct investment" by Chinese capital in the Hong Kong media market. Alibaba's Jack Ma is not the first Chinese businessman to directly invest in Hong Kong media, but the profile of Alibaba and the *Post* certainly made the acquisition eyebrow-raising. Although it is too early to tell if the acquisition would lead to significant differences in the *Post*'s approach to political reporting, the event could be a sign of the Chinese state's intention to exercise more direct influence on the Hong Kong media.

Without changes in ownership, the problem of media self-censorship is likely to persist or may become even more serious in the future. TVB, for example, have hitherto not repaired its image of being pro-government. Instead, merely two months after the end of the Umbrella Movement, there was news stating that about 20% of journalists in the organization, including many of those responsible for the original reportage of police violence in the "dark corner" scandal, had resigned. In numerous other events, such as the Mong Kok clashes in February 2016 and the Legislative Council election in September 2016, netizens continued to criticize TVB for exhibiting a conspicuous conservative and pro-government bias.

Meanwhile, the few pro-democracy or liberal-oriented media outlets could be facing their own problems of survival. In particular, Next Media Ltd., the corporation owning *Apple Daily*, is struggling with a sharp decline in revenue in its print businesses. It restructured and downsized its print magazine operation in mid-2015, implemented an outsourcing plan at its graphics department in June 2017, and then sold *Next Magazine* in July 2017. The series of events led to questions about the sustainability of the corporation at large, and even if the corporation can survive, it remains a question of whether the media outlet can still expend resources on investigative reporting. Cable TV, the paid television service regarded by pro-democracy citizens and the Umbrella Movement supporters as relatively trustworthy, was also facing severe business difficulties. After losing money for nine years consecutively, its parent corporation Wharf Holdings decided to "cut losses." The television station was sold to a new group of investors in April 2017, with questions hanging over the direction of future development of the company.

Generally speaking, beyond the survival of individual organizations, to the extent that the mainstream media are forced to cut down resources in face of the "business challenge" posed by digitization, high-quality journalism and critical reporting on public affairs are likely to suffer. As emphasized throughout the book, the information and reportage provided by mainstream media institutions remain crucial raw materials for further elaboration, interpretation, discussion, and reprocessing in the digital arena. The decline of quality and critical journalism could weaken the vibrancy of counter-public communications on the Internet.

Certainly, in line with the idea that social and political changes evolve dynamically as a result of the happening of events and the interactions among actors, the media system and its relationship with the pro-democracy movement could continue to evolve in ways that are not entirely predictable. The struggle for democracy in Hong Kong has long been an uphill battle. It will continue to be so.

Profiling the Umbrella Movement Participants

While this book provides an account of the occurrence and dynamics of the Umbrella Movement, focusing particularly on the role of the media, this appendix aims at providing a descriptive analysis of the basic characteristics of the participants for those interested in getting more information about the movement.

Profiling the participants of the Umbrella Movement is not a straightforward matter, however. Two issues need to be raised at the outset. First, what does it mean to have participated in the Umbrella Movement? Those who actually camped within the occupied areas undoubtedly had. But what about people who went to the site only a few times? Besides, does going to the occupied area entail participating in the movement? From our personal observations, there were citizens going to the occupied areas occasionally only as observers, sometimes because they in fact did not support the movement's cause, and sometimes because of professional reasons that compelled them to claim to be neutral. Of course, people who went to the occupied sites also included the anti-occupation protesters. Obviously, presence in the sites does not entail participation.

Putting the question the other way round, could an individual citizen who had not gone to the occupied site claim that one had participated in the movement through other activities in cyberspace or in places outside the occupied areas? In reality, it was very unlikely for a movement supporter who is active in cyberspace and yet not to have visited the occupied areas at all. But one could still raise the above as a conceptual question.

Having pointed out the murkiness of the notion of participation, we believe that it is inappropriate for us to impose a restrictive definition and try to identify the "real participants" during the onsite survey. Hence a participant, in the current analysis, is simply a person who was present in the occupied site and self-defined as such. This definition leaves open the possibility of significant variations in "modes of participation" among the participants—the participants could be in the occupied areas more or less frequently, and they could be more or less active in joining the various activities inside and outside the occupied areas. Nevertheless, the current operational definition of participation does rule out the possibility of participation without ever visiting the occupied area. Some scholars have argued for the significance of "digitally networked participation" (e.g., Theocharis, 2015). Even seemingly purely expressive acts can often be parts of wider mobilization processes. But in the case of the Umbrella Movement, it should be reasonable to treat physical presence in the occupied areas as a necessary feature of being a *movement participant*, since occupation of urban space constitutes the most important action being conducted.

Second, since the Umbrella Movement was extended over time and space, the profile of the participants that one could get from a protest onsite survey might differ depending on the date, time, and site of survey fieldwork. Conducting the survey during weekday nights probably would capture the most committed participants, whereas conducting the survey during weekends would capture a larger number of people who just visited the occupied areas occasionally. Some monitorial participants might be present mainly when major rallies and events occur. It should be noted that the two onsite surveys to be reported were conducted during weekends. This is partly due to practical concerns (the possibility of interviewing more people within a shorter period). This is also partly due to our belief that there is a need to take the occasional visitors seriously, since large-scale movements are impossible without huge numbers of people joining the action in a relatively more peripheral way.

Moreover, as the movement evolved from late September to mid-December, surveys conducted at different time points within the 79-day period may also produce different protester profiles. Therefore, strictly speaking, what the following analysis provides is not a single comprehensive profile of all participants in the movement; the findings should better be understood as snapshots of the movement participants taken at distinctive time-places. Nevertheless, we could still gain a good sense of the general profile of the movement participants from the findings, especially when the various snapshots produce similar results.

This appendix will discuss three aspects of the movement participants' profile. We will begin by analyzing the demographic characteristics and basic political orientations of the movement participants. We will then analyze the survey respondents' mode of participation in the movement. Finally, we will examine the respondents' self-proclaimed reasons to participate and their beliefs about the Umbrella Movement.

Demographics and Basic Political Orientation

Table A1 shows the demographics of the onsite survey respondents. The first three columns show the percentage distributions from the October 4–5 survey in Admiralty, the November 2 survey in Admiralty, and the November 2 survey in Mong Kok ("MK" hereafter). The "combined" column shows the figures when all respondents were treated as one sample, even though, as just noted, the figures in the first three columns are the more meaningful ones. The combined column was created only for further information. Moreover, for comparison, Table A1 also shows the demographics of the participants of the July 1 protest of 2007. The annual July 1 protest has been the most important series of large-scale contentious collective actions of the pro-democracy movement in Hong Kong since 2003 (Lee & Chan, 2011). But it took the conventional form of protest marches. The comparison could give us insights on whether the Umbrella Movement had attracted a different group of protesters.

The gender ratio of the participants in Admiralty in both early October and early November is close to 1:1, but there is a significant difference between Admiralty and MK, with participants in MK more likely to be men. This is probably related to the perception that the MK occupation was relatively less orderly and more conflictive, as some findings below will also suggest. Interestingly, when compared to the July 1 protests, the Umbrella Movement involved more equal participation by men and women.

The Umbrella Movement was widely regarded as having evolved into a student-led movement. Table A1 shows that, in all three surveyed time-places, more than 40% of the participants were 25 years old or below, whereas around 40% were between 26 and 40 years old. The November Admiralty survey registered the highest percentage of more mature or senior citizens. But even there, participants aged 41 or above constituted only 15.7% of the sample. Certainly, given the presence of these participants and a substantial proportion of participants between 30 and 40 years old, one should avoid treating the whole Umbrella Movement as a "student movement." But when compared to other large-scale protests in Hong Kong, it is true that the Umbrella Movement had a disproportionately large percentage of young participants. As Table A1 shows, 40.4% of the July 1 protesters in 2007 were 41 years old or above. This is about four times the percentage in the Umbrella Movement.

Participants in large-scale protests in Hong Kong often came from the more educated social strata. Nearly 60% of the July 1 protesters in 2007 had college education. The percentage of participants with college education was even higher in the Umbrella Movement. Close to 80% of the respondents in the October Admiralty survey had college education. The percentage of college-educated respondents went down in November, though.

Only about a quarter of the Umbrella Movement participants were current college students. But it was still a very substantial percentage, since current college students constituted only around 2% of the city's population.[1] Respondents who were university students at the time were asked to indicate their major. The majority of

Table A1 **Basic demographics of the protesters**

	October Admiralty	November Admiralty	November MK	Combined	2007 July 1 protest
Gender[b]					
Male	43.1	48.5	69.8	49.2	63.6
Female	56.9	51.5	30.2	50.8	36.4
Age[a]					
25 or below	48.8	44.7	51.5	48.5	28.3
26 to 40	42.9	39.7	35.9	41.0	31.3
41 to 55	5.9	11.5	9.2	7.5	28.9
56 or above	2.3	4.2	3.9	2.9	11.5
Education[a/b]					
Primary or below	1.0	12.6	3.1	3.5	3.8
Secondary	19.6	31.6	30.6	23.9	37.1
Tertiary or above	79.3	55.8	66.3	72.6	59.2
Current college students[b]	24.8	20.5	28.0	24.6	—
Major of current students[b]					
Social science	30.7	35.7	32.8	31.7	—
Arts	25.9	19.0	4.9	21.0	—
Business	14.2	19.0	27.9	17.5	—
Science and engineering	23.6	14.3	31.1	23.8	—
Law or medicine	5.7	11.9	3.3	6.0	—
Self-reported SES[a/b]					
Lower/grassroots	48.8	40.4	50.8	47.7	34.9
Middle	47.6	58.0	38.5	47.7	62.3
Upper	3.6	1.6	10.8	4.6	2.8

Notes: Entries are column percentages. When a variable is marked with superscript "a," the percentage distributions in the Admiralty surveys in the two months differ from each other significantly at $p < .05$ in a Chi-square test. When a variable is marked with superscript "b," the percentage distributions obtained from the two occupied areas in November differ from each other significantly at $p < .05$ in a Chi-square test. Total sample sizes for the five columns are 969, 273, 296, 1,538, and 577, respectively (same for the following tables).

current college students studied the social sciences or the arts. But interestingly, there was a significant difference between Admiralty and MK: a college student in MK was more likely to be a science and engineering major and very unlikely to be studying the arts.

Regarding self-reported socioeconomic status (SES), Table A1 shows that 48.8% of the respondents in Admiralty in early October regarded themselves as belonging to the lower or grassroots class, while 47.6% regarded themselves as belonging to the middle class. The middle-class "flavor" of Admiralty increased over the month: in early November, close to 60% of the Admiralty participants regarded themselves as middle class. This may be the result of the grassroots participants moving toward the MK occupation. MK itself can be considered a more grassroots district, and the MK occupied area had arguably taken up a more grassroots atmosphere.[2] In fact, more than 50% of the November MK respondents reported themselves as belonging to the lower or grassroots class.

More important, the Umbrella Movement registered a larger percentage of self-proclaimed grassroots participants when compared to the July 1 protest series. Only 35% of the July 1 protesters in 2007 regarded themselves as belonging to the lower class. The percentage is lower than that registered in the November Admiralty survey, where the percentage of self-proclaimed lower-class participants is already lowest among the three surveyed time-places. Given the self-reported character of the question and the high percentage of young participants in the Umbrella Movement, one possible reason for the relatively large percentage of lower-class participants in the Umbrella Movement is that young people have become more likely to see themselves as belonging to the lower class. This can be understood in relation to young people's increasingly critical attitudes toward inequalities in the society, as discussed toward the end of Chapter 2.

In fact, among the movement participants, age is significantly related to self-reported SES. Among participants aged between 10 and 25, 54.9% regarded themselves as belonging to the lower or grassroots class. The percentage of participants regarding themselves as such declined to 45.3% in the 26–40 group, and then declined further to only 26.2% and 26.8%, respectively, in the 41–55 group and the 56 or above group. The same correlation between age and SES also exists in the July 1 protest of 2007. The percentages of respondents who regarded themselves as belonging to the lower class in the July 1 protest of 2007 were 47.5%, 30.0%, 22.0%, and 35.6%, respectively, from the youngest to the oldest group. Comparatively, the percentage of people belonging to the youngest age group (25 or below) claiming themselves to belong to the lower class was still higher in the Umbrella Movement (54.9% vs. 47.5%). These findings hint at the frustrations toward social and income inequalities felt by the young participants in the Umbrella Movement.

In terms of political orientation, Hong Kong citizens vary in their degree of support for democracy (e.g., Sing, 2010), but we can presume the participants of the

Umbrella Movement to be supporters of democratization. Nevertheless, there are internal divisions among the democrats. Pro-democracy groups in Hong Kong can be placed on a continuum ranging from the most radical to the most moderate. The pro-democracy parties can also vary in terms of whether they primarily represent middle-class professionals (e.g., the Civic Party) or the grassroots (e.g., the Labor Party). The onsite survey thus asked the movement participants whether there was a political party that they supported in particular.

As Table A2 shows, a substantial proportion of the respondents did not support any political party. This is consistent with the findings reported in Chapter 2 on Hong Kong people's general distrust toward politicians and political parties. Only 31.2% of the October Admiralty respondents indicated a political party that they supported in particular. The percentage of party supporters went up somewhat in the November surveys, but there were still more than 55% of the respondents in both Admiralty and MK being non–party supporters.

Among the political parties, the Civic Party was relatively more popular in Admiralty. In contrast, the parties that were most popular among the MK participants were the League of Social Democrats, Civic Passion, and People Power, which were the three relatively radical groups. This pattern of party support, already discussed in Chapter 5, confirms general perceptions of the makeup of the two areas. The occupation in Admiralty, which is itself a financial district, tended to be more middle class–oriented (see Table A1), and the middle class–oriented Civic Party was also relatively more popular there. MK, in comparison, was more grassroots and attracted relatively more participants with radical orientations.

It is also worth noting that the Democratic Party, which is historically the biggest pro-democracy party in the city, was supported by only a small percentage of the participants. Although the Democratic Party was still, in late 2014, one of the biggest pro-democracy parties in the legislature,[3] its moderate stance on political matters was seemingly unwelcomed by citizens active in social movements.

The bottom of Table A2 shows the distribution of party support for different age groups. When conducting this analysis, the respondents from the three time-places were combined. The most important finding is the very substantial relationship between age and whether the participant supported any political party at all. For those aged 25 or below, more than 70% did not indicate support for any political party. The percentage of non–party supporters declined slightly to 65.4% for people between 26 and 40 and then sharply to 41.1% and merely 22.7%, respectively, for respondents between 41 and 55 and those aged 56 or above. It shows that the youngest participants, who were also the main group of participants, were largely alienated from the political party system.

It should also be noted that, among basic demographic factors, only age has such a substantial effect on whether one supports a political party or not. If we treat whether one supports a political party or not as a dichotomous variable, education does relate significantly to it: 52.8%, 61.4%, and 67.2% of respondents with primary,

Table A2 **Support for political parties**

By survey time-points	October Admiralty	November Admiralty	November MK	Combined
Democratic Party	4.2	3.7	3.1	3.9
ADPL	1.0	1.1	1.0	1.0
Civic Party[b]	13.4	17.6	10.5	13.6
Confed. of Trade Union	1.6	1.5	2.4	1.7
Labor Party[a]	1.9	6.6	3.7	3.1
League of Social Democrats	8.3	9.6	11.2	9.1
People Power	5.7	8.8	11.9	7.5
Civic Passion[b]	2.8	4.8	12.9	5.1
Others	3.2	4.8	4.7	3.8
None of the above[a]	68.8	59.0	57.4	64.9
By age groups	25 or below	26 to 40	41 to 55	56 or above
Democratic Party[c]	2.1	2.8	10.8	27.3
ADPL	1.2	0.5	2.7	2.2
Civic Party[c]	7.6	16.7	25.0	43.2
Confed. of Trade Union[c]	1.2	1.6	1.8	9.1
Labor Party[c]	2.2	3.1	8.0	0.0
League of Social Democrats	8.0	10.0	11.6	15.9
People Power[c]	8.7	5.1	11.6	11.4
Civic Passion[c]	6.3	3.8	8.0	0.0
Others	3.9	3.3	6.3	4.5
None of the above[c]	70.9	65.4	41.1	22.7

Notes: Entries are percentages. When a variable is marked with superscript "a," the percentage distributions in the Admiralty surveys in the two months differ from each other significantly at $p < .05$ in a Chi-square test. When a variable is marked with superscript "b," the percentage distributions obtained from the two occupied areas in November differ from each other significantly at $p < .05$ in a Chi-square test. When a variable is marked with superscript "c," significant differences ($p < .05$ in a Chi-square test) exist among the percentage distributions from the four age groups.

secondary, and tertiary education, respectively, did not support a political party. But in a multivariate analysis using both age and education to predict whether one supported a party or not, the effect of education becomes insignificant. In other words, the bivariate relationship between education and party support is only a result of the fact that the younger respondents were also better educated. Educational level itself does not have an independent impact on whether a respondent claimed to support a party or not.

The age groups also vary in terms of their favorite political parties. Among the most senior participants, the Civic Party and the Democratic Party were the most popular. For respondents between 26 and 55 years old, the Civic Party still stood out as the most popular. But for respondents aged 25 or below, the Civic Party was not more popular than the League of Social Democrats and People Power. In fact, the youngest protesters were particularly likely to support one of the three radical groups on the list *as long as they supported a certain party*. While only 8.7% of respondents aged 25 or below supported People Power, it actually corresponds to 29.9% of those in the age group who had proclaimed support for a specific party. In contrast, although 11.6% of those between 41 and 55 supported People Power, it corresponds to only 19.7% of the party supporters in the age group.

The survey asked the respondents to report their sense of belonging to Hong Kong and China through a 0–10 scale. Local and national identification has long constituted an important topic for academic research in the city (Lau & Kuan, 1988; Ma, 1999), and numerous empirical studies have shown that Hong Kong people's political attitudes are systematically tied to their local and national identification. People who identified themselves as "Hong Kongers" tended to hold more liberal and pro-democracy attitudes (e.g., Wong, 2002; Lee & Chan, 2005). Debates surrounding national and local identities were central to the anti–national education movement in 2012. The Umbrella Movement could also be understood as an act of the local society of Hong Kong protecting itself against the nation.

Indeed, the onsite surveys found that the participants exhibited a strong sense of belonging to Hong Kong *and* a very weak sense of belonging to China. The mean scores of sense of belonging to Hong Kong were between 7.3 and 7.6 on the 0–10 scale in the three surveyed time-places. In sharp contrast, the mean scores of sense of belonging to China were merely 2.30, 2.49, and 2.20 in the three time-places.[4]

There were some differences among age groups, but the relationship between age and sense of belonging to Hong Kong is not linear. Respondents aged 25 or below had a mean score of 7.63, and respondents aged 56 or above had a mean score of 7.99. The two mean scores are higher than those registered by respondents aged 26 to 40 and respondents between 41 and 55 (7.19 and 7.09, respectively). Similarly, there is no linear relationship between sense of belonging to China and age. Respondents aged 56 or above had a substantially higher mean score of 3.29 on the variable, whereas the mean scores for the three other age groups are—from the youngest to the relatively older ones—2.45, 2.25, and 2.23, respectively.

A weak sense of belonging does not entail an active urge to separate. The movement's insistence of adopting the label "Movement" instead of "Revolution" signified its lack of a desire to explicitly challenge the sovereign regime. But the Chinese government's reluctance to allow a more open electoral system in the city has undoubtedly undermined the positive affect that the already disgruntled citizens could have had toward China. Given the young people's already low levels of sense of belonging to China, the rise of discourses about Hong Kong independence after the Umbrella Movement was not surprising.

Mode of Participation

Political scientists typically use the term "mode of participation" to refer to the different types of activities that can be undertaken by citizens within a society to influence politics. Verba and Nie's (1972) classic study in the United States differentiated among voting, campaign activity, communal activity, and personalized contacting as the four major modes of participation in the American context. Recently, van Deth (2014) differentiated among conventional participation, unconventional or non-institutional participation, civic engagement, and expressive participation. Our use of the term mode of participation is both broader and narrower than the above conventional usage. While we are concerned with mode of participation within a movement, we are not concerned merely with types of activities. Given the character of the Umbrella Movement as a protest campaign extended over time and space, the survey questionnaire contains items related to five dimensions of people's mode of participation: time spent in the occupied areas, spatial location and coverage, companionship, participation leadership, and specific actions undertaken. The five dimensions cover the temporal and spatial aspects of a person's participation, the person's relationship with his or her co-participants, and the range of activities that the person had joined during the movement.

We can begin with time spent in the occupied areas. Table A3 summarizes the data. In the October Admiralty survey, which was conducted on the 7th and 8th day of the occupation (i.e., treating September 28 as the beginning), only 3.5% of the respondents reported that they had been in the occupied areas for "eight days or more," and 18.3% reported that they had been in the occupied areas for six or seven days. The majority of the respondents had spent two to five days in the occupied areas. In the November survey, a distinctive majority in both Admiralty and MK reported that they had visited the occupied areas for eight to 14 days, while more than 10% in both areas had visited the occupied sites for 14 days or more. There was no significant difference between the Admiralty and MK participants.

Besides number of days visiting the occupied areas, people also vary in terms of the actual amount of time they spent "per visit." More than 40% of the respondents in each surveyed time-place reported spending on average "four hours or fewer" in a visit to the occupied site. Around 40% in each surveyed time-place reported spending on average "more than four but fewer than eight hours" per visit. About 10% reported spending on average eight to 12 hours per visit. The percentages of respondents who spent more than 12 hours per visit differed

Table A3 **Time spent in the occupied areas**

By survey time-points	October Admiralty	November Admiralty	November MK	Combined
Number of days spent				
1	11.2	2.6	1.7	–
2–3	36.4	5.9	7.5	–
4–5	30.5	15.1	13.3	–
6–7	18.3	17.7	14.0	–
8–14/8 or more#	3.5	47.6	49.8	–
14 or above	–	11.1	13.7	–
Time spent per day[a]				
0–4 hours	45.3	44.0	41.7	44.4
4.5–8 hours	43.2	39.2	37.8	41.5
8.5–12 hours	9.0	10.1	10.4	9.5
More than 12 hours	2.4	6.7	10.1	4.7
Ever stayed overnight[a]	26.1	53.7	62.6	38.0

By age groups	25 or below	26 to 40	41 to 55	56 or above
No. of days spent (Oct)[c]				
1	9.1	12.5	23.2	0.0
2–3	30.7	42.3	33.9	50.0
4–5	32.6	29.2	28.6	22.7
6–7	23.3	13.3	14.3	18.2
8 or more	4.3	2.7	0.0	9.1
No. of days spent (Nov)				
1	2.3	2.0	3.7	0.0
2–3	9.2	3.4	5.6	9.1
4–5	16.9	12.3	13.0	0.0
6–7	16.9	13.7	20.4	9.1
8–14	44.1	55.4	44.4	50.0
14 or above	10.7	13.2	13.0	31.8

Table A3 (**Continued**)

By age groups	25 or below	26 to 40	41 to 55	56 or above
Time spent per day[c]				
0–4 hours	29.9	56.6	61.7	53.5
4.5–8 hours	49.7	34.7	33.6	32.6
8.5–12 hours	13.4	5.7	4.7	9.3
More than 12 hours	7.0	3.0	0.0	4.7
Ever stayed overnight[c]	46.4	31.6	31.3	16.3

Notes: Entries are percentages. # In October, "number of days spent" ranges from 1 day to "8 days or above." The distributions on "number of days spent" from the October and November surveys were not compared statistically. When a variable is marked with superscript "a," the percentage distributions in the Admiralty surveys in the two months differ from each other significantly at $p < .05$ in a Chi-square or Cramer's V test. When a variable is marked with superscript "c," significant differences exist among the four age groups.

somewhat across the three time-places. Only 2.4% in the October Admiralty survey reported spending such an amount of time. The corresponding percentage is slightly higher at 6.7% in the November Admiralty survey, and the November MK survey registered the highest percentage of respondents spending more than 12 hours per visit.

The percentage distributions obtained from the November Admiralty and November MK surveys did not differ from each other statistically significantly. Similarly, while the November MK survey registered the largest percentage of participants who had stayed overnight in the occupied areas, the difference between the figures from Admiralty and MK (53.7% vs. 62.6%) is not statistically significant. Nevertheless, the percentage of people who had stayed overnight increased substantially from October to November. This is understandable—as the movement went on, the percentage of people who had ever stayed overnight in the occupied areas would continue to increase.

Time spent in the occupied areas indicates the amount of a precious personal resource that a participant was willing to spend on the movement. Hence it can be taken as an indicator of a participant's commitment. But the amount of time that a participant could spend was also constrained by biographical availability (McAdam, 1986). A middle-aged person with a full-time job and two children at home would be relatively less available than a retired person or a university student. In fact, this is the pattern emerging from Table A3. Age does not have a linear relationship with time spent. On number of days spent in the occupied areas, the youngest and the oldest age groups reported relatively larger figures.

However, the oldest participants did not necessarily spend huge amounts of time in the occupied areas. They were also less likely to have stayed overnight. This probably relates to the bodily and health conditions of the senior citizens. As a result, the youngest participants stood out as the most committed participants when time spent per day and overnight stays are concerned. More than 20% of those aged 25 or below spent on average more than eight hours per visit, whereas the percentages for the other three groups range from 4.7% to 14.0% only. Nearly half of the youngest respondents had stayed overnight, whereas about 30% of those between 26 and 55 had done so. Only 16.3% of senior citizens had stayed overnight.

Table A4 addresses another dimension of citizens' mode of participation in the Umbrella Movement, namely, spatial location and coverage. In the October Admiralty survey, we asked the respondents to indicate whether they had also visited other occupied sites. As the table shows, many respondents did not simply stay in one occupied area. While the occupied areas in Central, Wan Chai, and Admiralty may not be easily differentiated from each other because the three districts are next to each other, it is notable that 46.1% of the respondents also visited Causeway Bay, and 48.0% also visited MK.

As the occupation continued, people had more chances to visit various areas. In the November Admiralty survey, as much as 82.1% of the respondents had visited MK. Similarly, more than 90% of the November MK respondents had visited Admiralty. In both MK and Admiralty, more than 60% of the respondents had visited the occupied site in Causeway Bay.

The bottom of Table A4 shows the within-movement mobility exhibited by different age groups. Interestingly, the youngest participants seemed to exhibit lower levels of spatial mobility when one considers the percentages of respondents who had visited Causeway Bay, Tsim Sha Tsui, and MK (only the Admiralty respondents were analyzed when whether one had visited MK was concerned). For instance, only 10.1% of the respondents aged 25 or below indicated that they had visited the Tsim Sha Tsui occupied site, whereas more than 20% of those aged 41 or above had done so. However, the pattern is reversed when visiting Admiralty by the MK respondents was concerned: 91.7% of the November MK respondents aged 25 or below had visited Admiralty, whereas only 70.0% aged 56 or above had done so.

While it is difficult to provide a concrete explanation of the reversed pattern of differences between age groups in the last two rows of Table A4, it should be acknowledged that, overall speaking, the flow of participants between Admiralty and MK was asymmetric at least over the first month of the movement. The November survey included a question asking the respondents where they had spent the largest amount of time since the beginning of the Umbrella Movement. In the Admiralty survey, 92.2% of the respondents claimed they had spent the largest amount of time in Admiralty, 5.6% said that they had spent the largest

Table A4 **Visited other sites or not**

By survey time-points	October Admiralty	November Admiralty	November MK	Combined
Have you been to:				
Central[a/b]	75.6	68.1	54.6	70.4
Wan Chai[b]	57.6	56.1	45.0	54.9
Causeway Bay[a]	46.1	68.5	63.7	53.8
Tsim Sha Tsui	11.0	15.3	20.6	13.7
MK[a]	48.0	82.1	–	–
Admiralty	–	–	92.9	–

By age groups	25 or below	26 to 40	41 to 55	56 or above
Have you been to:				
Central	69.3	72.0	62.9	78.9
Wan Chai	54.4	56.4	53.5	51.5
Causeway Bay[c]	49.0	59.2	57.1	58.3
Tsim Sha Tsui[c]	10.1	16.6	21.2	20.0
MK#[c]	49.1	61.8	63.2	70.0
Admiralty#[c]	91.7	94.0	81.8	70.0

Notes: Entries are percentages. When comparisons between age groups were made regarding whether the respondents have been to MK (Admiralty), only the Admiralty (MK) respondents were included. When a variable is marked with superscript "a," the percentage distributions in the Admiralty surveys in the two months differ from each other significantly at $p < .05$ in a Chi-square test. When a variable is marked with superscript "b," the percentage distributions obtained from the two occupied areas in November differ from each other significantly at $p < .05$ in a Chi-square test. When a variable is marked with superscript "c," significant differences ($p < .05$ in a Chi-square test) exist among the percentage distributions from the age groups.

amount of time in MK, and 2.2% claimed that they had spent the largest amount of time in other areas. In contrast, in the MK survey, only 58.2% claimed that they had spent the largest amount of time in MK, whereas 39.9% had spent the largest amount of time in Admiralty.

There are two main possibilities for a respondent who had spent the largest amount of time in one area to be included in the survey conducted in another area: either they were having an occasional visit to another occupied site, or they had "migrated" from one site to the other. The fact that 39.9% of the MK respondents had spent the largest amount of time in Admiralty suggests the possibility that some participants who spent their time primarily in Admiralty in the earliest days of the movement had "migrated" to MK later.

The dynamics of how participants flowed from one occupied area to the others certainly could not be easily mapped by a few survey questions. But the findings in Table A4 do signify the interconnectedness among the occupied areas. The various occupied areas were not split off from each other. They were interconnected in the sense that the participants did move around the various sites.

We can then turn to the companions that the participants had in the Umbrella Movement. Since the Umbrella Movement was not a single protest march occurring on a single day, the respondents might have different companions on different days. Therefore, the percentages shown in Table A5 refer to whether the respondents had ever visited (or stayed in) the occupied sites together with specific types of companions (or without companion).

More than 40% of the respondents in the October Admiralty survey had the experience of visiting the occupied areas alone, while about 80% in November had the experience of visiting the occupied areas alone. Similar to the July 1 protest (Lee & Chan, 2011), it was very common for the Umbrella Movement participants to have visited the occupied areas with others. Between 74% and 80% of the respondents in the three time-places had visited the occupied areas with friends. Around 30% to 40% had done so with classmates, while about 20% to 30% had visited the sites with family members.

Illustrative of the "self-mobilized" character of the Umbrella Movement, only 8.4% to 11.8% of the respondents in the three surveyed time-places had ever visited or stayed in the occupied areas with the social organizations that they belonged to. Similarly, only 2.2% to 5.9% of the respondents in the three time-places reported having visited the occupied areas with the social sectors they belonged to.

The bottom of Table A5 shows that young people were relatively less likely to have visited the occupied areas alone. Only 52.3% of the respondents aged 25 or below had done so, whereas the figure is 72.7% for respondents aged 56 or above. This is seemingly the result of the relative ease for young people to call upon their friends or classmates to act together. Nearly 90% of participants aged 25 or below had visited the occupied areas with friends, while 53.6% of the respondents aged 41 to 55 had done so, and the figure falls to merely 29.5% for those aged 56 or above. At the same time, more than 60% of respondents aged 25 or below had visited the occupied areas with their classmates. The corresponding percentages are understandably much lower for the other age groups.

Young people were less likely to have visited the occupied areas with their family members. Since most of the young participants were probably not yet married, only 6.6% of respondents aged 25 or below participated with their spouses, whereas nearly or more than half of the respondents at 41 or above had visited the

Table A5 **Companions at the protest**

By survey time-points	October Admiralty	November Admiralty	November MK	Combined
Alone[a/b]	43.3	78.0	81.1	56.7
With spouse	18.4	21.6	19.3	19.1
With family member[a]	18.6	31.1	24.3	21.9
With boyfriend/girlfriend	26.9	21.6	27.4	26.0
With friends[a]	80.1	74.4	78.4	78.7
With classmates[b]	41.9	43.2	33.4	40.5
With colleagues[a]	19.5	28.6	22.0	21.6
With organizations	8.8	8.4	11.8	9.3
With social sector[a]	2.2	5.9	5.7	3.5
By age groups	**25 or below**	**26 to 40**	**41 to 55**	**56 or above**
Alone[c]	52.3	58.8	65.2	72.7
With spouse[c]	6.6	26.5	48.2	52.3
With family member[c]	18.8	22.1	34.8	43.2
With boyfriend/girlfriend[c]	26.3	30.1	8.0	9.1
With friends[c]	88.3	77.1	53.6	29.5
With classmates[c]	60.6	26.1	5.4	2.3
With colleagues[c]	18.3	28.4	13.4	4.5
With organizations[c]	13.1	6.4	3.6	9.1
With social sector	3.6	3.4	4.5	0.0

Notes: Entries are percentages. When a variable is marked with superscript "a," the percentage distributions in the Admiralty surveys in the two months differ from each other significantly at $p < .05$ in a Chi-square test. When a variable is marked with superscript "b," the percentage distributions obtained from the two occupied areas in November differ from each other significantly at $p < .05$ in a Chi-square test. When a variable is marked with superscript "c," significant differences ($p < .05$ in a Chi-square test) exist among the percentage distributions from the various groups.

occupied areas with their spouses. Only 18.8% of participants aged 25 or below had visited the occupied areas with other family members, whereas more than one-third of respondents aged 41 or above had done so. Interestingly, the youngest participants were somewhat more likely to have participated together with the social organizations that they belonged to: 13.1% of the respondents aged 25 or below had done so, as opposed to less than 10% in the other three age groups. This is probably because many participating students were members of student associations or groups, and some student groups might have organized their members to act together.

When people participate in a movement with others, they could be the ones who call upon others to participate with them, or they could be the ones who are largely called upon to act by others. We use the term "participation leader" to refer to a person who contributes to the mobilization process behind a political activity by making people around him or her more likely to participate in the activity. The concern underlying the concept is the extent to which ordinary citizens can play a role in the mobilization process behind a political activity by influencing others. The concept of participation leadership is similar to the concept of opinion leadership in communication research (Katz & Lazarsfeld, 1955; Weimann, 1991). Both concepts deal with the flow of social influence through interpersonal networks. Opinion leaders, as Nisbet and Kotcher (2009) explicated, "did not necessarily hold formal positions of power or prestige in communities but rather served as the connective communication tissue that alerted their peers to what mattered among political events, social issues, and consumer choices" (p. 329). Similarly, the participation leaders are not necessarily the activity organizers and may not even be members of the organizing groups; they can simply be citizens who have exerted influences on other people's participation decision.

Social influence of the participation leaders can be exercised through interpersonal or impersonal communication (Huckfeldt & Sprague, 1995). That is, people can directly mobilize others to act or persuade others to support a cause. Alternatively, people can affect others simply through sending out signals about one's attitudes and/or behavioral decisions. In the Umbrella Movement, for instance, a person can send a signal to others regarding one's attitude by wearing a yellow (or blue) ribbon. Wearing a yellow ribbon by itself is not an act of interpersonal communication, but it does communicate one's attitude, and the signal may affect the calculation and decision of others.

Therefore, conceptually speaking, there are numerous possible indicators of participation leadership. But for simplicity, we focus only on direct mobilization, that is, whether the participants had tried to invite others to participate in the movement. Most of the respondents had indeed tried to invite others. In the October Admiralty survey, 40.4% of the respondents had invited others "once or twice," while 42.4% had invited others "many times." In the November Admiralty survey, 35.6% had invited others "once or twice," and 42.7% had invited others "many times." The figures from the MK survey were similar.

Young people were particularly active in inviting others to join the Umbrella Movement. More than half (54.3%) of the respondents aged 25 or below had invited others "many times." Only 10.1% in the group had never invited others. Among people between 26 and 40 years old, 34.1% had invited others "many times," whereas 23.1% had not invited others. Among people at 56 or above, only 19.5% had invited others "many times," and 51.2% had not invited others. These figures show that young people indeed constituted the "leaders" in the movement not only because of the leadership role played by HKFS and Scholarism in the movement at large, but also because of the leadership role the young participants played in the broader social mobilization process.

Finally, we can turn to the specific activities that the movement participants had engaged in. As discussed throughout the book, participants in the Umbrella Movement had engaged in a wide range of personalized activities. But there was also a range of activities that are more or less important for the sustaining or even survival of the movement. These include donating money and other resources to the movement, coordinating the delivery of materials and maintaining order within the occupied areas, setting up blockades in strategic areas, and confronting counter-protesters or the police at times.

Table A6 shows the extent to which the participants had joined various activities. The October Admiralty survey did not include many relevant items. But even in the very early stage, more than one-third of the participants had already helped deliver materials or maintain order in the occupied areas, and more than one-third had joined the civic seminars offered by volunteer teachers. Meanwhile, nearly 20% had joined discussions in the occupied areas about the directions or strategies of the movement.

By November, the percentages of participants who had joined such activities had risen substantially. More than 40% of the respondents in both occupied areas had joined discussions of strategies, and more than 50% in both areas had helped deliver materials or maintain order and attended civic lectures or seminars. At the same time, more than half of the respondents in both Admiralty and MK had helped protect the occupied areas when the police took action. More than 60% had donated material resources to the movement.

The MK participants were more likely than the Admiralty participants to have helped set up road blockades, handled the anti-occupation protesters, and protected the occupied area. But the Admiralty respondents were more likely to have participated in supportive actions outside the occupied areas. Some of these differences can be understood together with other differences between the two sites shown earlier. For instance, the higher percentages of people setting up blockades and handling the anti-occupation protesters in MK are consistent with the finding that supporters of the more radical political groups, which often emphasized direct and valiant actions, had a stronger presence in MK. There were arguably more participants in MK who were ready to engage in confrontations with counter-protesters or the police.

Table A6 **Participation in actions inside and outside the occupied areas**

By survey time-points	October Admiralty	November Admiralty	November Mong Kok	Combined (Nov. only)
a. Discussing movement directions/strategies in the occupied areas[a]	18.4	43.6	44.9	44.3
b. Delivering materials or maintaining order in the occupied areas[a]	36.6	55.7	60.1	58.0
c. Attending civic lectures or seminars in the area[a]	37.2	59.3	55.1	57.1
d. Setting up the blockade[b]	–	26.4	38.2	32.5
e. Handling the anti-occupation protesters[b]	–	36.3	53.0	45.0
f. Helping protect the occupied areas when police take actions[b]	–	52.4	63.5	58.2
g. Donating material resources	–	68.5	65.9	67.1
h. Donating money	–	13.2	10.8	12.0
i. Participating in actions outside the occupied areas to support the movement[b]	–	57.9	48.0	52.7

By age groups	25 or below	26 to 40	41 to 55	56 or above
a. Discuss strategies	49.2	40.8	37.5	54.5
b. Delivery materials[c]	61.8	61.7	42.9	40.9
c. Attend lectures	56.9	59.2	51.8	68.2
d. Set up blockades[c]	37.0	32.0	23.2	13.6
e. Handle counter-protests	46.9	42.7	46.4	50.0
f. Protect area	62.2	56.3	50.0	63.6
g. Donate resources[c]	71.8	71.8	48.2	45.5
h. Donate money	12.6	12.6	10.7	4.5
i. Participate outside	53.1	53.9	50.0	45.5

Notes: Entries are percentages. When a variable is marked with superscript "a," the percentage distributions in the Admiralty surveys in the two months differ from each other significantly at $p < .05$ in a Chi-square test. When a variable is marked with superscript "b," the percentage distributions obtained from the two occupied areas in November differ from each other significantly at $p < .05$ in a Chi-square test. When a variable is marked with superscript "c," significant differences ($p < .05$ in a Chi-square test) exist among the four age groups. For simplicity, when calculating the percentages for the "combined" column and when examining the differences between age groups, only respondents from the November survey were included in the analysis.

Nevertheless, the differences between areas in Table A6 are not substantial. In the end, the similarities between the participants in the two areas are more important than their differences. What the top half of Table A6 shows is that the participants in the Umbrella Movement were active on various fronts.

The bottom of Table A6 shows the differences between age groups in degree of activeness in various forms of actions. The results show that young participants were more active in setting up road blockades and in delivering materials and maintaining order. Among the November respondents aged 25 or below, 37.0% had helped set up road blockades, whereas only 23.2% of those between 41 and 55 and 13.6% of those aged 56 or above had done so. More than 60% of respondents age 40 or below had helped deliver materials or maintain order, whereas only around 40% of those in the two older groups had done so. Young people were also more likely to have donated material resources. More than 70% of participants aged 40 or below had done so, whereas less than half of those aged 41 or above had donated material resources.

However, there were no significant differences between age groups with respect to the other six items. The age groups were more or less equally active in confronting the counter-protesters, confronting the police, discussing movement strategies, donating money, attending civic lectures, and participating in supportive activities outside the occupied areas. On the whole, one should not exaggerate the differences among the age groups in degree of activeness.

Reasons to Participate and Beliefs about the Movement

After examining the participants' mode of participation, this section examines the participants' self-proclaimed reasons to participate and their beliefs and perceptions about the movement. The survey asked the respondents if they would agree that a list of reasons were important to their participation decision. The respondents indicated their answers with a five-point scale ranging from 1 = very unimportant to 5 = very important. Table A7 summarizes the descriptive statistics by showing the percentages of respondents recognizing a reason for participation as important (i.e., "important" or "highly important" in the five-point scale).

Self-reported reasons to participate in an action do not always reflect the most important factors driving participation as discernible through multivariate statistical analysis. This is partly because individuals are not always aware of the social and psychological forces behind their behavior, partly because of social desirability, and partly because people draw upon available cultural and discursive resources when making sense of their own behavior. But self-reported reasons are not meaningless. They reflect the degree to which the participants would find it appropriate to publicly acknowledge a reason for participation as important.

Table A7 **Reasons to participate in the movement**

By survey time-points	October Admiralty	November Admiralty	November Mong Kok	Combined
Reasons for participation				
Fight for election without filter	86.4	81.7	86.8	85.6
Fight for civil nomination[a]	76.6	66.3	72.3	73.9
Protect Hong Kong's liberty	89.7	87.2	88.9	89.1
The use of tear gas[a]	60.4	52.4	49.7	56.9
Police's handling of the protest[a]	–	48.7	50.0	49.5
Support and protect students[b]	72.4	70.0	58.4	69.3
Empower the movement	37.3	40.3	38.9	38.1
Experience mass protests[a]	12.3	18.7	17.6	14.4
Mobilized by friends	4.1	6.2	8.1	5.3
Mobilized by family/relatives	3.2	5.5	6.4	4.2
Call from HKFS[a]	12.9	19.0	14.2	14.2
Call from Scholarism	12.9	15.0	12.5	13.2
Call from OC Trio	6.2	7.7	7.1	6.6
Call from other organizations	5.4	7.0	6.8	5.9
By age groups	*25 or below*	*26 to 40*	*41 to 55*	*56 or above*
Fight for election without filter[c]	87.0	82.9	88.4	95.5
Fight for civil nomination	75.0	71.9	73.2	79.5
Protect Hong Kong's liberty	88.4	89.6	87.5	95.5
The use of tear gas[c]	50.6	62.0	62.5	68.2
Police's handling pf the protest[c]	45.8	52.9	48.2	59.1
Support and protect students[c]	61.8	74.7	79.5	86.4
Empower the movement[c]	34.5	36.7	53.6	72.7
Experience mass protests[c]	11.4	12.7	28.6	52.3
Mobilized by friends[c]	4.7	4.2	5.4	29.5
Mobilized by family/relatives[c]	2.2	3.4	7.1	34.1
Call from HKFS[c]	9.7	12.1	33.0	65.9
Call from Scholarism[c]	8.8	12.7	28.6	52.3
Call from OC Trio[c]	3.7	5.1	17.9	45.5
Call from other organizations[c]	4.3	4.2	16.1	29.5

Notes: Entries are percentages. When a variable is marked with superscript "a," the percentage distributions in the Admiralty surveys in the two months differ from each other significantly at $p < .05$ in a Chi-square test. When a variable is marked with superscript "b," the percentage distributions obtained from the two occupied areas in November differ from each other significantly at $p < .05$ in a Chi-square test. When a variable is marked with superscript "c," significant differences ($p < .05$ in a Chi-square test) exist among the percentage distributions from the four age groups.

The absolute majority of the participants understandably recognized "fighting for a filter-less election" and "protecting Hong Kong's liberty" as important reasons for their participation. That is, participants in a political activity are most likely to refer to the stated aims and espoused values of the activity as their main reason to participate. The results of the two items do not vary significantly across the three time-places. More than three-fourths of the respondents (76.6%) in Admiralty in October also regarded "fighting for civil nomination" as an important reason to join the movement. Interestingly, the percentage of respondents recognizing fighting for civil nomination as important declined somewhat to 66.3% in the November Admiralty survey.

Many respondents in the October Admiralty survey recognized the police's use of tear gas as an important reason driving them to act—a theme that Chapter 4 has addressed at length. Understandably, the importance of the police's use of tear gas as a reason for participation declined in November, but there were still around half of the respondents in both Admiralty and MK recognizing the use of tear gas as a reason for participation. There were also around half of the respondents in both areas recognizing the police's handling of the protesters as an important reason for participation.

Associated with the police's use of tear gas and handling of protesters is the idea of protecting and supporting the students. More than 70% of the respondents in Admiralty in October acknowledged it as an important reason for their participation. Interestingly, in November, there was a difference between Admiralty and MK. Since the main student groups HKFS and Scholarism had stayed largely in Admiralty, the Admiralty participants were more likely to recognize supporting and protecting the students as a reason for their participation.

Other items were recognized as important reasons for participation to much lesser extents. In all three surveyed time-places, only about 40% of the respondents regarded "empowering the movement" as an important reason for participation. Only between 12% and 19% in the three time-places regarded "experiencing mass protests" as an important reason for participation. More important, most respondents did not regard mobilization by other people and groups as important. At most, between 12% and 20% of the respondents in the three surveyed time-places regarded the calls to action issued by the HKFS and the calls issued by Scholarism as important. Notably, since the Umbrella Movement began, the two student organizations have taken over from OCLP to become the most recognized movement leaders. Only between 6% and 8% of the participants in the three surveyed time-places recognized the calls to action issued by the Trio as important to their participation decision. The participants also did not treat "other social organizations" or their own friends and family members as important sources of influence.

There is no significant difference between Admiralty and MK in the extent to which the participants were willing to treat the main organizers' calls to action as important reasons for participation. The main leaders of the movement were largely stationed in Admiralty, and during the movement, there was a perception among the public that the MK participants were less willing to follow the leadership of the main organizing groups. But the figures in Table A7 show that the participants in the two areas were equally likely (or equally unlikely) to recognize the mobilizing influence of the three organizers on themselves.[5]

The bottom of Table A7 shows the extent to which respondents belonging to different age groups recognized the various reasons for participation as important. Generally speaking, the basic pattern is largely the same for the different age groups: people were most likely to recognize the values and goals of the movement as important, followed by the police's use of tear gas and handling of the protesters, followed by the desire to empower the movement, and lastly followed by the mobilizing influences of the organizers and other groups and people.

Nevertheless, there are also significant and sometimes very substantial differences among the age groups. The young participants were significantly less likely to recognize almost the full range of possible reasons for participation as important. For instance, only 45.8% of the respondents aged 25 or below regarded the police's use of tear gas as an important reason for participation, whereas 59.1% of those aged 56 or above recognized it as important. Only about one-third of the respondents aged 25 or below regarded empowering the movement as an important reason for participation, whereas as much as 72.7% of those aged 56 or above treated the reason as important.

The same differences between age groups exist even on the items regarding the mobilizing influence of the HKFS and Scholarism. Although the two are student groups, the youngest respondents were not the most likely to acknowledge their mobilizing influence. Only less than 10% of respondents aged 25 or below recognized the calls for action issued by the HKFS and Scholarism as important reasons for participation. The percentages increased to around 30% for those between 41 and 55 and to more than 50% for the oldest group. These findings suggest that the youngest participants were the most adamant about the "independent" and "self-mobilized" character of their own participation in the movement.

We now turn to the respondents' other beliefs and perceptions about the Umbrella Movement. First, we focus on how the respondents understood the values and interests underlying the movement. We asked the respondents the extent to which they regarded "universal values," "democratization of China," and "local interests" as the foundational values of the Umbrella Movement. The notion of universal values is often appropriated by the democrats in their call for democratization and defense of human rights, press freedom, and other civil liberties in Hong Kong. Meanwhile, many democrats in Hong Kong were historically concerned with democratization not only of Hong Kong but also of China at large. However, increased conflicts between Hong Kong and China in recent years led to the rise of the localists, who regarded democratization of China as a non-issue. To the local-ists, Hong Kong citizens should simply focus on defending their local interests.

Respondents were asked to indicate the importance of the three notions to the Umbrella Movement using a five-point Likert scale (1 = very unimportant to 5 = very important). As Table A8 shows, the October Admiralty respondents treated

Table A8 **Perceived foundational beliefs of the movement and views on self-mobilization**

By survey time-points	October Admiralty	November Admiralty	November Mong Kok	Combined
Perceived foundational beliefs				
Local interest[b]	4.23	4.27	4.57	4.30
Universal values	4.46	4.34	4.46	4.44
Democratization of China[a]	3.54	3.35	3.25	3.45
Views on self-mobilization				
S-M movements are purer[a/b]	4.03	3.89	4.18	4.03
S-M can prevent hijacking[b]	3.83	3.74	4.09	3.87
S-M leads to loss of focus[b]	3.03	2.99	2.61	2.94
S-M leads to loss of leadership[a/b]	3.41	3.22	2.99	3.30
By age groups	25 or below	26 to 40	41 to 55	56 or above
Perceived foundational beliefs				
Local interest[c]	4.35	4.29	4.24	4.03
Universal values[c]	4.39	4.47	4.53	4.74
Democratization of China[c]	3.38	3.40	3.77	4.44
Views on self-mobilization				
S-M movements are purer[c]	3.96	4.07	4.28	4.36
S-M can prevent hijacking	3.89	3.79	4.01	4.05
S-M leads to loss of focus	2.93	3.00	2.78	3.03
S-M leads to lack of leadership[c]	3.24	3.41	3.22	3.13

Notes: Entries are mean scores on five-point Likert scales (1 = very unimportant / strongly disagree to 5 = very important / strongly agree). When a variable is marked with superscript "a," the mean scores in the Admiralty surveys in the two months differ from each other at $p < .05$ in an independent samples t-test. When a variable is marked with superscript "b," the percentage distributions obtained from the two occupied areas in November differ from each other at $p < .05$ in an independent samples t-test. When a variable is marked with superscript "c," significant differences ($p < .05$ in one-way ANOVA) exist among the four age groups.

universal values as the most important foundation of the movement, followed by local interests. Both obtain a mean score higher than 4. In contrast, the mean score obtained by democratization of China is much lower at 3.54, even though the mean score is still higher than the midpoint of the scale.

As the Umbrella Movement progressed, the importance of democratization of China fell further. The mean score of the item in the November Admiralty survey is significantly lower than the mean score obtained in the October survey. Besides, there was a significant difference in the mean scores on "local interest" in the November Admiralty survey and the November MK survey, already noted in Chapter 5. When compared to the Admiralty respondents, the MK participants treated local interest as more important. In fact, in the November MK survey, local interest is the notion registering the highest mean score.

There are also significant differences between age groups in perceived importance of the three notions. The youngest respondents were more likely to regard local interest as important to the movement. The mean score for the youngest group on the item is 4.35, whereas the mean scores for the other three groups are lower at 4.29, 4.24, and 4.03, respectively. In contrast, the young respondents were relatively less likely to acknowledge the importance of universal values and the quest for democratization in China. The youngest group had a mean score of 4.39 on universal values, whereas the other three age groups obtained mean scores from 4.47 to 4.74. The youngest respondents had a mean score of only 3.38 on perceived importance of democratization of China, while the oldest respondents had a mean score of 4.44. Nevertheless, it should be noted that, even among the youngest group, universal values was still perceived to be the most important to the movement.

Lastly, since the Umbrella Movement was widely regarded as the result of citizen self-mobilization, the survey asked the respondents their views about the possible advantages and disadvantages of citizen self-mobilization. The respondents in all three time-places generally agreed with the statements that "movements based on self-mobilization are purer" and "self-mobilization can prevent a movement from being hijacked."[6] The mean scores for the two statements in the three time-places are all around 4 on a five-point Likert scale.

The respondents were substantially less likely to agree with the two statements pointing toward the potential problems of citizen self-mobilization. In the October Admiralty survey, the statement "self-mobilization may lead to a loss of focus of the movement" obtained a mean score of 3.03, which means that the average respondent in the survey was basically neutral toward the statement. The mean score of the statement remains close to the midpoint of the scale in the November Admiralty survey, while the November MK respondents were more likely to disagree with it. Comparatively, the respondents were somewhat more likely to agree with the statement "self-mobilization may lead to the problem of lack of leadership." The mean score of the item in the October Admiralty survey is 3.41, which means that the average respondent from the survey tended to agree, though not very strongly, with the statement. The mean score of the item was lower in the November Admiralty survey, though it was still higher than the midpoint of the scale. Meanwhile, the mean score of the item was close to the midpoint of the scale in the November MK survey; that is, the average respondent in MK in November was neutral toward the statement.

As already pointed out in Chapter 5, the MK respondents were consistently more positive toward the notion of self-mobilization when compared to the Admiralty respondents. Meanwhile, were the youngest participants particularly positive toward the idea of self-mobilization? Interestingly, the bottom of Table A8 shows it was not the case. The four age groups do not differ significantly on level of agreement with "self-mobilization can prevent a movement from being hijacked" and "self-mobilization can lead to a loss of focus." There are significant differences among the mean scores of the four age groups on the other two items. But the youngest respondents were actually the least likely to see self-mobilized movements as purer. Also, while participants between 26 and 40 years old were the most likely to agree that self-mobilization can lead to the problem of lack of leadership, the youngest group had a mean score that is nominally higher than the mean scores for the two oldest groups. On the whole, when differences between age groups exist, the youngest group was less positive toward the idea of self-mobilization when compared to the two oldest groups.

Summary and Additional Remarks

To recapitulate, the Umbrella Movement participants were mostly young people under 40 years old and were mostly highly educated. About a quarter of the participants were current university students. When asked to self-report their social class, the participants were more or less evenly split between the middle class and the lower or grassroots class. But when compared to the July 1 protests in Hong Kong, participants in the Umbrella Movement were more likely to regard themselves as belonging to the lower or grassroots class.

The latter finding is significant given the prevalence of young and highly educated people in the movement. Political economists around the world have discussed the emergence of the "new poor": poor people are no longer confined to the geographical locations and social groups where they were conventionally found. Instead, as an editorial of the British newspaper *Independent* stated, "those meeting the definition of poor—a fluid concept—are increasingly young, in work, and living in private accommodation."[7] It is beyond the scope of this book to address the extent to which there is indeed the emergence of the "new poor" in Hong Kong. But as discussed in Chapter 2, young people have become increasingly critical toward income inequality and the dominance of big corporations. If they are not necessarily "objectively" in the conditions of poverty, young people nowadays have become more likely to subjectively identify themselves as, and with, the grassroots. The relatively high percentage of young people classifying themselves as belonging to the lower or grassroots class thus hints at the point that underlying the Umbrella Movement's demand for genuine democracy are broader concerns of social justice and equality. This reading of the Umbrella Movement would tie it even closer to a range of anti-austerity movements around the world in recent years (Della Porta, 2015).

The analysis examined five dimensions of the participants' mode of participation. Many of the participants spent a substantial amount of time in the areas, even though personal commitment and biographical availability led to inevitable variations. The participants visited different occupied areas, though many of them probably had a "base" in one of the occupied areas. People visited or stayed in the occupied areas, often together with their friends and family members. But a large percentage of participants had also visited or stayed in the occupied areas alone, showing that companionship was not necessary for participation. Most of the participants had tried to invite others to join the movement, and a substantial proportion had done so "many times." The participants were also active in onsite activities ranging from attending civic lectures offered by volunteer academics to building road blockades and confronting counter-protesters.

On the whole, the findings thus portray a form of truly active participation. In fact, the survey questions are by no means comprehensive. They certainly cannot capture all forms of actions undertaken by the participants, especially the more personalized and small group–based actions. The presence of a wide range of action opportunities constitutes part of the appeal of a large-scale and extended movement, as people can choose among the existing participation possibilities or sometimes even create their new and individualized possibilities, in the process constructing their own unique mode of participation in the movement.

One finding that emerges from the survey data and already discussed earlier in this book is the difference between the MK and Admiralty occupied areas. The MK participants were significantly more likely to be supporters of the more radical political parties and groups, more likely to regard themselves as belonging to the grassroots or lower class, and more active in confrontational actions such as building road blockades and confronting the police and counter-protesters. They put more emphasis on the importance of local interests and exhibited a more positive attitude toward the idea of self-mobilization. Combined together, the finding suggested the character of the MK occupation as relatively more local, grassroots, valiant, and masculine (as a matter of fact, there were substantially more men than women in the MK occupied area).

Movement participants and observers in Hong Kong should not be surprised by the above findings. Besides what we have already discussed in earlier chapters, the differences between the Admiralty and MK participants also hinted at the point that the characteristics of the urban environment in Hong Kong have implications on the occupation protests. The Admiralty occupation site, located in a financial district and surrounded by business buildings, might tend to attract participants with more middle-class and cosmopolitan orientations. These participants then helped further construct the actual atmosphere in the occupied area through their creative actions: building a self-study area, setting up a Lennon Wall, placing the tents in an almost overly orderly fashion, etc. The atmosphere created through such actions in turn tended to attract certain types of participants to come and/or stay.

The same applies to the MK occupation, which occurred in a grassroots residential and shopping district. Perhaps it is "reasonable" for a temporary temple of the God of Kwan to have been erected in MK instead of Admiralty. Besides, it is worth mentioning that local gangsters (or people who were reportedly gangsters) had tried to attack the occupation area in the district in the early days of the movement. It is unlikely to be a coincidence that attack by suspected gangsters occurred only in the grassroots residential district of MK and not in the financial district of Admiralty. In other words, the atmosphere and characteristics of an occupied area is also shaped by the interactions between the protesters and the movement's opponents.

Certainly, we did not have data about the MK participants in early October. Therefore we could not ascertain the degree to which the differences between the two areas were already existent in the early days of the occupation. But the onsite survey data do show that a substantial proportion of the MK participants in November had actually spent most of their time in the Admiralty area since the beginning of the movement. As we pointed out earlier, one possible interpretation of this finding is that some participants who were originally stationed in Admiralty had "migrated" to MK. If this interpretation is correct, the finding would become further evidence of the dynamic evolution of the occupation areas. It would also become a piece of evidence hinting at the tendency toward decentralization in the Umbrella Movement: while there were participants who "migrated" from Admiralty to MK in the first month of the movement, there was no evidence of "migration" of participants in the other direction. There was a net movement of people away from where the movement leaders were stationed.

Notes

Chapter 1

1. According to the polls conducted by the Centre for Communication and Public Opinion Survey at the Chinese University of Hong Kong. Results can be found at: http://www.com.cuhk.edu.hk/ccpos/research/taskforce-en.html.

2. For instance, just three days after the beginning of the protest, Voice of America published an online article discussing the role of social media in the Hong Kong protest. See http://www.voanews.com/content/social-media-documenting-not-driving-hong-kong-protests/2468696.html.

3. Article 45 of the Basic Law stipulates that: "The method for selecting the Chief Executive shall be specified in the light of the actual situation in the Hong Kong Special Administrative Region and in accordance with the principle of gradual and orderly progress. The ultimate aim is the selection of the Chief Executive by universal suffrage upon nomination by a broadly representative nominating committee in accordance with democratic procedures."

4. Throughout the book, family name goes first when a name is based on Chinese pronunciation, but family name goes second when the person uses an English name. For simplicity, when the person uses an English name, his or her Chinese first name is omitted.

5. Benny Tai, "The most lethal weapon of civil disobedience," *Hong Kong Economic Journal*, January 16, 2013, A16.

6. Scholarism achieved prominence in the public arena largely as a result of the anti–national education campaign that it led in 2012. The anti–national education movement succeeded in forcing the government to scrap the plan to turn national education into a core subject for primary schools. The protesting public worried that national education would become the subject through which the government could "brainwash" young children about the situation in China.

7. This was acknowledged by the Trio in the news both before and after the occupation, for example, http://rthk.hk/rthk/news/expressnews/20140926/news_20140926_55_1040133.htm.

8. This is based on personal observations by the authors. In late September, when the Trio announced the plan to start Occupy Central on October 1, they used the coded language of "the banquet" to refer to the occupation action because of the fear that talking about Occupy Central explicitly would allow the police to arrest them for openly inciting illegal actions. Around the time, many pro-democracy citizens claimed that they would "attend the wedding ceremony" but not "the banquet," meaning that they would go to support the occupiers without actually participating in the occupation.

9. Both the core leaders of the movement and many pro-movement academics were wary of China seeing the movement as having the aim of overthrowing the Communist Party. Hence

they rejected the notion of "revolution" and insisted that they were only demanding democracy for Hong Kong. Some movement participants and online media outlets continued to use the term "revolution," though.

10. In Hong Kong, the term "grassroots" is often used to replace the term "lower" in local parlance when discussing people and social classes at the lower echelons of the society.

11. General Kwan Yu was a historical figure treated as a god in the Taoist religion. Kwan is hailed in Chinese culture for his loyalty to his swear-brothers and is conventionally worshipped both by gangsters and in police stations in Hong Kong.

12. One of the opinion polls was conducted by the Centre for Communication and Public Opinion Survey at the Chinese University of Hong Kong in early November. The results showed that 67% of the general public believed that the protesters should retreat immediately: http://www.com.cuhk.edu.hk/ccpos/research/1411TaskForce_SurveyResult_141117_English.pdf.

13. One of the most interesting examples of on-site improvisatory actions was the frontline activists singing birthday songs when anti-occupation protesters went to the occupied areas and attempted to provoke the occupiers.

14. For example, during parts of the occupation campaign and especially in the Mong Kok occupation, some protesters were dissatisfied when the atmosphere in the occupied areas became too "carnivalesque."

15. In fact, toward the end of the occupation action, there were discussions among movement participants about the possibility of some of the prominent movement leaders joining the elections of the District Council and the Legislative Council in 2015 and 2016. This shows that the movement participants and leaders understood that they could not disregard the formal political institutions.

16. According to government statistics, the household broadband penetration rate was 82.9% in October 2014, and the mobile subscriber penetration rate was 238.4% (i.e., each citizen had 2.38 mobile numbers on average). The figures are available at: http://ofca.gov.hk/en/media_focus/data_statistics/key_stat/index.html.

Chapter 2

1. The figures were derived from http://www.police.gov.hk/ppp_en/09_statistics/poes.html (last accessed on December 7, 2015). By Hong Kong law, all public marches and rallies need to apply for a "letter of no objection" from the police. Even anti-government groups typically follow the procedure. Therefore, the police figures should be very close to the actual numbers of rallies and marches that were held in various years.

2. A search was conducted to derive articles mentioning any one of nine keywords: *kong-ji* (protest), *zap-wui* (rally), *zing-zo* (sit-in), *si-wai* (demonstration), *baa-gung* (labor strike), *baa-fo* (student strike), *maan-sai* (slow-driving), *zyut-sik* (hunger-strike), and *jau-hang* (marching). Cantonese pronunciation is used here as well as in other parts of the book unless otherwise indicated. The search was restricted to the main news pages and Hong Kong news sections.

3. The procedure does not capture all articles covering protests. But it should have captured a substantial proportion of relevant articles. The sample should suffice for the present purpose. Two assistants coded the articles after several rounds of training. Inter-coder reliability was calculated by the coders coding the same 188 articles derived from systematic sampling. All reported items have Scott's *pi* higher than 0.80 or percent of agreement above 95%.

4. We did not differentiate the civic groups further because it was impossible for the coders to recognize all civic associations and classify them properly; labor unions, in contrast, are more recognizable as such.

5. When only counting those protests with information about protest organizers, cross-tabulating a dichotomized variable "civic groups vs. other types of organizers" with the dichotomous period variable shows that the drop in percentages is statistically significant with $\chi^2 = 5.01, p < .03$.

6. Cross-tabulating a dichotomized variable "self-organizing citizens vs. other types of organizers" with the period variable shows that the increase is statistically significant with Cramer's $V = 0.089, p < .01$.

7. The separate dichotomous variables were recombined into a single dichotomous variable instead of summed into an internal level index because each dichotomous variable registered only a very small percentage of "1"s. Summation will produce a highly skewed item that may not be as meaningful as a simpler dichotomous variable.

8. The decrease in percentage in the case of violence or disruption in headline/lead is statistically significant with $\chi^2 = 7.33, p < .01$, whereas the decrease in percentage of violence or disruption in other parts of the article falls short of being statistically significant ($\chi^2 = 3.16, p = .076$).

9. The categories include "organizers/leaders," "participants," "target," "police/security," "mediator between protesters and targets," "counter-protesters," "observers/bystanders," and "others."

10. All surveys were conducted by university research centers using probability sampling and telephone interview. There can be minor variations among the surveys in the age range under study (e.g., some surveys interviewed citizens 15 or above, whereas others interviewed citizens 18 or above; some of the surveys included an age ceiling at 70). But this should not create huge influences on the mean scores of the efficacy items.

11. For instance, among the 299 members of the Standing Committee of the 12th Chinese People's Political Consultative Conference (since April 2014), 16 are representatives from Hong Kong. Among these 16 people, four are owners of media organizations in the city, while a fifth had worked as the CEO of Asia Television Ltd. in the past.

12. A series of events and controversies between 2013 and early 2014 signified the quick worsening of press freedom in Hong Kong. The events included news about Chinese banks withdrawing advertising from a few newspapers, a controversy surrounding the change of chief editorship in the liberal-oriented *Ming Pao*, the physical attack on the *Ming Pao* chief editor who had just stepped down from his position, and a radio station's decision to fire its popular and daring radio talk show host. The Hong Kong Journalists Association (2014) titled their annual report in 2014 "Press freedom under siege."

13. Wilson Wong, "Nothing to fear about the number of protesters on July 1? Weak society does not entail strong government," *Ming Pao*, July 10, 2009, A33.

14. "Netizens protested against the police's selective execution of law," *Metro Daily*, February 11, 2008, p. P01.

15. Sze Ka-yun, "Post-80s, rise?" *Hong Kong Economic Journal*, January 26, 2010, P16.

16. At most, a study by Wong and Wan (2009), drawing upon survey data in the mid-2000s, found a significant difference among age cohorts on value orientation at the bivariate level. But age ceases to significantly predict post-material orientation when other demographic factors are controlled.

17. While the surveys reported here adopted the format of the post-materialism questions utilized in the World Values Survey (WVS), the surveys did not use the exact set of WVS items. The purpose of the surveys is not to generate data for direct comparison with WVS. Besides, compared to face-to-face interviews adopted in WVS, there was the need to construct items that are more easily understandable to respondents in a telephone interview.

18. The break-off points are arbitrary, but choosing a different set of break-off points would not alter the overall pattern of results.

19. This is consistent with the aforementioned fact that survey studies in the 1990s in Hong Kong failed to find substantial between age-group differences in value orientation. It is worth noting here that the same pattern of findings—the youngest group being exceptionally more postmaterialist and the older age groups not differing from each other—can also be found using the 2013 World Values Survey data of Hong Kong.

20. According to government statistics, the Gini coefficient of Hong Kong stood at 0.525 in 2001, which rose further to 0.537 in 2011. The figures come from: http://www.hkeconomy.gov.hk/en/pdf/box-12q2-5-2.pdf.

Chapter 3

1. Benny Tai, "The most lethal weapon of civil disobedience," *Hong Kong Economic Journal*, January 16, 2013, A16.

2. Chan Kin-man, "Occupy Central with love and peace," *Ming Pao*, March 4, 2013, A27.

3. The search was limited to eight newspapers because the number of newspapers in the city varied over time. The limit was needed to make the figures more comparable. The eight newspapers are *Apple Daily, Oriental Daily, Sing Tao Daily, Ming Pao, Hong Kong Economic Times, Hong Kong Economic Journal, Wen Wei Po,* and *Ta Kung Pao.*

4. 823 of the 1,507 articles were published after the beginning of the occupation action on September 28. In other words, 684 articles were published in the nearly 9-month period in 2014 before the occupation began.

5. During the action in 2011, protesters occupied the open area on the ground floor of the Hong Kong and Shanghai Bank Building in Central. Neither traffic nor the bank's operation was disrupted. The occupation lasted for 11 months and ended only in September 2012, but the scale of the action was relatively small.

6. Whether the OC campaign involved a radicalization of the claims being made can be subjected to debate. As a matter of fact, the OC campaign, through a supporters' vote at the end of its third "deliberation day," had selected three proposals for a quasi-public referendum that would determine the "official position" of Occupy Central on the matter of electoral arrangement in 2017. Some radical groups mobilized their supporters to participate in the deliberation day in order to make sure that their proposals would be selected for the referendum. As a result, all three proposals selected by the deliberation day involved the component of civil nomination, that is, procedures for ordinary citizens to nominate candidates to stand in the Chief Executive election. Civil nomination, however, was already openly rejected by the Chinese government as unconstitutional. The vote after the deliberation day was therefore criticized by democrats of the moderate faction for ruling out more moderate proposals by various social groups. Nevertheless, it may be misleading to describe this process as "radicalization" of claims, since the Trio did not begin the campaign with a more moderate "official stance." It was a process through which the abstract idea of genuine popular election was concretized into an uncompromising emphasis on civil nomination.

7. The trekking protest was adopted from Korean farmer-protesters, who performed the action in Hong Kong during the anti-WTO protests in late 2005.

8. Kursk, "Goodbye to karaoke-style petition: New model for July 1 protest," *Ming Pao*, July 3, 2011, P03.

9. Ibid.

10. The four criteria were listed by Democratic Party's Emily Lau after the 2011 District Council elections as the way the Democratic Party would differentiate itself from the radical faction.

11. Lewis Loud, "The disappearance of the spirit of resistance," *Apple Daily*, May 8, 2013, A19.

12. However, one should not exaggerate the degree of violence advocated by the radical faction in Hong Kong. At least before the Umbrella Movement, the radical faction did not publicly advocate breaking windows, burning cars, and/or throwing stones at the police. The radical faction in Hong Kong is radical only in terms of their deviation from the mainstream Hong Kong society.

13. Fred Lam, "Peacefulness, rationality and non-violence," *Hong Kong Economic Times*, September 5, 2013, C07.

14. Benny Tai, "'Deliberation' is the radioactive element of the fight for genuine democracy," *Hong Kong Economic Journal*, April 12, 2013, A19.

15. Benny Tai, "Occupy Central is the means as well as the end," *Apple Daily*, July 9, 2013, A21.

16. Tang Fei, "Asking for advice from Professor Tai regarding the target of 'civil disobedience,'" *Ming Pao*, April 13, 2013, A24.

17. Benny Tai, "The target of 'civil disobedience': A response to vice-principle Tang Fei's question," *Ming Pao*, April 17, 2013, A32. In fact, at some point in the societal debate, Tai had claimed that the proposal of Occupy Central was put forward so that Occupy Central did not

need to be carried out; that is, it was hoped that the OC campaign could lead the government to listen to public opinion and put forward an electoral framework acceptable to the public.

18. Benny Tai, "The contrast in views on governance between 'Occupy Central' and 'anti-Occupy Central,'" *Apple Daily*, June 18, 2013, A21.

19. Onyin Wong, "Resistance by Occupy Central needs to 'raise the level,'" *Apple Daily*, February 18, 2013, A18.

20. Vivian Tam, "Calling the conscience of middle-aged people, Long Hair: if we don't do it, who do it?" *Ming Pao*, February 24, 2013, P03.

21. Benny Tai, "Non-violent action, civil disobedience, citizen awakening," *Hong Kong Economic Journal*, June 7, 2013, A23.

22. http://oclp.hk/index.php?route=occupy/eng_detail&eng_id=28. Last accessed on January 16, 2017.

23. Wong Siu-yee, "Benny Tai's 'nuclear blast in Hong Kong' attempts to destroy the rule of law," *Wen Wei Po*, April 17, 2013, A19.

24. Interestingly, the Rawlsian view on civil disobedience is indeed often criticized by social and political theorists as overly restrictive. See Cohen and Arato (1992).

25. Chan Kin-man, "Occupy Central with love and peace," *Ming Pao*, March 4, 2013, A27.

26. James Tien, "Why occupy Central?" *Ming Pao*, July 11, 2013, A43.

27. Benny Tai, "Is civil disobedience reasonable?" *Hong Kong Economic Journal*, August 30, 2013, A21.

28. "Benny Tai admits the strategy failed, alluded that Occupy Central would begin on October 1," *Sing Tao Daily*, September 3, 2014.

29. There were certainly other considerations behind the decision of having October 1 as the starting day. Since October 1 is also the National Day, the decision obviously was partly intended to enhance the symbolic impact of the action. But the point here is that the decision was also justified partly by referring to how starting on a public holiday could reduce the negative impact of the occupation on Hong Kong's economy and people's lives.

30. The poll was conducted by the Centre for Communication and Public Opinion Survey at the Chinese University of Hong Kong. The report is available at: http://www.com.cuhk.edu.hk/ccpos/research/1409TaskForce_SurveyResult_141028b.pdf

31. Benny Tai, "Three points about Occupy Central's view on the civil society," *Hong Kong Economic Journal*, September 13, 2013, A21.

32. Both surveys were telephone-based and conducted by the Centre for Communication and Public Opinion Survey at the Chinese University of Hong Kong. The target respondents were Cantonese-speaking Hong Kong residents aged between 18 and 70 in the September 2013 survey and those aged 15 or above in the 2014 survey. Methodologically, in both surveys, all telephone numbers from the 2005, 2007, and 2009 directories were compiled. The last two digits of the numbers were replaced by the full set of 100 double-digit figures from 00 to 99. Specific numbers were randomly selected by computers during the fieldwork. The most recent birthday method was adopted to select a respondent from a household. The sample sizes are 782 and 802 respectively, and the response rates are 40% and 37% (following AAPOR RR3) for the 2013 and 2014 surveys, respectively. Demographically, the 2013 survey oversampled women and people with high family income levels, whereas the 2014 survey oversampled people with high levels of education and income. Both surveys were weighted so that the samples match the Hong Kong population in age, sex, and education.

33. $F = 0.23$ and 1.23 respectively in one-way ANOVA, $p > .20$ in both cases.

34. $F = 4.11$ and 10.91 for activists' understanding and broad understanding respectively, $p < .02$ in both cases.

35. Interested readers could refer to Lee (2015b) for the analysis based on the 2013 survey.

36. "Learning" was indeed emphasized as part of the movement experience in the occupation campaign. Many academics offered "civic classes" in the "mobile classrooms" in the occupied areas.

Chapter 4

1. The "civic square" is the name given by social movement activists to the East Wing forecourt of the Government Headquarters. It was also the place where large-scale rallies and protests were conducted during the anti–national education movement in 2012. But in summer 2014, weeks before the Umbrella Movement, the Hong Kong government built fences to enclose the civic square. In late evening on September 26, 2014, the protesting student leaders called upon supporters to "retake the civic square." More than a hundred protesters climbed across the fences to enter the forecourt, and in the process the police arrested several protesters, including prominent leader of Scholarism Joshua Wong.

2. Allan Au, "The first in-take of tear gas is a sublimation in life," September 28, 2014. The article was in Chinese and the translation was done by the authors. The original Chinese article can be found at: http://aukalun.blogspot.hk/2014/09/blog-post_30.html (last accessed January 10, 2017).

3. http://www.oxforddictionaries.com/definition/english/monitor.

4. The survey was conducted by the present authors together with Professor Clement So at the School of Journalism and Communication at the Chinese University of Hong Kong.

5. ATV ceased its free television service operation in 2016 as the government decided not to renew its license. At the same time, ViuTV started operating its free television service in April 2016. ViuTV belongs to the same corporation as pay television service provider NOW TV.

6. The measure consists of whether the respondents have participated in past June 4 rallies, past July 1 protests, the 2012 anti–national education movement, the protests surrounding free television licensing in 2013, and "other protests and rallies."

7. In the surveys conducted by the Centre for Communication and Public Opinion Survey at the Chinese University of Hong Kong in September and November 2014, the respondents were asked to name up to four most important sources of public affairs information to them. More than 65% of the respondents in both surveys named TVB as one of the four sources, whereas *Apple Daily* constituted the distant second most mentioned news outlet with about 35% of the respondents naming it. Most of the other news outlets were mentioned by only 15% or less of the respondents. See Francis L. F. Lee, "Hong Kong citizens' media channel repertoire under the occupation movement," *Ming Pao*, December 4, 2014.

8. Some of the findings in the following analysis (up to Table 4.5) were presented in Tang (2015). But the present authors re-analyzed the data and the presentation and discussion of the findings here are original.

9. The six newspapers are *Apple Daily, Oriental Daily, Sing Tao Daily, Ming Pao, Hong Kong Economic Times,* and *Hong Kong Economic Journal.*

10. See: http://hkupop.hku.hk/chinese/popexpress/hkpolice/halfyr/datatables.html.

11. The term *hak-ging* is a combination of *hak-se-wui*, which literally means black society and is the term for gangster groups, and *ging-caat* (i.e., police).

12. The Chinese letter was last accessed on February 27 at https://www.facebook.com/tvbnewsopenletter.

13. *T*-value = 2.23, $p < .05$ in an independent samples t-test.

14. *T*-value = 4.02, $p < .01$ in an independent samples t-test.

15. If TV news exposure and newspaper reading frequency are averaged to form a mainstream media exposure index and used in the regression model instead of the two separate variables, mainstream media exposure would relate positively to attitude toward the police at $\beta = .09$, $p < .01$.

16. "Page-washing"—*sai-baan*—is a term used in local parlance to refer to having one's Facebook news feed being overwhelmingly dominated by messages about the same topic.

17. One clip of the early version of the news story that was still available on YouTube in February 2015 was at: https://www.youtube.com/watch?v=LvsrEF3gp-U. When the first author accessed the video on February 26, 2015, the video had had 517,383 views.

18. http://www.com.cuhk.edu.hk/ccpos/research/taskforce-en.html.

Chapter 5

1. From the organization's website: http://biglovealliance.org/index.php/en/about-us.

2. http://sampsonwong.hk/. Last accessed on January 10, 2017.

3. The song lyrics and music video is based on a song of popular star Andy Lau. Mocking Jer's version was developed based on a parody of a pro-government participant in the anti-occupation protest on August 17, 2014. The participant replied that she was going shopping when interviewed by a television journalist at the rally site. Her reply shows that she did not understand the purpose of the rally and was only mobilized by the pro-government groups to participate. Many pro-democracy citizens believe that many pro-government rally participants are similarly ignorant.

4. During the Tiananmen student movement in China in 1989, a large group of Hong Kong artists and singers also produced a song to support the student movement.

5. https://www.facebook.com/OccupyCentralMythKiller

6. https://www.facebook.com/pages/謠言終結者－和平佔領運動資訊/1486627231608268

7. The three variables need to be standardized before averaging because of their different scales. The time spent index has adequate reliability with Cronbach's alpha = 0.67.

8. The Cronbach's alpha value for frontline activism is 0.78, but the figure for support provision is only 0.37, which indicates low levels of reliability. Concretely, it means that participating in the four activities included in the index had only weak relationships with each other. People who have attended civic lectures, for instance, were not necessarily more likely to have donated money or material resources. However, for the purpose of parsimony of the analysis and based on the results of the factor analysis, the index of support provision was used.

9. It should be noted that, in the pattern matrix of the factor analysis, only one of the 21 items had a factor loading of larger than 0.30 on more than one factor.

10. The Cronbach's alpha of the index is 0.75.

11. The Cronbach's alpha values are 0.87 for online expressions, 0.75 for online debates, 0.61 for online explanatory activities, and 0.79 for mobile communication.

12. The Cronbach's alpha values are 0.83 and 0.86 for the two indices respectively.

13. The bivariate correlations among the four indices range from Pearson $r = 0.31$ between mobile communication and online explanatory activities to Pearson $r = 0.55$ between online expressions and online explanatory activities.

14. For instance, the public sentiment report was meant to be a response to the movement's call for the government to submit a supplementary report of Hong Kong's situation to the NPC. But submitting a report to the HKMO, as the critics pointed out, would be meaningless because the HKMO is not in a position to challenge the NPC's decision.

15. The selection committee is the body in charge of electing the Chief Executive and, following the NPC's decision on August 31, will continue to hold the exclusive right to nominate candidates for popular elections in the future. Many of the seats of the selection committee, especially the seats from the business sectors, were returned by elections in which only corporations, instead of individuals within the sectors, could vote. And the corporate vote system is a major means for China to ensure the dominance of the conservatives in the election committee. Abolishing corporate votes and establishing elections of the selection committee through voting by all individuals working within the various sectors is therefore a major method of democratizing the selection committee and thus the whole electoral system.

16. The Cronbach's alpha values are 0.80, 0.82, and 0.83 for the three indices respectively.

17. Cronbach's alpha are 0.71 and 0.57 for perceived positive outcome likelihood and perceived negative outcome likelihood respectively.
18. The two positive statements are correlated at $r = 0.44$, and the two negative statements are correlated at $r = 0.63$.
19. In fact, perceived likelihood of positive outcomes is not significantly related to perceived likelihood of negative outcomes ($r = .06, p > .05$), and perceived advantages of self-mobilization is also not related significantly to perceived disadvantages of self-mobilization ($r = -.02, p > .05$). It means that, at the individual level, a person who regards positive outcomes as likely to happen does not necessarily think that negative outcomes are less likely to happen. Similarly, a person who acknowledges the advantages of self-mobilization does not necessarily acknowledge the disadvantages of self-mobilization to lesser extents.
20. Technically, the distribution of the variable "number of likes" is highly skewed, with a small number of pages getting extraordinarily large numbers of likes. The natural logarithm of the variable was used in the analysis in order to reduce the skewness. The correlation between time of first post and the logged number of like variable remains basically the same: $r = -.19, p < .03$.
21. https://www.facebook.com/umbrellaparents/info/?tab=page_info.
22. When a Facebook page shares the contents or materials from another Facebook page, the heading of the news feed would invariably appear as "[name of Facebook page] shared [name of Facebook page]'s [type of content]." The number of times that a Facebook page has shared another Facebook page's content can therefore be derived through searching for the number of times the word sequence "shared [name of Facebook page]" appears in the corpus of news feeds.
23. The average correlation derived from random permutation is $-.008$, which suggests that the correlation of 0.095 cannot be just randomly produced.
24. "Other Facebook pages" is simply the residual category. It is the total number of Facebook pages that one page has liked minus the page of the main organizers, the number of pages of media organizations, and the number of pages of civic associations and political parties. These "other Facebook pages" cover a wide range, including pages of prominent individual public figures, pages of professional groups, and pages that cannot be easily classified.
25. Inter-coder reliability scores were calculated by having the two assistants coding the same systematically sampled set of about 300 posts. The reliability scores of all variables, measured in Scott's pi, are higher than .80.
26. In local movement parlance, "leftard" is a derogatory term used by some people to criticize left-leaning movement groups and activists for clinging to leftist ideas and principles without paying attention to what the reality of Hong Kong calls for.
27. Alternatively put, there could be spatial division within an occupation area. In the Mong Kok occupation, there was a well-known North-South division: the liberal-leftists camped mainly in the Northern part of the occupation, whereas the Southern part "belonged" to the localists (Yuen, 2017).
28. Mainstream pro-democracy parties included the Civic Party, the Labor Party, the Democratic Party, and the Association for the Democracy and People's Livelihood. Levels of support for some of these parties were low among the occupiers. Hence they were combined to simplify the analysis.

Chapter 6

1. Independent estimates by teams of academics put the number of rally participants at around 50,000 to 80,000, while the police estimated the number of participants to be around 110,000.
2. A summary of public opinion polls on the issue of electoral reform and Occupy Central was provided by the government in its Report on the Recent Community and Political Situation

in Hong Kong, published in January 2015 after the end of the Umbrella Movement. The report is available at: http://www.2017.gov.hk/filemanager/template/en/doc/rcps_report/rcps_report.pdf.

3. The results of the survey are available at: http://www.com.cuhk.edu.hk/ccpos/research/taskforce-en.html.

4. Ibid.

5. We set the period as beginning from September 1 to include those editorials published at a time when the happening of Occupy Central had become inevitable.

6. Chief Executive C. Y. Leung, in the middle of the Umbrella Movement, also asserted that the Umbrella Movement had been infiltrated by foreign forces. He claimed to have solid evidence in hand, but could reveal the evidence only at some appropriate moments. He had yet to provide the "solid evidence" to the public more than three years after the end of the Umbrella Movement.

7. The statement can be accessed at: http://www.isd.gov.hk/occupyresponse/eng/pdf/hkba_pr_20141028.pdf.

8. Interestingly, the various public pages belonging to the pro-establishment camp did not connect with each other at all. In fact, by the time of the writing of this book, all four pages mentioned here do not "like" the other three pages or any public pages of other political parties and groups of the pro-establishment camp.

9. The articles were read iteratively and interpreted in relation to the dynamics of the movement and the range of other poll findings present at the time. When reading news reports, attention was paid to the structure and organization of the texts, word choices, the use of sources and quotations, and other core elements of news discourses (van Dijk, 1988). When reading commentaries and editorials, attention was paid to how the invocations of the poll findings were articulated with broader discourses of the pro- and anti-movement camps.

10. All news articles were translated by the present author.

Chapter 7

1. A search in Wise News shows that the term *gong-duk* (the commonly used Chinese abbreviation for Hong Kong independence) appeared in only 133 articles in six newspapers between 2001 and 2003 (the six papers are *Apple Daily, Oriental Daily, Ming Pao, Sing Tao Daily, Hong Kong Economic Journal*, and *Hong Kong Economic Times*). The number surged to 556 in 2004 amid a heated debate surrounding patriotism at that time (Ming Pao Publishing, 2004), but then went down again to only 447 for the seven years between 2005 and 2011. As conflicts between Hong Kong and mainland China became more serious, the number of articles mentioning *gong-duk* surged to 490 and 411 respectively for 2012 and 2013. Notably, even in 2014, when the Umbrella Movement occurred, the number of articles mentioning *gong-duk* stayed at only around 519. Yet the figure surged to 1,747 in 2015 and then to 6,142 in 2016. Nevertheless, it should be noted that one important event leading to the prominence of Hong Kong independence in public discourse was the Policy Address by the Chief Executive C. Y. Leung in January 2015. Leung proactively singled out a student publication of the Hong Kong University and criticized it for promoting Hong Kong independence.

2. http://www.com.cuhk.edu.hk/ccpos/research/1607TaskForce_SurveyResult_160804_Eng.pdf.

3. http://www.com.cuhk.edu.hk/ccpos/research/taskforce-en.html.

4. One version of this argument is that the Hong Kong SAR government wants to provoke the oppositional forces into ever more radical actions so that, at some point, it could legitimately argue for the need of national security legislation.

5. For instance, see Wong Cheuk-ki, "Reconsidering the hardline style of Arthur Li: mob rule and the Internet generation," *Ming Pao*, February 13, 2016, p. B09; Yuen Ki-wang, "A cycle of reincarnation in fifth years." *Ming Pao*, February 14, 2016, p. P10.

6. The official reported about the case in response to a legislator's question. The transcript of the question and answer can be found at: http://www.info.gov.hk/gia/general/201411/05/P201411050605.htm.

7. See Tommy Cheung, "The pro-establishment camp has already taken the lead in the online discursive battle," *Hong Kong 01*, December 23, 2016. (Chinese online blog article published on https://www.hk01.com/.)

8. The radicalness of the idea of Hong Kong independence, the perceived immaturity of the two Youngspiration legislators in how they handled the controversy, plus the localists' strong criticisms of the democrats in the past led to a strong sense of ambivalence among the democrats regarding whether and to what extent they should support the localists in the controversy. This might partly explain why the pro-democracy media and Facebook pages seemed to be less active than the pro-government media and social media pages.

Appendix

1. According to government statistics, in 2013 to 2014, the publicly funded tertiary education institutions and a range of educational institutions offering self-financed degrees and sub-degrees combined to offer a total of around 140,000 full-time student places. The figures are derived from http://www.gov.hk/en/about/abouthk/factsheets/docs/education.pdf.

2. This difference between the class composition and "feel" of the two occupied areas can be signified by some of the most important "constructions" created by the movement participants in the area. While the Admiralty occupied area hosted the Lennon Wall, a sign of the international and cosmopolitan dimension of the movement, the Mong Kok area hosted the temporary temple for the God of Kwan, a very local and grassroots religion.

3. As of late 2014, the Democratic Party and the Civic Party had six seats each in the Legislative Council. They were the two biggest pro-democracy parties in the legislature. The Labor Party had four seats, while People Power, the Association for the Development of People's Livelihood (ADPL), and the League of Social Democrats had two, one, and one seat in the legislature respectively.

4. For both sense of belonging to Hong Kong and sense of belonging to China, the differences among the mean scores from the three time-places are not statistically significant.

5. The percentages of respondents recognizing the influence of the three leading groups are indeed slightly larger in Admiralty than in MK, but the differences are not statistically significant. The difference between the two areas would remain insignificant even if we combine the three main organizers together: 20.5% of the respondents in Admiralty in November recognized the influence of at least one of the three leading groups as important, whereas 16.9% of the November MK respondents recognized the influence of at least one of the three groups as important. The two percentages do not differ from each other significantly.

6. "Hijacking" is a term often used by people to criticize social groups, political parties, or public figures for trying to take advantage of a collective action by positing themselves as the leaders or representatives.

7. "The new poor: The social demography of poverty in modern Britain is changing fast—and tackling it will take more than slogans," *The Independent*, November 24, 2014.

References

Abramson, P. R. (1983). *Political attitudes in America: Formation and change*. San Francisco, CA: Freeman.

Achcar, G. (2013). *The people want: A radical exploration of the Arab uprising*. Berkeley: University of California Press.

Aday, S., Farrell, H., Freelon, D., Lynch, M., Sides, J., & Dewar, M. (2013). Watching from afar: Media consumption patterns around the Arab Spring. *American Behavioral Scientist, 57*(7), 899–919.

Ahy, M. H. (2016). Networked communication and the Arab Spring: Linking broadcast and social media. *New Media & Society, 18*(1), 99–116.

Alexander, J. (2005). *The civil sphere*. New York: Oxford University Press.

Allam, N. (2014). Blesses and curses: Virtual dissidence as a contentious performance in the Arab Spring's repertoire of contention. *International Journal of Communication, 8*, 853–870.

AlSayyad, N., & Guyenc, M. (2015). Virtual uprisings: On the interaction of new social media, traditional media coverage and urban space during the "Arab Spring." *Urban Studies, 52*(11), 2018–2034.

Anduiza, E., Cristancho, C., & Sabucedo, J. M. (2014). Mobilization through online social networks: The political protest of the indignados in Spain. *Information, Communication & Society, 17*(6), 750–764.

Au, A. K. L. (2016). Institutional logics as constitutive censorship: The case in Hong Kong broadcast news media. Unpublished PhD dissertation, School of Journalism and Communication, The Chinese University of Hong Kong.

Barranco, J., & Wisler, D. (1999). Validity and systematicity of newspaper data in event analysis. *European Sociological Review, 15*(3), 301–322.

Batziou, A. (2015). A Christmas trees in flames and other—visual—stories: Looking at the photojournalistic coverage of the Greek protests of December 2008. *Social Movement Studies, 14*(1), 22–41.

Bauman, Z. (1999). *In search of politics*. Stanford, CA: Stanford University Press.

Baumgartner, J. C., & Morris, J. S. (2010). My FaceTube politics: Social networking web sites and political engagement of young adults. *Social Science Computer Review, 28*(1), 24–44.

Beach, S. W. (1977). Social movement radicalization: Case of People's Democracy in Northern-Ireland. *Sociological Quarterly, 18*(3), 305–318.

Bennett, W. L. (2008). Changing citizenship in the digital age. In W. L. Bennett (Ed.), *Civic life online: Learning how digital media can engage youth* (pp. 1–24). Cambridge, MA: The MIT Press.

Bennett, W. L., & Iyengar, S. (2008). A new era of minimal effects? The changing foundations of political communication. *Journal of Communication, 58*, 707–731.

Bennett, W. L., Pickard, V. W., Iozzi, D. P., Schroeder, C. L., Lagos, T., & Caswell, C. E. (2004). Managing the public sphere: Journalistic construction of the great globalization debate. *Journal of Communication, 54*(3), 437–455.

Bennett, W. L., & Segerberg, A. (2011). Digital media and the personalization of collective action. *Information, Communication & Society, 14*(6), 770–799.

Bennett, W. L., & Segerberg, A. (2012). The logic of connective action. *Information, Communication & Society, 15*(5), 739–768.

Bennett, W. L., & Segerberg, A. (2013). *The logic of connective action.* New York: Cambridge University Press.

Biggs, M. (2013). How repertoires evolve: The diffusion of suicide protest in the twentieth century. *Mobilization, 18*(4), 407–428.

Boler, M., MacDonald, A., Nitsou, C., & Harris, A. (2014). Connective labor and social media: Women's roles in the "leaderless" Occupy movement. *Convergence, 20*(4), 438–460.

Boudreau, C., & Lupia, A. (2011). Political knowledge. In J. N. Druckman, D. P. Green, J. H. Kuklinski, & A. Lupia (Eds.), *The Cambridge handbook of experimental political science* (pp. 171–184). New York: Cambridge University Press.

Boykoff, J. (2006). *The suppression of dissent.* New York: Routledge.

Boyle, M. P., McLeod, D. M., & Armstrong, C. L. (2012). Adherence to the protest paradigm: The influence of protest goals and tactics on news coverage in US and international newspapers. *International Journal of Press/Politics, 17*(2), 127–144.

Bruns, A. (2008). *Blogs, second life, and beyond: From production to produsage.* New York: Peter Lang.

Buechler, S. (2011). *Understanding social movements.* Boulder, CO: Paradigm.

Cammaerts, B. (2012). Protest logics and the mediation opportunity structure. *European Journal of Communication, 27*(2), 117–134.

Carty, V. (2015). *Social movements and new technology.* Boulder, CO: Westview.

Castells, M. (2001). *The Internet galaxy.* Oxford: Oxford University Press.

Castells, M. (2009). *Communication power.* Oxford: Oxford University Press.

Castells, M. (2012). *Networks of outrage and hope.* Cambridge: Polity.

Cayli, B. (2013). Creating counter-publics against the Italian mafia: Cultural conquerors of web-based media. *Javnost—The Public, 20*(3), 59–75.

Chadwick, A. (2011). The political information cycle in a hybrid news system: The British prime minister and the "bullygate" affair. *International Journal of Press/Politics, 16*(1), 3–29.

Chadwick, A. (2013). *The hybrid media system: Politics and power.* Oxford: Oxford University Press.

Chaim, G. (1992). *Philosophical anarchism and political disobedience.* Cambridge: Cambridge University Press.

Chan, C. H., & Fu, K. W. (2014). Facebook pages in the occupation: Analysis of the Balkanized social media networks. *Ming Pao,* December 14, 2014, p. S07. (in Chinese)

Chan, C. H., & Fu, K. W. (2017). The relationship between cyberbalkanization and opinion polarization: Time-series analysis on Facebook pages and opinion polls during the Hong Kong Occupy Movement and the associated debate on political reform. *Journal of Computer-Mediated Communication, 22*(5), 266–283.

Chan, C. K. (2015). Contested news values and media performance during the Umbrella Movement. *Chinese Journal of Communication, 8*(4), 420–428.

Chan, J. M., & Lee, C. C. (1984). Journalistic paradigms on civil protests: A case study of Hong Kong. In A. Arno & W. Dissanayake (Eds.), *The news media in national and international conflict* (pp. 183–202). Boulder, CO: Westview.

Chan, J. M., & Lee, F. L. F. (2007). Media and politics in post-handover Hong Kong: An introduction. *Asian Journal of Communication, 17*(2), 127–133.

Chan, J. M., & So, C. Y. K. (2004). The surrogate democracy function of the media: Citizens' and journalists' evaluations of media performance. In S. K. Lau, M. K. Lee, P. S. Wan, and S. L. Wong (Eds.), *Indicators of social development* (pp. 1249–1276). Hong Kong: Hong Kong Institute of Asia-Pacific Studies.

Chen, W. C., Chang, H. H., & Huang, S. R. (2016). The arrival of the era of networked social movement? Exploring the Sunflower Movement participants' personal networks and social media use. *Journal of Humanities and Social Sciences, 28*(4), 467–501. (in Chinese)

Cheng, E. W. (2016). Street politics in a hybrid regime: The diffusion of political activism in postcolonial Hong Kong. *China Quarterly, 226,* 383–406.

Cheng, E. W., & Chan, W. Y. (2017). Explaining spontaneous occupation: Antecedents, contingencies and spaces in the Umbrella Movement. *Social Movement Studies, 16*(2), 222–239.

Cheng, E. W., & Yuen, S. (2017). Editors' introduction: Reimaging social movements in Hong Kong. In E. W. Cheng and S. Yuen (Eds.), *An epoch of social movements: The trajectory of contentious politics in Hong Kong.* Hong Kong: Chinese University of Hong Kong Press. (in Chinese)

Cheng, J. Y. S. (2014). The emergence of radical politics in Hong Kong: Causes and impact. *China Review, 14*(1), 199–232.

Cheng, Y. C., & Chen, P. L. (2016). Exploring online public participation in networked social movements: The case of Taiwan 318 movement. *Journal of Communication Research and Practice, 6*(1), 117–150. (in Chinese)

Cheung, C. K., & Leung, K. K. (2004). Economic and political conditions and modern and postmodern value orientations of Hong Kong citizens. *Social Science Journal, 41*(3), 347–361.

Cheung, P. T. Y. (2011). Civic engagement in the policy process in Hong Kong: Change and continuity. *Public Administration and Development, 31*(2), 113–121.

Colleoni, E., Rozza, A., & Adam, A. (2014). Echo chamber or public sphere? Predicting political orientation and measuring political homophily in Twitter using Big Data. *Journal of Communication, 64*(2), 317–332.

Coopman, T. M. (2011). Networks of dissent: Emergent forms in media based collective action. *Critical Studies in Media Communication, 28*(2), 153–172.

Corrigall-Brown, C. (2012). *Patterns of protest.* Stanford, CA: Stanford University Press.

Cottle, S. (2006). *Mediatized conflicts.* Buckingham: Open University Press.

Cottle, S. (2008). Reporting demonstrations: The changing media politics of dissent. *Media, Culture & Society, 30*(6), 853–872.

Creemers, R. (2015). The pivot in Chinese cybergovernance: Integrating Internet control in Xi Jinping's China. *China Perspectives,* no. 2015(4), 5–14.

Dalton, R. (2002). *Citizen politics.* Chatham, NJ: Chatham House.

De Fazio, G. (2012). Legal opportunity structure and social movement strategy in Northern Ireland and Southern United States. *International Journal of Comparative Sociology, 53*(1), 3–22.

DeGolyer, M., & Scott, J. L. (1996). The myth of political apathy in Hong Kong. *The Annals of the American Academy of Political and Social Science, 547,* 68–78.

Della Porta, D. (1999). Protests, protesters and protest policing. In M. Giugni, D. McAdam, & C. Tilly (Eds.), *How movements matter* (pp. 66–96). Minneapolis: The University of Minnesota Press.

Della Porta, D. (2015). *Social movements in times of austerity.* New York: Polity.

Della Porta, D., & Mattoni, A. (2015). Social networking sites in pro-democracy and anti-austerity protests: Some thoughts from a social movement perspective. In D. Trottier & C. Fuchs (Eds.), *Social media, politics, and the state* (pp. 39–64). London: Routledge.

Delli Carpini, M. X., & Keeter, S. (1996). *What Americans know about politics and why it matters.* New Haven, CT: Yale University Press.

DeLuca, K. M. (2005). *Image politics: The new rhetoric of environmental activism.* New York: Routledge.

DeLuca, K. M., & Peeples, J. (2002). From public sphere to public screen: Democracy, activism, and the "violence" of Seattle. *Critical Studies in Media Communication, 19*(2), 125–151.

DeLuca, K. M., Lawson, S., & Sun, Y. (2012). Occupy Wall Street on the public screens of social media: The many framings of the birth of a protest movement. *Communication, Culture & Critique, 5*(4), 483–509.

Di Cicco, D. T. (2010). The public nuisance paradigm: Changes in mass media coverage of political protest since the 1960s. *Journalism & Mass Communication Quarterly, 87*(1), 135–153.

Downey, J., & Fenton, N. (2003). New media, counter publicity and the public sphere. *New Media & Society*, 5(2), 185–202.

Earl, J., & Kimport, K. (2009). Movement societies and digital protest: Fan activism and other non-political protest online. *Sociological Theory*, 27(3), 220–243.

Earl, J., & Kimport, K. (2011). *Digitally enabled social change*. Cambridge, MA: MIT Press.

Earl, J., Kimport, K., Prieto, G., Rush, C., & Reynoso, K. (2010). Changing the world one webpage at a time: Conceptualizing and explaining Internet activism. *Mobilization*, 15(4), 425 – 446.

Earl, J., Martin, A., McCarthy, J. D., & Soule, S. A. (2004). The use of newspaper data in the study of collective action. *Annual Review of Sociology*, 30, 65–80.

Ekiert, G., & Kubik, J. (1998). Collective protest in post-communist Poland, 1989–1993: A research report. *Communist and Post-communist Studies*, 31(2), 91–117.

Einwohner, R. L. (2002). Motivational framing and efficacy maintenance: Animal rights activists' use of four fortifying strategies. *Sociological Quarterly*, 43(4), 509–526.

el-Nawawy, M., & Khamis, S. (2013). *Egyptian revolution 2.0: Political blogging, civic engagement, and citizen journalism*. Basingstoke: Palgrave Macmillan.

Eltantawy, N., & Wiest, J. B. (2011). Social media in the Egyptian Revolution: Reconsidering resource mobilization theory. *International Journal of Communication*, 5, 1207–1224.

Ems, L. (2014). Twitter's place in the tussle: How old power struggles play out on a new stage. *Media, Culture & Society*, 36(5), 720–731.

Erni, J. (2015). A legalist view on citizen actions in Hong Kong's Umbrella Movement. *Chinese Journal of Communication*, 8(4), 412–419.

Eveland, W. P., Jr. (2004) The effect of political discussion in producing informed citizens: The roles of information, motivation, and elaboration. *Political Communication*, 21, 177–193.

Falcon y Tella, M. J. (2004). *Civil disobedience*. Leiden: Martinus Nijhoff Publishers.

Fang, Q., & Forges, R. D. (2008). Were Chinese rulers above the law? Toward a theory of the rule of law in China from early times to 1949 CE. *Stanford Journal of International Law*, 44(1), 101–146.

Feldman, S., & Zaller, J. (1992). The political culture of ambivalence: Ideological responses to the welfare state. *American Journal of Political Science*, 36(1), 268–307.

Ferree, M. M., Gamson, W. A., Gerhards, J., & Rucht, D. (2002). *Shaping abortion discourse: Democracy and the public sphere in Germany and the United States*. New York: Cambridge University Press.

Finkel, S. E., & Muller, E. N. (1998). Rational choice and the dynamics of collective political action: Evaluating alternative models with panel data. *American Political Science Review*, 92(1), 37–49.

Fraile, M. (2013). Do information-rich contexts reduce knowledge inequalities? The contextual determinants of political knowledge in Europe. *Acta Politica*, 48(2), 119–143.

Freeman, L. C. (2008). Centrality in social networks: Conceptual clarification. In L. C. Freeman (Ed.), *Social Network Analysis* (Vol. 3) (pp. 355–380). London: Sage.

Frith, J. (2015). *Smartphones as locative media*. New York: Polity.

Fuchs, C. (2014). *OccupyMedia! The occupy movement and social media in crisis capitalism*. Winchester: Zero Books.

Fung, A. Y. H. (2007). Political economy of Hong Kong media: Producing a hegemonic voice. *Asian Journal of Communication*, 17(2), 159–171.

Gamson, W. A. (1968). *Power and discontent*. Homewood, IL: Dorsey.

Gamson, W. A., & Herzog, H. (1999). Living with contradictions: The taken-for-granted in Israeli political discourse. *Political Psychology*, 20(2), 247–266.

Gamson, W. A., & Meyer, D. (1996). Framing political opportunity. In D. McAdam, J. McCarthy, & M. Zald (Eds.), *Comparative perspectives on social movements* (pp. 275–290). New York: Cambridge University Press.

Gamson, W. A., & Modigliani, A. (1987). The changing culture of affirmative action. In R. G. Braungart & M. M. Braungart (Eds.), *Research in political sociology*. (Vol. 3) (pp. 137–177). Greenwich, CT: JAI Press.

Gamson, W. A., & Modigliani, A. (1989). Media discourse and public opinion on nuclear power: A constructionist approach. *American Journal of Sociology, 95*(1), 1–37.

Gamson, W. A., & Wolfsfeld, G. (1993). Movements and media as interacting systems. *Annals of the American Academy of Political and Social Science, 528,* 114–125.

Gerbaudo, P. (2017). Social media teams as digital vanguards: The question of leadership in the management of key Facebook and Twitter accounts of Occupy Wall Street, Indignados and UK Uncut. *Information, Communication & Society, 20*(2), 185–202.

Gil de Zúñiga, H., Jung, N., & Valenzuela, S. (2012). Social media use for news and individuals' social capital, civic engagement and political participation. *Journal of Computer-Mediated Communication, 17,* 319–336.

Gitlin, T. (1980). *The whole world is watching.* Berkeley: University of California Press.

Giugni, M. (2004). *Social protest and policy change.* Lanham, MD: Rowman & Littlefield.

Giugni, M. (2009). Political opportunities: From Tilly to Tilly. *Swiss Political Science Review, 15,* 361–368.

Giugni, M. (2011). Political opportunities: Still a useful concept? In M. Hanagan & C. Tilly (Eds.), *Contention and trust in cities and states* (pp. 271–283). Berlin: Springer.

Gladwell, M. (2010). Small change: Why the revolution will not be tweeted. The New Yorker, October 4, 2010. http://www.newyorker.com/magazine/2010/10/04/small-change-malcolm-gladwell (last accessed on August 30, 2015).

Gonzalez-Bailon, S., & Wang, N. (2016). Networked discontent: The anatomy of protest campaigns in social media. *Social Networks, 44,* 95–104.

Haciyakupoglu, G., & Zhang, W. Y. (2015). Social media and trust during the Gezi protests in Turkey. *Journal of Computer-Mediated Communication, 20*(4), 450–466.

Hajek, M., & Kabele, J. (2010). Dual discursive patterns in Czech activists' Internet media communication. *European Journal of Communication, 25*(1), 43–58.

Han, R. B. (2015). Defending the authoritarian regime online: China's "voluntary fifty-cent army." *China Quarterly, 224,* 1006–1025.

Hanneman, R. A., & Riddle, M. (2005). *Introduction to social network methods.* University of California, Riverside. Published in digital form at http://faculty.ucr.edu/~hanneman/nettext/index.html.

Hara, N., & Huang, B. Y. (2011). Online social movements. *Annual Review of Information Science and Technology, 45,* 489–522.

Harris, B. D., Morgan, C. V., & Gibbs, B. G. (2014). Evidence of political moderation over time: Utah's immigration debate online. *New Media & Society, 16*(8), 1309–1331.

Hayes, G. (2006). Vulnerability and disobedience: New repertoires in French environmental protests. *Environmental Politics, 15*(5), 821–838.

Hepp, A. (2012). *Cultures of mediatization.* London: Polity.

Herbst, S. (1993). *Numbered voices.* Chicago: University of Chicago Press.

Hjarvard, S. (2013). *The mediatization of culture and society.* London: Routledge.

Ho, K. L., & Leung, S. W. (1995). Materialism and political attitude. In S. K. Lau, M. K. Lee, P. S. Wan, & S. L. Wong (Eds.), *Indicators of Social Development: Hong Kong 1993* (pp. 229–257). Hong Kong: Institute of Asia-Pacific Studies, Chinese University of Hong Kong.

Ho, K. L., & Leung, S. W. (1997). Post-materialism revisited. In S. K. Lau, M. K. Lee, P. S. Wan, & S. L. Wong (Eds.), *Indicators of Social Development: Hong Kong 1995* (pp. 331–358). Hong Kong: Institute of Asia-Pacific Studies, Chinese University of Hong Kong.

Ho, M.-S. (2015). Occupy Congress in Taiwan: Political opportunity, threat, and the Sunflower Movement. *Journal of East Asian Studies, 15*(1), 69–97.

Hong Kong Journalists Association (2014). Press freedom under siege: Grave threats to freedom of expression in Hong Kong. Annual Report of the Hong Kong Journalists Association, July 2014. http://www.hkja.org.hk/site/Host/hkja/UserFiles/file/annual_report_2014_Final.pdf. (last accessed January 22, 2016).

Howard, P. N., & Hussain, M. M. (2013). *Democracy's fourth wave? Digital media and the Arab Spring.* New York: Oxford University Press.

Huckfeldt, R., & Sprague, J. (1995). *Citizens, politics, and social communication*. New York: Cambridge University Press.

Hussain, M. M., & Howard, P. N. (Eds.) (2013). *State power 2.0: Authoritarian entrenchment and political engagement*. Farnham, Surrey: Ashgate.

Inglehart, R. (1977). *The silent revolution*. Princeton, NJ: Princeton University Press.

Inglehart, R. (1990). *Culture shift in advanced industrial societies*. Princeton, NJ: Princeton University Press.

Ip, K. M. (2014). *Silent revolution: A hundred years of anti-corruption efforts in Hong Kong*. Hong Kong: Chung Hwa Bookstore. (in Chinese)

Iyengar, S. (1990). Shortcuts to political knowledge: Selective attention and the accessibility bias. In J. Ferejohn & J. Kuklinski (Eds.), *Information and the democratic process* (pp. 160–185). Champaign: University of Illinois Press.

Iyengar, S., & Hahn, K. S. (2009). Red media, blue media: Evidence of ideological selectivity in media use. *Journal of Communication, 59*(1), 19–39.

Jenkins, J. C., & Perrow, C. (1977). Insurgency of powerless: Farm worker movements (1946–1972). *American Sociological Review, 42*(2), 249–268.

Jenkins, J. C., & Wallace, M. (1996). The generalized action potential of protest movements: The new class, social trends, and political exclusion explanations. *Sociological Forum, 11*(2), 183–207.

Johann, D. (2012). Specific political knowledge and citizens' participation: Evidence from Germany. *Acta Politica, 47*(1), 42–66.

Johnston, H. (2014). *What is a social movement?* London: Polity.

Kamel, S. H. (2014). Egypt's ongoing uprising and the role of social media: Is there development? *Information Technology for Development, 20*(1), 78–91.

Katz, E., & Lazarsfeld, P. F. (1955). *Personal influence*. New York: Free Press.

Kaufhold, K., Valenzuela, S., & Gil de Zúñiga, H. (2010). Citizen journalism and democracy: How user-generated news use relates to political knowledge and participation. *Journalism & Mass Communication Quarterly, 87*(3–4), 515–529.

Kim, Y. H., Chen, H. T., & Gil de Zúñiga, H. (2013). Stumbling upon news on the Internet: Effects of incidental news exposure and relative entertainment use on political engagement. *Computers in Human Behavior, 29*(6), 2607–2614.

Kim, Y. M. (2009). Issue publics in the new information environment: Selectivity, domain specificity, and extremity. *Communication Research, 36*(2), 254–284.

King, A. (1975). Administrative absorption of politics in Hong Kong: Emphasis on the grass roots level. *Asian Survey, 15*, 422–439.

Kitschelt, H. P. (1986). Political opportunity structure and political protest: Anti-nuclear movements in four democracies. *British Journal of Political Science, 16*, 57–85.

Kitschelt, H. P. (1993). Social movements, political parties, and democratic theory. *The Annals of the American Academy of Political and Social Science, 528*, 13–29.

Klandermans, B. (1997). *The social psychology of protest*. Oxford: Blackwell.

Koopmans, R. (2004). Movements and media: Selection processes and evolutionary dynamics in the public sphere. *Theory and Society, 33*(3–4), 367–391.

Kolb, F. (2007). *Protest and opportunities*. Chicago: University of Chicago Press.

Kovach, B., & Rosenstiel, T. (1999). *Warp speed: America in the age of mixed media*. Washington, DC: The Century Foundation Press.

Kriesi, H. (2004). Political context and opportunity. In D. A. Snow, S. A. Soule, & H. Kriesi (Eds.), *The Blackwell companion to social movements* (pp. 67–90). Oxford: Blackwell.

Ku, A. S. (2001). The "public" up against the state: Narrative cracks and credibility crisis in postcolonial Hong Kong. *Theory, Culture and Society, 18*(1), 121–144.

Ku, A. S. (2004). Negotiating the space of civil autonomy in Hong Kong: Power, discourses and dramaturgical representations. *China Quarterly, 179*, 647–664.

Ku, A. S. (2007). Constructing and contesting the "order" imagery in media discourse: Implications for civil society in Hong Kong. *Asian Journal of Communication, 17*(2), 186–200.

Kuo, L. S. (2016). Social movement and "theatrical" news/documentary photography: The case of photos of "The Sunflower Movement." *Journal of Communication Research and Practice, 6*(1), 79–115. (in Chinese)

Lam, J. T. M. (2002). The 2000 Legislative Council elections: An assessment of democratic development in Hong Kong. In H. C. Kuan, S. K. Lau, & T. K. Y. Wong (Eds.), *Out of the shadow of 1997?* (pp. 289–308). Hong Kong: The Chinese University Press.

Lam, W. M. (2004) *Understanding the political culture of Hong Kong.* New York: M. E. Sharpe.

Lau, S. K. (1982). *Society and politics in Hong Kong.* Hong Kong: Chinese University Press.

Lau, S. K., & Kuan, H. C. (1988). *The ethos of the Hong Kong Chinese.* Hong Kong: The Chinese University Press.

Lavine, H. (2001). The electoral consequences of ambivalence toward presidential candidates. *American Journal of Political Science, 45*(4), 915–929.

Le, E. (2004). Information sources as a persuasive strategy in editorials: *Le Monde* and the *New York Times. Written Communication, 20*(4), 478–510.

Lee, F. L. F. (2006a). Collective efficacy, support for democratization, and political participation in Hong Kong. *International Journal of Public Opinion Research, 18*(3), 297–317.

Lee, F. L. F. (2006b). Election interpretation and institutional repair in political transition: An analysis of the post-election campaign in the 2006 Legislative Council Election in Hong Kong. *Communication & Society, 1,* 69–90. (in Chinese)

Lee, F. L. F. (2007). Strategic interaction, cultural co-orientation, and press freedom in Hong Kong. *Asian Journal of Communication, 17*(2), 134–147

Lee, F. L. F. (2008). Local press meets transnational activism: News dynamics in an anti-WTO protest. *Chinese Journal of Communication, 1*(1), 57–78.

Lee, F. L. F. (2010). The perceptual bases of collective efficacy and protest participation: The case of pro-democracy protests in Hong Kong. *International Journal of Public Opinion Research, 22*(3), 392–411.

Lee, F. L. F. (2014). *Talk radio, the mainstream press, and public opinion in Hong Kong.* Hong Kong: Hong Kong University Press.

Lee, F. L. F. (2015a). Press freedom and political change in Hong Kong. In G. Rawnsley & M. Y. Rawnsley (Eds.), *The Routledge Handbook of Chinese Media.* London: Routledge.

Lee, F. L. F. (2015b). Internet alternative media use and oppositional knowledge. *International Journal of Public Opinion Research, 27*(3), 318–340.

Lee, F. L. F. (2015c). Internet, citizen self-mobilisation, and social movement organisations in environmental collective action campaigns: Two Hong Kong cases. *Environmental Politics, 24*(2), 308–325.

Lee, F. L. F. (2016). Impact of social media on opinion polarization in varying times. *Communication & the Public, 1*(1), 56–71.

Lee, F. L. F., & Chan, J. M. (2005). Political attitudes, participation, and Hong Kong identities after 1997. *Issues & Studies, 41*(2), 1–35.

Lee, F. L. F., & Chan, J. M. (2009a). The organizational production of self-censorship in the Hong Kong media. *International Journal of Press/Politics, 14,* 112–133.

Lee, F. L. F., & Chan, J. M. (2009b). The political consequences of ambivalence: The case of democratic reform in Hong Kong. *International Journal of Public Opinion Research, 21*(1), 47–64.

Lee, F. L. F., & Chan, J. M. (2011). *Media, social mobilization, and mass protests in post-colonial Hong Kong.* London: Routledge.

Lee, F. L. F., & Lin, A. M. Y. (2006). Newspaper editorial discourse and the politics of self-censorship in Hong Kong. *Discourse & Society, 17*(2), 331–358.

Lee, F. L. F., & Tang, G. K. Y. (2013). Economic development, political change, and Hong Kong young people's postmaterial turn. Working paper in Hong Kong Culture & Society series, School of Journalism and Communication, Chinese University of Hong Kong, JcMotion Publishing. (in Chinese)

Lee, J. K., Choi, J. Y., Kim, C. S., & Kim, Y. H. (2014). Social media, network heterogeneity, and opinion polarization. *Journal of Communication, 64*(4), 702–722.

Lee, P. S. N., So, C. Y. K., & Leung, L. (2015). Social media and Umbrella Movement: Insurgent public sphere in formation. *Chinese Journal of Communication, 8*(4), 356–375.

Lemert, J. (1981). *Does mass communication change public opinion after all?* Chicago: Nelson Hall.

Leung, D. K. K. (2015). Alternative Internet radio, press freedom and contentious politics in Hong Kong, 2004–2014. *Javnost—The Public, 22*(2), 196–212.

Leung, D. K. K., & Lee, F. L. F. (2014). Cultivating an online counter-public: Examining usage and political impact of Internet alternative media. *International Journal of Press/Politics, 19*(3), 340–359.

Leung, L. (2009). Mediated violence as "global news": Co-opted "performance" in the framing of the WTO. *Media, Culture & Society, 31*(2), 251–270.

Lewis, J. (2001). *Constructing public opinion.* New York: Columbia University Press.

Li, J. F. (2007). Socialist rule of law with Chinese characteristics. *Issues & Studies, 43*(1), 115–157.

Lippmann, W. (1922). *Public opinion.* New York: Macmillan.

Lui, T. L. (2003). Rearguard politics: Hong Kong's middle class. *Development Economy, 41*(2), 161–183.

Lui, T. L., & Chiu, S. W. K. (Eds.) (2000). *The dynamics of social movements in Hong Kong.* Hong Kong: Hong Kong University Press.

Lupia, A. L., & Sin, G. (2003). Which public goods are endangered? How evolving technologies affect the logic of collective action. *Public Choice, 117*, 315–331.

Luskin, R. (1990). Explaining political sophistication. *Political Behavior, 12*(4), 331–361.

Ma, E. K. W. (1999). *Culture, politics, and television in Hong Kong.* New York: Routledge.

Ma, L. Y. (2014). The cognitive and affective framing processes in the Tsoi Yuen resistance movement in Hong Kong. Unpublished PhD dissertation, Chinese University of Hong Kong, Hong Kong.

Ma, N. (2005). Civil society in self-defense: The struggle against national security legislation in Hong Kong. *Journal of Contemporary China, 14*(4), 456–482.

Ma, N. (2007). *Political development in Hong Kong.* Hong Kong: Hong Kong University Press.

Ma, N. (2011). Value changes and legitimacy crisis in post-industrial Hong Kong. *Asian Survey, 51*(4), 683–712.

MacKinnon, R. (2013). *Consent of the networked.* New York: Basic Books.

Mansbridge, J. (2001). The making of oppositional consciousness. In J. Mansbridge & A. Morris (Eds.), *Oppositional consciousness* (pp. 1–19). Chicago: University of Chicago Press.

Marmura, S. (2008). A net advantage? The Internet, grassroots activism and American Middle-Eastern policy. *New Media & Society, 10*(2), 247–271.

McAdam, D. (1982). *Political process and the development of black insurgency, 1930–1970.* Chicago: The University of Chicago Press.

McAdam, D. (1986). Recruitment to high-risk activism: The case of freedom summer. *American Journal of Sociology, 92*, 64–90.

McAdam, D. (1996). Political opportunities: Conceptual origins, current problems, future directions. In D. McAdam, J. McCarthy, & M. Zald (Eds.), *Comparative Perspectives on Social Movements* (pp. 23–40). New York: Cambridge University Press.

McAdam, D., & Sewell, W. H., Jr. (2001). It's about time: temporality in the study of social movements and revolutions. In R. R. Aminzade, J. A. Goldstone, D. McAdam, E. J. Perry, W. H. Sewell Jr., S. Tarrow, and C. Tilly (Eds.), *Silence and voice in the study of contentious politics* (pp. 51–88). New York: Cambridge University Press.

McAdam, D., & Simpson, R. J. (2005). "There will be fighting in the streets": The distorting lens of social movement theory. *Mobilization, 10*(1), 1–18.

McCarthy, J. D., & McPhail, C. (1998). The institutionalization of protests in the United States. In D. S. Meyer & S. Tarrow (Eds.), *The social movement society* (pp. 83–110). Lanham, MD: Rowman & Littlefield.

McCarthy, J. D., McPhail, C., & Smith, J. (1996). Images of protest: Dimensions of selection bias in media coverage of Washington demonstrations, 1982 and 1991. *American Sociological Review, 61*(3), 478–499.

McCluskey, M., Stein, S. E., Boyle, M. P., & McLeod, D. M. (2009). Community structure and social protest: Influences on newspaper coverage. *Mass Communication & Society, 12*, 353–371.

McCulloh, I., Armstrong, H., & Johnson, A. (2013). *Social network analysis with applications.* Hoboken, NJ: Wiley.

McFarlane, T., & Hay, I. (2003). The battle for Seattle: Protest and popular geopolitics in the Australian newspaper. *Political Geography, 22*(2), 211–232.

McHendry, G. F., Jr. (2012). Whale wars and the axiomatization of image events on the public screen. *Environmental Communication, 6*(2), 139–155.

McLeod, D. M., & Hertog, J. K. (1998). Social control and the mass media's role in the regulation of protest groups: The communicative acts perspective. In D. Demers & K. Viswanath (Eds.), *Mass media, social control and social change* (pp. 305–330). Ames: Iowa State University Press.

Melucci, A. (1989). *Nomads of the present: Social movements and individual needs in contemporary society.* London: Hutchinson.

Mercea, D. (2014). Towards a conceptualization of casual protest participation: Parsing a case from the Save Rosia Montana campaign. *East European Politics and Societies, 28*(2), 386–410.

Messing, S., & Westwood, S. J. (2014). Selective exposure in the age of social media: Endorsements trump partisan source affiliation when selecting news online. *Communication Research, 41*(8), 1042–1063.

Meyer, D. S., & Tarrow, S. (1998). A movement society: Contentious politics for a new century. In D. S. Meyer & S. Tarrow (Eds.), *The social movement society* (pp. 1–28). Lanham, MD: Rowman & Littlefield.

Mico, J. L., & Casero-Ripolles, A. (2014). Political activism online: Organization and media relations in the case of 15M in Spain. *Information, Communication & Society, 17*(7), 858–871.

Milkman, R., Luce, S., & Lewis, P. (2013). *Changing the subject: A bottom-up account of Occupy Wall Street in New York City.* Working Paper for The Murphy Institute, The City University of New York. Available online at: http://sps.cuny.edu/filestore/1/5/7/1_a05051d2117901d/1571_92f562221b8041e.pdf.

Ming Pao Publishing (Ed.) (2004). *The debates on patriotism.* Hong Kong: Ming Pao Publishing. (in Chinese)

Molaei, H. (2015). Discursive opportunity structure and the contribution of social media to the success of social movements in Indonesia. *Information, Communication & Society, 18*(1), 94–108.

Mueller, C. (1999). Claim "radicalization?" The 1989 protest cycle in GDR. *Social Problems, 46*(4), 528–547.

Mutz, D. (2006). *Hearing the other side.* New York: Cambridge University Press.

Ng, C. H. (2008). The core values movement. In T. L. Lui, E. K. W. Ma, & C. H. Ng (Eds.), *Cultural politics in Hong Kong.* Hong Kong: Hong Kong University Press. (in Chinese)

Nisbet, M. C., & Kotcher, J. E. (2009). A two-step flow of influence? Opinion-leader campaigns on climate change. *Science Communication, 30*(3), 328–354.

Norris, P. (2000). *A virtuous circle.* New York: Cambridge University Press.

Oegema, D., & Klandermans, B. (1994). Why social movement sympathizers don't participate: Erosion and nonconversion of support. *American Sociological Review, 59*, 703–722.

Oliver, P. E., & Maney, G. M. (2000). Political processes and local newspaper coverage of protest events: From selection bias to triadic interactions. *American Journal of Sociology, 106*(2), 463–505.

Oliver, P. E., & Myers, D. J. (1999). How events enter the public sphere: Conflict, location, and sponsorship in local newspaper coverage of public events. *American Journal of Sociology, 105*(1), 38–87.

Olorunnisola, A. A., & Martin, B. L. (2014). Influences of media on social movements: Problematizing hyperbolic inferences about impacts. *Telematics and Informatics, 30*(3), 275–288.

Opp, K. D. (1994). Repression and revolutionary action: East Germany in 1989. *Rationality and Society, 6*, 101–138.

Opp, K. D. (2004). "What is is always becoming what ought to be": How political action generates a participation norm. *European Sociological Review, 20*(1), 13–29.

Opp, K. D., & Roehl, W. (1990). Repression, micromobilization, and political protest. *Social Forces*, 69(2), 521–547.

Ostman, J. (2012). Information, expression, participation: How involvement in user-generated content relates to democratic engagement among young people. *New Media & Society*, 14(6), 1004–1021.

Papacharissi, Z. (2016). Affective publics and structures of storytelling: Sentiment, events and mediality. *Information Communication & Society*, 19(3), 307–324.

Pearce, K. E., & Kendzior, S. (2012). Networked authoritarianism and social media in Azerbaijan. *Journal of Communication*, 62(2), 283–298.

Penney, J., & Dadas, C. (2014). (Re)tweeting in the service of protest: Digital composition and circulation in the Occupy Wall Street movement. *New Media & Society*, 16(1), 74–90.

Peters, J. (2015). *The marvelous clouds*. Chicago: University of Chicago Press.

Poell, T., Abdulla, R., Rieder, B., Woltering, R., & Zack L. (2016). Protest leadership in the age of social media. *Information Communication & Society*, 19(7), 994–1014.

Poon, K. (2008). *The political future of Hong Kong: Democracy within Communist China*. London: Routledge.

Popkin, S. (1991). *The reasoning voter*. Chicago: University of Chicago Press.

Price, V., & Zaller, J. (1993). Who gets the news? Alternative measures of news reception. *Public Opinion Quarterly*, 57(2), 133–164.

Prior, M. (2007). *Post-broadcast democracy*. New York: Cambridge University Press

Quill, L. (2009). *Civil disobedience*. New York: Palgrave Macmillan.

Rawls, J. (1973). *A theory of justice*. Oxford: Oxford University Press.

Rowen, I. (2015). Inside Taiwan's Sunflower Movement: Twenty-four days in a student-occupied parliament, and the future of the region. *Journal of Asian Studies*, 74(1), 5–21.

Rucht, D. (1998). The structure and culture of collective protest in Germany since 1950. In D. S. Meyer & S. Tarrow (Eds.), *The social movement society* (pp. 29–58). Lanham, MD: Rowman & Littlefield.

Salem, S. (2015). Creating spaces for dissent: The role of social media in the 2011 Egyptian Revolution. In D. Trottier & C. Fuchs (Eds.), *Social media, politics, and the state* (pp. 171–188). London: Routledge.

Schaefer, A. (2015). Differential learning in communication networks: Interpersonal communication moderating influences of news media usage on political knowledge. *International Journal of Public Opinion Research*, 27(4), 509–543.

Schudson, M. (1992). *Watergate in American memory*. New York: Basic Books.

Schudson, M. (1998). *The good citizen*. Cambridge, MA: Harvard University Press.

Seligson, M. A. (1980). Trust, efficacy and modes of political participation: A study of Costa Rican peasants. *British Journal of Political Science*, 10, 75–98.

Sing, M. (2000). Mobilization for political change: The pro-democracy movement in Hong Kong (1980s–1994). In T. L. Lui & S. W. K. Chiu (Eds.), *The dynamics of social movement in Hong Kong* (pp. 21–54). Hong Kong: Hong Kong University Press.

Sing, M. (2004). *Hong Kong's tortuous democratization: A comparative analysis*. London: Routledge.

Sing, M. (2010). Explaining mass support for democracy in Hong Kong. *Democratization*, 17(1), 175–205.

Small, M. (1995). *Covering dissent*. New Brunswick, NJ: Rutgers University Press.

Sniderman, P., Brady, D., & Tetlock, P. E. (1991). *Reasoning and choice: Explorations in political psychology*. New York: Cambridge University Press.

Snow, D. A., & Benford, R. D. (1988). Ideology, frame resonance, and participant mobilization. In B. Klandermans, H. Kriesi, & S. Tarrow (Eds.), *From structure to action: Social movement participation across cultures* (pp. 197–217). Greenwich, CT: JAI Press.

Snow, D. A., Rochford, R. B., Worden, S. K., & Benford, R. D. (1986). Frame alignment processes, micromobilization, and movement participation. *American Sociological Review*, 51, 464–481.

So, A. (1999). *Hong Kong embattled democracy: A societal analysis.* Baltimore, MD: Johns Hopkins University Press.

So, A. (2011). The development of post-modernist social movements in the Hong Kong Special Administrative Region. In J. Broadbent & V. Brockman (Eds.), *East Asian social movements* (pp. 365–378). New York: Springer.

So, C. Y. K. (2015, August 13). Traditional news media are still the main turf. *Ming Pao*, p. A32. (in Chinese)

So, C. Y. K., & Chan, J. M. (2007). Professionalism, politics, and market force: Survey studies of Hong Kong journalists, 1996–2006. *Asian Journal of Communication, 17*(2), 148–58.

Soule, S. A., & Earl, J. (2005). A movement society evaluated: Collective protest in the United States, 1960–1986. *Mobilization, 10*(3), 345–364.

Sparks, C. (2015). Business as usual: The UK national daily press and the Occupy Central Movement. *Chinese Journal of Communication, 8*(4), 429–446.

Staggenborg, S. (1991). Critical events and the mobilization of the pro-choice movement. *Research in Political Sociology, 6*, 319–345

Staggenborg, S. (2001). Beyond culture versus politics: A case study of a local women's movement. *Gender & Society, 15*(4), 507–530.

Stein, L. (2009). Social movement web use in theory and practice: A content analysis of US movement websites. *New Media & Society, 11*(5), 749–771.

Stephens, N. (2012). Tyranny of the perceived majority: Polling in the U.S. news media before the invasion of Iraq. *Critical Studies in Media Communication, 29*(3), 220–237.

Suhay, E., Blackwell, A., Roche, C., & Bruggeman, L. (2014). Forging bonds and burning bridges: Polarization and incivility in blog discussions about Occupy Wall Street. *American Politics Research, 43*(4), 643–679.

Sunstein, C. (2009). *Going to extremes.* Oxford: Oxford University Press.

Sunstein, C. (2017). *#Republic: Divided democracy in the age of social media.* Princeton: Princeton University Press.

Tai, B. Y. T. (2008). An unexpected Chapter Two of Hong Kong's constitution: New players and new strategies. In Ming Sing (Ed.), *Politics and government in Hong Kong: Crisis under Chinese sovereignty* (pp. 220–245). London: Routledge.

Tang, G. K. Y. (2015). Mobilization of images: Effects of TV screen and mediated instant grievances in the Umbrella Movement. *Chinese Journal of Communication, 8*(4), 338–355.

Tang, G. K. Y., & Lee, F. L. F. (2013). Facebook use and political participation: The impact of exposure to shared political information, connections with public political actors, and network structural heterogeneity. *Social Science Computer Review, 31*(6), 763–773.

Tarrow, S. (1989). *Democracy and disorder: Protest and politics in Italy, 1965–1975.* New York: Oxford University Press.

Tarrow, S. (1998). *The power in movement.* New York: Cambridge University Press.

Tarrow, S. (2013). *The language of contention: Revolutions in words, 1688–2012.* New York: Cambridge University Press.

Taylor, V. (1989). Social movement continuity: The women's movement in abeyance. *American Sociological Review, 54*, 761–775.

Theocharis, Y. (2015). The conceptualization of digitally networked participation. *Social Media + Society, 1*(2), doi:10.1177/2056305115610140

Theocharis, Y., Lowe, W., van Deth, J. W., & García-Albacete, G. (2015). Using Twitter to mobilize protest action: Online mobilization patterns and action repertoires in the Occupy Wall Street, Indignados, and Aganaktismenoi movements. *Information, Communication & Society, 18*(2), 202–220.

Thompson, J. B. (1995). *The media and modernity.* Stanford, CA: Stanford University Press.

Thompson, J. B. (2000). *Political scandal.* London: Polity.

Thompson, J. B. (2005). The new visibility. *Theory, Culture & Society, 22*(6), 31–51.

Thorson, K., Driscoll, K., Ekdale, B., Edgerly, S., Thompson, L. G., Schrock, A., et al. (2013). YouTube, Twitter and the Occupy Movement: Connecting content and circulation practices. *Information, Communication & Society, 16*(3), 421–451.

Tilly, C. (1978). *From mobilization to revolution.* Reading, MA: Addison Wesley.

Tilly, C. (1995). *Popular contention in Great Britain, 1758–1834.* Cambridge, MA: Harvard University Press.

Ting, K. F., & Chiu, C. C. H. (2000). Materialistic values in Hong Kong and Guangzhou: A comparative analysis of two Chinese societies. *Sociological Spectrum, 20*(1), 15–40.

Tremayne, M. (2014). Anatomy of protest in the digital era: A network analysis of Twitter and Occupy Wall Street. *Social Movement Studies, 13*(1), 110–126.

Tripp, C. (2013). *The power and the people: Paths of resistance in the Middle East.* New York: Cambridge University Press.

Tsui, L. (2015). The coming colonization of Hong Kong cyberspace: Government responses to the use of new technologies by the Umbrella Movement. *Chinese Journal of Communication, 8*(4), 447–455.

Tufekci, Z. (2013). "Not this one": Social movements, the attention economy, and microcelebrity networked activism. *American Behavioral Scientist, 57*(7). 848–870.

Tufekci, Z., & Wilson, C. (2012). Social media and the decision to participate in political protest: Observations from Tahrir Square. *Journal of Communication, 62*(2), 363–379.

Valenzuela, S., Arriagada, A., & Scherman, A. (2012). The social media basis of youth protest behavior: The case of Chile. *Journal of Communication, 62*(2), 299–314.

Van Deth, J. W. (2014). A conceptual map of political participation. *Acta Politica, 49,* 349–367.

van Dijck, J. (2009). Users like you? Theorizing agency in user-generated content. *Media, Culture & Society, 31*(1), 41–60.

van Dijk, T. A. (1988). *News as discourse.* Hillsdale, NJ: Lawrence Elbaum Associates.

Veg, S. (2017). The rise of "localism" and civic identity in post-handover Hong Kong: Questioning the Chinese nation-state. *China Quarterly, 230,* 323–347.

Verba, S., & Nie, N. (1972). *Participation in America.* Chicago: University of Chicago Press.

Wada, T. (2012). Modularity and transferability of repertoires of contention. *Social Problems, 59*(4), 544–571.

Walgrave, S., & Verhulst, J. (2011). Selection and response bias in protest surveys. *Mobilization, 16*(2), 203–222.

Wang, Z. (2012). *Never forget national humiliation.* New York: Columbia University Press.

Weaver, D. A., & Scacco, J. M. (2013). Revisiting the protest paradigm: The Tea Party as filtered through prime-time cable news. *International Journal of Press/Politics, 18*(1), 61–84.

Weimann, G. (1991). The influentials: Back to the concept of opinion leaders? *Public Opinion Quarterly, 55,* 267–279.

Wilkes, R., & Ricard, D. (2007). How does newspaper coverage of collective action vary? Protest by indigenous people in Canada. *The Social Science Journal, 44,* 231–251.

Wolover, D. J. (2016). An issue of attribution: The Tunisian revolution, media interaction, and agency. *New Media & Society, 18*(2), 185–200.

Wong, K. Y., & Wan, P. S. (2009). New evidence of the postmaterialist shift: The experience of Hong Kong. *Social Indicators Research, 92*(3), 497–515.

Wong, T. K. Y. (2002). Identity in the 2000 Legislative Elections. In H. C. Kuan, S. K. Lau, & T. K. Y. Wong (Eds.), *Out of the shadow of 1997? The 2000 Legislative Council election in the Hong Kong Special Administrative Region* (pp. 165–181). Hong Kong: The Chinese University Press.

Xu, K. B. (2013). Framing Occupy Wall Street: A content analysis of the *New York Times* and *USA Today. International Journal of Communication, 7,* 2412–2432.

Yang, G. B. (2016). The premature death of emotion: The civilization process of Internet emotional mobilization. Paper presented at the Communication Technologies and New Media Events Workshop, Chinese University of Hong Kong, Hong Kong, January 2016.

Yang, Q. H., & Liu, Y. (2014). What's on the other side of the great firewall? Chinese web users' motivations for bypassing the Internet censorship. *Computers in Human Behavior, 37*, 249–257.

Yuen, S. (2017). Mong Kok. Paper presented at the Workshop on the Umbrella Movement, January 4–5, 2017, City University of Hong Kong, Hong Kong.

Yuen, S., & Cheng, E. (2017). Neither repression nor concession? A regime's attrition against mass protests. *Political Studies, 65*(3), 611–630.

Yung, B., & Leung, L. Y. M. (2014). Diverse roles of alternative media in Hong Kong civil society: From public discourse initiation to social activism. *Journal of Asian Public Policy, 7*(1), 83–101.

Zhao, S. S. (2004). *A nation-state by construction*. Stanford, CA: Stanford University Press.

Zhu, Q. F., Skoric, M., & Shen, F. (2017). I shield myself from thee: Selective avoidance on social media during political protests. *Political Communication, 34*(1), 112–131.

Index

dark corner incident, 99–100, 102–104,
167–168, 205

decentralization, 10, 104, 108, 121, 124, 139–140,
142, 147–149, 186, 196, 198, 202, 233

degree of involvement, 108, 116, 127, 186

Democratic Party, 144, 212–214, 238, 242, 244

democratization, 3, 24, 38, 48–49, 51, 65, 143, 180,
188, 200, 212, 228, 230
democratization of China, 143–146, 198,
228–230

discourse of corporate hegemony, 47–48, 84–86,
88, 131

discourse of opportunities, 47–48, 84–86, 88

District Council, 197, 236, 238

distrust, 143, 188, 198
toward media, 102
toward police, 100, 103
toward politicians/political parties, 38, 43, 212

diversification/diversity (of protests), 13, 27–29, 37

echo chamber, 17, 202

efficacy, 34–35, 50, 58, 83, 86, 100, 237
collective efficacy, 34–35, 71–72, 83, 85–88, 101
external efficacy, 34–35, 65, 71–72, 83, 85–86,
88, 101
internal efficacy, 34–35, 71–72, 85, 88, 101

Egypt, 80, 182, 193–194

escalation of action, 178

Eu, Audrey, 154

eviction, 4, 76, 105, 149, 161, 165, 178–179, 186

Facebook, 15, 23, 71, 93–95, 102, 109–110, 114,
128, 166, 168, 198, 204, 242, 244
Facebook page, 21–23, 108, 113, 128–142, 146,
167, 169, 182, 203–204, 242
Facebook post, 128, 130–133, 139–141,
167–169, 204

fifty-cents, 165

foreign intervention frame, 152–153, 155,
157–158, 160, 168–169

fragmentation, 202–203

frame, 20–21, 151–152, 155, 169, 188–189
collective action frame, 189–190
counter-frame/counter-framing, 20, 151–153,
162, 165, 169, 177, 190
diagnostic, 183, 189
personal action frame, 8–9, 183, 189–190
prognostic, 183, 189

frontline activism, 117–120, 142, 185, 241

Gandhi, 62, 157

gangsters/triad societies, 98, 164, 171, 233, 236

generalized action potential, 34, 53

generation, 26, 42–44, 46, 48, 84, 200, 202, 243

Ghonim, 182–183

Golden Forum, 109–110, 145–147

High Court, 159–160

Ho, Denise, 105–107

Hong Kong and Macau Affairs Office/HKMO,
122, 241

Hong Kong Commercial Daily, 152, 155, 158–159,
162, 175

Hong Kong Economic Journal, 50, 64, 153, 158,
235, 237–240, 243

Hong Kong Economic Times, 152, 157–158, 238,
240, 243

Hong Kong Federation of Students/HKFS, 4–6,
9, 91, 93, 106, 114, 121–125, 130, 134–140,
147–149, 159, 166, 168, 173, 178, 187,
197–198, 201, 223, 226–228

Hong Kong independence/independence of Hong
Kong, 56, 143, 199–200, 215, 243–244

Hong Kong Indigenous, 201

Hong Kong Research Association/HKRA, 170

Hong Kong Shield, 105, 131–132, 135

hunger strike, 178, 236

identity, 29, 56, 63, 105, 189, 199, 203

ideological package, 152, 189

improvisation, 5, 181–182

Indignados, 7, 16, 187

Inmedia, 64, 109–110, 142, 145–147

instant provocation, 77, 90–91

insurgent public sphere, 165

integrated media environment, 19–21, 64, 77,
103, 169

internal dissension, 5, 10, 142, 147–149

Internet control, 165

interpersonal discussion, 65, 69, 100

July 1 protest, 13, 24–25, 29, 34, 37, 39–41, 49,
55–57, 92, 94, 97–98, 196–197, 209–211,
220, 231, 238, 240

June 4, 92, 240

Justice Alliance, 166

karaoke-style (protest/resistance), 57, 238

King, Martin Luther, 61–62, 157

Labor Party, 144–145, 212–213, 242, 244

labor strike, 54–55, 236

Lai, Jimmy, 154–155, 159

Lam, Carrie, 122